The Joan Palevsky   Imprint in Classical Literature

In honor of beloved Virgil—

"O degli altri poeti onore e lume . . ."

—Dante, *Inferno*

The publisher gratefully acknowledges the generous contribution to this book provided by the Jane K. Sather Professorship in Classical Literature Fund.

SATHER CLASSICAL LECTURES

Volume Seventy-One

Laughter in Ancient Rome

Laughter in Ancient Rome

Laughter in Ancient Rome

On Joking, Tickling, and Cracking Up

Mary Beard

UNIVERSITY OF CALIFORNIA PRESS

Berkeley · Los Angeles · London

University of California Press, one of the most
distinguished university presses in the United States,
enriches lives around the world by advancing scholarship
in the humanities, social sciences, and natural sciences. Its
activities are supported by the UC Press Foundation and
by philanthropic contributions from individuals and
institutions. For more information, visit www.ucpress.edu.

University of California Press
Oakland, California

Library of Congress Cataloging-in-Publication Data

Beard, Mary.
    Laughter in ancient Rome : on joking, tickling, and
cracking up / Mary Beard.
        p.   cm. — (Sather classical lectures ; volume
seventy-one)
    Includes bibliographical references and index.
    ISBN 978-0-520-27716-8 (cloth, alk. paper) —
    ISBN 978-0-520-95820-3 (electronic)
    1. Laughter—Rome—History—To 1500.   2. Latin
wit and humor—History and criticism.   3. Rome—
Social life and customs.   I. Title.
BF575.L3B38   2014
152.4'30937—dc23   2013040999

Manufactured in the United States of America
23 22 21 20 19 18 17 16 15 14
10 9 8 7 6 5 4 3 2 1

In keeping with a commitment to support
environmentally responsible and sustainable printing
practices, UC Press has printed this book on Natures
Natural, a fiber that contains 30% post-consumer waste
and meets the minimum requirements of ANSI/NISO
Z39.48-1992 (R 1997) (Permanence of Paper).

Contents

Preface

When I gave the Sather Lectures at Berkeley in the fall of 2008, I had the time of my life. I hope that this book captures some of the fun we all had then in thinking about what made the ancient Romans laugh—how, when, and why Romans cracked up (or said they did).

Laughter in Ancient Rome remains, in part, very close to the lectures as they were delivered, but in part it is very different. Each lecture focused on particular aspects of Roman laughter—from the jokes of the emperor through the "monkey business" of the stage to the sometimes learned (and sometimes silly) speculation of Roman intellectuals on why people laugh when they are tickled. I tried to weave discussion of theory and method into the fabric of these case studies—and to continue it late at night in Berkeley's welcoming bars and cafés.

The explorations in part 2 are still recognizably (I hope) based on the lectures I gave. Those late-night discussions, however, have been adapted into a series of new chapters, which form part 1. Here I face directly some of the big questions that hover over any history of laughter—and of Roman laughter in particular. Can we ever know how, or why, people in the past laughed? What difference does it make that we barely can explain why we ourselves laugh? Is there such a thing as "Roman" (as distinct from, say, "Greek") laughter? I imagine that most readers will start with part 1 and move on to part 2, but it is not forbidden to start by dipping into part 2 and then move back to the more general—and wide-ranging—studies in part 1.

I am trying to get under the skin of laughter at Rome. This book is not a comprehensive survey of Roman laughter (indeed I am not sure what any such survey would look like, still less that it would be feasible, interesting, or useful to produce). Instead, it is intended to be a series of encounters with—to borrow the Russian poet Velimir Khlebnikov's memorable term—the "laughterhood" of Rome: the jokers and jesters, the gigglers and chortlers, the theorizers and moralizers.[1] It will put center stage some of the less appreciated byways of ancient literature (from the *Philogelos,* the "Roman jokebook," to Macrobius' learned and witty treatise *Saturnalia*), and it will try to shed new light on Roman culture and some of its best-known classics—Virgil's *Eclogues* and Apuleius' unsettling novel, *The Golden Ass,* to name but two—by looking through the lens of laughter.

Inevitably, *Laughter in Ancient Rome* reflects my own interests and expertise as a social and cultural historian. I am focusing on laughter as a shifting and adaptable cultural form, whatever its human physiological roots. I do not pretend to be a neurologist, and (as several footnotes will make clear) I remain far from convinced that neuroscience is much of a help in understanding the cultural and historical variability of laughter. My focus is also, as the title blazons, on the culture of Rome rather than of Greece. But, as we shall see, classical antiquity is not easy to divide into two neat halves, one Greek, one Roman, so I am constantly in dialogue with Stephen Halliwell's great book *Greek Laughter* (2008)—which I explicitly reference only to indicate disagreement or to highlight discussions particularly relevant to my argument. I have also remained fairly resolutely "pagan" in my focus, for which I apologize to those who would like more on the rich Jewish and early Christian debates about laughter.

My aim is to make the subject of Roman laughter a bit more complicated, indeed a bit messier, rather than to tidy it up. I have little patience with approaches that think they can explain and control the slippery phenomenon of laughter. To be honest, I am getting fed up with being told that laughter is all about power (true, but what cultural form isn't?) or that it is prompted by incongruity (sometimes, to be sure, it is, but the hilarity of satire or slapstick is not easily explained that way). This book is a reply to some of those oversimplifications and a long-considered provocation—reminding us of the puzzling centrality of laughter at Rome and challenging us to think about Roman culture a little differently through laughter.

We start from two occasions in Rome when laughter was explicitly written into the ancient script: an encounter in the Colosseum, and a joke on the comic stage.

CHAPTER I

Introducing Roman Laughter

Dio's "Giggle" and Gnatho's Two Laughs

COLOSSEUM, 192 CE

In 192 CE, a young Roman senator sitting in the front row of a show at the Colosseum in Rome could hardly restrain his laughter at what he saw. It was not a good moment to be caught laughing.

The emperor Commodus himself was hosting the spectacles, to a presumably packed crowd of some fifty thousand people—senators, as was the rule, in the ringside seats with the best view, while the women and slaves were squashed at the very back, high up and hardly able to see the bloody conflicts playing out more than a hundred feet beneath them in the arena. It could be that, for this particular show, some people had decided to stay away, for the story had got around that the emperor—the star of the spectacle, as well as its host—was intending to dress up as Hercules and fire deadly arrows into the audience. Perhaps this was one of those occasions when it was safer to be a slave (or female) and in the back row.[1]

Rich and poor, scared and fearless, the audience needed stamina. The proceedings went on all day for fourteen days. The seats were hard, and those with money and sense must have brought cushions, drinks, and picnics. Everyone knew that applause for the emperor's antics—as gladiator, wild-beast hunter, and god look-alike—was required. On the first day, he killed a hundred bears, "hurling spears at them from the balustrade around the arena" ("a display of marksmanship rather than of courage," as one eyewitness tartly observed).[2] On other days, his animal victims were brought to him on the floor of the arena but safely restrained in nets, and after lunch he would follow up these beast hunts with some mocked-up gladiatorial combat (at which he was of course always victorious) before the regular fighters came out to please the crowd.

It was during these shows, which took place just a couple of months before Commodus' assassination on 31 December 192, that our senator nearly burst into laughter but managed to disguise the telltale signs of mirth on his face by plucking some laurel leaves from the wreath he was wearing and chewing on them hard. Or that is what he tells us in his own account.[3]

The senator in question was the historian Cassius Dio, whose family—originally from Bithynia, in modern Turkey—had been active in imperial Roman politics for generations.[4] Dio himself became a leading player in the political life of the early third century CE: he was consul for the first time in around 205, during the reign of the emperor Septimius Severus, and again in 229, as the colleague of the emperor Severus Alexander; among other appointments, he served as governor of the provinces of Africa, Dalmatia, and Pannonia. But he is now better known as the author of an eighty-volume history of Rome, written in Greek, covering the period from the mythical arrival of Aeneas in Italy up till his own day, well over a millennium later, in the third century CE—and it is in one of the later books of this history that we learn of the stifled laugh. As Dio himself explains, the whole project took him more than twenty years, starting in the late 190s, first to research and then to write. Almost a third survives in its original form; for much of the rest (including the events of 192), we depend on more or less accurate medieval summaries of, or excerpts from, Dio's text.[5]

The particular prompt for Dio's half-stifled laughter was one memorable moment of imperial histrionics. After noting the emperor's threats of Herculean violence against the audience in general, Dio's account turns to Commodus' assault on the senators in their—dangerously exposed—seats at the front:

> He did something else along the same lines to us senators, which gave us good reason to think that we were about to die. That is to say, he killed an ostrich, cut off its head, and came over to where we were sitting, holding up the head in his left hand and in his right the bloody sword. He said absolutely nothing, but with a grin he shook his own head, making it clear that he would do the same to us. And in fact many would have been put to death on the spot by the sword for laughing at him (for it was laughter rather than distress that took hold of us) if I had not myself taken some laurel leaves

from my garland and chewed on them, and persuaded the others sitting near
me to chew on them too—so that, by continually moving our mouths, we
might hide the fact that we were laughing.[6]

This glimpse of life in the dangerous front line of Roman imperial politics is one of the rare occasions where, across almost two thousand
years, Roman laughter seems to come truly alive. We recognize the sen-
sation that Dio describes; we can almost feel what he must have felt. In
fact, his short account of how he desperately tried to conceal his laughter is bound to resonate with anyone who has ever bitten their lip, their
chewing gum, or their eraser to prevent some dangerous or embarrass-
ing hilarity from erupting in an entirely inappropriate setting, to disguise or contain the telltale quivers of face and mouth. Replace the
laurel leaves with candy, and it is one of those moments when the
Romans seem just like us.

Some might now say that Dio was in danger of "getting the giggles"
or "corpsing," which is how we often envisage that struggle between,
on the one hand, discretion, obedience, or politeness and, on the other,
the laughter that stubbornly refuses to be put down. But there are in
Dio's language none of the gendered associations that come with the
English word *giggle*—the sound, as Angela Carter memorably put it,
that "expresses the innocent glee with which women humiliate men in
the only way available to them."[7] Nor does Dio use the Greek word
kichlizein, often translated as "giggle" and with its own significantly
eroticized implications; indeed, on one occasion, it is explicitly defined
as "the laughter of prostitutes."[8] What Dio was trying to keep to himself was *gelōs* or *gelan*, the standard Greek word, from Homer to late
Roman antiquity and beyond, for "laughter" or "to laugh" (and the
root of some of the modern technical terminology of laughter—the
adjective *gelastic* and the noun *agelast*, "nonlaugher"—which, I am
afraid, will inevitably crop up in the chapters that follow).[9]

There is, of course, something curiously gratifying about a story that
casts the excesses of Roman imperial power as the object of laughter.
Dio's account of Commodus' threats in the amphitheater—both menacing and ridiculous as they were—suggests that laughter could be one of
the weapons of those opposed to Roman autocracy and the abuse of
power: one response by the disaffected was violence, conspiracy, or
rebellion; another was to refuse to take it seriously.

This is not the only occasion in Dio's *History* when laughter plays a
role in the clash between Roman power and its subjects. There is
another, even less well-known story in his account of Rome's expansion

at the beginning of the third century BCE, almost five hundred years earlier—which brought the Romans into conflict with the Greek town of Tarentum in South Italy. At the start of hostilities, the Romans dispatched envoys to Tarentum, dressed in their formal togas, intending to use this costume to impress their adversaries. When they arrived, according to Dio at least (there are other versions), the Tarentines laughed at the Romans' dress, and one man managed to shit all over the clean Roman clothes of the chief envoy, Lucius Postumius Megellus. This went down well with the locals but provoked a predictable response from Postumius: "'Laugh,' he said, 'laugh while you still can! For you will be crying for a very long time, when you wash these clothes clean with your blood.'" The threat, of course, came true; Roman victory meant that the Tarentines did shortly pay with their blood.[10]

What made the Tarentines laugh? In part, maybe, it was a laugh of derision or scorn (that certainly is how, in Dio's account, Postumius took it when his toga was aggressively fouled). But Dio implies that the sheer silliness of the formal Roman dress was also a factor in causing the Tarentines to crack up. In other words, this combination of laughter, power, and menace matches the much later story from the Colosseum. Power is met, and spontaneously challenged, by laughter. In the case of Tarentum there is an added extra: a clear hint that the cumbersome and hopelessly impractical Roman toga could look as funny to non-Romans in the ancient world as it now does, in the modern, to us.

Dio's stifled laughter in the arena raises three important sets of questions, which this book will explore. First, what prompted the Romans to laugh? Or, to be realistic, what prompted urban elite male Romans to laugh? For we have almost no access to the laughter of the poor, of the peasants, of slaves, or of women—except in the descriptions that urban elite males give.[11] In the ancient world, as often now, one way of marking difference among different social groups was to assert that they laughed differently, and at different things. Second, how did laughter operate in Roman elite culture, and what were its effects? What political, intellectual, or ideological jobs did it do? How was it controlled and policed? And what does that tell us about how Roman society worked more generally? Third, how far can we now understand or share the Roman culture of laughter? Were there some aspects of it in which the Romans really were "just like us"? Or will modern historians of Roman laughter always resemble anxious guests at a foreign party—joining in with the hearty chuckling when it seems the polite thing to do but never quite sure that they have really got the joke?

These are big questions, which I hope will open up new perspectives on the social and cultural life of ancient Rome, as well as contribute some classical insights to the cross-cultural history of human laughter—and I mean primarily laughter, not humor, wit, emotion, satire, epigram, or comedy, even though all those related subjects will make occasional appearances in what follows. A second look at Dio's description of the scene in the Colosseum reveals just how complicated, intriguing, and (sometimes unexpectedly) revealing those questions can be. Simple as it may seem at first sight, there is more to the narrative of Dio's laugh than a straightforward, first-person account of a young man resourceful enough, in the deadly power politics of second-century Rome, to suppress his laughter, and so save his skin, just by chewing on some laurel leaves. For a start, in Dio's account the strategy adopted is definitely chewing, not—as would be more familiar to us—biting. Of course, it is tempting to tell the story as if it exactly matched the modern cliché of the desperate laugher who crunches on some convenient implement to repress his laughter ("Dio recorded how he had *kept himself* from laughing . . . by chewing desperately on a laurel leaf," as one modern historian summarized the event[12]). But Dio makes clear that he was not actually preventing himself from laughing but rather exploiting the movement of his jaws on the leaves as a clever disguise—an alibi, even—for the movement that his laughter produced.

WHY DID DIO LAUGH?

One tricky issue is how power operated on different sides of this laugh. The idea that Dio's half-concealed outburst amounted to an act of subversion or resistance to Commodus' tyranny is, of course, one compelling way of seeing it. And that would fit with the views of many modern theorists and critics who characterize laughter as an "unruly force" and "a site of popular resistance to totalitarianism."[13] In these terms, Dio's laugh was a spontaneous and powerful weapon in the standoff between a vicious autocrat and an apparently supine Senate: not only because it was an expression of senatorial opposition but also because it acted more positively, to make Commodus seem ridiculous, to cut him down to size. As in the story of the Tarentines, it is impossible to exclude the element of derision: a person who prompts us to laugh is, by definition, laughable (or *laugh-able*, a term whose ambiguities will be a recurrent theme in this book[14]).

But that is only part of the picture. For laughter, in its various guises, can be a weapon *of* the ruling power, as well as against it. And in this story the emperor himself was (as I have translated it) grinning, as he shook his own head while waving the ostrich's at the frightened, bemused—or amused—senators. The word Dio uses is *sesērōs* (from the verb *sesērenai*), which means literally "parting the lips" (it is also used of "gaping" wounds) and can carry a friendly or more often, as presumably here, a threatening sense.[15] No doubt the emperor's gesture is to be distinguished from Dio's simple "laugh" (which is what my translation aims to do, though possibly introducing misleading modern associations with the word *grin*). But this is nevertheless another of those words—of moving the lips and mouth—that make up the wide vocabulary of laughter and its cognates in ancient Greek.

Roman power relations of all kinds were displayed, negotiated, manipulated, or contested with a laugh. For every laugh in the face of autocracy, there was another laugh by the powerful at the expense of the weak—or even laughter imposed upon the weak by the strong. That, in a sense, is one message of the sneer of Postumius at the Tarentines ("Laugh, laugh . . ."), and it is more obviously the moral of a chilling anecdote about one of Commodus' predecessors, the emperor Caligula: he had forced a man to watch the execution of his own son in the morning, then invited him to dinner in the afternoon—and forced him to laugh and joke.[16] Laughter, in other words, flourished amid the inequalities of the Roman social and geopolitical order.[17]

Even trickier is the question of what exactly Dio was laughing at. Why did the display of the emperor brandishing the ostrich head have the senator reaching for his garland? We are not dealing with a joke here. Although the study of laughter and the study of jokes often go together (and the second part of this chapter looks at the relationship between some Roman laughter and some Latin verbal jokes), most laughter in most cultures has nothing to do with jokes at all. So was it, as Dio himself implies, that the sight of the emperor dressed up in the costume of an arena fighter (or rather dressed down, with bare feet and wearing just a tunic) and proudly decapitating an ungainly bird with the longest, and silliest, neck in the world could not help but appear ridiculous—whatever the menace that might lie behind it? Was it as if the emperor had turned himself into a parody of that heroic and mythical decapitator Perseus, brandishing his sword and the head of the Gorgon Medusa?[18] Or was the laughter, as most recent commentators have imagined, produced by the terror of the occasion—what we would call a nervous laugh, and nothing to do with the potentially comic aspects of the display at all?[19]

Laughter often produces these interpretative dilemmas. The most common response to any outburst of laughing is the question "What are you (or they) laughing at?" or rather "*Why* are you (or they) laughing?" (for, despite some powerful theories to the contrary, laughter is not always laughter *at*[20]). There is, of course, no definitive, right answer, least of all from the mouth of the laugher. In fact, any answer given is rarely an independent or objective explanation but almost always part of the debates, contestations, fears, paradoxes, hilarities, transgressions, or anxieties that produced the laughter in the first place. In this case, imagine that Dio had not managed to control himself but had been caught chortling by one of Commodus' henchmen, who proceeded to challenge him as to why he was laughing. It is not hard to guess roughly what he might have said—something, perhaps, to do with a joke that his neighbor had just whispered in his ear, or with that bald man in the row behind (and certainly not to do with the antics of the emperor).[21] Nor is it hard to guess how he might have presented the scene in the safety of his home later that evening: "Of course, I just laughed at him . . ." For if laughter is, or can be, political, so too are all those claims people make about having laughed—and the reasons they give (true or false) for doing so.

These are certainly some of the factors at work in Dio's account of this occasion in his *History*. It is such an appealing description, and it is so easy for us to empathize with what seems close to a very modern struggle to keep the "giggle" in, that we are liable to overlook its literary and political artifice and to imagine that we are (however remotely) eyewitnesses of a Roman laugh. But, of course, we are not. This is a carefully crafted analysis, chosen for excerption in a medieval digest (whose compiler no doubt found it a vivid and pointed tale of imperial transgression), originally written some two decades after the events it describes—a moment when it must have seemed wise for any writer to distance himself from the tyrant-emperor Commodus. And distance himself is exactly what Dio does by claiming to have laughed at the antics not from fear but at the sheer absurdity of the scene ("It was laughter rather than distress that took hold of us," as he insists, against all those who would accuse him of nervous laughter). The very point of his account lies in the retrospective, and possibly tendentious, interpretation that it offers. To say "I found this funny" or, even better, "I had to conceal my laughter, else I would have been put to death" simultaneously indicts and ridicules the tyrant while casting the writer as a down-to-earth, genial observer not taken in by the ruler's cruel but empty posturing.[22] Which is no doubt just what Dio intended.

HAHAHAE, 161 BCE

My second instance of laughter was to be heard less than a mile away from the site of the Colosseum, more than four hundred years earlier, in 161 BCE. Laughter of a very different kind, it occurred on the stage of a Roman comedy, not in a spectacle played out under the eye of a threatening emperor but in the course of one of those festivals of fun, games, and worship of the gods that had been, in some form or other, a part of Roman urban culture as far back as we can trace it.[23] This was not theater as we now know it, nor even, in our terms, a "stage." In the second century BCE, there were still no permanent theater buildings in Rome; performances took place in the open air, in temporary wooden structures sometimes erected around the steps of a temple (most likely to provide a convenient block of seating for the audience—which cannot have amounted to more than a few thousand). In the case I shall be exploring, the theater was probably put up on the Capitoline Hill, around the temple of the Great Mother (Magna Mater).[24]

It must have been a jolly and lighthearted atmosphere—perhaps even raucous. Roman comedies typically featured entangled boy-wants-girl intrigues and a series of more or less stock characters (the clever slave, the mean brothel keeper, the boastful but rather stupid soldier, and so on), each recognizable by its distinctive theatrical mask. As specialists have long insisted, most of the Roman comedy that survives has strong links with its Greek predecessors.[25] I shall return to these in chapter 4; for the moment, I am concentrating on the Roman context. Whatever the laughter erupting from the audience, I shall focus first on a couple of instances of laughter between the actors onstage, written into the comic script. They introduce an even more subtle laughter narrative than Dio's account of his giggle in the Colosseum and show how knowingly a Roman writer could exploit the tricky dilemmas of what a laugh could mean.

These two cases of scripted laughter come from *The Eunuch,* by Publius Terentius Afer (now usually known as Terence), which was first performed in 161 BCE. It has always been the most popular of Terence's plays, was given an immediate second showing, and reputedly earned its author the unprecedented sum of eight thousand sesterces from the official sponsors.[26] The memorable plot involves all the usual romantic intrigues but owes its extra punch to an outrageous scenario of disguise and cross-dressing—in which a lusty, love-sick young man (Chaerea) pretends to be a eunuch in order to get up close to the (slave) girl of his affections (Pamphila), who belongs to a courtesan called Thais. It is a marker of the almost unbridgeable gulf between ancient sexual politics and our own that the "happy ending" comes after Chaerea has used his eunuch disguise to rape Pamphila, as a prelude to the wedding bells that ring for them in the finale of the play.[27] One version of the ancient production notes claims that the precise occasion of the play's first performance was the Roman festival of the Megalesia, in honor of the Great Mother (hence the suggestion that the performance may well have taken place around the steps of her temple). If that is correct, then the context itself must have given the plot a curious piquancy. For the priests of the Great Mother, the so-called Galli, who lived in the temple precinct, were themselves eunuchs, reputedly self-castrated—as Roman writers loved to dwell on, and to decry—with a sharpened flint. Eunuchs and their look-alikes, in other words, would have been on view both inside and outside this drama.[28]

At two points in the play, one of the characters, Gnatho (Gnasher), a typically ancient comic combination of jokester, sponger, and flatterer, erupts in a peal of laughter: *hahahae*. These are two of only a dozen or so occasions in which classical Latin literature explicitly represents the sound of laughter, and for that reason alone they are worth looking at carefully; we do not need, as we normally do, to *infer* laughter as part of a comic exchange, since we are explicitly told when and where it occurred. As another tale from the very front line of Roman laughter, it is well worth the effort to decode. The complexity; the multiple perspectives; the twists and turns among joker, recipient, and observers (on- and offstage); and the sheer difficulty in getting the joke are all part of the point.

The scripted laughter is part of a series of exchanges between the sponger Gnatho and Thraso, a blustering soldier in the service of some unidentified Eastern monarch, who feature in one of the play's intricate subplots (which may have been as difficult for some of the ancient audience to follow in detail as for us—indeed a bit of bafflement was all part of the fun). The soldier not only is Gnatho's meal ticket but had also been the owner of Pamphila and is himself in love with Thais (in fact he had given young Pamphila to Thais as a love gift). In the scenes in question, Thraso is bragging about his various exploits to Gnatho, who (as the professional sponger's role in life demands) plays the flatterer and laughs at the jokes, in the hope of free dinners in return—while the dramatist insinuates just how insincere his performance is.[29] Their conversation is overheard by Parmeno, a bungling slave (whose master is, of course, also in love with Thais and is Thraso's rival for her affections). Unseen and unheard by the others, he chips in the occasional aside.

The bluff soldier starts by talking up his close relationship with his royal boss, who "trusted me with his whole army, and all his plans." "Amazing" is Gnatho's simultaneously unctuous and caustic reply (402–3). Thraso then goes on to boast of putting down one of his fellow officers, the commander of the elephants, who was jealous of his influence with the king: "Tell me, Strato," he claims to have quipped, "are you so fierce because you're in charge of the wild animals?" "What an amazingly smart and clever thing to say," chimes in Gnatho with transparent insincerity (414–16). Another self-promoting story from Thraso follows. It's the one about "how I scored a hit at a dinner party against a man from Rhodes"—and it's the one that prompts the laughter:

> *Thraso:* This young Rhodian guy I'm telling you about was at a party with me. Actually I had a bird in tow. And he began to make a pitch for her and take the piss out of me. So I say to him, "Answer me this, smartass. Are you trying to pick up the tidbits, when you're such a tasty morsel yourself?"
>
> *Gnatho: hahahae*
>
> *Thraso:* What's the matter?
>
> *Gnatho:* Oh the wit of it! The cleverness! The neatness! Unbeatable! But hang on, did *you* make that joke up? I thought it was an old one.
>
> *Thraso:* Had you heard it before?
>
> *Gnatho:* Loads of times. It always goes down very well.
>
> *Thraso:* But it's mine.
>
> *Gnatho:* I can't help feeling sorry for the silly young reprobate, having that said to him.[30]
>
> *Parmeno* (out of earshot): God, you don't deserve to get away with that.
>
> *Gnatho:* What did he do, tell me.
>
> *Thraso:* He was finished. Everyone who was there—they just died of laughter. And ever since they've had a lot of respect for me.
>
> *Gnatho:* And so they should. (422–33)[31]

Less than a hundred lines later, there is another bout of laughter. Thraso has grown tired of waiting for Thais to come out of her house, so has decided to go off, leaving Gnatho to hang around for her. Parmeno this time speaks within earshot:

> *Thraso:* I'm off. (*To Gnatho:*) You stay and wait for her.
>
> *Parmeno:* Of course, it really isn't proper for the commanding officer to be out walking in the street with his lady friend!
>
> *Thraso:* Why should I waste words on you? You're just like your master!
>
> *Gnatho: hahahae*
>
> *Thraso:* What are you laughing at?
>
> *Gnatho:* At what you just said, and at that story about the guy from Rhodes— whenever I think about it. (494–98)[32]

There can be no doubt whatsoever that this repeated *hahahae* is meant to indicate Gnatho laughing. For a start, Terence tells us so, with his "What are you laughing at?" ("Quid rides?" 497). What is more, ancient commentators on the play reiterate the point ("Here the sponger has also inserted the sound of laughter [*risus*]"[33]), and on several occasions Roman scholars in late antiquity refer in general terms to this way of representing laughter on the page ("*Hahahae* is the sound of joy and laughter [*risus*]"[34]). But even if we did not have these direct pointers, we would hardly mistake the sound. Unlike the barking of dogs, the grunting of pigs, or the croaking of frogs—which different languages render in bewilderingly different ways ("oink oink," says the Anglo-American pig, "röf röf röf" or "uí uí" the Hungarian, "soch soch" the Welsh)—laughter in almost all world languages, and in entirely different linguistic families, is rendered as (or includes within its repertoire) some variant on *ha ha, hee hee,* or *tee hee.*[35] Or, to quote Samuel Johnson's typically pointed exaggeration, "Men have been wise in many different modes; but they have always laughed the same way."[36]

But *why* is Gnatho laughing? Identifying the sound of his laughter is one thing; as with Dio's anecdote, understanding its cause is quite another.

The first outburst follows Thraso's story of the Rhodian, whose punch line I translated as "Answer me this, smartass. Are you trying to pick up the tidbits, when you're such a tasty morsel yourself?" That was an attempt to give the line some point in modern terms. The Latin literally means "You are a hare: do you chase after delicacies?" ("Lepu' tute's, pulpamentum quaeris?" 426). So what was there in these words to cause Gnatho to crack up? Commentators both ancient and modern have disagreed about that (sometimes relying on different readings of the Latin text).[37] But recent critics have usually followed the lead of the fourth-century commentary of Aelius Donatus in referring to the role of the hare as a delicacy on the Roman dinner table: "A hare, which is itself a delicacy, should not be seeking *pulpamenta,* which are tasty morsels of meat used as hors-d'oeuvres"; or as Donatus' text more crisply glosses it (*Eun.* 426), "You are seeking in another what you have in yourself."[38] The implications are of course erotic, as the context makes clear: the young Rhodian is flirting with Thraso's "bird" when he should be the object of erotic attention himself. There is further support for this in another part of Donatus' lengthy note (much less often quoted in modern scholarship), which collects evidence for the sexual overtones of the hare; it includes the view—wonderfully appropriate to the plot of *The Eunuch*—that the hare is an animal "of uncertain sex, now male, now female."[39]

Dissected in this clinical way, Thraso's witticism may seem to lose whatever capacity to raise a laugh that it might once have had (following the iron rule, which goes back to antiquity itself, that a joke explained is a joke lost[40]). Yet the bare bones of the joke that are revealed could fit comfortably enough into several modern theories of joking technique, from Sigmund Freud's *Jokes and Their Relation to the Unconscious* to the numerous modern and ancient discussions that see incongruity (and/or its resolution) at the heart of what makes us laugh. So here the impossible, nonsensical incongruity from which the joke starts (the young Rhodian is not a hare) is economically resolved as we realize that the "hare" and the "delicacies" can have quite different referents in the erotic encounter of the dinner party, or, to put it in the terms of one leading current theory, the clash between the culinary and the erotic "script" is gradually resolved in favor of the latter.[41]

Why on earth the resolution of incongruity, or whatever is supposedly going on within the Freudian unconscious, should cause that distinctive vocal and bodily response we know as *laughing* is a question that no modern theory—not even Freud's—satisfactorily answers.[42] But in this case, that problem is sidestepped, for we quickly suspect that it is not actually the joke that is making Gnatho laugh after all. Gnatho is laughing because he is a sponger, and the ancient cliché was that spongers flattered their patrons by laughing at their jokes, whether they were funny or, more likely, not. This *hahahae* is not a spontaneous reaction to a hilarious one-liner but a well-practiced response to his patron's verbal posturing masquerading as a spontaneous reaction. Gnatho is laughing to please. This is another aspect of that complex relationship between laughter and power that I have already highlighted.

Thraso's instant retort—"What's the matter?" ("Quid est?" 427)—
may indicate that not even he was taken in. Donatus thought that in
asking that question, the stupid soldier was simply fishing for compliments for his bon mot (compliments that he did indeed receive, albeit
insincerely: "Oh the wit of it!"). But Thraso's challenge could equally
well suggest that Gnatho's pseudospontaneity had been all too easy to
see through. His laugh had convinced nobody, not even the gullible
character it had been intended to hoodwink.

As if to avoid the awkward confrontation, Gnatho quickly changes
the subject and moves to the attack. Was it Thraso's joke anyway? Was
he not just recycling an old one, as if it were his own? Was it, in other
words, no more spontaneous than Gnatho's enthusiastic response to it?
The sponger claims he has already heard it "loads of times," and maybe
we should imagine that he had. For it is a joke we find elsewhere in
Latin literature, quoted in a late antique text but attributed to a writer
even earlier than Terence.

Near the end of that strange collection of imperial biographies known
as the *Augustan History,* concocted under a variety of pseudonyms
probably in the late fourth century CE, the author stops to puzzle at
how, in 284, the new emperor Diocletian quoted a line from Virgil
immediately after he had killed Aper, the praetorian prefect and a
potential rival, in full view of the army. Was that not an uncharacteris-
tically literary gesture for such a military man as Diocletian? Perhaps
not as uncharacteristic as it may seem, the biographer concedes. After
all, he observes, soldiers had a habit of quoting well-known bits of
poetry, and they were shown doing so in comic plays: "For, in fact, 'Are
you trying to pick up the tidbits, when you're such a tasty morsel yourself?' is a saying of Livius Andronicus." Thraso's joke, if you believe
this account, was a classic quote from Rome's first Latin dramatist,
active a good seventy years before Terence.[43]

Of course, the biographer might simply have got it wrong: from the
perspective of the late fourth century, it might have been easy to confuse
two venerable early Latin writers and to attribute a line of Terence to
his predecessor Livius Andronicus. But if he was right, then Terence
was making Thraso pass off as his own invention a gag that was already,
in 161 BCE, decades old.[44] For the audience, no doubt part of the joke
was precisely that: the pushy soldier claiming as his own clever quip a
one-liner that most of them knew already.

New or old, the joke scored a hit against the young Rhodian at the
dinner party. Or so Thraso recounts, leading us into another familiar

topic in the ancient and modern theory of laughter that we have already glimpsed in Dio's *History*: laughter as derision.[45] Thraso was laughing at the boy, so aggressively that Gnatho purports to feel sorry for the victim (a backhanded compliment to the force of Thraso's wit, which—as his aside indicates—is more than Parmeno, who overhears it, can take). The effect on the other dinner guests was dramatic: "They just died of laughter." Cracking up, as we all know, can be painful; it can reduce you to helpless incapacity. "Dying of laughter" is an ancient image no less than a modern one. In fact, it was sharply literalized in a series of stories about men who really did die laughing: the fifth-century BCE painter Zeuxis (who expired, according to one Roman writer, as he laughed at his own painting of an old woman), for example, or the philosopher Chrysippus at the end of the third century BCE (according to Diogenes Laertius, writing centuries later, under the Roman Empire, it was the sight of an ass eating figs and drinking unmixed wine that finished him off).[46] The "death" of Thraso's fellow diners was part of an established ancient tradition.

The next outburst of *hahahae* prompts more questions. Fed up with waiting for Thais to return, Thraso tells Gnatho to wait for her. This draws an ironic quip from Parmeno, who is now fully part of the conversation: of course Thraso should not hang around, he appears to agree; after all, it isn't the done thing for a commanding officer to be seen in the street with his mistress. Thraso, who is many ranks below a "commanding officer," realizes that he is being sent up and turns on the slave ("Why should I waste words on you? You're just like your master!"), before Gnatho again laughs.

What, as Thraso himself asks, causes the laughter this time? Is it Thraso's retort to Parmeno? Or is it also, as Gnatho goes on to claim, the recollection of "that story about the guy from Rhodes"? (Gnatho presumably calculates that not even the gullible Thraso would think that the rather lame response of "just like your master" was capable of raising much of a laugh.) Or is it, more likely, Parmeno's joke about the "commanding officer," which Gnatho can hardly admit to Thraso—who was its target—had caused him to crack up (hence the smokescreen about the "guy from Rhodes" again)? In short, we have just one *hahahae* and at least three possible causes for the laughter that it signals. Part of the interpretative fun for the audience or reader (and indeed for the characters themselves) must come from weighing one possible cause against another, puzzling out how the laughter is best explained.[47]

AUDIENCE REACTION

How, more generally, can we approach the laughter of the people in the audience, rather than those on the stage? Unlike Dio in the Colosseum, those who came to watch *The Eunuch* were encouraged, even supposed to laugh—but at what, and why?

Of course, we cannot know for certain how the audience reacted at a Roman comedy: whether, when, or how enthusiastically they laughed. If ancient theatergoers were like their modern equivalents in this respect (and that is of course a big if), part of their experience will have been shared. Many people will have laughed at the same things. They will have cheered, cried, chuckled, and applauded together: that, after all, is part of the common bond of theater. Yet at the same time, some reactions would necessarily have been more personal and idiosyncratic. Individual members of the audience would have laughed at different things, or at the same things for different reasons. And some would not have laughed at all. Most of us have had the uncomfortable experience of being in a theater (or in front of a television, for that matter), our lips barely curling, while those round about us were laughing with gusto; the louder they laugh, the less we feel we can join in and the more stony our faces become. It was similar, we may imagine, in the Roman theater. Laughter acts both to incorporate and to isolate. The history of laughing is, as we shall see, about those who don't (or won't) get the joke as well as about those who do.[48]

Yet we have seen enough by now to make a good guess at various likely ancient responses to these episodes in *The Eunuch*. I have already suggested that Thraso's quip about the young Rhodian may have raised a laugh precisely because the soldier was trying—implausibly—to pass off an old joke as his own invention (as if today someone claimed to have just thought up "Waiter, waiter, there's a fly in my soup . . ."). But there was more to it than that. Some members of the audience may have refused to laugh (or laughed only halfheartedly) for the simple reason that it was a very old joke, one that they had heard many times before and did not much want to hear again. For others, laughter might have been prompted by the sheer familiarity of the quip. As the cliché goes, old jokes are the best—in the sense that they cause us to crack up not through the disruptions of incongruity or the pleasures of derision (as many a modern theory has it) but through the warm recollection of all the other occasions on which just the same joke has worked as intended. Laughter is as much about memory, and about the ways we have learned to laugh at certain cues, as it is about uncontrollable spontaneity.[49]

Laughter's prompts and objects are also wider ranging than we often acknowledge. Here, for example, some may have laughed because Thraso's "joke" was *not* funny—and because Gnatho's transparently unspontaneous laughter neatly exposed, in no more than those three syllables (*hahahae*), the mechanisms of flattery, the vulnerability of both patron and client, and the slipperiness of laughter as a signifier. The audience, in other words, was laughing at the constituents, causes, and social dynamics of laughter itself. The laughter—and its different interpretations and misinterpretations, uses and misuses, within these scenes—is part of the joke.[50]

This self-reflexivity is underlined by the simple fact that, in these two passages of *The Eunuch,* laughter is explicitly written into the script. To be sure, there may have been a good deal of laughter, on- as well as offstage, in Roman comedy. Certainly, modern translators of Plautus and Terence regularly introduce "laughter" into the stage directions, to bring the plays to life: phrases, in brackets—such as *laughing uproariously, with a laugh, still laughing, laughing uncontrollably, laughing, trying to conceal his laughter,* and *laughs still more*—litter English versions of these comedies, even though nothing like them is to be found in the Latin originals.[51] But here Terence's insistence, twice, on Gnatho's *hahahae,* his explicit introduction of laughter into the dialogue of his play, makes this a particularly loaded moment—one in which characters, audience, and readers cannot dodge the question of what this laughter (or laughter more generally) is all about.

The same is true of the other dozen or so cases of scripted laughter in classical Latin literature. These are all found in comedy, both Plautus and Terence, with just one possible exception: a short, and puzzling, fragment of the poet Ennius ("*hahae,* the shield itself fell down"), which could equally well come from a comedy or a tragedy.[52] Taken together, they add to the range of circumstances in which Roman laughter might erupt and the range of emotions it might reflect, for, as we have already seen, both in the amphitheater and in the exchanges between Gnatho and the soldier, the idea that laughter is caused by jokes, or clever wit, is only one part of the story. So, for example, in one of these passages we may recognize the laughter prompted by (self-)satisfaction: the *hahae* of Ballio the pimp, in Plautus' *Pseudolus* (1052), as he congratulates himself on outwitting the clever slave of the title. Elsewhere we catch chuckles of sheer pleasure: in Terence's *Heauton Timorumenus,* or *Self-Tormentor* (886), when the elderly Chremes laughs in delight at the tricks that yet another clever slave has played.[53]

But at the same time, these instances of comic laughter, explicitly scripted, repeatedly point audience and reader to many of the tricky interpretative dilemmas that laughter raises. Can we pin down exactly what it is that makes anyone laugh (even ourselves)? How can laughter be misunderstood or mistaken? Is a person who laughs potentially as vulnerable to the power of laughter as a person who is laughed at? It will not escape the attention of either audience or readers of the plays that in their laughter, both Ballio and Chremes have got things terribly wrong. For all his laughter of self-congratulation, Ballio has not outwitted Pseudolus at all but has actually been caught by a trick played by the slave that is even cleverer than the poor pimp can imagine. Likewise, Chremes is not, as he believes, the beneficiary of his slave's wiles but himself their dupe and victim. It is as if the scripted laughter here serves to draw attention to laughter's perilous fragility and the many possible constituents and interpretations of a single laugh.

UNDERSTANDING ROMAN LAUGHTER

In this chapter I have looked in detail at the choreography of two particular moments of Roman (written) laughter, from a pair of authors living four centuries apart—one writing in Greek, the other in Latin; one a historian with an ax to grind about laughter stifled in the Colosseum, the other both portraying and prompting laughter in the comic theater. They serve as a useful frame for what follows in the rest of the book, for, although I shall occasionally explore material later than Dio, and although I shall sometimes focus on visual images, I shall for the most part be drawing on Latin and Greek writing between the second century BCE and the second century CE.

These examples have also opened up some of the key issues that will be central to the rest of my discussion. Beyond the dilemmas of interpretation and understanding that I have highlighted throughout, they have prompted reflection on the uncertain and disputed boundary between "faked" and "real" laughter. (When we join in the guffaws at a joke we do not quite understand, are we pretending to laugh—or just laughing differently?) They have shown how laughing could act to exclude as well as include, offer friendly support as well as hostile derision, both reaffirm and contest hierarchies and power. And Thraso's quip about the hare turned out to be a reminder that Roman jokes could have complicated histories stretching over many centuries. Indeed we shall meet others, in the chapters that follow, whose histories stretch for thousands of years, right up to our own day.

As I have hinted, one big question that hovers over the whole of the book is this: How comprehensible, in any terms, can Roman laughter now be? How can we understand what made the Romans laugh, without falling into the trap of turning them into a version of ourselves? Some readers may already have felt uneasy about some of my procedures in exploring those passages of *The Eunuch*. It was not simply that the process of dissection spoiled the joke about the young Rhodian; even more to the point, the dissection was founded on the assumption that if only we worked hard enough at it, the joke would make sense to us too, that it could be translated into terms we understand. Of course, that must sometimes be so (if it were not, then the whole of culture of Roman laughter would be lost to us, and my project stillborn). But in any individual case we must not assume that successful translation between the Roman world and our own is possible. There is a danger that the question "What made the Romans laugh?" might be converted, by an act of spurious empathy, into the question "What do I think would have made me laugh, if I were a Roman?"

We can see this in more vivid form if we reflect on how and why modern audiences laugh at performances of Roman comedy. Part of the time it is because the jokes can be shared across the centuries. But part of the time it is because the translator, director, and actors have worked very hard to make the plays funny in modern terms—using idiom, nuance, expression, gesture, costume, and staging designed to trigger laughter for us (but bearing very little resemblance to anything Roman). What is more, at least some of the audience will have gone to the play already committed to the spirit of the enterprise, determined to find a Roman comedy funny—and at the same time laughing at themselves for doing so. It is surely this combination of factors that explains the success enjoyed in 2008 by the stand-up comedian Jim Bowen with a retelling of a selection of the jokes from the one surviving ancient jokebook, the *Philogelos* (Laughter lover), probably compiled in the late Roman Empire (discussed in detail in chapter 8).[54] Some of those jokes are still capable of raising a laugh (indeed, more than that: some of them are the direct ancestors of our own jokes). But there were other reasons for Bowen's success: he used a translation of the jokes that closely echoed the modern idiom and rhythms of stand-up, the audience had come to the show (or tuned in on the online site) determined to laugh, and

Bowen played up the absurdity of the whole occasion—to the extent that many of the most determined laughers were also laughing at themselves for laughing at these very, very old, Roman jokes.

So who, if anyone, was the joke on? This is a question I shall come back to in the next three chapters, which reflect on the theory and history of Roman (and other) laughter—before focusing, in the second half of the book, on particular key figures and key themes in the story of Roman laughter, from the jesting orator to the ridiculous monkey.

Part One

CHAPTER 2

Questions of Laughter, Ancient and Modern

THEORIES AND THEORY

Marcus Tullius Cicero—the Roman world's most renowned orator (and also one of its most infamous jokesters)—was curious about the nature of laughter. "What is it?" he asked. "What provokes it? Why does it affect so many different parts of the body all at once? Why can't we control it?" But he knew that the answers were elusive, and he was happy to profess his ignorance. "There is no shame," he explained in his treatise *On the Orator* in the mid-50s BCE, "in being ignorant of something which even the self-proclaimed experts do not really understand."[1]

He was not the only one. A couple of centuries later, Galen, the prolific medical writer and personal physician to (among others) the emperors Marcus Aurelius and Commodus, admitted that he was stumped about the physiological cause of laughter. In his essay *On Problematical Movements,* he reckoned he could account for other types of involuntary bodily motion. Imagination, for example, might explain why a man gets an erection on catching sight of (or even just thinking about) his lover. But laughter, he was prepared to concede, defeated him.[2]

For well over two thousand years, laughter has baffled and intrigued. Ambitious theorizing and ingenious speculation about its nature and causes have gone hand in hand with frank expressions about the impossibility of ever solving its mystery. Beyond the specific prompts to any individual outburst ("Why are you laughing?" or "Quid rides?"), laughter as a phenomenon demands explanation, yet it always seems to defeat any explanation offered. In fact, the more ambitious the theories are, the more striking laughter's victory seems to be over those who would control, systematize, and explain it.

To study the "laughterhood" of ancient Rome involves reflecting on when, why, and how Romans laughed, but also on how they tried to make sense of laughter, what they—or at least those who had the leisure to think and write—thought it was, and what might cause it. So this chapter will start by exploring some of the wide range of Roman theorizing on the subject and some of the sources of Roman ideas. Where did they look when they wanted to explain why they laughed? Was Aristotle (and in particular his discussion of comedy in the lost second book of the *Poetics*) really the origin of most ancient thought on the subject? Was there such as thing, as has often since been claimed, as "the classical theory of laughter"?

The chapter will move on to consider modern theories of laughter, partly to point up their relationship with their ancient predecessors (for almost every modern social or psychological theory on this subject—I am not referring to neuroscience here—turns out to have some precedent in the Greco-Roman world). But there are some even more fundamental questions to be broached. What resources are at our disposal when we attempt to make some sense of laughter, either now or in the past, at home or abroad? What wider cultural purposes do theories of laughter serve? When we ask, for example, "Do dogs laugh?," what is that question about? It is not usually, I think we can safely say, about dogs.

But first let us get a flavor of Roman speculation about laughter—and its diversity—starting with some of the theories and observations scattered throughout the vast encyclopedia (the *Natural History*) of that obsessive Roman polymath Gaius Plinius Secundus—or Pliny the Elder, as he is now usually known.

ROMAN QUESTIONS—AND OURS

Pliny was inquisitive about laughter—as he was inquisitive about almost everything else in his world. (It was, in a way, his scientific curiosity that killed him, when he went fatally close to the fumes of Vesuvius in the eruption of 79 CE). In the thirty-seven books of the *Natural History*, with, as he boasted, its "twenty thousand facts worth knowing," he returned to the subject several times. At what age do human infants

begin to laugh? he wondered. Where in the body does laughter originate? Why do people laugh if you tickle them under their arms?[3]

Those are familiar enough questions, and they continue to exercise
modern students of laughter even now. Less comfortably familiar are
some of Pliny's answers. Human infants, he confidently assures his readers, do not laugh until they are forty days old, except for Zoroaster, the
ancient Iranian prophet, who laughed on the very day he was born—presumably a mark of his superhuman quality.[4] Pliny also identifies various
organs in the human body that are responsible for laughter. One is the
diaphragm, "the main site of merriment" ("praecipua hilaritatis sedes"),
as he calls it. Its importance in producing laughter is proved, he explains,
by the ticklishness of the armpits. For, in Pliny's version of human anatomy, the diaphragm extends right up to the arms; scratching the armpits,
where "the skin is finer than anywhere else in the body," directly stimulates the diaphragm and so causes laughter.[5] But the spleen is involved
too. Or at least "there are those who think that if the spleen is removed
[or reduced], a man's capacity for laughter is removed at the same time,
and that excessive laughter is caused by a large spleen."[6]

Elsewhere in Pliny's encyclopedia we find all kinds of fantastic tales
about laughter—earnestly recounted, however weird they may seem to
us. There is, for example, the curious fact about Crassus (the grandfather of the more famous Marcus Licinius Crassus, killed at the battle
of Carrhae in 53 BCE), who, "so they say," never once laughed in his
whole life. His story leads off a long discussion of people with strange
bodily peculiarities: from Socrates, who always wore the same facial
expression and never seemed happy or sad, to Antonia (the daughter of
Mark Antony), who never spat, and a certain Pomponius, "a poet and
a man of consular rank," who never belched.[7]

Plants and a variety of other natural features have a part to play too.
Pliny tells of the marvelous *gelotophyllis* (laughter leaves) that grew in
Bactria, a region on the borders of modern Afghanistan and Uzbekistan,
and along the banks of the river Borysthenes (the modern Dnieper). If it
was consumed in a mixture of myrrh and wine, it produced hallucinations
and laughter, which could be controlled only by an antidote of "pine-nut
kernels, with pepper and honey in palm wine." Was this a cannabis plant,
as some modern readers of Pliny have hoped? Or was it, more prosaically,
as one dictionary has it, "probably a sort of crowfoot"?[8]

Also in the Eastern Roman Empire, in what is now central Turkey,
Pliny points to two extraordinary springs, Claeon (Weeping) and Gelon
(Laughing), so called—he explains—from the Greek words for the effect

that drinking from each one had. Springs had a definite association with ancient laughter. Pomponius Mela, for example, a Roman geographer and contemporary of Pliny, refers to another pair on "the Fortunate Islands" (probably the Canaries): the water of one would make you laugh to death; the other, luckily, was an effective antidote. But it was Pliny's story that made a particular impression on Sir William Ramsay, an intrepid Scot from Aberdeen and late nineteenth-century explorer of Asia Minor, who took it so seriously that he tried to locate the very springs, in rural Phrygia. Having resolved in 1891, he wrote, "to test out every spring at Apameia," he found two that neatly fitted the bill—though, oddly, he seems to have identified them on the basis of the sound their water made ("We could hear the bright, clear, cheerful sound with which the 'Laughing Water' ripples forth. . . . No one who goes to these two fountains and listens will entertain the slightest doubt that they are 'the Laughing' and 'the Weeping'"). Pliny, by contrast, was referring to the water's power: one spring made you laugh, the other cry.[9]

Where Pliny found his information is not always clear. Occasionally (and perhaps more often than modern critics tend to acknowledge) it came from personal observation or inquiry. That is almost certainly the case for one part of his discussion of the role of the diaphragm in producing laughter, which ends by noting a much more ghoulish version of the phenomenon of underarm tickling. It can be seen both on the battlefield and in gladiatorial shows, he claims, when the diaphragm is punctured, rather than merely scratched, that the result can be death—accompanied by laughter. The idea that wounds to the diaphragm could provoke laughter from military casualties had a long history in Greek scientific writing, going back at least to the fourth century BCE. But it may well have been Pliny himself, from his experience as a spectator in the Roman arena, who made the connection with the deaths of gladiators.[10]

In general, however, Pliny was proud to have assembled his information from earlier writers—so proud that, at the beginning of the *Natural History,* he insists that he has drawn on some two thousand volumes by one hundred authorities in compiling his twenty thousand facts, and he systematically lists those he has used for each book of his encyclopedia.[11] In a very few instances, we can more or less pinpoint the source of his material on laughter. For example, the story of the two springs, "Weeping" and "Laughing," almost certainly derived from the work of the fourth-century Greek scientist, philosopher, and pupil of Aristotle Theophrastus, or at least it follows directly on from the tale of another extraordinary spring in the same region (this one "threw up masses of stones") for which Pliny explicitly references Theophrastus.[12] For the most part, though, it is a matter of conjecture from which of his named sources, or from where exactly in the rich tradition of Greek and Roman speculation on laughter, Pliny has gleaned any particular theory or piece of information. It is a question of spotting the similarities and postulating connections. So, for example, to judge from their similarity to a discussion in Aristotle's fourth-century treatise *Parts of Animals,* many of Pliny's remarks—gladiators aside—on the importance of the diaphragm in the production of laughter almost certainly go back ultimately to Aristotle himself or to one of his followers.[13]

A rich and varied tradition of speculation it certainly was, in Rome especially—as Roman writers drew on their classical and Hellenistic Greek predecessors, refining and adapting their theories, and adding some distinctively Roman contributions of their own. Even if we leave aside, for the moment, their discussions of the ethics of joking and laughter (when it is proper to laugh, at what, and for what purpose), Pliny's remarks are just one small glimpse into Roman opinion about the causes and characteristics of laughter, ranging from the frank expressions of bafflement we have already noted to yet more ingenious and learned theorizing.

Galen may have despaired of revealing the physiological roots of laughter. But he had theories aplenty about the comic nature of apes and monkeys. These were animals that, as we shall see in chapter 7, could usually be guaranteed to raise a laugh among the Romans, and Galen knew them very well, for the simple reason that—given the impossibility or unacceptability of human dissection at that period—he based much of his anatomical and physiological theory on the dissection of apes. For him, the laughter they provoked was a question of imitation or, as we might put it, caricature. "We laugh particularly," he wrote, "at those imitations that preserve an accurate likeness in most of their parts but are completely wrong in the most important ones." So we laugh at the ape, Galen argues, as a caricature of the human being: its "hands," for example, are very like our own in every respect, except the most important—the ape's thumb is not opposed to its fingers, making it useless and "utterly laughable" (*pantē geloios*). This is a rare ancient reflection on what makes something visually laughable.[14]

Others had different observations. Plutarch, writing in the early second century CE about the role of laughing and joking at dinner, stresses what we would call the social determinates of laughter. What people laugh at, he insists, depends on the company in which they find themselves (you can laugh at a joke with your friends that you could not bear to hear in the company of your father or your wife). And he points to the way in which social hierarchy impacts on laughter. The success of a joke depends on who is telling it: people will laugh if a man of humble origins jokes about the low birth of another; the same quip from an aristocrat will be taken as an insult.[15]

That question of why people laugh at jokes was also posed, and answered, by Roman theorists of rhetoric, Cicero included. After side-stepping the general problems of the nature of laughter in *On the Orator*, he turns—in the voice of Julius Caesar Strabo, the main character in this part of the long dialogue—to the specific ways an orator can exploit laughter and to what raises a laugh and why. "The main, if not the only, prompts to laughter," he says, "are those sayings which highlight and point the finger at something unseemly but in no unseemly fashion." Or as Quintilian put it more snappily, just over a century later, "laughter is not so far from derision" (better in Latin: "a derisu non procul abest risus").[16] But the investigation that follows in Cicero's dialogue (as also in Quintilian's textbook on oratory) is more varied and nuanced than that summary might suggest. In analyzing the rhetoric of joking, Cicero identifies all kinds of features that may provoke laughter—from mimicry and "pulling faces" to the unexpected and the "incongruous" (*discrepantia*).[17] And it is Cicero who is the earliest surviving source for something close to the modern cliché in the study of laughter that nothing is less funny than the analysis of a joke: "'My view,' said Caesar, 'is that a man, even if he is not unamusing, can discuss anything in the world more affably than wit itself.'"[18]

These Roman theories and observations take us into that intriguing intellectual no-man's-land between the utterly familiar and the disconcertingly strange—between, for example, that simple question of "What makes people laugh?" (and which of us has not asked that?) and the unbelievable tales of magical springs and overactive spleens. But even that dichotomy proves to be less stable than we might at first imagine. This is partly the problem of how slippery and deceptive apparently familiar ideas can be. When Cicero wrote that "incongruity," as I have translated the Latin *discrepantia,* was a cause of laughter, just how close to modern "incongruity theories" of laughter—which we shall shortly explore—was he? Or, if we identify Pliny's *gelotophyllis* as cannabis, which we now believe is a good, chemical source of the giggles, does that make Pliny a more familiar and reliable witness than if we opt for the dictionary definition of "crowfoot" (which is not usually thought to have laughter-inducing properties at all)?[19] But perhaps even more destabilizing is the way that those extravagant and implausible views of the ancients can prompt us to look again at some of our own scientific "truths" about this subject. What, after all, is to count as a plausible explanation of why we laugh? In the end, is one theory of modern neuroscience, that the site of laughter is located in the "anterior part of the human supplementary motor area" in the left frontal lobe of the brain, any more believable, or at least any more useful, for most of us on an everyday basis than Pliny's mad ideas about the diaphragm and the spleen?[20]

ARISTOTLE AND "THE CLASSICAL THEORY OF LAUGHTER"

It is surprising, given the extraordinary diversity of these Roman speculations on laughter and its causes, that modern studies so often refer, in the singular, to "the classical theory of laughter." This theory has become definitively associated with Aristotle, who still casts his heavy shadow over modern studies of laughter—the first systematic analyst, so it is often said, of the whole subject, and the one who canonically formulated (even if he did not originate[21]) two major claims. The first is that man is the only animal to laugh, or—to put it in its stronger form— that laughter is a property of the human being (man, that is, can be defined as "the animal that laughs"). The second is that laughter is essentially derisory or is the expression of the laugher's superiority over, and contempt for, the butt of his laughter. Scholars working in later periods all too often assume that ancient speculation on laughter essentially followed a single tradition more or less defined by Aristotle and his followers, in the so-called Peripatetic school that he established.[22] In fact, it is not uncommon, even for classicists, to try to identify a direct source for most Roman writing on laughter in the works of Aristotle or later writers of his school (Theophrastus and Demetrius of Phaleron being popular candidates).[23]

So was all ancient analysis of laughter in effect a series of "footnotes to Aristotle"?[24] Before proceeding much further in exploring what Roman writers had to say about the subject, we need to look critically, and in some detail, at Aristotle's contributions to theories of (and about) laughter and to consider how clear and systematic they may have been. This will involve broaching some of the arguments that surround perhaps the most famous "lost work" of antiquity: the second book of his

Poetics, which once formed the sequel to his analysis of the nature of tragedy, with its famous views of catharsis, pity, and fear. It was here, it is usually supposed, that Aristotle tackled the subject of comedy.

I am not claiming that Aristotle's work on laughter had no influence on Roman approaches. Roman writers on science, rhetoric, and culture were undoubtedly indebted to, and in dialogue with, their Aristotelian predecessors; in fact, I have already noted that Pliny cites Theophrastus as one of his authorities in the *Natural History* and seems to reflect some Aristotelian observations in his discussion of the role of the diaphragm in laughter. But the common idea that Aristotle's work on the subject—insofar as we can recover it—represented a systematic theoretical position amounting to something that could be called "the classical theory of laughter" is (at the very least) a drastic oversimplification, or, to put it bluntly, wrong. The truth is that many of the often-quoted, "classic" remarks by Aristotle—intriguing and intelligent though they may individually be—are little more than asides, and not part of a developed theory at all. Even the lost second book of the *Poetics*—with whatever it had to say of the nature, causes, and ethics of laughter as it occurred in the comic theater—hardly justifies the exaggerated significance often optimistically attributed to it.

This book has been one of the great controversies (or holy grails) of classical studies, and it has been hugely mythologized. A few mavericks have denied that it ever existed;[25] many more have been entranced by the lure of what has been lost and have debated how its contents are to be reconstructed. Most famously of all, it has been given a starring role in a best-selling modern novel. Umberto Eco's clever fantasy *The Name of the Rose* reenacted the destruction of this elusive text. At the climax of the mystery story (which also argues for the "liberating, anti-totalitarian" power of laughter as a weapon against oppressive authority), the very last manuscript copy of Aristotle's precious treatise, held in a murder-ridden medieval monastery, is literally consumed by a laughter-hating librarian—before the whole place goes up in flames.[26]

Eco's novel dramatizes not only the opposition to laughter by the authorities of the medieval church but also the belief, held by many students of both ancient and modern culture, that Aristotle's second book of the *Poetics* would have offered the missing link to "the classical view of laughter." As Quentin Skinner once remarked, in trying to answer the question of why ancient Greek statues so rarely appear to smile, "It's odd that the phenomenon we would call good-natured laughter seems to have been a notion completely foreign to the ancient

Greeks. It's a terrible shame that Aristotle's treatise on comedy is lost, for *he would surely have explained.*"[27]

Others have tried to show that it is not quite as lost as is usually assumed. Hints of what it contained have been gleaned from other works of Aristotle. More radically, a quarter of a century ago, Richard Janko made a bold attempt to revive a much older idea that a short treatise known as the *Tractatus Coislinianus,* preserved in a tenth-century manuscript now in Paris, is none other than a skeletal summary of the second book of the *Poetics.* If so, it would confirm the contents of the book as both a literary analysis of comedy and a discussion of the sources of (comic) laughter, from words to actions—for instance "using vulgar dancing" or "when someone who has the power [to choose] lets slip the most important and takes the most worthless."[28]

This idea has never won much support: the majority view is that the *Tractatus* is a muddled, mediocre confection, possibly Byzantine, which preserves at most a few traces of thirdhand Aristotelian reflection.[29] Yet in any case, the more fundamental question is whether that lost book really did contain the key to ancient analysis of comedy—and whether, as Skinner wrote, it "would surely have explained" what we want to know about Greek laughter and its theories. There is no clear sign that it would, and some telling hints that it would not. For why—in the pointed words of Michael Silk (who has done more than most to dispel the shadow of Aristotle over ancient laughter)—were those "Aristotelian pearls of wisdom on comedy" lost in the first place and "ignored by all of subsequent antiquity"? Disconcerting as this may seem, Silk's presumption is that "all or most of what Aristotle in fact said on the subject was perfunctory—and maybe *Tract. Coisl.* reflects it—and that there were no pearls there to be ignored anyway."[30]

Who can know? This brisk dismissal may do Aristotle an injustice. But it is certainly hard to resist the conclusion that the loss of the second book of the *Poetics* (assuming, of course, that there was one) has contributed to its modern fame and exaggerated its ancient significance. We are dealing here with a powerful combination of our own emotional investment in those tantalizing books that have slipped through the net and—let's be honest—the convenience (in the absence of any firm evidence) of being able to reconstruct an Aristotelian view to suit our own various purposes. Indeed it may well be, as Silk again has hinted, that the "theory of comedy" in the *Poetics* owes much more to the inventive zeal of modern Aristotelians than to the mixed bag of observations and aperçus that Aristotle himself offered. The plain fact is that they are lost.[31]

If we focus instead on Aristotle's remarks on laughter that do survive, we get a very different impression from that which is often presented, and again much more of a mixed bag. For they include plenty of ideas *about* laughter but nothing that remotely approaches a theory *of* laughter—in the sense of a coherent explanatory model, a defined methodology, and a panoply of argument directed at the subject in hand. Aristotle certainly had powerful and systematic theories of other topics, but there is no sign of that in the case of laughter.[32] His longest discussion on the subject occupies a couple of modern pages in the *Nicomachean Ethics,* where he advocates, as so often, the virtuous middle way between two extremes. To be "well-turned" or "witty" (*eutrapelos*) is a desirable characteristic of a "gentleman" (as the Greek *eleutheros* is conventionally, but awkwardly, translated). Too much joking is the mark of a "buffoon" (*bōmolochos*), too little the mark of a "boor" (*agroikos*): both are to be avoided.[33] But the two main elements of what has become known as "the classical theory of laughter" are found elsewhere.

The claim that human beings are the only animals that laugh is a subsidiary argument in Aristotle's discussion of the human body, in particular the role of the diaphragm. In a perilously circular explanation, he asserts that the fact that "humans alone are susceptible to tickling is due (a) to the fineness of their skin and (b) to their being the only living things that laugh." There is in this no suggestion that laughter is a distinguishing property of the human being. Despite the popular assumption about this aspect of his "theory," he is certainly not defining man as "the animal that laughs."[34]

The other claim, that laughter is a form of derision and a display of superiority, is more complicated. It derives in part from the discussion in the *Nicomachean Ethics* where Aristotle refers to some forms of joking (*skōmma*) as "a kind of abuse" or "a reproach" (*loidorēma ti*).[35] But in its popular form, it is drawn mainly from two passages in two different treatises. In the first, surviving book of the *Poetics,* he has a few words to say, in passing, on the subject of comedy: "A representation of people worse than us, not in the full sense of bad, but what we laugh at, is a subdivision of the ugly/shameful [*tou aischrou*]. The laughable is some kind of fault and ugliness/shame [*aischos*] that involves no pain or harm—such as, obviously, a comic mask [literally a 'laughable face,' *geloion prosōpon*], which is ugly [*aischron*] and distorted but free of pain."[36] This is often put together with a second passage, from Aristotle's *Rhetoric,* where he discusses the character of different groups of an orator's potential audience (for without knowing what his listeners are like, the orator will never successfully persuade them). The young, Aristotle explains, are fickle, passionate, argumentative, and highly principled; also, "they are fond of laughter, and therefore witty [*eutrapeloi*]. For wit is educated insolence [*pepaidumenē hubris*]."[37]

It is hard to know how exactly to translate these passages, or to know what point Aristotle was trying to make. The key extract from the *Poetics* raises all kinds of questions. What kind of fault—moral or physical (shame or ugliness?)—underlies the laughable? Whose pain, or lack of it, does Aristotle have in mind? What implications does this discussion of comic drama have for laughter off the stage?[38] The other passage, from the *Rhetoric*, is even more puzzling, largely because of the strange oxymoron, even "joke," in the phrase "educated insolence" (*pepaidumenē hubris*). For, as critics have often seen, *hubris* (which can mean anything from "excess" through "outrage" to "violence" or "rape") cannot be "educated," but that very word *pepaidumenē* has, in any case, an ambiguous root, *paid-*, which signifies both "education" and "childishness" or "play."[39] What is Aristotle trying to say about wit, apart from being witty himself?

It is clearer what is he not saying. First, there is rather less about derision than is usually supposed. It is true that creative translation can turn his definition of wit into "educated *abuse*," but the famous lines from the *Poetics*—though they refer to the subject of laughter as being "some kind of fault" and so suggest an element of derision—explicitly reject the idea of pain; there is no reason to see "scoffing" here.[40]

Second, even though some of these passages do share an interest in laughter prompted by ridicule (or laughter at another's expense), Aristotle certainly does not suggest that this is laughter's only cause, function, or stylistic register. If he were suggesting that, he would have been a very poor reader of Greek literature and culture, in which (*pace* Skinner's assertion that it was a completely "foreign" notion) there was plenty of "good-natured laughter."[41] In fact, Aristotle himself, in another passage in the *Rhetoric*, explicitly places laughter and the laughable into the class of "pleasant things." Whatever exactly he may have meant by this, it has seemed so incompatible with the idea of derision that several editors of the text have rejected it as a later addition—not by Aristotle.[42]

The fact is that Aristotle's ideas about laughter were numerous and not necessarily mutually compatible. One sixth-century commentary on a philosophical textbook (*The Introduction*) by Porphyry even states that Aristotle in his *History of Animals* claimed that man was not the only animal to laugh: herons did too. True or not (and the laughter of the heron is found in no text of Aristotle that we still possess), he approached the subject from a variety of angles, and his views cannot be reduced, or elevated, to a single, systematic "classical theory of laughter."[43]

It is also important to underline that there was almost certainly a much looser link than is often assumed between this diverse Aristotelian theorizing and later Roman writing about laughter. Roman theorists were not wholly dependent on what Aristotle had said before, or on the works of his immediate followers. With these, we confront the problem of loss on an even bigger scale than with the second book of the *Poetics*. Almost none of the key texts of Aristotle's Peripatetic successors between the fourth and second centuries BCE survive, beyond a few sentences and some disputed titles. This makes it impossible to prove that they are not the source for any individual claim we may find in Roman discussions. But the signs are that—in laughter as in so many other areas—there was significant Roman input into the dialogue with earlier Greek thought. The argument that laughter is a property of man may even have been an innovation of writers of the Roman period, developing Aristotle's almost casual observation that (leaving aside the possible distraction of the heron) man is the only animal that laughs. At least, we find that theory regularly in Roman imperial writers—and never in earlier surviving literature.

In the words of Porphyry, for example, writing in Greek in the third century CE, "Even if a man does not always laugh, he is said to be laughing not in that he always laughs but that he is of such a nature as to laugh—and this holds of him always, being connatural, like neighing of horses. And they say that these are properties in the strict sense, because they convert: if horse, neighing; and if neighing, horse." Or, as Porphyry implies: if man, laughing; and if laughing, man.[44] For obvious reasons, this became a very loaded set of ideas in the controversies of early Christian theology, for if Jesus were known to have laughed, that would have major implications for those crucial debates about how his status—divine or human—was to be defined. Indeed, this is an issue that animates and divides Eco's fictional monks in *The Name of the Rose*: Did Jesus laugh, or didn't he?[45]

More generally, Roman discussions of laughter are only rarely a precise match for the Aristotelian theories that do survive in the works of Aristotle. It is clear enough, for example, that Pliny's views on tickling are Aristotelian in a broad sense, focusing on the role of the diaphragm in the production of laughter. But it is equally clear that Pliny's account is significantly different from the version of tickling in *On the Parts of Animals:* Pliny suggests that it is direct irritation of the diaphragm that raises a laugh; Aristotle had argued instead that it was the heat generated by the irritation that actually produced the laughter. Pliny also has a different view from Aristotle on the first occurrence of a baby's laughter (Pliny's babies do not laugh at all until forty days old, while Aristotle's laugh and weep while asleep), and it was surely somewhere else that Pliny picked up that story about Zoroaster, which is found in Iranian sources as well. To claim that all Pliny's variants derive from some lost Peripatetic follower of Aristotle would be a mere act of faith.[46]

Much the same is true of Cicero's discussion of laughter in *On the Orator.* This contains some material almost certainly derived from the Aristotelian tradition (Aristotle had, for example, already highlighted "incongruity" as a cause of laughter[47]). But most recent investigations of this dialogue have identified much less Demetrius of Phaleron (and his elusive, possibly nonexistent, treatise *On the Laughable*) and many more Roman elements, themes, and theories than was once thought. In fact, one of the main distinctions that structures Cicero's argument—that between *cavillatio* (extended humor) and *dicacitas* (immediate witticisms)—seems to have little to do with anything we can find (or reconstruct) in earlier Greek works on the subject: these were, in Elaine Fantham's words, "old-fashioned Roman terms" making "a Roman distinction."[48]

I shall come back to the relationship between Greek and Roman laughter, in both theory and practice, in chapter 4. At this point let me emphasize two important tenets that underpin the rest of this book. First, there is no such thing as "the Aristotelian theory of laughter," or at least not in those precise terms. Aristotle generated all kinds of ideas about laughter, a range of speculations and aperçus on aspects of the subject as diverse as tickling, the mechanisms of jokes, comedy, derision, the role of laughter in social life, and the importance of play. But there is no reason to suppose that Aristotle developed a systematic theory of laughter, or even that he necessarily saw laughter as a unitary phenomenon and field of inquiry.

Second, however influential some of Aristotle's views were (and they certainly were influential), they did not delimit ancient approaches to laughter, still less did they amount to anything that might be called "*the* classical approach to laughter." In both Greece and Rome, views about laughter multiplied and took root—some more strongly than others—in many different contexts, from the philosophical schools (for it was not only the Peripatetics who had things to say on laughter[49]) to the emperor's dinner table, from the rhetorical classroom to the bar and the brothel. To put it simply, there was—as we have already glimpsed—a lot of very varied talk about laughter in antiquity.

Just as there is in the modern world. And it is to this that we now turn, and to another shadow that hangs heavily over recent studies of laughter: the so-called three theories of laughter. These are, in a sense, the younger siblings of "the classical theory," and they too need to be gently dethroned before we move on.

"THE THREE THEORIES OF LAUGHTER"

The range of modern writing on laughter is truly daunting. My own university library holds around 150 books with *Laughter* somewhere in the title, published in English in the first decade of the twenty-first century. Leaving aside assorted memoirs, novels, and collections of poetry that managed to squeeze the word on to their title page (*Love, Laughter and Tears at the World's Most Famous Cooking School* and the like), these books range from popular psychology and self-help manuals through the philosophy of humor and the anatomy of the joke to the history of the chuckle, the chortle, the snigger, and the giggle in almost any period or place you can imagine (right back to the origins of laughter in the caves of primitive humans).

Behind these monographs—both weighty and popular—lies an even wider array of specialist articles and papers investigating yet more aspects of the subject, in ever finer detail: from the use of laughter in health education films in Dutch colonial Java or the sound of laughter in the novels of James Joyce to the patterns of laughter between interviewer and respondent in telephone surveys and that old classical chestnut of when, and how, babies first start to laugh or smile.[50] Not to mention all the radical philosophical, political, and feminist celebrations of laughter that would no doubt have confirmed the worst fears of the starchy Lord Chesterfield—whose notorious advice to his son in the 1740s was that a gentleman should at all costs avoid laughing out loud.[51] Wyndham Lewis and others, for example, urged laughter "like a bomb" in their 1914 Vorticist manifesto. And modern French feminism has often put laughter at center stage—rescuing the monstrous, snaky-headed, cackling Gorgon of classical mythology from Sigmund Freud's revulsion (to parade instead her beauty and her laughter) and making laughter a defining characteristic of that complex amalgam of female body and text that has become known as *l'écriture féminine* (inadequately translated as "women's writing"). The text is "the rhythm that laughs you" ("le rythme qui te rit")—as Hélène Cixous memorably, but somewhat mystically, wrote.[52]

There is far too much written—and still being written—on the subject of laughter for any one person to master; nor, frankly, would it be worth their while to try. But when confronted with the product of centuries of analysis and investigation, stretching back as we have seen into antiquity itself, it is tempting to suggest that it is not so much laughter that is the defining property of the human species but rather the drive to debate and theorize laughter.

It is partly in response to the sheer profusion of views and speculation about laughter across various fields of inquiry that a "second-order" level of theorizing has developed—which divides theories of laughter into three main strands, with key theorists taken to represent each one. There are few books on laughter that do not offer, somewhere near the beginning, as I am about to do, a brief explanation of these theories of what laughter is, what it signifies, and how it is caused. I am more suspicious than many commentators of the oversimplification that this metatheorizing often entails, but I am struck that each of the three—more or less distinctly—echoes some strand of ancient theorizing (hence my phrase *younger siblings*). We are still discussing laughter in ways that are closely linked to the ancient Greeks and Romans.[53]

The first we have already touched on in discussing Aristotle. It is the so-called superiority theory, which argues that laughter is a form of derision or mockery. Laughter, in other words, always has a victim: we always laugh, more or less aggressively, at the butt of our jokes or the object of our mirth, and in the process we assert our superiority over them. Apart from ancient writers (including Quintilian, with his snappy slogan about *risus* being close to derision, *derisus*), the most celebrated theorist of superiority is the seventeenth-century philosopher Thomas Hobbes. "The passion of Laughter," he wrote in *The Elements of Law*, "is nothyng else but a suddaine Glory arising from some suddaine Conception of some Eminency in our selves, by Comparison with the Infirmityes of others"—a much-quoted sentence, whose catchword of "Sudden Glory" has often been reused, even recently as the title of a book on the history of laughter.[54] But superiority theory is not only an aspect of the philosophy and ethics of laughing. Evolutionary biology chimes in, with some reconstructions of laughter's origins among the earliest humans: the idea, for example, that laughter derives directly from "the roar of triumph in an ancient jungle duel" or that the laugh (or the smile) originated in an aggressive baring of the teeth.[55]

The second is known as the incongruity theory and sees laughter as a response to the illogical or the unexpected. Aristotle gives a very simple example of this: "On he came, his feet shod with his—chilblains." This raises a laugh, Aristotle explains, because the listener expects the word *sandals,* not *chilblains.*[56] But a much bigger team of modern philosophers and critics can be marshaled as supporters of this theory, albeit with a wide range of nuances and emphases. Immanuel Kant, for example, claimed that "laughter is an affection arising from a strained expectation being suddenly reduced to nothing" (another of the most famous slogans in the study of laughter). Henri Bergson argued that laughter is provoked by living beings acting as if they were machines—mechanically, repetitively, stiffly. More recently, the linguistic theories of Salvatore Attardo and Victor Raskin have set the resolution of incongruity at the heart of verbal jokes—as in "'When is a door not a door?' 'When it's a jar.'"[57]

Experimental science has a role here too. One of the most celebrated experiments in the history of laboratory-based studies of laughter is the weight discrepancy test. Subjects are asked to lift a series of weights, similar in size and appearance and varying only slightly in heaviness, and to rank them from heaviest to lightest. Then another weight is introduced, similar in appearance but substantially heavier or lighter than the rest. The subjects regularly laugh when they lift the new weight—because, it is argued, of the incongruity between it and the others. In fact, the heavier or lighter the new weight is, the more strongly they laugh: the greater the incongruity, in other words, the more intense the laughter.[58]

The last of the trio is the relief theory, best known from the work of Sigmund Freud but not invented by him. In its simplest, pre-Freudian form, this theory sees laughter as the physical sign of the release of nervous energy or repressed emotion. It is the emotional equivalent of a safety valve. Rather like the pressure of steam in a steam engine, pent-up anxiety about death, for example, is "let off" when we laugh at a joke about an undertaker.[59] (Cicero may be hinting at something along these lines when he defends his own controversial joking in the midst of the civil war between Caesar and Pompey.[60]) Freud's version of this idea is considerably more complicated. In his *Jokes and Their Relation to the Unconscious,* he argues that the energy released in laughter is not the energy of the repressed emotion itself (on the safety-valve model) but the psychic energy that would have been used to repress the thoughts or feelings if the joke had not allowed them to enter our conscious minds. A joke about an undertaker, in other words, allows our fear of death to be expressed, and the laughter is the "letting off" of the surplus psychic energy that would otherwise have been used to repress it. The more energy it would have taken to repress the fear, the bigger the laugh will be.[61]

These three theories can be a convenient shorthand: they bring some order to the complicated history of speculation on laughter, and they highlight some striking similarities in the way that it has been understood across the centuries. But beyond that, they run into serious problems—both in terms of the individual theories of laughter themselves and as an overarching scheme for classifying the field of study as a whole. For a start, none of the theories tackles laughter in its widest sense. They may try to explain why we laugh at jokes, but they do not address the question of why we laugh when we are tickled. Nor do they explore the social, conventional, domesticated laughter that punctuates so much of human interaction; they are much more interested in the apparently spontaneous or uncontrollable type.[62] To put it another way, they are more concerned with Dio's laugh than with Gnatho's—and not even, for the most part, with the act of laughing itself.[63] The first two theories do not begin to explain why the physical response we know as laughter (the noise, the facial contortion, the heaving of the chest) should be prompted by the recognition of superiority or incongruity. The relief theory does face that question directly, but Freud's suggestion—that the psychic energy that would have been deployed in repressing the emotion is somehow converted into bodily movement—is itself deeply problematic.[64]

In practice, most of these attempts to theorize "laughter" focus more narrowly on the related, and somewhat more manageable, categories of "the comic," "jokes," or "humor." The titles of some of the most famous books on the subject make this focus clear: Freud was writing explicitly about jokes; the full title of Bergson's treatise is *Laughter: An Essay on the Meaning of the Comic;* Simon Critchley's excellent recent study, which includes a good deal about laughter, is titled *On Humour.*

Even within these limits, it is a general rule that the more features and varieties of laughter that a theory sets out to explain, the less plausible it will be. No statement that begins with the words "All laughter . . ." is ever likely to be true (or at least if true, too self-evident to be interesting). Superiority theory, for example, throws a good deal of light on some classes of joking and laughing. But the more it aims at being a total and totalizing theory, the less light it throws. It needs desperate ingenuity to explain on the basis of superiority why we laugh at puns. Could it really be that the verbal jousting they imply takes us back to ritualized contests for supremacy in the world of primitive man? Or could it possibly be a question of displaying human superiority over language itself? I very much doubt it.[65]

And whatever we make of Freud's attempt to describe the mechanism of laughter generated by a dirty joke, when the same principles are extended to the question of why we laugh at (say) the exaggerated movements of clowns, the result is itself almost laughable. Still arguing that a saving of psychic energy must be involved, Freud claims that in watching the clown, we will compare his movements to those that we ourselves would use in achieving the same goals (walking across a room, maybe). We must generate psychic energy to imagine performing his movements, and the bigger the movements that have to be imagined, the more psychic energy will be generated. But when it is finally clear that this is surplus to requirements—in comparison with that needed to imagine our own more economical movements—the extra energy is discharged, in laughter.[66] This is, to be sure, a brave attempt to impose some systematic, scientific consistency across a range of different types of laughter. But its sheer implausibility must prompt us to wonder what we can expect from a general theory of how and why people laugh. For rather like Aristotle, modern theorists—whatever their grander aims may be—are almost always more revealing and stimulating in their speculations, aperçus, and theories *about* laughter than in any overarching theory *of* laughter.

There is also a problem, however, with the tripartite scheme itself. Convenient shorthand it may be. But it is also dangerously oversimplifying and encourages us to shoehorn long, complicated, nuanced, and not always consistent arguments into its tidy but rigid framework. The truth is, of course, that the theoretical landscape in this area is much messier than "the theory of the three theories" would suggest. This is clear enough from the fact that the same theorists crop up, in modern synoptic accounts, as key representatives of different theories. Bergson, for example, is assigned to both incongruity and superiority: incongruity because he argued that laughter arises when human beings are perceived to be acting "mechanically," when—in other words—a human behaves like a machine; superiority because for Bergson the social function of laughter was to mock, and so discourage, such inelasticity ("Rigidity is the comic, and laughter is its *corrective*").[67] Even Aristotle can be differently pigeonholed. To be sure, his elusive "theory of laughter" (or comedy) is usually seen as a classic case of superiority theory, but he also crops up as an advocate of incongruity and, rather less plausibly, of relief.[68]

In fact, through the long history of studies of laughter, the works of the "founding fathers" have more often been raided than read; they have been selectively summarized to provide an intellectual genealogy for many different arguments; and slogans have been extracted that rarely reflect their original inchoate, uncertain, and sometimes self-contradictory complexity. It can often be a shock to go back to the original texts and discover what exactly was written and in what context. The famous quotation from Hobbes, for example, about laughter "arising from some suddaine Conception of some Eminency in our selves, by Comparison with the Infirmityes of others" reads rather differently when we realize that it continues with the phrase "or with our owne formerly": it is still a theory of superiority, but referring to self-criticism as well as the mockery of others. And Quentin Skinner has emphasized how Hobbes, in discussing laughter in the *Leviathan* in apparently similar terms, suggests that it actually reveals a sense of inferiority on the part of the laugher. Laughter, Hobbes wrote there, "is incident most to them, that are conscious of the fewest abilities in themselves; who are forced to keep themselves in their own favour, by observing the imperfections of other men. And therefore much Laughter at the defects of others, is a signe of Pusillanimity." This is a rather different view of what lies behind that Sudden Glory than any simple version of superiority theory would suggest.[69]

The hundreds of pages that Freud wrote on the subject of jokes, humor, and the comic (comprising also a good deal about laughter) have probably been more selectively appropriated and tendentiously quoted than any other work on the subject. Freud's "theory" is a dazzling and confusing mixture: an attempt to reach a consistent, scientific approach (most implausibly, as we have seen, at its edges) standing alongside a range of speculations—some of which have little to do with his main argument, and some of which seem flatly contradictory. Freud offers probably the most extreme example of critics and theorists mining the work to extract different "key points" to back up their own arguments. So, in addition to the "relief theory" of laughter, one recent writer on Roman satire has stressed Freud's observation on the complex psychosocial dynamics of the joke (among the teller, the listener, and the joke's victim); another, writing on theatrical laughter in Greece, has emphasized instead Freud's insistence that "we scarcely ever know what we are laughing at"; another, concerned with Roman invective, invokes

Freud's distinction between tendentious and innocent jokes and his discussion of the role of humor in humiliation; and so on.[70] All these aspects are there. But it is salutary to wonder, if Freud's *Joke* book—like the second book of Aristotle's *Poetics*—were one day to be lost, what kind of reconstruction could be made from the various summaries and quotes. My guess is that it would be a very far cry from the original.

One of the aims of this book is to preserve some of this disorder in the study of laughter, to make it a messier rather than a tidier subject. There will be much less on the three theories than you might expect.

NATURE AND CULTURE?

It will already be clear, I hope, that what has made laughter such an intriguing and compelling object of investigation for more than two thousand years is also what makes it such a tricky and sometimes intractable one. One of the most difficult questions is whether laughter should be thought of as a unitary phenomenon at all: Should we even be looking for a theory that might put under the same explanatory umbrella the ultimate causes (or the social effects) of the laughter produced by a hearty tickling, a good joke, or a mad emperor brandishing an ostrich head in the arena—let alone that often rather subdued version that regularly punctuates and reinforces human conversation? Scrupulous caution might suggest that these are significantly different signals, with different causes and effects. Yet in all kinds of ways, laughter as a response does feel very similar across its different manifestations, both for the laugher and for the audience.[71] Besides, it is often impossible to draw a clear boundary between its various types. The laughter of polite punctuation can slip imperceptibly into something much more uproarious; most of us, in Dio's position, would not be certain whether we were laughing out of nervousness or at the ridiculous antics of the emperor; and when someone is being tickled, it is common for even the observers, who are not themselves being tickled, to laugh.

But even more crucial is the question of how far laughter is a "natural" or a "cultural" phenomenon—or, perhaps better, how far laughter directly challenges the simplicity of that binary division. As Mary Douglas summed it up, "Laughter is a unique bodily eruption which is always taken to be a communication." Unlike sneezing or farting, it is taken to mean something. This is a distinction that Pliny missed in one of his observations on laughter that I have already quoted. For although he grouped together Crassus "who never laughed" with Pomponius "who never belched," in fact they make an awkward pairing. Even in this negative aspect, "not to laugh" is a social signifier in a way that "not to belch" (probably) is not.[72]

This ambiguity of laughter, between nature and culture, has a tremendous impact on our attempts to understand how laughter in general operates in human society and more specifically how far it is under our conscious control. "I couldn't help laughing," we often say. Is that true?

To be sure, some laughter really does seem to be, and feels, uncontrollable—and not only that produced by tickling. Whether with Dio chewing on his laurel leaf in the arena or a BBC newsreader who cannot prevent herself corpsing on air, sometimes laughter erupts (or nearly does) whether we want it to or not, entirely outside our conscious design or control. Such incidents are presumably the clearest cases of what Douglas had in mind when she wrote of a "bodily eruption" that is also "taken to be a communication." However unwilled the eruptions may be, the observer or listener will still ask themselves what the laugher is laughing at and what message is being conveyed.

But the idea of laughter's uncontrollability is much more complicated than these simple stories may suggest. We have already seen several Roman instances in which laughter could be held back or released more or less to order, and we have noted the very fuzzy boundary between spontaneous and unspontaneous laughter. Indeed, as we saw in the previous chapter, even the narrative of Dio in the arena is more subtly nuanced than it at first appears. The fact is that most laughter in the world is relatively easy for the laugher to control. Even the effects of tickling are more subject to social conditions than we imagine: you cannot, for example, produce laughter by tickling yourself (try it!), and if tickling is carried out in a hostile rather than a playful environment, it does not cause laughter. Besides, even the most ticklish sites of the body are differently identified in different cultures and at different times. The underarm is more or less universal, but whereas we would stress the soles of the feet, one member of Aristotle's school, responsible for a relevant section of the long scientific compendium known as the *Problems*, had quite other ideas: we are, he claimed, most ticklish "on the lips" (because, he went on to explain, the lips are near "the sense organ").[73] Tickling does not, in other words, as we sometimes imagine, produce a wholly spontaneous, reflex response.[74]

Nonetheless, the dominant myth of uncontrollability has an important function in our view of laughter and in its social regulation. For the long tradition of policing and controlling laughter—stretching back to antiquity itself—regularly relies on that image of a wild, unbounded, potentially dangerous, natural eruption to justify all the careful rules and regulations that are so often proposed. By a nice paradox, the most stringent mechanisms of cultural control are sustained by the powerful myth that laughter is an uncontrollable, disruptive force that contorts the civilized body and subverts the rational mind.

In practice, most people, most of the time, manage to manipulate two strikingly incompatible views of laughter: the myth of its uncontrollability on the one hand and the everyday experience of laughter as a learned, cultural response on the other. Anyone who has ever brought up young children will remember the time and effort it takes to teach them the standard rules of laughter: in simplest terms, what to laugh at and what not to laugh at (clowns, yes; people using wheelchairs, no; *The Simpsons,* yes; the fat lady on the bus, no). And some of the rough justice that children inflict on their peers centers on the proper and improper uses of laughter.[75] This is a theme in literature too. For example, in his fantastic prose-poem *Les Chants de Maldoror,* the Comte de Lautréamont offers an uncomfortably vivid image of the rules of laughter—or rather, of what it would be like to misunderstand them. In the first canto, his title character, the miserable misanthrope, scarcely human, Maldoror, notices people laughing and wants to follow suit, even though he does not see the significance of the gesture. So, in uncomprehending imitation, he takes a pocketknife and cuts the corners of his mouth to make "a laugh," before realizing that he has not made a laugh at all but only a bloody mess. It is a clever reflection on our capacity to learn to laugh and on the idea of laughter as the property of the human being (is Maldoror a human?). And, as always with such stories, we are left with the nagging doubt that Maldoror's first instincts might perhaps have been more right than wrong: that maybe laughter is nothing more than a (metaphorical) knife applied to the lips.[76]

LAUGHING DIFFERENTLY

Another aspect of learning to laugh is found in the cultural specificity of the objects, style, and rhetoric of laughter. Whatever the physiological universals that may be involved, people in different communities, or parts of the world, learn to laugh at different things, on different occasions, and in different contexts (as anyone who has tried to raise a laugh at a conference abroad will readily attest). But it is also a question of *how* people laugh and the gestures that accompany the laughter. Indeed, it is part of our expectations and stereotypes of foreign cultures that they laugh differently. Even the most sophisticated theorists can have strikingly rough-and-ready views about these ethnic differences. For Nietzsche, Hobbes's opposition to laughter (giving it a "bad reputation," or bringing it "into disrepute," as another translation puts it) was just what you would expect from an Englishman.[77]

The classic anthropological example of how people laugh differently comes from the Pygmies of the Ituri Forest in what is now the Democratic Republic of the Congo. As Mary Douglas described it, not only do the Pygmies "laugh easily" compared with other, more dour and solemn tribes, but they laugh in a distinctive way: "They lie on the ground and kick their legs in the air, panting and shaking in paroxysms of laughter."[78] To us this might seem a flamboyant and contrived display, but the Pygmies have so internalized the conventions of their culture that it is, for them, quite "natural."

It is not, however, quite so simple. This description of the Pygmies raises some tricky questions about the nature and culture of laughing and reintroduces some of the literary, discursive, and second-order issues that I touched on in chapter 1. Pygmy laughter, and the paroxysms that go with it, is a favorite standby of students of laughter, a convenient example of cultural diversity in the ways that people laugh. But what is the evidence for it? So far as I can tell, the information is derived from just a single source—a best-selling book called *The Forest People,* by the popular anthropological writer Colin Turnbull. This account was driven by Turnbull's romantic view of the Pygmies, as happy, open, gentle folk, living an idyllic existence, blissfully in harmony with their exotic rain-forest world (in stark contrast, as he claimed in a later book, with the unpleasant, grim mountain people of central Uganda). Exuberant laughter was just one of the signs of the Pygmies' cheerful lifestyle: as Turnbull described it, "When pygmies laugh it is hard not to be affected; they hold on to each other as if for support, slap their sides, snap their fingers, and go through all manner of physical contortions. If something strikes them as particularly funny they will even roll on the ground." Turnbull was "subjective, judgmental and naïve" and almost certainly an unreliable witness of Pygmy culture. Quite how unreliable we will probably never know. But in any case, the more interesting question is why his testimony on Pygmy laughter should have been so widely repeated, even by scholars such as Douglas, who in other respects would have little time for Turnbull's brand of anthropology.[79]

It is partly, no doubt, that even the most hardheaded among us are loath to discard this happy, colorful image of the little Pygmy kicking his legs in the air, despite the reservations we may have about Turnbull's ethnographic observation (and despite the fact that his description actually stopped short of the leg kicking). But there are more discursive issues at work here too. For the behavior of Pygmies, as it is so often told and retold, no longer has much direct relationship with what the real people of the Ituri Forest do, or once did—still less with why they laughed in that way or with what consequences. Their story has become a literary cliché, a shorthand that—in our second-order reflections on laughter— usefully stands for the extreme case of a foreign people who laugh differently. In our own cultural calibration of laughter, the Pygmies have come to mark one end of the spectrum, with the no less overquoted Lord Chesterfield standing for complete control or repression at the other.[80] Nietzsche's view of the English as all lying toward what we might call the Chesterfield end of the laughter spectrum is a hint of how culturally relative such calibration can be. It is hard not to wonder how the Pygmies would have described Turnbull's style of laughter.

"DO DOGS LAUGH?": RHETORIC AND REPRESENTATION

The study of laughter—in the present as much as in the past—is always bound up with literary representation, discursive practice, imagery, and metaphor. And it repeatedly faces the question of where the boundary between literal and metaphorical laughter lies and what the relationship is between them. Sometimes we find it relatively unproblematic to embrace metaphorical readings. If a Roman poet, for example, writes of glittering water or a houseful of flowers "laughing" (*ridere*), that is usually taken as a metaphor for the sparkling gaiety of the scene (rather than some learned hint at the etymology of the verb or its Greek equivalent).[81] But metaphorical uses of "laughing" also lurk just beneath the surface of some of the most apparently scientific, experimental discussions of laughter. Nowhere is this more striking (or more often neglected) than in the old Aristotelian question of whether human beings are the only animals that laugh.

This has been the subject of much inconclusive scientific investigation going back at least to Charles Darwin, who was, for obvious reasons, keen to stress that chimpanzees appeared to laugh when they were tickled. More recent scientific observers have identified a characteristic "open-mouth display" or "play face" in primates engaged in nonserious activities—and have occasionally claimed to detect some chimps and gorillas using jokes and puns in their rudimentary sign language. Some biologists, not to mention devoted dog owners, have concluded that there is also such a thing as canine laughter (a conclusion that prompted Mary Douglas's famous article "Do Dogs Laugh?"), while a few have even interpreted the high-pitched chirping that rats produce when they are tickled as a form of protolaughter (the nape of the neck is said to be one of their most ticklish zones, though they chirp enthusiastically with a "full body" tickle too).[82]

Unsurprisingly, these interpretations have been contested from many angles. The "laughter" of primates, for example, is articulated differently from that of humans. The universal pattern in humans is for the characteristic *ha-ha-ha* to be produced in one single exhalation, followed by silence during inhalation. Not so among the primates. Their panting laughter is vocalized during both the in and the out breath. Is this, as some would have it, just a variant on the same spectrum of laughter? Or does it indicate, as others think, that we are dealing with a significantly different type of response—and that the primates are not, in our terms, laughing at all? The chirping of rats (which is, incidentally, at such a high frequency that it is inaudible to the human ear) remains even more deeply controversial, with many scientists resisting any connection to human laughter at all.[83] But even if we were to concede that similar neural pathways are involved in all these phenomena, and that there are at least some evolutionary links between the rats' chirping and the humans' chortling, there is a much more pressing question that is almost always sidestepped: What would we mean if we were to say that dogs or apes or rats "laugh"?

Most people would agree that the devoted dog owners, in detecting laughter in their pets, are driven by a desire to anthropomorphize and to incorporate the animals into the world of human sociality, by projecting onto them that key human characteristic of laughter. Or as Roger Scruton observed, with slightly different emphasis, when we hear hyenas (for example) "laughing" at one another, it is an expression not of *their* amusement but of *ours*.[84] But even in the apparently more rigorous discourse of experimental science, the boundary between laughter as a metonym of humanity and laughter as a physical or biological response is a tricky one. Once again we find an important blurring of the simple distinction between nature and culture. For the claim that a rat can "laugh" is always liable to imply something more about that species in general, and our relationship with it, than just that the neurons in its brain operate in a particular way. Any study of laughter cannot help but raise questions about the language of laughter and about the ordering of our cultural and social world, in which laughter is such a key signifier.

These are just some of the puzzles that, for me, make the study of laughter in general so compelling: simultaneously enriching and frustrating, eye-opening and opaque. And, of course, when we turn to the study of laughter in the past—when the giggles and chuckles are long since inaudible—those puzzles become even more intriguing. How do those contested boundaries between nature and culture, between the rhetoric and the physical manifestations of laughter, impact on how we understand laughter in history? And what exactly are we interested in, anyway? Is it what made people laugh? Is it the social, cultural, and political effects of laughter? Its function? Or how it was discussed, debated, and explained?

In the next chapter I shall look briefly at some of the questions that govern any historical study of laughter, Roman or otherwise, and I shall reflect (critically) on one final theorist whom no book on past laughter can afford to ignore: Mikhail Bakhtin, whose work lies behind numerous attempts to tell the story of changing patterns of laughter from the Middle Ages on (and has influenced studies of antiquity too). In chapter 4, I shall continue to broach some of the basic ground rules for thinking about the issues that we face in exploring Roman laughter, in particular how we might negotiate that necessarily fragile boundary between what counts as Greek and what as Roman—between, in other words, *risus* and *gelōs*.

CHAPTER 3

The History of Laughter

IS THERE A HISTORY OF LAUGHTER?

Human beings, we can safely say, have always laughed. But did people in the past laugh differently from us? And if so, how—and, just as important, how can we know? We have already glimpsed in chapter 1 the appeal and the frustrations of trying to understand a couple of outbursts of Roman laughter. In this chapter, I want to look harder at these issues, across a wider range of Roman material. We shall discover how scholars have ingeniously rewritten the texts of Roman jokes as they have come down to us, to make them funnier (in our terms). And we shall briefly reflect on the particularly tricky question of visual images. How can we identify visual depictions of a laughing face? (It's not as easy as you might think.) And how can we decide which images might have caused Romans—or which Romans—to crack up?

I shall also move outside the ancient world, to more general questions of how we might historicize the chuckles and chortles, giggles and guffaws of our forebears. There is, in fact, a long history to the history of laughter. Already in 1858, Alexander Herzen observed—in what has become something of a slogan among more recent scholars—that "it would be extremely interesting to write a history of laughter."[1] Interesting it certainly would be. Yet the exact terrain of that history is hard to define. Are we dealing with a history of the theory of laughter, and its protocols and rules (whether broken or obeyed)? Or are we focusing on the much less manageable, much more elusive subject of the practice of laughter in the past? Or some inextricable combination of the two?[2]

And what kind of changes can we hope to track over time? Here we need to consider the work of another modern analyst of the culture of laughter, the Russian critic Mikhail Bakhtin. In many ways as important and innovative as Sigmund Freud in the study of laughter, Bakhtin has foisted some misleading myths onto the subject of Roman laughter, which I am afraid I must dispel. But his work also raises bigger questions about how we describe and understand long-term developments in an area such as this. What exactly is it that changes when we say that laughter changes across the centuries? I suggest that we can usefully shine the historical spotlight on laughter, that we can approach the subject *historically* (what else is this book attempting to do?), but that we can no more tell a linear history of laughter than we can devise a universal theory of laughter. In fact, I would argue that many so-called histories of laughter turn out to be loaded stories of human progress and refinement. When Romans reflected on the laughter of the past (and we ourselves are not so very different in this respect), part of the point was to show that their predecessors had laughed more coarsely, or more lustily, than they did—to construct a version of history in which laughter acted as a marker of increasing sophistication.

But we will start in December 1976, with a famous lecture delivered by the historian Keith Thomas on the place of laughter in Tudor and Stuart England. This lecture, though published only in a weekly magazine, was programmatic and has been extremely influential on approaches to the history of laughter, particularly in the English-speaking world.[3]

PAST LAUGHTER

Thomas posed the fundamental question. "Why," he asked his audience, "should laughter concern the historian"—rather than be of interest merely to the social anthropologist, the literary critic, or the psychologist? Because, he insisted, "to study the laughter of our ancestors, to go on reading until we can hear the people not just talking but also laughing is to gain some insight into changing human sensibilities."

The project that Thomas sketched out was both important and impossible. I mean *impossible,* because, of course, however hard we read, we cannot "hear the people . . . laughing" (or talking, for that matter) in any period of history before the late nineteenth century, and it may be dangerously self-deceiving to imply, even metaphorically, that we can. But his project nonetheless remains important, for some equally obvious reasons. It almost goes without saying that we could write a better and "thicker" description of any historical society if we understood the protocols and practice of its laughter. Who laughed, at what, when? When was laughter out of order? What were the appropriate subjects or occasions for a chuckle?

Let's take just a couple of examples from the Roman world. At least one writer of the imperial period, in his discussion of good manners at dinner, accepted that bald men or those with odd-shaped noses were fair game for a laugh but that blind people were emphatically not and that those with bad breath or dripping, snotty noses fell somewhere in between. This may not tell us much about real-life laughter, even among the elite, in the Roman Empire. Prohibitions of this sort are often perilous guides to popular practice, for, as we know from our own experience, the strongest prohibitions are sometimes aimed at the commonest features of everyday life (the modern equivalents—"No swearing!" or "Do not litter!"—are no sure indications of the prevalence, or otherwise, of foul language or of trash in the streets). But these laughter regulations are nonetheless a precious glimpse into one version of a Roman hierarchy of bodily transgression and abnormality; they hint at one way in which acceptable behavior and acceptable appearance might be calibrated—that is, measured on a spectrum from what was legitimately laugh-able to what was absolutely not.[4]

Likewise, the imagined "geography" of Roman laughter offers an intriguing sideways glance at ancient representations of cultural difference. Much as modern anthropologists have imagined the hysterical Pygmy, Roman writers pictured a world in which different peoples, countries, or cities could be characterized by their different styles of laughter, by the different objects of their mirth, or by the different degrees to which they themselves were laughable. On the one hand were those who repeatedly became the butt of laughter (such as the poor citizens of ancient Abdera, in northern Greece, whose supposed stupidity—as we shall discover in chapter 8—was often good for a laugh); at the other were people who simply laughed too much and were far too keen, so it was said, on the frivolous pleasures of laughing and joking.

The population of the Egyptian city of Alexandria—largely Greek by ethnic origin—was a case in point. In an extraordinary lecture to the Alexandrians, delivered at the end of the first or the beginning of the second century CE, the orator and intellectual Dio Chrysostom attacked their apparently well-known passion for jocularity. "Please be serious, just for a moment, and pay attention," he starts. "Because you're always so full of fun and frivolity; in fact, one might say that you're never found wanting when it comes to fun and pleasure and laughter." He goes on to compare the laughter of "certain barbarians" with that of the Alexandrians. These barbarians, he claims, induce in themselves apparently drunken laughter by inhaling the fumes of incense (another candidate for an ancient reference to cannabis); the Alexandrians, by contrast, reach that state without chemical assistance, just by frivolous banter and joking, "through ears and voice," as Dio puts it. And, he berates them, "you play the fool even worse than the barbarians do, and you stagger around, as if you'd been hitting the bottle."[5]

In his dissection of the culture of the Germans, the Roman historian Tacitus offers a bleaker view of ethnic differences, pointing to some significant absences of laughter among the barbarians. He notes that in Germany—unlike at Rome—"nemo . . . vitia ridet"; that is, "nobody laughs off vices," or "nobody [merely] ridicules vices." But it is, of course, an observation that reflects back on the morals and practices of the Romans themselves. The implication is that in their primitive state of simplicity, the Germans take vice more seriously than simply as a subject of laughter or ridicule.[6]

I am not for a moment trying to suggest that Roman elite culture had a fixed template of the different ways in which laughter operated across the empire and beyond or that it would be possible simply to map the varieties of laughter found among the different peoples of the Roman world. It is, however, clear that laughter was one of the coordinates—shifting and unstable as it no doubt was—that Romans used to characterize cultural difference, as well as to define (and occasionally critique) themselves.

Yet these examples of Roman "laughter thinking" tend to make the history of laughter seem an easier subject than it is. For the further you move away from the rules, protocols, and moral exhortations associated with laughter and the nearer you get to what Thomas meant by "hearing" the laughter of the past, the murkier the waters become. That is to say—as those two scenarios with which I opened this book highlight—trying to recognize the situations, jokes, emotions, or words that actually prompted (or might have prompted) laughter in the past takes us right to the heart of the classic dilemmas of all historical understanding. How familiar or foreign is the world of past time? How comprehensible is it to us? How far does the process of historical study necessarily domesticate (or refamiliarize) material that may be much stranger than we let it seem? Questions of laughter raise these issues in a particularly acute form: for if it is hard to access the day-to-day culture of laughter of our contemporary neighbors just the other side of a national or cultural boundary, how much harder must it be to access that of people separated from us by centuries?

We do not need to go back two millennia to see the problems. Anyone who has ever dipped into those diligent nineteenth-century newspaper accounts of meetings or debates that systematically record the occurrence of laughter throughout the text—"(Laughter)," "(Prolonged laughter)," "(Muffled laughter)"—will often have been baffled as to what prompted the mirth or why some things prompted more uproarious hilarity than others. It is not simply that we fail to spot the long-forgotten topical references or that we have no access to the gestures and visual effects that may have contributed to the laughter. We are also dealing with a series of strikingly alien and sometimes quite mysterious social conventions about what provoked laughter or when laughter was required.

But what makes it more complicated is that it isn't always mysterious. If some laughter in the past is baffling, some does seem relatively easily comprehensible. As we have seen, it is not hard to empathize (correctly or not) with Dio's half-smothered outburst in the Colosseum. Jokes too can sometimes operate across the centuries. Mark Twain nicely sent up the familiarity of very old gags in his 1889 satire *A Connecticut Yankee in King Arthur's Court* (now itself ironically, more than a hundred years since its publication, an example of just the kind of continuity he was discussing). At one point in his stay at Camelot, Twain's time-traveler hero, who has been transported back centuries to the Arthurian court, listens to the performance of the court wit, Sir Dinadan, and offers this judgment: "I think I never heard so many old played-out jokes strung together in my life. . . . It seemed peculiarly sad to sit here, thirteen hundred years before I was born, and listen again to poor, flat, worm-eaten jokes that had given me the dry gripes when I was a boy thirteen hundred years afterwards. It about convinced me that there isn't such a thing as a new joke possible. Everybody laughed at these antiquities—but then they always do; I had noticed that, centuries later."[7] At the end of this book we shall reflect further on the capacity of some Roman jokes, written more than two thousand years ago, still to raise a laugh (or not). Should we imagine some universal human psychology of laughter? Or have we successfully learned to find those jokes funny—or have we inherited, no doubt unconsciously, some of the ancient rules and conventions of laughter?

One problem, then, is not whether historical laughter is familiar or strange to us (it is both) but how to distinguish the familiar elements from the strange and how to establish where the boundary between the two lies. We always run two different and opposite risks: both of exaggerating the strangeness of past laughter and of making it all too comfortably like our own.

By and large, classicists have erred on the side of familiarity, wanting so far as possible to join in the laughter of the Greeks and Romans, and they have often worked very hard to find and explain the funny points in ancient comedy and the quips, jokes, and other kinds of repartee signaled in Roman literature. Sometimes they have had to "emend"—or even effectively to rewrite—the ancient texts as they have come down to us to rescue the jokes they once contained. These desperate measures are not necessarily as illegitimate as they might appear at first sight. Inevitably there is a potentially large gap between what any ancient writer originally wrote and the version of their works, copied and recopied, that has reached the modern reader. The medieval monks who transcribed by hand so many works of classical literature could be very inaccurate, especially when they did not fully understand what they were copying or did not see its significance. Not unlike the complicated system of Roman numerals (whose details were almost invariably garbled in the scribal process), jokes were a common area for error. The errors can be glaring. One particularly dim copyist, for example, when transcribing the discussion of laughter in the second book of Cicero's *On the Orator*, systematically replaced the word *iocus* ("joke") with *locus* ("place," in the sense of "passage in a book"). He removed the laughter at a stroke, but his mistake has been straightforward, and uncontroversial, to correct.[8]

Sometimes, however, more radical ingenuity has been required. In the sixth book of his *Handbook on Oratory*, Quintilian (writing in the second century CE) also turned to the role of laughter in the repertoire of the orator. In the text we have—an amalgam of manuscript copies and the suggestions of now centuries of academic editors—many of his examples of what might prompt laughter in a speech seem at best flat, at worst garbled or close to nonsense, hardly the witticisms that Quintilian cracked them up to be. In a notable study of these, Charles Murgia claimed to have restored some point to a series of key passages. Thanks to his clever reconstructions of Quintilian's original Latin, several of the jokes, puns, and wordplays have apparently been brought back to life. But the nagging question is: Whose joke is it? Has Murgia really taken us back to the Roman quip, or has he actually adjusted the Latin to produce a satisfactorily modern joke?[9]

One snatch of repartee, quoted with approval by Quintilian, gives a good idea of the intricacy, technical complexity, and deep uncertainty of the whole process of getting and reconstructing these ancient gags. It is worth looking at in some detail. The passage in question is a courtroom exchange between an accuser and a defendant called Hispo, whose wise-crack we are supposed to admire. The text in the most recent printed edition of Quintilian goes like this: "When Hispo was being charged with pretty outrageous crimes, he said to his accuser, 'Are you measuring me according to your own standards?'" Or in Latin: "Ut Hispo obicienti atrociora crimina accusatori, 'me ex te metiris?'"[10] This text is the product of much hard work by modern scholars "improving" what is preserved in the manuscripts. *Atrociora* (pretty outrageous) has replaced the next-to-meaningless *arbore* (tree) of the manuscript versions. *Metiris* ("measure," from the verb *metiri*) has been substituted for the word *mentis* (which looks as if it might come from the verb *mentiri*, with an *n*, meaning "to lie"—but it would be a hopelessly ungrammatical form). And *me ex te* (me according to your standards) has been incorporated to complete the sense.[11] But even with these emendations, the exchange seems decidedly lame, hardly the kind of thing to raise much of a laugh.

Murgia intervened, partly by going back to the manuscript version and partly by going beyond it. On his reading, the prosecutor was conducting his case "in language marred by barbarisms" (*obicienti barbare crimina accusatori,* replacing *arbore* with *barbare* rather than *atrociora*). Hispo instantly defended himself, and cleverly raised a laugh, by responding, exactly as the manuscripts have it, with a glaring barbarism. "Mentis," he said, or "You is lying," as Murgia translates it—so trying to capture something of the jarring note sounded by the ungrammatical Latin (*mentis* being, as he interprets it, an intentionally awkward active form of a verb that ought have been used in the passive form, *mentiris*). It certainly seems to make a funnier point: Hispo replies to an accuser who is attacking him in bad and barbarous Latin with some very bad, barbarous, and ungrammatical Latin indeed.[12]

But is it what Quintilian wrote? It is hard entirely to banish the suspicion that Murgia may have cleverly emended the usual version of Quintilian's text to make it funny for us. "Mentis," or "You is lying," does, to be sure, stick close to the manuscripts, right or wrong, but "in language marred by barbarisms" has little support beyond the fact that it contributes to a joke that sounds plausible enough to the modern ear.[13] And maybe it is rather too plausible. Maybe Hispo's joke really was feeble by our standards, even if it prompted Roman laughter for reasons we cannot now recapture. Or maybe, despite the spotlight Quintilian gives to it, it was feeble by the standards of most Romans too.

The truth is that one of the categories to which historians and theorists of laughter have paid the least attention is the "bad joke" (in Latin usually *frigidus*, a "cold joke")—although, as Twain captured so nicely, in the day-to-day world of laughing and jesting, bad jokes are ubiquitous, can play an important part in defining what counts as good to laugh at, and may tell us as much about laughter's history and culture as "good" ones.

Recently, in a wide-ranging study of the "funny words" in the Latin comedies of Plautus (the major predecessor of Terence, writing in the late third or early second century BCE), Michael Fontaine has been even more ambitious than Murgia.[14] Fontaine's project has been to rescue the puns throughout these plays, not only those that the plodding medieval monks overlooked but those that he claims had been lost in antiquity itself, almost as soon as the plays reached written form.[15] He conjures up some exuberant—and indeed quite laughable—moments in Plautine comedy. To take one of the very simplest examples, in Plautus' *Rope,* a character who has struggled to shore after a shipwreck declares that he "is freezing," *algeo.* Fontaine here suggests a pun on the Latin word *alga,* or "seaweed," as if the word meant "covered in seaweed," and he goes on to imagine that part of the joke is that the character in question was dressed in a seaweed costume.[16]

Who knows? Like many of the other conjectures in the book, this is learned, ingenious, and even quite funny. But whether Fontaine is revealing (as one commentator has it) jokes that have "lain dormant . . . for centuries"[17] or offering pleasing modern inventions that rescue the jokes *for us* is a moot point. In fact, this kind of approach should prompt us to think harder about the criteria available for figuring out exactly which lines in an ancient comedy were likely to have provoked ancient laughter. How much laughter we would have heard in the Roman comic theater, and at what particular moments in the script, is a trickier question than it might seem.

VISUAL LAUGHTER

An even starker instance of the modern dilemmas in recapturing Roman laughter is found in ancient visual images. The first problem is to decide when ancient paintings or sculptures are attempting to represent laughter or smiles—or, more precisely, it is hard to decide what counts as an ancient visual representation of laughter or smiles. There is very little as straightforward as Terence's instantly recognizable *hahahae*.[18]

To our eyes, obvious laughers seem to be few and far between in the surviving repertoire of Greco-Roman art, though why that should be is less clear. To focus just on sculpture, a recent survey of scholars in the field elicited disappointing answers to the question of why there is so little laughter captured in ancient marble or bronze: "The prime reason is one of genre. Greek sculpture is broadly religious," ventured one; "Because laughter distorts the body" or "[It] has to do with the issue of decorum," others suggested; "A limitation of the sculptor's technique," another rather desperately hazarded.[19] Of course, as is well known, the facial expression of many early Greek statues (especially the so-called *kouroi* and *korai* of the seventh to early fifth centuries BCE) is regularly called the "archaic smile," but it is far from certain that it represented a smile in our sense of the word—rather than, to take just a couple of modern suggestions, a sense of animation or of aristocratic contentment.[20] And no less ambivalent are those apparently laughing Gorgons (are they really grimacing?), comic masks (are they intended to be grotesque rather than laughing?), and satyrs (who sport an uncontrolled animalistic rictus more than a laugh perhaps).[21]

These uncertainties are not, in fact, restricted to the art of the classical world. Surprising as it may now seem, it was only in the late nineteenth century that one of the best-known paintings of a laughing subject—Frans Hals's seventeenth-century *The Laughing Cavalier* (see fig. 1)—was given that title or even referred to as an image of laughter. What prompted the new description (or why it stuck so firmly) is difficult to determine. But it is largely thanks to its now-familiar title that we treat this painting so unquestioningly as an image of a laugher rather than of a man with "a disdainful half-smile and provocative air"—or, for that matter, a man of uncertain expression with an upturned moustache.[22]

But if the identification of laughers in art is tricky, it is even trickier to identify the images that might have elicited laughter from a Roman viewer. In a major book, *Looking at Laughter*, John Clarke attempted to do just that. He assembled an extraordinary range of Roman art, from grotesques to caricatures, from parodies to the ancient equivalent of strip cartoons, and tried to use it to open up the world of popular, lusty, raucous, and sometimes rude Roman laughter. It is a hugely engaging study and, what is more, brings to our attention some intriguing—and largely forgotten—Roman images. But at the same time, it confronts us with another version of the problem I have just been pondering. How do we know that Romans, or some Romans, laughed at these images? To put it another way, who is laughing here? Is it the Romans? Or us? Or is it us trying to imagine—even impersonate—the Romans?[23]

Take one of Clarke's prime examples: not in this case a forgotten image, but the famous mosaic on the floor of the entrance hall of the so-called House of the Tragic Poet, showing a ferocious dog greeting the visitor and underneath the words *CAVE CANEM*—"Beware of the Dog" (see fig. 2). It is one of a group of three such entranceway mosaics in Pompeii apparently depicting the domestic guard dog for the visitor to walk over (which now decorate thousands of modern tourist souvenirs, from postcards to fridge magnets). For Clarke, they all would have prompted ancient laughter, because of the double take between illusion and reality, but the example in the House of the Tragic Poet would have elicited more chuckles than the others precisely because of the associated writing. That *CAVE CANEM* served to draw attention to the fact that the dog in question was only an illusion, to "unmask the humor of the artifice"—and so to prompt laughter.[24]

I share Clarke's view of the importance of illusion and imitation in producing Roman laughter. Less convincing is his attempt to explain the social function of the laughter that might have erupted at the entranceway to these houses—where he reaches too easily for that overused term *apotropaic*. Entrances, he suggests, were dangerous liminal spaces in the Roman imagination; a peal of laughter in the hallway was good defense against the evil eye.[25] But—apotropaic or not—none of this cut much ice with his fellow art historian Roger Ling. In an otherwise warm review of Clarke's book, Ling insisted that the mosaic was not funny at all but meant in deadly earnest. It was intended to alert visitors—with both the words and the picture—to "the creature that awaited unwelcome intruders." That is to say, "it was no joke!"[26]

There is no sure way that we can decide between these alternatives—between what might be, on Clarke's part (or my own), overenthusiasm for the unearthing of laughter where it might never have occurred and down-to-earth common sense, bordering on a failure of imagination, on the part of Ling. Yet this opposition reminds us of another side to the discursive complexity of laughter, at once baffling and intriguing. Notwithstanding all those grand theories of laughter, there is nothing that, intrinsically, causes human beings to crack up; there is nothing that systematically and unfailingly guarantees laughter as a response, even within the norms and conventions of an individual culture. Incongruity, as one theory would have it, may often prompt laughter, but not all examples of incongruity do so, and not for everyone. A joke that raises chortles at a wedding will almost certainly not do so at a funeral—or as Plutarch noted (see pp. 27–28), what makes you laugh in the company of friends will not do so when you are with your father or your wife.

Over and above any psychological or evolutionary determinants, what makes words, gestures, or events seem laugh-able is that, for whatever reason, the culture in question has defined them as such (or at least as potentially such), has encouraged its members to laugh at them in certain contexts, and, by processes that I suspect are now entirely irrecoverable, has made that laughter appear "natural." So whether *CAVE CANEM* provoked laughter among Roman visitors to the House of the Tragic Poet depends on how far they had learned to see, in Clarke's terms, the unmasking of visual artifice as laugh-able or how far they saw the image, as Ling would have it, as an information notice about a dangerous dog—or how far both readings were possible, according to different circumstances, moods, or viewers.

It is for these reasons, despite all the possible perils of studying "written laughter," that this book concentrates on those cases, more numerous than you might expect, where Roman literature makes laughter explicit—where its eruption is signaled, discussed, or debated—rather than focusing on images or texts that may (or may not) have been intended to raise a laugh. So there is less in what follows on the laughter that might have been prompted by paintings or sculpture or that might have been heard in the comic theater; there is much more on the stories that Romans told about particular occasions of laughter, of all sorts, and on their discussions of its functions, effects, and consequences.

ENTER BAKHTIN

In framing his manifesto for a history of laughter, Keith Thomas had much more in mind than the question of how to spot the joke in any particular period of the past. He was interested in tracking historical changes in the principles and practice of laughter and in thinking about how they might be explained. As he put it, in broaching this subject, he aimed "to gain some insight into *changing* human sensibilities."[27]

So in his survey of Tudor and Stuart laughter, he pointed to a general shift over that period from the outspoken, popular, coarse, often scatological forms of laughter (including all the carnivalesque forms of inversion—"the 'holiday humour' which accompanied those occasions of licensed burlesque and disorder which were an annual feature of most Tudor institutions") toward an atmosphere that was much more controlled and "policed." The "rites of misrule" were gradually eliminated, he observed, and there was a narrowing of the subjects seen fit for ridicule: much less jesting about bodily deformity, a growing aversion to crude scatology, and a marked tempering of open ribaldry at the expense of clerics and the social hierarchy. We are not far, on Thomas's model, from the world of antigelastic decorum notoriously summed up in Lord Chesterfield's advice to his son in the mid-eighteenth century, much quoted in the history of laughter (and its absences): "Frequent and loud laughter is the characteristic of folly and ill manners. . . . In my mind there is nothing so illiberal, and so ill-bred, as audible laughter."[28]

What caused the change? Thomas suggested a variety of factors. He noted, for example, a more general emphasis in this period on bodily control as a marker of a social hierarchy—of which laughter, and its associated bodily disruptions, was just one aspect.[29] He stressed the growing cultural importance of the middle class, for whom the old inversionary rituals of laughter (assuming as they did a binary division of English society into high and low) no longer seemed so pointed or so relevant: "Lords and servants could exchange places, but for the middle classes, who had no polar opposite, role-reversal was impossible." He also reflected on the increasingly "precarious" position of some key institutions over the sixteenth and seventeenth centuries, which acted to discourage, rather than to encourage, laughter. "Once the underlying security of medieval religion had gone, laughter had to be kept out of the churches. Once the social hierarchy was challenged, the laughter of carnival and festive inversion seemed a threat rather than a support. Once the aristocracy had been temporarily dethroned, during the Commonwealth, it seemed imperative to build a wall of decorum which would safeguard its position thereafter."[30]

It is perhaps surprising that in the course of this, Thomas did not mention the name of Mikhail Bakhtin, a Soviet theorist and the author of *Rabelais and His World*—an extraordinarily influential study of François Rabelais's controversial classic of the mid-sixteenth century, his multivolume satiric novel *Gargantua and Pantagruel*.[31] For Thomas's characterization of feasts of misrule and other forms of inversionary carnivalesque celebrations has much in common with Bakhtin's account of laughter in *Rabelais and His World*—which has inspired, or underpinned, many recent attempts to explore historical developments in (to translate Bakhtin literally) European "laughter culture." In fact, after Aristotle and the three theories, Bakhtin represents the most recent shadow to hang heavily over modern discussions of laughter and its history. But unlike the theorists I considered in chapter 2, he was concerned not with the causes of laughter but with universal patterns of how laughter operates (between high and low) and, in particular, with its social and political operations within medieval and Renaissance culture—and (like Thomas) with the story of how those operations changed.

The book originated in Bakhtin's doctoral dissertation. Written in the 1930s and defended amid controversy in the late 1940s (several of the examiners wished to fail it[32]), it was first published in Russian in 1965 and in English in 1968. Although—or perhaps because—Bakhtin had been consistently marginalized by the Soviet authorities, *Rabelais* quickly became influential among historians and critics in the West.[33] In truth, the book is complicated and in places—unless the English translation, on which most Western readers have relied, is very misleading—allusive, epigrammatic, and arguably self-contradictory.[34] It is also wide-ranging, making theoretical contributions to a number of very different fields. But historians have nevertheless extracted from it a powerful view of the development in the uses of laughter in the West, which forms the essential background to Bakhtin's exploration of Rabelais's extravagant satire and its later reception. In very broad terms, it runs along the following lines.

Bakhtin identified a clear distinction in the High Middle Ages between the popular culture of carnival—with its stress on the unbridled, all-embracing, life-giving force of laughter, often mediated through "the lower bodily stratum" (or "bums, farts and other transgressions," as Vic Gatrell glossed it[35])—and the decidedly nonlaughing, agelastic culture of the state and the church. These two spheres were brought together in Rabelais and other sixteenth-century writers when, for a brief period, high literary culture embraced vernacular, popular humor—"laughter in its most radical, universal and at the same time gay form emerged from the depths of folk culture" to take its place in the "sphere of great literature and high ideology." From the seventeenth century on, however, the "people's festive laughter" was diluted. Partly under the influence of early modern absolute monarchy, the true culture of carnival disintegrated, to be replaced by mere mockery, "erotic frivolity," and an attenuated, ironic, bourgeois version of the earlier lusty festivities. It became, in other words, light entertainment, not liberation.[36]

These ideas have been inspirational, exercising a powerful influence on many leading critics and historians. "Bakhtin's concepts of 'carnivalization'. . . 'grotesque realism' and the like are so frequently employed that it is difficult to remember how we managed without them."[37] Yet at the same time—in whole or in detail—they raise a series of well-known, and much-discussed, problems. His characterization of the honest, earthy, incorporating laughter of carnival has certainly appealed to the nostalgia and the dreams of many decidedly unearthy, deskbound scholars, but in its simplest form it hardly stands up to historical scrutiny. Indeed, establishment apparatchiks though they may have been, several of Bakhtin's doctoral examiners were rightly skeptical of his hard-line views on the popular character of medieval laughter ("I am afraid that when we evaluate the popular or non-popular nature of a movement only from the perspective of laughter, then we will diminish any notion of popular character," as one, not unreasonably, put it[38]).

Many later critics have had equally severe reservations about Bakhtin's notion that carnivalesque laughter was a wholly positive and liberating force. For, of course, carnival could be a site of conflict, fear, contestation, and violence too. Or alternatively, the temporary, licensed transgression that carnival allowed could be seen as a defense of the orthodox social and political hierarchy rather than a challenge to it (the price that the people paid for a few days of inversionary fun was knowing their place for the remaining 360-something days of the year).[39] There is also the question of whether the culture of church and state was quite as agelastic as Bakhtin claimed (courtiers and clerics laughed too) or whether the laughter associated with the lower bodily stratum was in general restricted to the common people. Whatever their expressions of disapproval, the elite too have often found (and still find) that farts and phalluses can prompt laughter. In the eighteenth century, for example, as Gatrell has insisted, saucy comic prints were often "unmitigatedly 'low' by polite standards" but nonetheless aimed at an elite audience ("Indicators of low manners in high places multiply as this book progresses," he sharply observes).[40]

There are, however, two other problems with Bakhtin's approach that are particularly relevant to my project.

SATURNALIAN FUN

The first problem is a specifically classical one: namely, Bakhtin's reconstruction of the Roman festival of Saturnalia as an ancient ancestor of carnival, and so a key component in the "laughterhood" of ancient Rome. This rather flimsy idea is, for classicists, one of Bakhtin's most misleading legacies and deserves more challenge than it usually receives. I need to explain why the fun, games, and laughter of the Saturnalia are not at center stage in this book.

The Roman religious festival of the god Saturn took place over a number of days in December.[41] Involving both civic and domestic celebrations, it is one of the least understood but most confidently talked about of all Roman rituals—partly because of the easy assumption that it somehow represents the Roman origin of "our" Christmas (parties and presents in midwinter) and partly because it has been cast as a popular inversionary ritual, standing, conceptually at least, at the head of the whole Western tradition of carnival (a temporary topsy-turvy world, full of popular laughter and of the lower bodily stratum). This model of the festival was not entirely Bakhtin's creation. You can find superficially similar approaches in James Frazer's *Golden Bough,* as well as in Nietzsche[42]—and in any case, many modern specialists in ancient ritual may never have read *Rabelais and His World.* But the trickle-down effect has been strong, and the continuing popularity of this approach must largely be a consequence of the powerful impact (direct or indirect) of Bakhtin, who wrote of the "essence of carnival . . . most clearly expressed and experienced in the Roman Saturnalias [*sic*]" and of the inversionary "crowning and uncrowning of a clown" and the "tradition of freedom of laughter" during the festival—of which "faraway echoes" were still to be detected, he claimed, in later carnivalesque ceremonies.[43]

Indeed, classicists often present the festival itself, along with a range of associated "Saturnalian literature," in even more strongly carnivalesque terms. It is commonly said, for example, that a whole series of hierarchical role reversals defined the Saturnalia: that slaves were waited on at dinner by their masters; that anyone (from slave to clown) could be chosen by lot to be the master of ceremonies, or "king," of the festival; that the festal dress for the free population was the *pilleus,* which was the distinctive headdress of the ex-slave; and even that the slaves actually took charge of their households while the festivities lasted. What is more, the occasion is supposed to have featured the kind of "exuberant gorgings and even more excessive drinking bouts" that we associate with carnival, as well as the general license to gamble (strictly controlled for the rest of the year), to party, to speak your mind (no matter what your station in life)—and to laugh.[44] Against this background have been set all

kinds of well-known literary manifestations of the topsy-turvy Saturnalian spirit: from the satiric free speech of Seneca's skit on the deification
of the emperor Claudius, the *Apocolocyntosis* (often imagined to have
been written for the Saturnalia of 54 CE),[45] to Horace's clever characterization of his slave Davus (who is given a chance to expose his master's vices in a poem explicitly set at the Saturnalia),[46] not to mention the
whole world of Roman comedy, where the (temporary) victories of the
clever slave over the dim master, and the laughter they provoke, can
seem reminiscent of the (temporarily) inversionary world of Saturnalian
carnival.[47]

The trouble is that there is much less ancient evidence for this proto-
carnival than is usually assumed. It is true that the Romans wrote up the
Saturnalia in ludic terms: we certainly have evidence for its sense of
play, its parade of freedom (which Horace's Davus is imagined to
exploit when he points up the failings of his master), and its suspension
of normal social rules (togas off, gaming boards out).[48] But some of the
most distinctive features of the Bakhtinian carnival—the gross overcon-
sumption, the emphasis on inversion, on the lower bodily stratum, and
even the laughter—are much harder to document. The references we
have to increased wine allowances or special food are neither restricted
to the Saturnalia nor treated by Roman writers as particularly gross.[49]
And beyond the fantasy of the poor old emperor Claudius shitting himself in the *Apocolocyntosis*[50] (which may or may not be a strictly Saturnalian work), there is little hint of carnivalesque scatology: most Saturnalian wit comes across as rather refined, or at least verbal, and even the
role of laughter is relatively subdued. In fact, the elite literary jesting
that we witness in Macrobius' late-antique literary celebration *Saturnalia* may not be as untypical (or as "late") as is often imagined.[51]

More significant, though, the idea of role reversal, so characteristic
of carnival, is a much flimsier construction than is usually allowed.
There are, it is true, a couple of (late) references in ancient literature to
slaves being served by their masters at the Saturnalian dinner.[52] Even so,
some of the apparently key passages disappear on closer examination:
the notion, for example, that the slaves ruled the household at the Saturnalia is the result of some imaginative repunctuation of a sentence of
the philosopher Seneca, while other passages have been no less imagina-
tively (mis)translated.[53] And—whether the drawing of lots was rigged
or not—the most famous "Saturnalian king" to have come down to us,
indeed the only one we know by name, turns out to have been the
emperor Nero.[54]

In fact, the emphasis in most ancient writing is not on reversal as such but on the social equality that apparently ruled during the festival. As Bakhtin himself acknowledged, ancient accounts stress that the Saturnalia represented not so much an overturning of social distinctions but rather a return to a primitive world in which such distinctions did not yet exist. In line with this, we find repeated emphasis on the fact that masters and slaves sat down together at dinner and that anyone was allowed to speak freely to anyone else across social boundaries. It is significant too that in their *pillei,* free Romans wore the costume not of slaves but of ex-slaves—a mediating category, which leveled rather than reversed social distinctions.[55]

Of course, the real-life Saturnalia must have come in many very different forms, and the views of the slaves and the poor (which we don't have) were unlikely to have been the same as those of the rich (which we do). But it is hard to resist the conclusion that in casting the festival in the mold of an inversionary carnival, Bakhtin and others have misrepresented, or highly selectively presented, what was for the most part a rather prim—or at least paternalistic[56]—occasion as a raucous festival of belly laughs and the lower bodily stratum. For this reason, though laughter may have been one element at a good Saturnalia, I shall not put much emphasis on the festival.

NARRATIVES OF CHANGE

The second problem with Bakhtin's approach—also raised by Thomas's essay—is far broader. It is the question of the very nature and status of a historical account of laughter. What kind of history are we telling when we try to tell "the history of laughter"? What is it a history *of?*

However we choose to contest many of the details of Bakhtin's account, from his interpretation of an ancient festival to his reading of Rabelais, there is one underlying principle that guides his work and that he shares with—or has bequeathed to—Thomas and many other scholars: namely, the idea that it is possible, not merely that "it would be *interesting,*" in Herzen's famous phrase, to write a diachronic history of laughter as a social phenomenon. There is, of course, a compelling logic here. If laughter—its practice, customs, and objects—is found in different forms, according to context, place, or period, then it follows that laughter must necessarily be capable of change. If it can change, then surely we should be able to write a developmental history that delineates and even attempts to account for the transformation.

True. But the process is much trickier, in both theory and practice, than any such simple logic makes it seem. For the attempt to write a diachronic history raises once more, and in yet more acute form, all those questions about the relationship between laughter and the cultural discourse of laughter that I have already touched on (see pp. 7–8, 24, 45–46). To put this at its simplest, what is it that changes over time? Is it the practice of laughter as it was seen and heard? Or the rules, protocols, and discursive conventions that surrounded it? Or is it partly both? In which case, how can we now distinguish between those two aspects?

We certainly cannot assume that laughter was more restrained in a period when the rules governing its occurrence were more insistent. It is perfectly conceivable that raucous chuckles might ring out pretty much as before (though perhaps in tactically changed locations) in the face of new prohibitions. One critic has recently—and aptly—described the British eighteenth century as "an impolite world that talked much about politeness."[57] And it may well have been that the behavior of the unfortunate Chesterfield son remained more or less unaffected by the strictures against "audible laughter" laid down by his obsessive father—whose advice was regarded in some quarters as maverick as soon as it was published (and certainly not as the orthodoxy that it is often presented as today).[58]

Likewise, Thomas in his lecture repeatedly pointed to areas of continuity even where he wished to show drastic change: the feasts of misrule, with their raucous burlesques, gradually faded over the seventeenth century (except, as he concedes, "annual occasions of burlesque and misrule lingered in many small communities until the nineteenth century"); rough forms of ridicule were tempered (albeit "among the common people these new attitudes were slower to take root. . . . Rough music and charivari continued in the villages"); jokes in general became more delicate by 1700 (though "middle-class delicacy took time to triumph. . . . Jest-books were really not cleaned up until the early nineteenth century").[59]

But that is only one side of the story. For we must also assume that over time, new rules and protocols could have a major impact on where and when and at what laughter erupted. Or alternatively, we might infer that some of those new protocols were developed precisely to reflect "changing sensibilities" in the practice of laughter. After all, we don't now laugh at cuckolds, one of Thomas's key examples of Tudor ribaldry (or do we?).

These problems are tricky enough, but they are only the start of the intriguing methodological and heuristic dilemmas entailed in laughter's history. We might want to argue, for example, that his father's rules necessarily made Chesterfield Junior's laughter different, even if it continued in outwardly the same way (laughing in the face of prohibition is never the same as laughing with approval). We might also want to suggest that the attempt to separate laughter practice from laughter discourse is unhelpful or even actively misleading: "laughter" as an object of study is an inextricable combination of bodily disruption and discursive interrogation, explanation, and protocol. Or is that combination merely a useful alibi for our inability to "hear," as Thomas would have it, the laughter of past times and its changing registers?

The closest comparison that I know—and one that helps us appreciate the perils and rewards of the history of laughter—is the history of sex and sexuality. We can track important changes in the discursive practices surrounding sex and in the regimes of policing and control that claimed to govern sexual conduct in the past. But it remains much less clear how these related to changes in what people actually did in bed and with whom, or the pleasure they derived: restrictive talk does not necessarily correlate with restrictive behavior, though it may do. It is also well known, of course, that the history we choose to tell of the sexual conduct of our predecessors is almost always deeply loaded and ideological, often as much an implicit judgment of ourselves as a scrutiny of the past—whether a celebration of our own "tolerance" or a lament for our "prudishness."

Much the same is true in histories of laughter, which show a repeating pattern almost no matter what period or what culture is concerned. On the one hand we find commentators and critics focusing on, and indeed ridiculing, the occasional extreme agelasts of the past or particularly agelastic moments. It is to this tendency that Lord Chesterfield owes his fame, likewise that cliché of Victorian humorlessness "We are not amused."[60] Agelasts indeed, as the Romans also found, can be very laughable. On the other hand, the overall developmental story is almost invariably similar to that told by Thomas and, with significantly different nuances, by Bakhtin—a version (as Thomas himself saw) of "the civilizing process."

Diachronic histories of laughter regularly tell of the taming of the crude, the bawdy, the cruel and lusty. They may look back in nostalgia to a time when laughter was more honestly earthy (as Roger Chartier observed of contemporary discussions of medieval carnival, they always sited the truly carnivalesque some time in the past[61]). Or they may take pride in the growing refinement that has outlawed the crudity of earlier forms of laughter or spared some innocent victims of ridicule. So far as I have been able to discover, there is no culture in the world that claims to laugh more coarsely or more cruelly than its predecessors. *Earthy* is only ever a retrospective designation. The modern history of laughter, in other words, is always bound up with a judgment (whether good or ill) on social and cultural progress.[62]

Much the same was true in ancient Rome. Admittedly, there are no ancient narrative accounts of the history of Roman laughter. But the contrast between the controlled, sophisticated, or mild laughter of *now* and the earthy, fearless, or crude laughter of the past is a striking theme in Roman writing. The details differ from author to author, the precise argument (and moral) of some of the passages concerned is hard to follow, not to say deeply controversial, and the idea of a chronological development correlates in sometimes complicated and contradictory ways with ideas of foreign influence. But the basic message that ancient writers tried to convey is clear: if you go back far enough in Roman time, you find a culture of ribald, jocular laughter that has—for better or worse—been lost or is on the point of being so.

Cicero, for example, could write nostalgically in a letter of 46 BCE of his affection for "native witticisms," now so overlaid by foreign traditions "that there is hardly a trace of old-style wit to be seen." It is only in his friend Paetus (to whom the letter is flatteringly addressed) that he can now "spot any likeness of the ancient native jocularity [*festivitas*]."[63] Both Livy and Horace refer back to the rough, caustic traditions of rustic Latin jesting and to the abusive, ribald—and frankly mysterious— "Fescennine verses," or *Fescennina licentia*, much enjoyed, Horace claims, by "farmers of yore" (*agricolae prisci*).[64] In fact, as Emily Gowers suggests, Horace's famous "Journey to Brundisium" in *Satires* 1.5 can be read not simply as the travelogue of an uncomfortable trip south from Rome or a pointed commentary on the politics of the 30s BCE but as a journey into the history of Roman laughter and satire: the central episode takes us back to its deepest roots, staging a comic duel between a pair of scurrilous, grotesque, jesting clowns, Sarmentus and Messius Cicirrus. Horace's own style of laughter is much more up-to-date and refined than that: the poet, as Ellen Oliensis rightly insists, "takes care to locate himself very definitely in the audience, far above the satiric boxing ring."[65]

The idea of a native Italic tradition of jocularity—"la causticité des vieux Latins"[66]—has been appealing to modern scholars. It has been seen as a powerful factor in the development of the distinctive tradition of Latin satire, and the lingering traces of the "Fescennine" spirit have been sought out in all kinds of places where they sometimes do, and sometimes do not, belong.[67] But whether this Roman reconstruction accurately reflects the historical reality of the shifts and developments of Roman laughter (whatever exactly we mean by the term) is as hard to disentangle as any narrative of any history of laughter anywhere or at any time. In part it presumably does; in part it cannot. But which parts?

In exploring the case studies that are the focus of the second half of this book, I shall be alert to signs of historical change and shall keep an eye out for the perspective of ancient authors themselves on the history of Roman laughter. But for what are now—I trust—obvious reasons, I shall not set out to tell a diachronic story of how laughter changed at Rome over the centuries. I have no doubt that there were all kinds of differences in the "laughterhood" of Rome between the campfire world of the small, early settlement by the Tiber in (say) the seventh century BCE and the multicultural metropolis of Augustan Rome in the first century. And again, I am sure that the culture of laughter in the "pagan" empire was different, in crucial respects, from that of its Christian successor. I am, however, far from sure how confidently we can describe (still less account for) those changes or whether we have sufficient evidence, particularly for the earlier period, to make a useful attempt. My focus in what follows is broadly, and intentionally, synchronic, concentrating for the most part on the Roman world from the second century BCE to the second century CE.[68]

But first we need to ask what exactly the culture of Roman laughter might mean, what its basic coordinates are, and how far it can be distinguished from Greek laughter.

CHAPTER 4

Roman Laughter in Latin and Greek

LAUGHING IN LATIN

The study of Roman laughter is in some ways an impossible project. That is partly what makes it so intriguing, so special, so enlightening, and so worthwhile. As I hope I have made clear already (perhaps too clear for the tastes of some readers), the laughter of the past is always likely to frustrate our most determined efforts to systematize and control it. Anyone who—with a straight face—claims to be able to offer a clear account of why or how or when Romans laughed is bound to be oversimplifying. But in the inevitable confusion (in the mess left in laughter's wake), we still learn a lot about ancient Rome and about how laughter in the past might have operated differently. This is a subject (like many, to be honest, in ancient history) in which the process of trying to understand can be as important and illuminating as the end result.

But process isn't everything, and we should not entirely accept defeat before we begin. Whatever the tricky problems that I have been enjoying so far, there are also some striking and relatively straightforward observations to be made about how laughter works in the Latin language and in Latin literature. In fact, to investigate Roman laughter is to engage with some of the most basic and familiar words in Latin (those that even the rawest beginner is likely to have encountered), as well as some rather more recondite vocabulary. It also involves exploring some of the less-trodden byways of Latin literature, as well as throwing fresh light on some of the most canonical Latin texts we have.

One of most important of these observations concerns the Latin vocabulary of laughter. It is only a slight exaggeration to say that there is just one word in Latin for "laughing." In modern English, we are used to a range of subtly nuanced (even if elusive) terms for *laugh*: from *chuckle* and *chortle* through *giggle, titter,* and *snigger* to *howl* and *guffaw*—not to mention such related words as *grin, beam, smile,* and *smirk*. Ancient Greek too has a wide range of laughter vocabulary, from the standard *gelan* and its compounds through variants such as *kanchazein* (a more robust form) and *sairein* (e.g., Commodus' grin; see p. 6) to the delightfully onomatopoeic *kichlizein* (not far from our *giggle*) or *meidian* (often translated as "smile"). In Latin we are dealing, for the most part, with just the word *ridere,* its compounds (*adridere, deridere, irridere,* and so on), and its various cognates as adjectives and nouns (*risus,* "laughter"; *ridiculus,* "laughable"). All of these signal some form of audible, physical reaction or gesture broadly and recognizably akin to laughter as we know it. Dictionary definitions and some modern critics try to calibrate these variants precisely, from *deridere,* for example, signaling derision to *irridere* ridicule or laughing at. Yet the terms are almost certainly much less fixed, referentially, than such definitions imply.[1]

The confidence with which it is often assumed, for example, that *adridere* always refers to supportive laughter or, pejoratively, flattery, is quite misplaced. True, sometimes it does: Ovid tells his learner lover to make a good impression by joining in the laughter (*adride*) whenever his would-be girlfriend laughs; the hallmark of comic toadies is "to offend no one and be a total yes-man" (*adridere omnibus*); and Horace uses the word in the context of sympathetic laughter.[2] But it is certainly not always so supportive, as phrases such as "laughing savagely" (*saevum adridens*) make absolutely clear.[3] In fact, in another passage of Terence's *Eunuch,* Gnatho exploits the potential double entendre of the word when he reflects on his life as a scrounger and his relationship with the (rather dim) guys who are his meal tickets: "I don't set out to make them laugh at me, but actually *eis adrideo* and compliment their wit at the same time." The joke here turns on the possible slippage in the phrase *eis adrideo* between "I flatter them" and "I laugh at them." Is Gnatho merely toeing the subservient line, or is he hinting to the audience that he has the upper hand in dealing with the likes of Thraso? Who, in other words, is laughing at whom? The ambivalence is half-seen and half-missed by one late antique commentator, who wrote simply that Terence had used "*arrideo* instead of *irrideo*."[4]

Some modern critics have been even more confident than this in suggesting which Latin word should be used where, even inserting the "correct" term where necessary. One glaring case concerns the text of an epigram of Martial. The poem is a squib addressed to one Calliodorus, who fancies himself a great jester and so dinner party guest, and according to the manuscript tradition includes the phrase *omnibus adrides*. The most recent editor, with staggering self-confidence, has simply replaced this with *omnis irrides*. Why? Because, he explains, "*adrides must* mean either 'you smile at approvingly' . . . or 'you please.' . . . Neither fits Calliodorus. . . . The word for his activity can *only* be *irrides*."[5] Such rewriting is the price you have to pay if you want to preserve neat linguistic boundaries.

Beyond *ridere* and its linguistic family, there are few Latin alternatives. Occasionally, words such as *renidere* (shine out) do metaphorical duty for some shades of laughter or facial expression (*renidere* is, more or less, "to beam").[6] *Rictus* can refer (unflatteringly) to the open mouth or gaping jaws that are inevitably part of the laughing process, as well as to the bared teeth of an animal.[7] Elsewhere, *cachinnare* or (more commonly) the noun *cachinnus* can be used for a particularly raucous form of laughter or for what we might call "(a) cackle." As one late Roman grammarian, Nonius Marcellus, put it, it had been used to signify "not just laughter [*risus*] but a stronger sound."[8] The words have a catchy onomatopoeic ring but again are harder to pin down than dictionary definitions imply and prove resistant to the very precise classification that we might like to impose on them.

It is true that a contrast between *cachinnare* and (mere) *ridere* is sometimes more or less spelled out. Cicero, for example, at one point in his broadside against Verres, the infamous governor of Sicily, turns to attack Verres' nasty sidekick Apronius, for humiliating a supposedly upstanding member of the Sicilian elite; Cicero pictures a banquet at which "his fellow guests laughed [*ridere*], Apronius himself cackled [*cachinnare*]."[9] Likewise, in what was effectively his manifesto poem, the satirist Persius was clearly trying to outdo his predecessor Horace in describing his own reaction to the folly of the world as *cachinnare*, not Horace's gentler *ridere*.[10]

However, the word is not always so loaded, so aggressive, or so loud. It is the pleasant sound of laughter (*cachinni*), along with wine, wit, and a pretty girl, that sums up the atmosphere of a friendly party at the poet

Catullus' house; it is the laughter of disbelief (*cachinnasse*) with which, in Suetonius' biography, Vespasian's grandmother reacts to the unlikely omen that her grandson will become emperor; and it is the furtive giggles of servant girls (*furtim cachinnant*) laughing at their mistress behind her back.[11] What is more, metaphorical usage too reflects that range. *Cachinnare* and *cachinni,* both verb and noun, are used to evoke the sound of water—from the pounding of the ocean to the gentle rippling of Lake Garda.[12] Cackles or giggles or ripples? We should always hesitate before assigning too rigid or precise a value to Latin terms for "laughing" or "laughter."

LATIN SMILES?

So far I have not pointed to a word that corresponds to our own *smile.* I mean that curving of the lips that may, or may not, be a preliminary to a fully vocalized laugh—but is independently one of the most powerful signifying gestures in the modern Western world. From "Smile, please" to smiley faces, it underpins for us all kinds of human interaction, signaling warmth, greeting, wry amusement, disdain, affection, confidence, ambivalence, and much more. It is hard for us to imagine social life happening without it, yet it is hard to find a Latin equivalent.

In ancient Greek the position appears somewhat simpler. The word *meidiaō* may be much more distant from our *smile* than that standard translation implies. In Homer and other early writers, *meidiaō* can also be a sign of hostility, aggression, or superiority, and in general it seems to be treated as a gesture of the face as a whole rather than just the lips.[13] But as Halliwell shows, it does overlap in part with our usage, notably because unlike laughter, and like our "smiling," it makes no noise (or as he more carefully puts it, "It is impossible . . . to show that *meid-* terms ever imply vocalisation").[14] In Latin there is no specific term of that sort. When Virgil evoked the "smiling" gods of Homer, he often fell back on another compound of *ridere,* that is *subridere,* which technically means a "suppressed or muffled laugh," even a "little laugh."[15]

Renidere (to beam) can also, metaphorically, signal a silent facial expression that seems akin to a smile. This is how the poet Catullus has Egnatius famously reveal his urine-cleaned teeth: "Egnatius . . . renidet." And Robert Kaster, in exploring the world and the text of Macrobius' *Saturnalia,* has not only translated the word as "smile" but also suggested that these "smiles" play a particular role in articulating the learned discussion that is staged in the dialogue. Phrases such as

"Praetextatus smiled" (*Praetextatus renidens*) tend to greet an ignorant, out-of-place comment by some (usually inferior) participant in the discussion, and they invariably herald a pronouncement by an expert "which admits no contradiction." Kaster is an acute observer of the structure of this late antique debate and of the hierarchies within it. But it is far less clear than he suggests that this "beaming" is a close match for our own category of grandly supercilious smiling—those "gestures of magnificent condescension," as he puts it.[16]

Other, more discursive, metaphorical uses of the word outside Macrobius—admittedly often centuries earlier than the *Saturnalia*—are varied but revealing. Catullus certainly likens the expression (*renidet*) to laughing, but Egnatius' determined display of his white teeth is an absurd form of laughter (*risus ineptus*) and so is itself laughable. In Ovid, *renidens* is (twice) the expression of foolish optimism on the face of young Icarus, in Livy it is that of the boastful trickster, and Quintilian also uses it of a misplaced sign of pleasure (*intempestive renidentis*).[17] Repeatedly, as with the Greek *meidiaō*, the emphasis is on the facial expression as a whole (*hilaro vultu renidens, renidenti vultu, renidens vultu*[18]), not specifically the lips—as is also once made explicit in Macrobius: *vultu renidens*.[19] For the most part, the common defining feature of this gesture seems to be the facial "glow" (of confidence, whether well-placed or misplaced) rather than the oscular curve, or "smile" as we know it.[20]

So did the Romans smile? At the risk of falling into the trap of overconfident classification that I have been criticizing, my working hypothesis is "by and large, in our terms, no." But that is not (simply) for linguistic reasons, and it needs to be argued rather carefully. The cultural significance of smiling may be reflected in, but is not wholly circumscribed by, language. Several modern European languages (English and Danish, for example—like ancient Greek) have separate word groups, from separate linguistic roots, that distinguish "smile" from "laugh." Others (notably the Romance descendants of Latin) do not. Reflecting those Latin roots, modern French uses *sourire* for "smile," just as Italian uses *sorridere* (both derived directly from *subridere*; respectively cognate with the French *rire* and the Italian *ridere*). Yet both of these modern cultures have an investment in the social significance of smiling, as distinct from laughter, no less intense than that of (for example) their modern Anglo-American counterparts.

Nonetheless, the linguistic patterns of Latin do seem to accord with other negative hints which suggest that smiling was not a major part (if a part at all) of Roman social semiotics. Only the most hard-line ethologists, neuroscientists, and their followers hold to the human universality of such facial gestures—whether in form, type, or meaning.[21] Crucially important for me is that we find in Roman literature none of those distinctions between smiling and laughing drawn by the likes of Lord Chesterfield (for whom a silent smile was a sign of decorum, in contrast to "loud peals of laughter"),[22] and—whatever is going on in Macrobius—we see no clear evidence that smiling as such was a significant player in Roman social interactions in general. "Keep smiling!" and the like were sentiments unheard of in Rome, so far as I can tell, and as Christopher Jones has shown, two Romans meeting in the street were likely to greet each other with a kiss, where we would smile.[23]

Of course, arguments from silence are always perilous, especially when the process of spotting the smile is necessarily an interpretative one. But it is hard to resist the suggestion of Jacques Le Goff that (in the Latin West at least) smiling as we understand it was an invention of the Middle Ages.[24] This is not to say that the Romans never curled up the edges of their mouths in a formation that would look to us much like a smile; of course they did. But such curling did not mean very much in the range of significant social and cultural gestures at Rome. Conversely, other gestures, which would mean little to us, were much more heavily freighted with significance: Caesar scratching his head with one finger, which would now indicate no more than an annoying itch, could give Cicero the hint that Caesar posed no danger to the Roman Republic.[25]

There is an important lesson in this. It has become standard practice when translating not only *subridere* but also *ridere* itself and its other cognates into English to use the word *smile* where it seems more natural to us than *laugh* (even some famous lines of Virgil have been the victim of this tendency; see pp. 84–85). This has a doubly misleading effect. It tends to give smiling a much bigger presence in Roman cultural language than it deserves—or ever had. And in offering an apparently "better" translation, it tends to erode the potential foreignness of Roman patterns of laughter, to make them look increasingly like our own. To be sure, we cannot absolutely prove that there was no strong and meaningful Roman tradition of smiling that lurked underneath the general rubric of *ridere*. We need to remain alert to that possibility. But we should also resist the easy temptation to reconstruct the Romans in our own image. So even where *laugh* may seem awkward, I shall use it as the first option in translating *ridere* and its compounds and cognates: that is not to say that even the English word *laugh* captures exactly what the Romans meant by *ridere*, but it is certainly less misleading than *smile*. And that awkwardness is, after all, part of the historical point.

JOKES AND JESTS

We are not simply dealing with the poverty in the Latin vocabulary of laughter compared with the richness of (say) Greek, or with a simple lack of cultural discrimination in classifying laughter's various forms. We are dealing with a *different* richness of vocabulary and perhaps with a significantly different set of cultural priorities. For however few the Latin terms for laughter may be, the terms for what may provoke it—in the forms of jokes and witticisms—are legion. To list just some: *iocus, lepos, urbanitas, dicta, dicacitas, cavillatio, ridicula, sal, salsum, facetiae*. We can no more define the precise difference between *dicacitas* and *cavillatio* than we can define how exactly *chortle* differs from *chuckle*. But the contrast with the Greek range of vocabulary—which is overwhelming dominated by two words for joke, *geloion* and *skōmma*—is striking.[26] Whatever the origin and history of these terms (on which see further chapter 5), their range and variety point to a Roman cultural concern with the *provocation* of laughter and with the relationship between the laugher and whoever prompted the laughter (both joker and butt).

Interestingly, Roman popular sayings also seem to reflect these priorities. Proverbs and slogans about laughter are common in modern English-speaking culture: "He who laughs last laughs longest," "Laugh and the world laughs with you" (or, to quote a Yiddish proverb, "What soap is to the body, laughter is to the soul"). Overwhelmingly, they treat laughter (and its effects) from the point of view of the person who laughs. Romans also sloganized laughter, but much more frequently these slogans stressed the role of the joker rather than the laugher ("It's better to lose a friend than a jest,"[27] "It's easier for a wise man to stifle a flame within his burning mouth than keep his *bona dicta* [wit or quips] to himself"[28]) or focused on the relationship between the laugher and the object of their laughter or on questions of who or what was an appropriate target for a jest ("Don't laugh at the unfortunate"[29]). To put this another way, where most modern theory, and popular interest, is firmly directed toward the laugher and to laughter's internal coordinates, Roman discussions tended to look to the human beings who caused laughter, to the triangulation of joker, butt, and laugher—and (as we shall see in the next chapter) to the vulnerability of the joker, no less than of the person joked about.

LATIN LAUGHTER—OFF THE BEATEN TRACK

One of the pleasures of tracking down Roman laughter is that it leads to some extraordinary—surprising and even startling—works of Latin literature still somewhat off the beaten track, unfamiliar even to most professional classicists. We find all kinds of glimpses into Roman laughter in some unexpected places, and there is no shortage of them. They include long discussions that broach, directly or indirectly, the question of what makes people laugh, reflect on the protocols and ethics of laughing, or use laughter as a marker of other cultural values at Rome. No discussion of laughter is ever neutral.

So, for example, laughter features as one diagnostic of the emperor's mad villainy or perverse extravagance in the biography of the third-century CE emperor Elagabalus—which belongs to that strange, partly fictional, partly fraudulent, but hugely revealing collection of imperial lives known as the *Augustan History* (or *Historia Augusta*—the history, that is "of the emperors," *Augusti*).[30] In what is almost a parody of a pattern that we shall see repeated in the lives of earlier emperors in less tendentious accounts (see chapter 6), Elagabalus outdid his subjects in laughter as much as in everything else. In fact, he sometimes laughed so loud in the theater that he drowned out the actors ("He alone could be heard")—a nice indication of the social disruption caused by gelastic excess. He also used laughter to humiliate. "He had the habit too of inviting to dinner eight bald men, or else eight one-eyed ones, or eight men with gout, or eight deaf men, or eight with particularly dark skin, or eight tall men—or eight fat men, in their case to raise a laugh from everyone, as they could not fit on the same couch." It was not so much the mad replication that caused the laughter but rather his slapstick exposure of the victims' fatness. There was a similar comic style in his experiment with a Roman prototype of whoopee cushions: "Some of his less prestigious friends he would sit on airbags, not cushions, and he had these deflated while they were dining, so that the men were often suddenly found under the table in the middle of their meal."[31] This is a combination of power, dining, laughter, and practical jokes to which we shall return.

An even richer discussion that often goes unnoticed (or is merely pillaged for some of the individual jokes it contains) is found in the second book of Macrobius' *Saturnalia*. Writing in the context of a highly learned, late antique subculture, Macrobius (through the scripted contributions of his various characters) offers the closest thing we have from the ancient world to an extended history not so much of laughter but of joking, and, indirectly at least, he reflects on different styles of jokes and on the nature and importance of "old jokes."

The scene is simple. In keeping with the lighthearted atmosphere of the festival, the Saturnalia, that provides the dramatic context of the work, each of the discussants in turn picks a joke from the past to recount to the others (Hannibal and Cato the Elder are the earliest Roman "jokers" cited, though—true to type—the Greek character in the discussion, Eusebius, contributes a quip from Demosthenes, and the Egyptian Horus picks an epigram of Plato's).[32] This leads on to a rather more systematic anthologizing of the quips of three historical characters—Cicero, the emperor Augustus, and his daughter, Julia—and occasionally to wider reflections on laughter.[33] In part, Macrobius' account matches the standard historical template, with its emphasis on *antiqua festivitas* and the fearlessness, if not the rudeness, of the jokers of earlier times.[34] But it also carefully shows what hangs on the choice of a favorite joke and how that choice may relate to character. Predictably, it is one of the uninvited guests, the oddball bully Evangelus, the man most concerned to undermine the atmosphere of literary high culture, who chooses the joke about sex; the buttoned-up grammarian Servius can hardly bear to tell a joke at all and in the end settles for a dry piece of wordplay.[35]

The final section of their discussion turns, significantly, to another key institution of Roman laughter: mime (in Latin, *mimus*). This particular form of dramatic display was not, as its name in English might suggest, a silent affair, dependent on gesture alone, but a performance with words, sometimes improvised, sometimes scripted, and both male and female actors. Its precise character and history are much less understood than modern textbook accounts sometimes suggest, as is its precise relationship to another ancient genre—pantomime. But two features are clear. First, mime could sometimes be very bawdy, and our genteel debaters of the *Saturnalia* are careful to stress that they will not actually bring the mimes into their banquet, only a selection of the jokes—so avoiding the bawdiness (*lascivia*) but reflecting the high spirit (*celebritas*) of the performances.[36] Second, it was the one and only cultural form at Rome whose primary, perhaps even sole, purpose was to make you laugh. So Roman writers repeatedly stressed—and that was the message blazoned on the tombstones of some mime actors.[37]

I shall later argue (see pp. 167–72) that the hilarity so strongly associated with mime is one aspect of the more general importance of imitation and impersonation in the production of Roman laughter, from actors to apes. But Macrobius' discussion already gestures in that direction with a series of stories about the competition between two pantomime actors, Pylades and Hylas, to present convincing imitations of mythical characters. In the cleverest of these, the audience is reported to have laughed at Pylades, who was playing the mad Hercules, because he was stumbling around "and wasn't maintaining the manner of walking appropriate to an actor." He took off his mask and berated them: "Idiots," he said, "I'm playing the part of a madman." In a nice twist, the audience turns out to have been laughing at a man for what they imagined was a bad piece of acting, when in fact it was a perfect example of (laughable) impersonation.[38]

Sometimes it is not a lengthy discussion, such as Macrobius', but just a couple of unnoticed words in some little-read text that can shed unexpected light on the operations and significance of laughter in Roman culture. The collected volumes of Roman oratorical exercises that go under the general title of *Declamations* have recently attracted some keen scholarly attention, but even so they are still relatively underexploited. A combination of rhetorical training and after-dinner entertainment, these exercises usually started from a fictional (or at least fictionalized) legal case, on which the learner orators or celebrity after-dinner speakers would take different sides, for defense or prosecution. The collections gathered together some of these cases, along with excerpts from particularly notable speeches by famous rhetorical showmen; they represent, in a sense, both a manual of models to imitate and a compilation of oratorical "greatest hits."[39]

One telling example, from the collection compiled by the elder Seneca in the early first century CE, concerns a (fictionalized) version of the case of Lucius Quinctius Flamininus, who was expelled from the Senate in 184 BCE for inappropriate conduct while holding office.[40] Several shorter and slightly different variants survive elsewhere in Latin literature,[41] but the declamation centers on the relationship between Flamininus and a prostitute, whom—in his infatuation—he had taken with him when he left Rome to govern his province. At dinner there one evening, she remarked that she had never seen a man's head cut off, so to please her, Flamininus had a condemned criminal executed right in front of her in the dining room. Then, in the fictionalized world of the declamation, he was accused of *maiestas* (often translated as "treason" but better as "an offense against the Roman state").[42]

The oratorical highlights focus not on the rights and wrongs of the execution of the criminal as such (the man had, after all, been condemned to death anyway) but on its context. The declamation is in fact a treasure-house of Roman clichés on the proper separation of the official business of state from the pleasures of ludic entertainment and the jocular world of the dinner party. Many of the quoted speakers found snappy ways of summing up this underlying issue. Taking "the forum into a feast" (*forum in convivium*) was no better than taking "a feast into the forum" (*convivium in forum*), quipped one. "Have you ever seen a praetor dining with his whore in front of the rostra?" asked another, referring to the raised platform in the Forum from which speakers traditionally addressed the Roman people.[43]

Held up for specific criticism is the fact that the executioner was drunk when he killed the man and that Flamininus was wearing slippers (*soleae*), both signs of private pleasure rather than official duty. But another marker of transgression lies in the "jokes" being made of the serious business of state. An execution has been turned into "a dinner table joke" (*convivales ioci*), Flamininus is himself accused of "joking" (*ioci*), and the woman is said to have been "making fun" (*iocari*) of the fasces, the symbols of Roman power. In fact, according to one of these rhetorical reenactments of the terrible scene, when the unfortunate victim was brought into the room, the prostitute laughed (*arridet*)—not, as the translation in the Loeb Classical Library has it, with very different implications, "smiled."[44] There is, I suspect, a sexual resonance here; laughter was often associated with ancient prostitutes, so it is exactly what you might expect this, or any, whore to do.[45] But more than that, the single word *arridet* (emphatically at the end of the sentence) underlines the irruption of gelastic frivolity into the world of state business.[46]

What happened next, however, brings into focus a different role of laughter in the social interaction around this dinner table. The whole occasion is written up in decidedly melodramatic terms (we are asked to imagine at one point that the unfortunate criminal misreads the scene as the preliminary to a pardon and actually thanks Flamininus for his mercy). But what did the other guests do once the execution had been carried out? One man wept, one turned away, but another laughed (*ridebat*)—"to keep in with the prostitute" (*quo gratior esset meretrici*).[47]

This is laughter provoked by something quite different from the jokes of Macrobius. Jocular and (transgressively) ludic though the laughter of this whole scene may be, there are no verbal quips to prompt the outbursts. We see instead the laughter of (inappropriate) pleasure on the part of the woman and the laughter of flattery, or (to put it more politely) of social alignment, on the part of another dinner guest. This is another example of that nexus of signals implied by a laugh—from pleasure to approval to outright sycophancy—to which we shall return.

CLASSIC LITERARY LAUGHS: THE LESSONS OF VIRGIL'S BABY

The study of laughter does not merely reanimate some less-known works of Latin literature; it also encourages us to look again, through a different lens, at some of the most canonical. We have already glanced at Horace's *Satires* and at Catullus. There are many more cases where laughter plays a role, sometimes disputed, in the most famous Latin classics to have survived from the Roman world: from Ovid's *Art of Love*, with its parodic set of instructions to young women on how to laugh,[48] through Virgil's reference to Venus' laugh, which enigmatically seals the discussion between her and Juno at the beginning of *Aeneid* 4 (and with it the fate of Dido),[49] to the opening of Horace's *Art of Poetry*, where he lists the kinds of representational incongruities that would, he claims, make anyone laugh ("If a painter wanted to put a horse's head on a human neck . . . would you be able to keep your laughter in?").[50]

The most famous, and controversial, of all such references to laughter, however, is the especially puzzling end to Virgil's puzzling fourth *Eclogue*. This poem was written around 40 BCE, against the background of promising attempts—fruitless as they proved in the long term—to secure peace in the civil war between Octavian (the future emperor Augustus) and Mark Antony. It heralds the coming of a new golden age for Rome, embodied in or brought about by the birth, imminent or recent (the chronology is vague), of a baby boy. Virgil celebrates this baby in messianic terms (hence the title "Messianic Eclogue" often given to the whole poem)—"the boy under whom . . . a golden race shall rise up throughout the world" and so on. But who was the baby? This has been a major source of dispute for centuries, with suggestions ranging from the yet unborn child of either Octavian or Mark Antony (both of whom turned out, inconveniently, to be girls) through a purely symbolic figure for the return of peace to Jesus—whose birth, this idea goes, Virgil was unwittingly prophesying.[51] But almost equally controversial has been the significance of the last four lines of the poem (60–63), which address the baby and focus on the "laughter" (*risus*) exchanged between him and his parent(s). What is this *risus*, and whose *risus* is it anyway?

Once more, the details of the argument focus on exactly what the Latin author wrote and how accurately the medieval manuscripts, on which we rely, reflect that. The main issue comes down to the origin and direction of the "laughter" and depends on the difference of just a few letters. The crux is this. In the poem's final couplet, was Virgil thinking of the *risus* of the baby, directed either to his *parenti* (singular, dative case, presumably his mother[52]) or to his *parentes* (plural, accusative case, meaning mother *and* father)? Or did he mean that the *risus* of the *parentes* (here a nominative case) was directed at the baby? And what hangs on this? The argument is technical and ultimately, let me warn you, inconclusive—and it involves Latin words that to the innocent eye are identical (or almost so), even if they point to significantly different interpretations. But it is also very instructive and well worth pursuing in all its intricacy. For it puts laughter right back into the heart of a debate about one of the most classic of all classical texts while exposing the pitfalls of not reflecting carefully enough on the linguistic rules and cultural protocols of Roman laughter.

All the main surviving manuscripts run:

Incipe, parve puer, risu cognoscere matrem
(matri longa decem tulerunt fastidia menses);
incipe, parve puer: cui non risere parentes,
nec deus hunc mensa, dea nec dignata cubili est.

Literally, this means "Begin, little boy, to recognize your mother with *risus* (to your mother ten months [of pregnancy] have brought long distress); begin, little boy: he on whom his parents have not *risere*, no god thinks worthy of his dinner table, no goddess worthy of her bed." The idea (frankly "enigmatic" as it is[53]) must be that the starry, divine future of the child depends on his parents' warmth for him now, reflected in their *risus* toward him.

But most modern editors of the poem have thought this so enigmatic, not to say unconvincing, that they have chosen to adjust the text in order to change the nature of the interaction described. Instead of having the parents (*parentes*) direct their *risus* toward the baby (*cui*), they have the baby (*qui* substituted for *cui*) directing his *risus* toward his parent—that is, his mother (*parenti*). On this reading, the interaction of the final two lines runs as follows:

Incipe, parve puer: qui non risere parenti,
nec deus hunc mensa, dea nec dignata cubili est.

Or, "Begin, little boy: those who have not *risere* on their parent, no god thinks worthy of his dinner table, no goddess worthy of her bed." In other words, it is what the baby himself does that paves the way for his future greatness.

There are some strong reasons for making these changes. In general, the revised text seems to make better sense. For one thing, the phrase "Begin, little boy" seems to demand some action on the part of the baby, not—as our manuscript reading would have it—on the part of the parents. For another, the idea that the entirely "natural" response (*risus*) of the parents to their child should be prophetic of his future seems hard to fathom. What is more, although there is no direct support for it in any of the manuscripts of Virgil, this does seem to be much closer to the text that Quintilian had in front of him just a century or so after Virgil wrote—as we know, because he refers to this particular passage in discussing a tricky point of Roman grammar.[54]

But whether these changes are correct or not (and I doubt that we shall ever firmly settle this), the questions here also turn the spotlight on to laughter—or more precisely, on to what difference thinking harder about laughter might make to our understanding of the text. For critics of these lines tend to fall back on a series of overconfident assumptions about the linguistic and social rules that governed Roman *risus*—and on all kinds of claims about what *ridere* and *risus* can (or *must*) mean. This is a place where we find many false certainties about Roman laughter on show.

So, for example, there is an alternative and less drastic emendation in line 62—which retains the idea that it is the *risus* of the baby but changes just one letter of the manuscript version. It replaces *cui* with *qui* but keeps the plural *parentes* found in the manuscripts, to read "qui non risere parentes." Assuming that *parentes* is in the accusative case, this would mean "those who have not *risere* at their parents." It is, at the very least, an economical solution, but it has often been rejected on the grounds that "*rideo* with the accusative can *only* mean 'laugh at' or 'mock'" (and so would suggest, ludicrously, that the baby here was ridiculing his parents). In fact, that is simply false; as the most careful critics have conceded, there are numerous examples in Latin of *ridere* being used with an accusative object in an entirely favorable sense.[55]

From a different angle, many scholars have seized on Pliny's statement that human children do not laugh until they are forty days old—except for Zoroaster, who laughed (*risisse*) from the moment he was born. In this way, they argue, through his hints at supernaturally precocious laughter, Virgil is claiming divine status for the child. Maybe. But the fact is, we have no idea how old Virgil's baby is meant to be, we have no idea how widespread in the Roman world Pliny's factoid about the chronology of laughter was, nor does the closest parallel passage (as we shall shortly see) provide any justification for that religious interpretation.[56] There have also been firm (and conflicting) views expressed on whose *risus* is meant earlier, in line 60 (*risu cognoscere matrem*, or "to recognize your mother with *risus*"). Must this be the *risus* of the baby, in recognition of his mother? Or could it be her *risus*, which allows the baby to recognize her?[57] The Latin is, of course, consistent with either (or indeed both simultaneously).

Perhaps more important, though, underlying almost all recent interpretations of these lines we can detect a decidedly sentimental tinge. Even one of the most hardheaded Latinists, Robin Nisbet, suggests that the scene's "humanity" (whatever he means by that) is a good indication that "a real baby is meant" rather than some abstract symbol of peace and prosperity, and some critics, even when they are not arguing for a prophetically Christian reading of the text, evoke a scene that is frankly closer to an image of the adoring Virgin Mary and baby Jesus than to anything we know from pagan Rome.[58] This sometimes chocolate-box tone is underpinned by what has become the standard translation of *risus* and *ridere* here, "smile" rather than "laugh": "Begin, little boy, to recognize your mother with a *smile*."[59] It conjures up a picture of the loving smiles that bind mother and son and resonate powerfully in our understanding of babies and parenthood. How misleading is this?

So far I have avoided this issue, by keeping largely to the Latin terms. But not only should "smile" never be the translation of first resort for *ridere;* in this case there is also a clear suggestion in one of Virgil's closest predecessors for this scene that a vocalized laugh is definitely meant. Virgil most likely drew and adapted this scene from Catullus, who in his wedding hymn for Manlius Torquatus imagines the future appearance of Torquatus junior, a baby sitting on his mother's lap, stretching out his hands to his father, and "sweetly laughing to him with his little lips half open" (*dulce rideat ad patrem / semihiante labello*).[60] This is not the curved lips of a silent smile; it is a laugh, and that is what we should think of in the Virgilian scene too.

It is perhaps easier for those not so embedded in the traditions of Virgilian scholarship to see the wider possibilities here, and their different perspectives can be instructive. For modern theorists of literature and psychoanalysis who have reflected on the role of laughter as a metaphor of communication, this passage has had a particular importance, even if it has rarely been discussed at length. Georges Bataille, for example, referenced Virgil's words in a famous essay on the subject. "Laughter," he wrote, "is reducible, in general, to the laugh of recognition in the child—which the following line from Virgil calls to mind."[61] Julia Kristeva, likewise, hinted at the scene described by Virgil when she theorized the crucial role of laughter in the relationship between mother and baby and in the baby's growing sense of its own "self."[62] These ideas found an echo in the work of the cultural critic Marina Warner, who commented directly on the final lines of *Eclogue* 4 in the course of a more general discussion of (in her words) "funniness." She had no difficulty in translating Virgil's *ridere* as "laugh" and in seeing a point to that laughter: "'Learn, little boy, to know your mother through laughter.' Did he [Virgil] mean the child's laughter? Or the mother's? Or, by omitting the possessive, did he want his readers to understand that recognition and laughter happen together at the very start of understanding, identity, and life itself?"[63]

This is a radically different type of reading from those I have just reviewed. Many classicists would, I suspect, be reluctant to follow Warner, still less Bataille or Kristeva, and this is not the place for a lengthy discussion on the strengths and weaknesses of their arguments.[64] But at the very least, in interpreting this contested passage so differently and in their conviction that we are dealing with vocal laughter, they offer a powerful reminder of how dangerous it is to assume that we know how Latin *risus* worked—let alone to impose some version of "baby's first smile" on the culture of ancient Rome.

ROMAN LAUGHTER IN GREEK

Roman laughter was not, however, merely laughter in *Latin*. So far in this chapter I have focused on Latin literature, but already by the second century BCE, Rome had a bilingual literary culture, in which laughter could be debated and discussed in both Latin and Greek.

In fact, both incidents of Roman laughter that I chose to discuss in the first chapter of this book are classic examples of this kind of linguistic and literary bilingualism. The first (pp. 1–8) describes an incident that took place in the Colosseum at Rome, in a fearful and funny stand-off between the emperor Commodus and a group of the Roman political elite; it was taken from a history of Rome written in Greek by a Roman senator whose original home was in the Greek-speaking province of Bithynia, in what is now Turkey. The second (pp. 8–14) was taken from a Latin comedy originally performed in the second century

BCE at (almost certainly) a religious festival in the city of Rome. But—in a form of literary syncretism long debated by scholars of Greco-Roman comedy—it was in fact a Romanized adaptation and conflation of two plays by the late fourth-century Athenian dramatist Menander. Neither of these survives beyond some fragmentary snatches recovered from Egyptian papyrus and excerpts quoted by later authors, but, from even the few passages we have, it is clear that some of the funny lines I discussed earlier go back, with adjustments, to one of Menander's plays.

The question is not whether these two stories deserve their place in an exploration of Roman laughter. Of course they do: each in its different way unfolds within a Roman institutional framework, and each is told by a "Roman" writer (Dio a Roman senator, Terence probably an enfranchised ex-slave). But they raise the question of where we might want to draw the line. There is in particular a vast amount of surviving literature written in Greek in the period of the Roman Empire, when the Greek world was under Roman political and military control—from the satires of Lucian to the lectures of Dio Chrysostom and the boy-gets-girl novel (*Leucippe and Cleitophon*) by Achilles Tatius, not to mention the biographies and philosophy of Plutarch, the histories of Dio and Appian and Dionysius, or the wearisome hypochondria of Aelius Aristides and the interminable (fascinating to some) medical treatises of Galen. Does it all count as Roman? Does "Roman" laughter potentially include the laughter of the whole Roman Empire, from Spain to Syria? What is the difference between Greek and Roman laughter? I have already pointed to some mismatches in the vocabulary of laughing and jesting in the Latin and Greek languages. How far does that indicate significant cultural differences that we should be taking into account?

These reflections gesture toward a lively, wider debate among historians and archaeologists about the very nature of "Roman" culture. Complex as this debate has become, one simple question largely sums it up: what do we mean by that superficially unproblematic adjective *Roman* (whether "Roman laughter" or "literature," "sculpture" or "spectacle," "politics" or "pantomime")? Which Romans are we talking about? The wealthy literate elite? Or the poor, the peasants, the slaves, or the women? And even more to the point, are we thinking of the term geographically, chronologically, or more integrally linked to political and civic status or to distinctive norms of behavior and culture? Can, for example, an intellectual treatise written in Greek by an Athenian aristocrat in the second century CE count as Roman because Athens was then part of the Roman Empire? Would it be more convincingly Roman if the

Greek writer was (like Dio) simultaneously a Roman senator or if we knew that the work was read and debated by Latin speakers in Rome itself?

There are, of course, no right answers to these questions. The most influential recent studies have insisted on disaggregating any unitary notion of "Roman" culture while also arguing against any simple progressive model of cultural change across the ancient Mediterranean.[65] No one would now think of the early city of Rome as a cultural vacuum that was gradually filled, in a process neatly labeled "Hellenization," thanks to its contacts with the Greek world. (The Roman poet Horace would, I suspect, have been horrified to discover that his words "Captured Greece took captive its rough conqueror" would be dragged out of context and turned into a slogan for the simple inferiority of Roman versus Greek culture.[66]) Likewise, few historians would now characterize growing Roman influence in the West as a straightforward process of "Romanization"—or, alternatively, think in terms of a clear standoff between "Roman" cultural forms and those of the more or less resistant "natives."

Instead they point to a shifting cross-cultural multiplicity of "Romannesses," formed by an often unstable series of cultural interactions summed up in a range of sometimes illuminating, sometimes overseductive, sometimes (I fear) quite misleading metaphors, such as constellation, hybridity, creolization, bilingualism, or crossbreeding.[67] In fact, in some of the most radical work, even the basic descriptive language of ancient cultural difference and ancient cultural change in the Roman Empire seems to have been turned inside out and upside down. So, for example, in Andrew Wallace-Hadrill's wonderfully heady study *Rome's Cultural Revolution,* the very opposition between Roman and Greek (Hellenic) culture is drastically subverted. That is to say, Wallace-Hadrill offers a series of powerful arguments for seeing Rome as a prime engine of "Hellenization," "Hellenization" as one aspect of "Romanization," and ultimately "Roman" influence as a driver behind the "re-Hellenization" of the Hellenic world itself![68]

These vertiginous issues inevitably lurk in the background of any book such as this one. But my most pressing questions are rather narrower and more manageable. For a start, we have to face the fact that we have almost no access whatsoever to the culture of laughter among the nonelite anywhere in the Roman world. Whether the style of "peasant laughter" really was as different from that of the urban elite as we often imagine, who knows? (We shouldn't forget that the supposed lustiness of the peasant can be as much an invention of the sophisticated city dweller as an accurate reflection of the gelastic life of simple peasant society.)[69] In any case, to study "Roman laughter" is now necessarily to study laughter as it is (re)constructed and mediated in a range of elite literary texts. The question is: which ones, and particularly which ones of those produced in Greek or partly rooted in the Greek world? Is there a line to be drawn? Where? Does Plutarch—Greek essayist, priest at the sanctuary of Delphi, and avid student of "Roman" culture—belong in this book, in Stephen Halliwell's *Greek Laughter,* or in both? Are we in danger of confusing "Greek" with "Roman" laughter? And how much does it matter?

There can be no hard-and-fast rules. Recent critical approaches to the Greek culture of the Roman Empire have stressed many different, sometimes contradictory, aspects: its emphatically Hellenic (even "anti-Roman") coordinates, its active role in the reformulation of the very categories of "Greek" and "Roman" or in supporting the political and social hegemony of Rome over Greece, and so on.[70] In practice, the modern dividing line between "Greek" and "Roman" has sometimes come down to little more than subject matter (if the work in question is about Rome, it tends to be treated as Roman; if about Greece, then it's seen as Greek—despite the fact that the bifocal, Greco-Roman perspective of Plutarch and others makes nonsense of that procedure). Perhaps even more often, to be honest, it comes down to the territorial divisions of the modern academy. On the one hand, scholars of classical Greek literature tend to embrace and interpret this material as somehow an extension of their territory (it is, after all, written in "their" language and constructively engages with its classical Greek predecessors). Many Roman cultural historians, on the other hand, would claim it as part of their remit (it was written in "their" period and often gestures directly or indirectly to the power structures of the Roman empire). The truth is, there is no safe path to be trodden between seeing this literature in terms of (on the one hand) *being Greek* or (on the other) *becoming Roman*—to conscript the titles of two of the most influential modern contributions to this whole debate.[71]

I shall proceed with some very basic methodological guidelines in mind. First, that the "Greek" and "Roman" cultures of laughter in the period of the Roman Empire were simultaneously both foreign to each other and also so mutually implicated as to be impossible to separate. Simply by virtue of language, some sense of cultural difference could always be mobilized. We have to imagine, for example, that when Virgil had his text of Homer in front of him and was considering how he would reflect the Greek word *meidiaō* in his own epic (see p. 73), he necessarily pondered on the different senses of Greek and Latin words for laughter and what might hang on them. And we caught a glimpse (on p. 78) of paraded ethnic preferences in joking among the elite diners at Macrobius' Saturnalian dinner party: Greek, Egyptian, and Roman. We certainly need to keep alert for hints of cultural difference. But for the most part, there is little to be gained (and much to be lost) by attempting to prize apart the gelastic culture of imperial literature, still less by distributing these culturally multifaceted texts on one side or the other of some notional "Roman"/"Greek" divide (Plutarch's *Roman Questions* in, *Leucippe and Cleitophon* out; Apuleius' Latin version of the story of "Lucius the Ass" in, the parallel Greek version out). Elite Romans, wherever in the empire they lived, learned to "think laughter" in debate with both Greek and Latin texts. We are dealing, in large part at least, with a shared literary culture of laughter and "laughterhood," a bilingual cultural conversation.

My second guideline serves to limit that very slightly. If we do imagine Roman imperial culture as a conversation (to add, I confess, yet another metaphor to those of hybridity, constellation, and the rest), I have chosen to concentrate on those literary works written in Greek where we can most confidently point to an explicitly Roman side in that script, rather than merely a generalized sociopolitical Roman background. That is sometimes through characters clearly labeled as Roman being featured in a dialogue (as we find, for example, in Plutarch's *Table Talk*) or through specifically Roman subject matter and context (such as the names, currency, and events that form part of the background to the gags in the late antique "jokebook" the *Philogelos,* or "Laughter lover").

What is striking is how powerful the Roman intervention in that conversation can be. In fact, as we shall now see, some of the traditions of laughter that may appear superficially to be more or less pure "Greek" turn out to be much more "Roman" than we usually assume. Sometimes we find that what we take as notable traditions of classical Greek laughter are very largely constructions of the Roman period. Occasionally we find that the Greek idiom of laughter adapts to ideas and expressions that are distinctively Latin. And when—conversely—Roman authors take over Greek jokes, we have evidence for the creative adaptation of the original material for a Roman audience. Here again, Terence's *Eunuch*—with Gnatho the sponger, Thraso the soldier, and the joke about the young Rhodian—offers a nice glimpse of the "Romanization" of Greek laughter and the archaeology of a Roman joke while introducing some of the bigger issues of the final section of this chapter.

TERENCE'S GREEK JOKE

The comedies of Plautus and Terence have long provided revealing instances of the intricacy of Roman engagement with Greek culture—and the philological work of Eduard Fraenkel in the 1920s underpins many discussions of this.[72] The plays are explicitly drawn from Greek models, but the dramatists actively reworked the "originals" into something significantly different, with a new resonance in the Roman context. For example, whatever its Greek source (which is still debated), Plautus' *Amphitruo* closely engages with that most distinctive of all Roman celebrations: the triumphal procession, held in honor of military victory. Plautus in fact comes close to adapting whatever his (Greek) original was into a comic parody of the origins of the (Roman) triumph.[73]

In Terence's *Eunuch,* this creative adjustment goes right down to the individual jokes, so adding a further twist to the scenes of laughter that I looked at in the first chapter—and an important coda to my treatment there. The prologue of the play states clearly that its models were two late fourth-century plays of Menander: *The Eunuch* and *The Toady* (*Kolax*), from which the characters of the soldier and the sponger/flatterer (or toady) were drawn. We have, from various papyrus scraps and quotations, more than a hundred lines of *The Toady,* and these confirm that the characters of Gnatho and Thraso went back to that source (even if they were known by different names in Menander's play).[74] In fact, a brief snatch of dialogue, quoted by Plutarch, seems likely to have been the inspiration for one of the exchanges between the two that I quoted in chapter 1—a classic example of a willfully misleading explanation for an outburst of laughter. This, as we saw (p. 11), is Terence's version:

> *Gnatho: hahahae*
>
> *Thraso:* What are you laughing at?
>
> *Gnatho:* At what you just said, and at that story about the guy from Rhodes—whenever I think about it.

And this, to judge from Plutarch (who is discussing the problems of dealing with flatterers), is the "original" passage in *The Toady,* which Terence took over. The sentiment is strikingly similar, and the words are attributed to the sponger/flatterer of the title:

I'm laughing when I think about the joke
You made against the Cypriot.[75]

Whether that explanation for laughter was as wickedly misleading in Menander's play as in Terence's, we do not have enough information to say (though Plutarch's claim that the toady was "dancing in triumph" over the soldier with these words suggests that it was). But one thing seems certain: in each play there was some comic reference back to an earlier joke—yet the exact terms of that joke were different. In *The Eunuch,* it was a joke about the Rhodian boy ("chasing after delicacies"). In Menander, it is some (lost) gag about a "Cypriot"—perhaps, as some critics have proposed, connected with the old Greek saying about Cypriot bullocks eating dung (so all Cypriots are "shit eaters").[76]

If so, we can only guess what lay behind Terence's change. Perhaps the Cypriot bullock joke was simply not part of the Roman repertoire and was likely to fall flat in front of Terence's first audience. Perhaps he entirely rewrote the joke to make a topical allusion to Roman political relations with Rhodes. But maybe Terence changed only the nationality of the quip's antihero (the boy chasing the delicacies), from Cypriot to Rhodian; after all, in his *Eunuch,* the desired girl came from Rhodes, and maybe there was an intentional link. If so, that would give a deeper resonance, for the more learned members of the Roman audience, to the idea that it was an old joke (see p. 13). In fact, it was so old that it went back not just to Livius Andronicus but (plus or minus the Cypriot–Rhodian switch) to the age of Menander in the fourth century BCE. Here, in other words, the Greek inheritance was not merely adjusted to a different comic context; it was turned into an integral part of the Roman joke itself.

THE ROMAN SIDE OF GREEK LAUGHTER

Classicists have long tussled with the ways that Roman writers reinvigorate (or recycle) their Greek predecessors, pointing to a characteristic combination of similarity and difference found throughout Roman (re)-use of Greek cultural forms, right down to the laughs. But they more rarely look at the relationship from the other side. To conclude this chapter, and to think more about potential "Roman" aspects of "Greek" laughter, I am taking a cue from Andrew Wallace-Hadrill and from Tony Spawforth, who have both argued for a wide-ranging cultural impact of Rome on the Greek world (from the style of lamps made in Roman Athens to the "cultural comportment" of the imperial Greek elite).[77] Some of the traditions often assumed to be those of classical Greece owe a lot in various ways to the cultural conversations of the (Greco-)Roman Empire.

One of the most memorable symbols of Greek laughter is the fifth-century BCE philosopher Democritus, from the northern Greek city of Abdera—who has gone down in history as "the laughing philosopher," celebrated in that role not only in antiquity but also by modern artists and writers as diverse as Peter Paul Rubens and Samuel Beckett. Often paired with Heraclitus (his opposite—"the weeping philosopher"), Democritus crops us time and again in ancient writing in his iconic role as "the laugher" (or as the "laughter expert").[78] When, for example, Cicero is settling down in *On the Orator* to a discussion of the role of laughter in oratory and wants to brush aside the impossible question of what laughter actually is, he writes, "We can leave that to Democritus";[79] others tell how Democritus' mockery of his fellow countrymen gave him the nickname Laughing Mouth or made him, as Stephen Halliwell has put it, the "patron saint" of satiric wit ("Democritus used to shake his sides in perpetual laughter," wrote Juvenal, even though there was much less in his day to provoke ridicule—no flummery, no togas with purple stripes or sedan chairs).[80]

But by far the richest account of Democritus' laughter is found in what is, in effect, an epistolary novella comprising a series of fictional letters written in Greek, exchanged between the citizens of Abdera and the legendary Greek doctor Hippocrates—now preserved among the writings associated with Hippocrates (spuriously, in the sense that almost certainly none are from his own hand).[81] In this story, the Abderites (who have their own cameo part to play in the history of laughing and joking, as we shall see in chapter 8) are increasingly concerned about the sanity of their famous philosopher, for the simple reason that he was always laughing, and at the most inappropriate things. "Someone marries, a man goes on a trading venture, a man gives a public speech, another takes an office, goes on an embassy, votes, is ill, is wounded, dies. He laughs at every one of them,"[82] they write in their exasperation to Hippocrates, asking him to come to Abdera to cure Democritus. The doctor agrees (and the novella includes some comic touches among the preparations—from transportation to arrangements for his wife during his absence). But as we learn from the letters, when he encounters the patient, he soon discovers that Democritus is not mad at all: he is rightly laughing at the folly of humanity ("You think there are two causes of my laughter—good things and bad things. But I laugh at one thing—mankind"[83]).

En route to this (happy) conclusion, there is plenty of opportunity for the various parties to offer their views of what laughter is for. In fact, the novella is one of the most extended philosophical treatments of laughter to survive from the ancient world. But what I want to underline here is that there is no evidence whatsoever for any particular association between Democritus and laughter before the Roman period. The earliest reference we have to this connection is that casual aside in Cicero, while the Hippocratic novella is almost certainly to be dated to the first century CE, several centuries after the deaths of both of its protagonists.[84] Democritus' own writing, so far as we can reconstruct it, was principally concerned with theories of atomism and a much more moderate ethical stance than the "absurdist" position that the novella implies. How or why he had been resymbolized by the first century CE in these very different terms, we can only conjecture.

We find a broadly similar pattern in another significant symbol of Greek laughter—that is, the tradition of distinctively "Spartan" laughter. Sparta is the only city in the ancient world, outside the realm of fiction (see pp. 181–83), where there was said to have been a statue, even a shrine and a religious cult, of Laughter; it was attributed to the mythical lawgiver Lycurgus.[85] Moreover, the boot-camp atmosphere of classical Sparta is supposed to have included a prominent role for laughing and jesting. The young Spartiates were said to learn both to jest and to endure jesting in their "common messes" (*sussitia*), and the Spartan women were supposed to ridicule those young men who failed to meet the standards of the training system.[86] The surviving references to Spartan quips and witticisms emphasize their down-to-earth frankness, even aggression (such as the retort of the lame Spartan fighter who was laughed at by his peers: "Idiots, you don't need to run away when you fight the enemy"[87]). Tempting as it may be to use this evidence to fill in some of the many gaps in what we know of classical (fifth- and fourth-century BCE) Spartan culture,[88] the fact is that it all comes from writers of Roman date—principally, but not only, Plutarch. It must in part reflect a nostalgic construction of Spartan "exceptionalism," with these supposed "primitive" traditions of laughter being used, retrospectively, to mark out the oddity of the Spartan system.[89]

Of course, in both these cases we should be careful not to overclaim. We would get a very odd view of ancient history if we assumed that no traditions existed before the first surviving reference to them ("absence of evidence is not evidence of absence," as the old inferential cliché goes). It would be implausible to imagine that, in his casual aside, Cicero invented Democritus' connection with laughter; much more likely he was referring (with what degree of knowledge is not clear) to some preexisting commonplace. On the evidence we have, it is impossible to be certain exactly when the popular metamorphosis of Democritus— from atomist to laugher—took place.[90] There is certainly a deeper prehistory to the traditions of Spartan laughter too: Plutarch, in fact, cites a third-century BCE source for the "shrine of Laughter," and many of those anecdotal quips attributed to famous Spartans of the past may well have had an even earlier origin.[91] Yet the fact remains that— selected, adjusted, and embellished as they must have been—the traditions about Democritus and the Spartans have come down to us in the literature of the Roman Empire. In a scholarly world in which historians have tried to push so many traditions back to the glory days of classical Greece, it is important to remember that many of the details, the interrelationships, the cultural nuances (even if not the entire traditions themselves) are the product of the Greco-Roman imperial world.

One final example gives us a nice glimpse of the two-way traffic in "laughter culture"—not only from Greece to Rome but also from Rome to Greece. One of the slogans of British eighteenth-century urbanity was "Attic salt"—the traditions of elegant wit particularly associated with ancient Athens. The same Lord Chesterfield who so disdained "audible laughter" was a tremendous advocate of this particular style of jest, as he wrote to his long-suffering son: "That same Attic salt seasoned almost all Greece, except Boeotia; and a great deal of it was exported afterward to Rome, where it was counterfeited by a composition called Urbanity, which in some time was brought to very near the perfection of the original Attic salt. The more you are powdered with these two kinds of salt, the better you will keep, and the more you will be relished."[92] Poor Lord Chesterfield could not have been more wrong in his chronology, or in suggesting the transmission of "Attic salt" from Greece to Rome. It is true that Roman writers admired Athenian wit: they saw it as a form to be imitated, and in their cultural geography of wit they put the Athenians in prize position, followed by the Sicilians and then the Rhodians.[93] But so far as we can tell, the idea of wit as salt (*sal*) was originally a Roman idea, defined in Latin and part of a range of Roman cultural tropes that (as we shall see) linked jesting and laughing to the sphere of dining and the repertoire of cooking. "Attic salt" was not a Greek term, but it was the Romans' way of describing their own construction of Athenian wit.

No Athenians, so far as we know, ever congratulated themselves on their "Attic salt." In classical Greece, the word *hals* (salt) was not part of the terminology of jesting. Eventually, however, the idea did spread eastward. Some Greeks of the Roman period apparently adopted, incorporated, and maybe adjusted this characteristically "Roman" perspective on laughter. In the second century CE, we find Plutarch referring to the wit of Aristophanes and Menander as *hales*—their "little pinches of salt."[94] We should make sure not to underestimate the Roman aspects of that often inextricable mixture that is the Greco-Roman culture of laughter.

. . .

It is to various aspects of that inextricable mixture that we now turn. The issues that I have been discussing in these first four chapters underlie the explorations in the second part of this book of particular aspects of Roman laughter and of some of the distinctive characters who have a particular role to play in the "laughterhood" of Rome. We shall encounter laughing emperors, plenty of monkey business, and some passable jokes—but first the funniest man in the Roman world, Marcus Tullius Cicero, and some of his fellow orators. There have been several excellent studies of uses of wit and laughter in the Roman courtroom, but I shall focus on the dilemmas confronting the joking orator trying to raise a laugh from his audience in order to expose some of the ambiguities and anxieties of the culture of laughter in ancient Rome.

FIGURE 1. Frans Hals, *The Laughing Cavalier* (1624). This painting—which we now take for granted as an image of a laughing man—raises the question of how confidently we can identify laughter in the art of the past.

FIGURE 2. Mosaic—"Beware of the dog"—from the House of the Tragic Poet, Pompeii (first century CE). How can we decide if this image was intended to make visitors laugh?

FIGURE 3. Bronze statuette of an actor with an ape's head (Roman date). This nicely symbolizes the overlap between the mimicry of actor and of monkey.

FIGURE 4. A boy with a performing monkey, from an original painting (first century CE) in the House of the Dioscuri, Pompeii. The ape becomes an actor.

FIGURE 5. Parody of Aeneas, escaping from Troy, with his father and son—with ape heads (from an original painting, first century CE, from Pompeii).

FIGURE 6. Rembrandt's self-portrait as Zeuxis (c. 1668). Notice the painting of the old lady in the background.

Part Two

CHAPTER 5

The Orator

CICERO'S BEST JOKE?

Let's start this chapter with a puzzle. In the middle of his long discussion of the proper role of laughter in oratory—in the sixth book of his training handbook for would-be public speakers—Marcus Fabius Quintilianus (or Quintilian, as I have been calling him) turns to discuss double entendres. "Although there are numerous areas from which jokes [*dicta ridicula*, literally "laughable sayings"] may be drawn, I must stress again that they are not all suitable for orators, especially those that rest on double entendre [*amphibolia* in his Latinized Greek]." He proceeds to quote a couple of puns that do not meet his high standards, even though uttered by Cicero himself. One is an abusive slur on the low birth of a candidate for political office, a fairly unsubtle play on two similar-sounding Latin words: *coquus* (cook) and *quoque* (also). The candidate in question was said to be the upwardly mobile son of a cook (*coquus*); when Cicero overheard the man canvassing for support, he is supposed to have gibed, "I will vote for you *too* (*quoque*)." This kind of joking is so beneath the elite orator, Quintilian explains, that he had thought of banning it entirely from the rhetorical repertoire. But he concedes that there is one absolutely splendid (*praeclarum*) example of the genre, which "on its own is sufficient to prevent us condemning this whole class of joke."[1]

That example also came from the mouth of Cicero, in the year 52 BCE, when he was defending Titus Annius Milo against the charge of murdering the radical and controversial politician Publius Clodius Pulcher. Cicero's performance in this trial is usually regarded as unsuccessful, if not ignominious (a substantial majority of the jury convicted Milo of the crime). But Quintilian paints Cicero's rhetorical role rather more honorably. Part of the case, he explains, hinged on timing, including the exact moment of Clodius' death. So the prosecutor repeatedly pressed Cicero to say precisely when Clodius was killed. Cicero replied with a single word: *sero*, punning on its two senses, both "late" and "too late." The point is that Clodius died late in the day—but also that he should have been got rid of years before.[2]

It is not hard to see the joke here. The puzzle is why on earth Quintilian should have deemed it such an outstanding instance of a provocation to laughter that it rescued all jokes of this type from what would otherwise have been a complete ban. What was so especially good about this one?

The main focus of this chapter is laughter in Roman oratory and the chortles and chuckles of the Roman courtroom. What jokes were best at getting the audience to crack up? When should a speaker try to make his listeners laugh (and when not)? What were the pluses and minuses of using laughter to attack an opponent? Just how aggressive was public laughter in Rome? And what is the relationship between joking, laughter, and falsehood (or outright lying)? We shall meet virtuoso performers who raised a laugh by mimicking the posh voices of their adversaries, we shall come across some funny words that were surefire prompts to mirth (*stomachus*—that is "stomach"—was apparently one that was always likely to get a Roman going), and we shall glimpse a hilarious competition in making pig noises between a peasant and a professional jokester. I also hope that by the end of the chapter, we may have a better idea of why that particular quip on the time of Clodius' death attracted Quintilian's fulsome praise.

CICERO AND LAUGHTER

My leading character throughout the chapter is, of course, the most infamous funster, punster, and jokester of classical antiquity: Marcus Tullius Cicero. It is true that Cicero now, even among many scholars, has more of a reputation for humorless pomposity than for engaging wit. "Cicero can be a fearful bore," as one of his best twentieth-century biographers wrote (perhaps saying rather more about herself than about him), and more recently another senior classicist (jokingly) dismissed him as the kind of man who would have been no fun at all as a dinner companion.³ But in antiquity, both in his lifetime and as he was reinvented over the centuries that followed, one of Cicero's trademarks, for better or worse, was his capacity to get people laughing—or his sometimes irritating inability to refrain from doing so.⁴

This is a major theme in Plutarch's biography, written some 150 years after Cicero's death. From the very first chapter (where Plutarch repeats a joke that Cicero made on his own name, which means "chickpea" in Latin), the *Life* returns again and again to the theme of the famous orator's use of laughter: sometimes to his witty bons mots, sometimes to his ill-advised tendency to crack a gag in very inappropriate places. Plutarch admits that Cicero's exaggerated sense of his own importance was one of the reasons for his unpopularity in some quarters, but he also attracted hatred because he attacked people indiscriminately, "just to raise a laugh," and Plutarch quotes a variety of his gibes and puns—against a man with ugly daughters, against the son of a murderous dictator, and against a drunken censor ("I'm afraid the man will punish me—for drinking water").⁵

One of the most notorious occasions of Cicero's ostentatious use of laughter was during the final civil war of the Republic—between Julius Caesar and Pompey—which was the prelude to Caesar's autocratic rule. After much hesitation, Cicero joined Pompey's camp in Greece in the summer of 49 BCE before the battle of Pharsalus, but he was not, says Plutarch, a popular member of the squad. "It was his own fault, as he did not deny that he regretted having come . . . and he did not hold back from joking or making witty gibes at his comrades; in fact, he himself was always going about the camp without a laugh, and frowning, but he made others laugh, quite against their will." ("So why not employ him as guardian of your children?" he is said to have quipped, for example, at Domitius Ahenobarbus, who was promoting a decidedly unmilitary type to a command position on the grounds that he was "mild-mannered and sensible.")⁶

Several years later, after Caesar's assassination, Cicero replied to some of these criticisms in a pamphlet now known as the second *Philippic,* a vicious attack on Mark Antony—who, among other things, had clearly leveled, or repeated, some of the charges of inappropriate jocularity.⁷ Like Plutarch, Antony had most likely objected to Cicero's habit of making his comrades laugh in such awful circumstances, and against their will (effectively an assertion of his control over their "uncontrollable" outbursts of laughter). In a characteristic rhetorical sweep, Cicero at first brushes the accusation aside: "I'm not even going to respond about those jokes you said I made in the camp." But then he does offer a brief defense: "To be sure, that camp was full of gloom, I admit. But all the same, even if they are in dire straits, men do still take some relaxation from time to time; it's only human. Yet the fact that the same man [Antony] finds fault both with my melancholy and with my jesting is a powerful proof that I took a moderate line in both respects."[8] Cicero justifies laughter as a natural human reaction even in troubled times while also pleading moderation in his conduct.[9]

It is, however, in his comparison of Cicero and the Greek orator Demosthenes, which forms the postscript to this pair of parallel lives, that Plutarch offers his most pointed comments on Cicero's use of laughter. These were the two greatest orators of the Greco-Roman world (hence their treatment as a pair), but their use of laughter was starkly different. Demosthenes was no joker, but intense and serious, even—some would say—morose and sullen. Cicero, on the other hand, was not only "addicted to laughter" (or perhaps "quite at home with laughter," *oikeios gelōtos*); he was, in fact, "often carried away by his joking to the point of buffoonery [*pros to bōmolochon*], and when, to get his own way in the cases he was pleading, he handled matters that deserved gravity with irony, laughter, and mirth, he neglected decorum."[10]

Plutarch quotes a telling Roman quip about Cicero's jocularity. During his consulship, in 63 BCE, he was defending Lucius Licinius Murena against charges of bribery, and in the course of his defense speech (a version of which still survives), he made tremendous fun of some of the absurdities of Stoicism—the philosophical system vociferously espoused by Marcus Porcius Cato, one of the prosecutors. When "clear laughter" (the Greek word is *lampros*, literally "bright") spread from the audience to the judges, Cato, "beaming" (*diameidiasas*), simply said, "What a *geloios* we have for a consul."[11]

The Greek word *geloios* has been translated into English in several different ways: "What a *funny* consul we have!" "What a *comedian* we have for a consul."[12] But what did Cato say in his original Latin? One possibility is that he called Cicero a *ridiculus consul*. If so, it will have been a nice joke, because *ridiculus*—one of the most basic terms of Latin laughter vocabulary—was a dangerously ambiguous word. For, in a way that constantly destabilized Roman discussions of laughter, *ridiculus* meant "laugh-able" or "prompting laughter" in two ways: on the one hand, it could refer to something that people laughed at, the butt of laughter (more or less "ridiculous" in the modern sense); on the other hand, it was someone or something that provoked people to laugh (and so it could imply something like "witty" or "amusing"). As we shall find in what follows, this was a pressing ambiguity in Roman culture, exploited and debated in various ways. Here, if Cato really did say that Cicero was a *ridiculus* consul, he was cleverly pointing the finger at his rival, insinuating that such a smart jokester was also a man that the audience should laugh *at*.

Quintilian's discussion of Cicero and laughter enriches this picture. He lays out a similar comparison between Demosthenes (whom "many people think had no capacity for raising laughter in a judge" or even that he firmly wanted nothing to do with it) and Cicero ("whom many think had no moderation in it"). Quintilian himself is rather more charitable on both counts. Demosthenes did not actively dislike jokes, he insists, but was simply not very good at them. As for Cicero ("whether I judge correctly on this, or whether I am swayed by my inordinate passion for this outstanding orator"), he displayed a wonderful *urbanitas* (wit or urbanity), and "both in his everyday conversations and in his debates in court and cross-examination of witnesses, he uttered more witty remarks [*facete*] than anyone else." In fact, Quintilian suggests, Cicero probably did not actually coin some of the rather vulgar sayings often attributed to him.[13]

Nonetheless, on several occasions in the lengthy discussion that follows, Quintilian finds himself wondering whether certain Ciceronian bons mots were not quite appropriate for a gentleman orator. As we shall see, two antitypes of joker—the vulgar opposites of the cultured wit—stalk discussions of the rhetoric of laughter: the mime actor, or *mimus* (who has a large part to play in chapter 7), and the *scurra* (a curious amalgam of jester, scrounger, and man-about-town, who features in this and the next chapter). Quintilian concedes that some of Cicero's tactics for raising a laugh were uncomfortably close to those of the *mimus* or the *scurra*. And he was not the only one to have those qualms. One well-known story, found both in Macrobius and in one of the declamations of the elder Seneca, explicitly pits Cicero in a contest of wits against Decimus Laberius, a writer of mimes (when an encounter in the cramped seats at some spectacle or play leads to a competitive exchange of gibes).[14] Macrobius also treats it as common knowledge that Cicero's enemies used to call him a *consularis scurra* ("a *scurra* of consular rank").[15] In fact, another possibility is that Cato exclaimed in Latin, "What a *scurra* we have for a consul!" There is no Greek equivalent of the word *scurra*, and Plutarch might reasonably have resorted to *geloios* as a rough translation.[16]

In seeking to explain Cicero's dubious reputation in this area, Quintilian partly casts the blame on his secretary Tiro, "or whoever it was who published the three volumes on this subject." The "subject" he is referring to is wit or jesting, and this trio of books appears to have been a collection of Cicero's *bona dicta* (jokes), not all of which were quite up to scratch. For the problem with jokebooks throughout history is that they are often padded out with some decidedly feeble, or risky, specimens. "If only," Quintilian continues, "he had been more sparing in the number of jokes [*dicta*] he included and shown more judgment in selecting than eagerness in collecting them. It would not have exposed Cicero so much to his critics."[17] We know little of this multivolume compendium of wit and wisdom, but it was not the only such publication of the great orator's bons mots. In a surviving letter of 46 BCE, Cicero writes to thank his friend Gaius Trebonius, who had just sent him, as a gift, a book containing a collection of his own witticisms. A perfect present for a narcissist, one might say. But here also there was perhaps a problem with the selection, or lack of it ("Whatever I've said seems to you to be *facetum* [witty]," Cicero writes, "but it might not seem the same to others"). Luckily, Trebonius must have had a gift for packaging the quips: "As *you* tell them, they become *venustissima* [ever so smart]," Cicero writes in ironically grateful mode. "In fact, readers will almost have used up all their laughter before they get to me."[18]

It is presumably these long-lost collections that lie behind the "jokes of Cicero," the series of "one-liners" we find assembled on a more modest scale in Macrobius and in Quintilian himself. My own particular favorite is his nice swipe at the apparently diminutive husband of his daughter, Tullia: "Seeing his son-in-law Lentulus, a short chap, kitted out with a long sword, he said. 'Who tied my son-in-law to his sword?'"[19] But we should also note another variant on the *sero* joke among these, suggesting that the pun between "too late" or "a bit late" and "late in the day" was something of a classic. It is one of the gags that Cicero made in Pompey's camp during the civil war. When he first arrived at the camp, after all his vacillations, people said to him, "You've got here a bit late [*sero*]"—perhaps the equivalent of a sardonic "Better late than never." "I've not come at a late hour [*sero*]," he retorted. "I don't see anything ready for dinner yet [*nihil hic paratum*]."[20] Indeed, Cicero's *dicta,* or *facetiae* (as they came more often to be called), were a staple of Renaissance wit and learning and regularly find a place in jokebooks and other such compendia at least up to the eighteenth century.[21] It is only the modern world that has tended to forget that Cicero was such a "laughter lover."

Not that it is likely that Cicero really coined all these jokes ascribed to him. Quintilian was not merely being protective of his hero in suggesting that he had been credited with some feeble specimens that he had never uttered. In a letter written from Cilicia (where he was the provincial governor) in 50 BCE, Cicero complains that "everybody's *dicta* are ascribed to me" and jokingly ticks off his correspondent—whose name, appropriately, was Publius Volumnius Eutrapelus (*eutrapelos* means "witty" in Greek)—for not making a stand on Cicero's behalf and denying his authorship of the weak imposters; at the same time he flatters himself (or pretends to flatter himself) that his authentic witticisms were stamped with his individual style. "Don't you protest?" he writes. "After all, I was hoping that I had left such a distinctive brand of quips that they could be recognized in and of themselves."[22]

The truth is, of course, that "great men" attract, as much as they utter, bons mots and that jokes migrate among them (nicely demonstrated by the very same gag being attributed to Cicero by Quintilian and to Octavian, the future emperor Augustus, by Macrobius).[23] But whether they were authentic or not, the important point is that in antiquity, Cicero was known for his jokes as well as his speeches and treatises, and he had a decidedly edgy reputation for laughter.

CONTROLLING LAUGHTER?

Despite the air of gravitas that has become Cicero's modern hallmark, some particular aspects of his laughter, wit, and "humor" (a term we cannot resist, though it is treacherous to apply to the ancient world) have remained on the scholarly agenda.[24] Recently, for example, Gregory Hutchinson and others have explored how Cicero's *Letters* exploit jocularity, badinage, and the culture of shared laughter in constructing epistolary relationships. Laughter and joking in the *Letters,* as Hutchinson points out, are generally treated as companionable, rather than aggressive, and are often a marker that "the addressee is especially trusted, or especially akin in mind"; when Atticus is away, Cicero writes to him that he has no one with whom he can "joke freely."[25]

But an even more influential strand of discussion has concerned the role of humorous invective in Ciceronian speeches and its implications for social and cultural control. Amy Richlin's important study *The Garden of Priapus,* first published in 1983, laid much of the groundwork for this—arguing (in a way that is now taken for granted) that the sexual humor in Roman satire, epigram, lampoon, and invective was closely related to hierarchies of power. On Richlin's model, when Cicero ridicules the sexual behavior of his opponents (casting them on the wrong side of the boundaries that lay between proper, normative Roman maleness and a variety of transgressive antitypes—the pathic, the "softy," the *cinaedus,* the *mollis*), he is using wit and laughter as one weapon in the struggle for dominance.[26] This is humor founded not on goodwill but on aggression. It is a classic case of a type of joking that Freud labeled tendentious (as opposed to innocent)—in which, as he put it, "by making our enemy small, inferior, despicable or comic, we achieve in a roundabout way the enjoyment of overcoming him—to which the third person [that is, in Ciceronian oratory, the audience], who has made no efforts, bears witness by his laughter."[27]

A decade after Richlin's study appeared, Antony Corbeill, in *Controlling Laughter,* developed these ideas at length, with a primary focus on Cicero's speeches and a wider range of targets in mind, from the sexual effeminacy that was one of Richlin's main concerns to all kinds of bodily peculiarities—such as gout or disfiguring swellings or even "funny" names. For Corbeill, Cicero's use of laughter at his opponents, whether in the courtroom, the senate, or the assembly, was a powerful mechanism of both exclusion (for it served to isolate the enemy and present him as beyond the social pale) and persuasion (for it united the laughing audience in the affirmation of their shared "ethical standards"). To put it even more strongly, aggressive communal laughter at the deviant, or rather at the man Cicero chose to present as such, was a means of "simultaneously creating and enforcing the community's ethical values. Jokes become a means of ordering social realities." One instructive instance of this is Cicero's attack on Vatinius in 56 BCE, a speech that seems to revel in mocking the grotesque appearance (bull neck, bulging eyes, and nasty swellings, or *strumae*) of its target while correlating Vatinius' physical ugliness with his moral and political failings. As the audience joins together in laughter, so Corbeill's logic goes, "Cicero becomes the society's moral spokesperson, inveighing against the outrage Vatinius embodies."[28]

This has been an extremely influential approach. In fact, most historians of Roman public life and public speaking would now regard Cicero's use of laughter both as a powerful means of attack and as an equally powerful mechanism for reinforcing, or constructing, social norms.[29] It is also an overwhelmingly aggressive (and frankly not very funny) approach to oratorical laughter, which I hope to nuance—or supplement—in the rest of this chapter. I am not looking to overturn it.

I have no doubt whatsoever that laughter in the Roman Forum, court-room, or Senate house could act to isolate the deviant while reaffirming shared social values, nor do I have any doubt that Roman laughter could sometimes be, in Quintilian's words, "not far from derision."[30] But there was much more to it than that, which has not recently received the attention it deserves.

My focus will be on Cicero's discussion of the use of laughter in public speaking, its benefits and—more especially—its risks. I shall concentrate not on his speeches but on the central chapters of the second book of his essay *On the Orator,* which (even if not quite the "mini treatise" on laughter that it is sometimes cracked up to be[31]) is nevertheless the most substantial, sustained, and challenging discussion of laughter, in any of its aspects, to have survived from the ancient world—a fact that is all too easy to forget in our hunt for the lost views of Aristotle (pp. 29–31).

It is in *On the Orator,* more than in any other of his surviving works,[32] that Cicero offers both theoretical analysis and concrete examples of what was most likely to rouse a Roman audience to laughter, how laughter could be provoked, and with what consequence for speaker, listeners, or the butt of the joke. The truth is that when we read his speeches, we are usually second-guessing what was funny, when exactly the audience would have laughed—and how enthusiastically. It is one thing to talk generally about the humorous invective of the speech against Vatinius; it is quite another to judge which precise passages would have provoked the most hilarity (were all those physical oddities equally funny?) or how the words might have been delivered in order to do that. But just as Terence's *hahahae* enabled us to pinpoint a precise moment of laughter, the discussion in *On the Orator* gives explicit information (at least as Cicero saw it) on particular outbursts of laughter, even occasionally calibrating its intensity, and reflects on some of the major principles that guide a Roman orator in exploiting jocularity and laughter. It is a discussion that faces questions of laughter itself—its causes and effects—head on.

Cicero's discussion points his readers to important sides of the laughing process beyond the familiar topics of derision and control (indeed, derision is not an especially prominent theme here). We learn about the physical nature of laughter; about different ways of raising a laugh from an audience, from funny words to funny faces; and about what was off limits as a proper subject of laughter. But one crucial undercurrent is the risk associated with provoking laughter. Laughter was always in danger of rebounding: it was not only the orator's opponent who could be isolated and exposed by raising a laugh; its provocation could also expose and isolate the orator himself. The two senses of *ridiculus* ("he makes us laugh" versus "the one we laugh at") were always perilously close. You had to be careful in playing for laughs.[33]

CICERO ON THE (JOKING) ORATOR

Cicero wrote *On the Orator* in the middle 50s BCE, shortly after his return from exile, when he was trying, with only limited success, to recover his power and influence in the city of Rome.[34] Extending over three books, it is not primarily a rhetorical training manual with rules for budding speakers (though it includes plenty of nitty-gritty technical advice) but rather a more general consideration of the nature of the ideal orator and the skills (physical, intellectual, personal, moral, philosophical) that such a man requires. It was written against the background of long-standing debates, going back at least to fifth-century BCE Greece, on the morality of rhetoric (how far was effective persuasion necessarily deceptive?), its relations with philosophy and other forms of knowledge, whether rhetoric was a discipline that could be taught, and if so how.[35]

Following the example of Plato—to whom there is a direct reference near the start of the first book—Cicero composed his treatise in the form of a discussion among a group of learned Roman "amateurs" in the art of oratory.[36] Its dramatic date is 91 BCE, and its cast of characters is carefully chosen to match. The leading roles are taken by Lucius Licinius Crassus, at whose villa the discussion is set, and Marcus Antonius, both renowned orators of the period and mentors of the young Cicero. They are joined by other discussants, who are imagined to be present for all or part of the two days over which the debates take place. These include the much younger Gaius Aurelius Cotta (Cicero's informant of the contents of the discussion, according to the dramatic fiction) and—to give him his full name—Gaius Julius Caesar Strabo Vopiscus (an indirect ancestor of Caesar the dictator), who takes the lead in the discussion of laughter.[37]

Over the three books, the discussion covers a wide range of topics, from the power or harm of eloquence and the kind of knowledge a good orator needs (book 1) through the various means of oratorical persuasion (book 2) to issues of style and various forms of delivery (book 3). For the most part, the debate is fairly gentle. Although the Platonic literary and philosophical background is clear, this is not the kind of dialogue in which a Socrates-like figure uses his dazzling intellectual firepower and quick repartee to trounce the opposition and impose his own arguments on the assembled company, and readers. Here we find a much less aggressively antagonistic style of debate, with extended contributions by the main participants and less repartee (which may be what Cicero meant when he wrote in a letter that he had adopted the "Aristotelian mode" in *On the Orator*[38]). Where there are disagreements between the various characters (as on the question of the knowledge required by the ideal orator, in book 1), it is usually assumed, rightly or wrongly, that Cicero's views are broadly those of the character of Crassus.[39]

For a relatively hard-core work of ancient oratorical theory, *On the Orator* has recently attracted a surprising amount of attention from Roman historians and critics in general. There has been a lively interest in—among other things—its distinctively "Roman" character (notwithstanding its obvious and open debts to earlier Greek discussion), its relationship to the politics of the period (both that of its dramatic date and that of its composition), and its role in Cicero's self-fashioning as a "new man," as well as in the performative aspects of Roman oratory and masculinity. (It would, I suspect, come as a surprise to Cicero that his treatise has been discussed, at length, in the course of a chapter headed "Love.")[40] The discussion of the oratorical uses of laughter takes up more than seventy chapters (or around one-fifth) of book 2, toward the center of the whole work.[41] Following an account of various other means of persuasion, largely fronted by Antonius, the words in this section are almost entirely given to the character of Julius Caesar Strabo—and are presented as light relief from what has been a rather lengthy exposition up to this point. As Antonius remarks, "I'm already worn out by the tough path my argument has taken and shall take a rest while Caesar is talking, as if I were in some convenient inn."[42] In tune with this, throughout the section we find laughter and a bit of banter among the participants.[43]

Modern critics tend to mislead when they describe these chapters as a digression specifically on "humor" or "wit" or "Witz und Humor." To be sure, those topics take a substantial part in the discussion, and they provide the link from the previous section, on how to appeal to the audience ("Attractive too, and often extremely effective, are jokes and witticisms"[44]). But when the character of Strabo (as I shall call him from now on) takes the floor in this debate, his principal subject is laughter, divided—as Strabo insists—into five subfields: (a) what laughter is, (b) where it comes from, (c) whether an orator should want to provoke (*movere*) laughter in his audience, (d) how far, and (e) what the different categories of "the laughable" (*ridiculum*) are.[45] The first three subfields get only brief discussion. The final pair, especially the last one, are given much fuller treatment.

As a piece of Ciceronian writing—which of course it is, despite some wild ideas that it was based on a treatise by Strabo—it is brave and innovative but occasionally, let's be honest, can seem a bit muddled. Thanks to the careful analysis by Edwin Rabbie, no one any longer seriously imagines (as once they did) that it is little more than a scissors-and-paste job, merely regurgitating earlier discussions of laughter by Greek theorists, with a few Roman examples thrown in along the way.[46] This is not, of course, to deny any engagement on Cicero's part with the Greek rhetorical and philosophical tradition on laughter. Strabo explicitly refers to Greek books "on the laughable" (*de ridiculis*), which he claims to have read.[47] And several observations, as well as some of the terminology used, appear to reflect an Aristotelian or at least a Peripatetic influence: from the first word of the section, where *suavis* (agreeable) is probably the equivalent of the Aristotelian *hēdus,* to the more general idea that the "locus . . . et regio quasi" (the field . . . and as it were the province) of the laughable lies in "what you might call the dishonorable or ugly," which echoes what Aristotle says in the *Poetics* and was most likely one line that his followers took.[48] The engagement is hardly surprising: almost anyone with any intellectual credentials who was trying to write about any ethical subject in the first century BCE would have been bound to think about what the Peripatetics had to say.[49]

But more important, it is also an emphatically "Roman" work. Some of the crucial distinctions that Cicero draws (such as that between *cavillatio* and *dicacitas*—"wit spread throughout a speech" versus "individual barbs") rely on characteristically Latin terminology and have, so far as we can tell, no direct precedent in Greek theorizing.[50] All the examples that he gives of laughter and bons mots are drawn from Roman history and oratory (not just thrown in, they are integral to his argument and sometimes even seem to lead it[51]). Besides, when Strabo refers to earlier Greek works on "the laughable," he does so not to follow their theories but to dismiss them: "I had rather hoped," he says, "that I would be able to learn something from them . . . but those who tried to impart any systematic theory of the subject showed themselves so silly [*insulsi,* literally "lacking in salt"] that there was nothing else to laugh at in them but their silliness [*insulsitas*]."[52]

In other words, what we have in this long discussion of oratorical laughter is a characteristically Roman cultural product: Roman practice and tradition, theorized by a Roman intellectual in dialogue with his Greek predecessors.

THE ARGUMENT: STRUCTURE, SYSTEM, AND TERMINOLOGY

The details of this lengthy argument on laughter are in places difficult to fathom, individual passages (and jokes) are opaque, and the text is frequently corrupt and inaccurate.[53] All the same, the gist of the section is clear enough. After Antonius has handed over to Strabo to discuss the new topic (because he is so outstanding at *iocus* and *facetiae*), Strabo starts (218) by laying down a basic distinction: *facetiae* (wit) is divided between what the "ancients" (*veteres*[54]) called *cavillatio* (extended wit) and *dicacitas* (barbs). Neither of these forms of wit can be taught, he claims, as both depend on natural facility, and he backs this up with a number of examples designed to show not only how useful such witticisms can be but also how impossible it would be to be trained in them. One of the most memorable (220) is a quick gibe (a case of *dicacitas*) made by Strabo's half-brother, whose name, Catulus, literally means "Puppy." He was challenged by his opponent in some courtroom, presumably in the course of a case of theft: "Why are you barking, Puppy Dog [*Catule*]?" "Because I see a thief" was Catulus' instant retort.[55]

Some general conversation among the participants follows (228)—including some banter about which of them is really best at joking. But they end up giving the floor back to Strabo and agreeing that even if laughter raising is not a discipline that can be taught as such, there are nevertheless some practical guidelines (*observatio quaedam est*) that he could discuss and explain. At this point (235), Strabo outlines his five questions about laughter (see p. 109). He briefly waves aside the first three. The problem of the nature of laughter itself he leaves to Democritus; even the supposed experts do not understand it, he claims. On the question of its origin, he pinpoints, without much explanation, "what you might call the dishonorable or ugly" (236). And third, yes, there are several reasons why an orator should try to raise a laugh: *hilaritas* brings goodwill, everyone is impressed by cleverness, it crushes or makes light of or deflects an opponent, it reveals the speaker as a refined and witty (*urbanus*) individual, and most of all, it relieves the austerity of a speech and gets rid of offensive suggestions that cannot easily be dealt with by reason.

The next question—of how far an orator should use laughter—is treated at much greater length, over eleven chapters (237–47). Here Strabo issues a series of warnings about circumstances in which laughter is not appropriate (people do not laugh at serious wickedness or misery, for example) and about what kind of laughter raising is off limits for the orator. Particularly to be avoided is the laughter associated with the *scurra* or with the mime actor (*mimus*).[56] And he gives a series of examples that point up the boundary between the acceptable and the unacceptable. Crassus, he explains (telling of an incident involving one of his fellow discussants), once raised a big laugh in a public gathering by a flagrant take-off of a very posh opponent—getting up and imitating his facial expression, his (presumably posh) accent, and even the pose he adopted in his statues (242).[57] But Strabo stresses that this kind of display "has to be handled with the greatest of caution": a hint of mimicry is perfectly allowable (so that a listener "may imagine more than he actually sees"), but too much is the mark of the mime actor. Crassus' showmanship was dangerously marginal. Other golden rules include not to seize every opportunity that presents itself for raising a laugh, always to do so for a point (not simply for the sake of laughter itself), and not to seem to have prepared a joke in advance. He quotes a quip against a one-eyed man ("I'll come and dine with you, because I see you've got space for one"). This was the joke of a *scurra*, because it was premeditated, it would have applied to all one-eyed men (not just its immediate target), and it was unprovoked (246).

It is in the course of this section on how far an orator should exploit laughter that the character of Strabo first introduces the distinction between wit *dicto* (in verbal form: a joke that depends on the exact words in which it is told) and wit *re* (in substance: one that can be told differently and still prompt laughter). That contrast becomes the main organizing principle of the long final discussion (248–88), on the different categories of "the laughable." Here Strabo reviews the main types of witticism under those two headings, including jokes from ambiguity, from the intrusion of the unexpected, from wordplay, from the inclusion of lines of verse (257–58—not a familiar modern category of the laughable), from words taken literally, from witty comparisons or images, from understatement, from irony, and so on. But throughout, warnings about the inappropriate use of laughter are again repeatedly voiced. In fact, near the start of this discussion on categories, there is a short digression (251–52) on the tactics for raising a laugh that, however effective they may be, the orator should avoid. These include clownish mimicry and silly walks, grimacing, and obscenity. The bottom line is that not everything that raises laughter (*ridicula*) is also witty (*faceta*), and it is wit that we look for in the ideal orator.

This diversion on laughter comes to an end with Strabo running out of steam in his classification ("I feel I have rather overdone my division into categories") and offering a perfunctory summing-up of what prompts laughter: disappointing expectations, ridiculing other people's character, comparison with something more dishonorable, irony, saying rather silly things, or criticizing what is foolish. If you want to speak in a joking way (*iocose*), he finally insists, you must be naturally equipped for it and have a face to fit. Not a "funny" face, but quite the reverse. "The more severe and sterner a man's expression, the more 'salty' [*salsiora*] his remarks are usually thought to be" (288–89). And on that cue, he hands back to Antonius to resume the tougher road of oratorical theory on more serious themes.

There are all kinds of intriguing puzzles and problems in this discussion of laughter that go far beyond the precise sources for the arguments. As often in Cicero's dialogues, the selection of characters has been one topic of interest. Why choose Strabo to front the discussion? There is no reason whatsoever to suppose that he had (as Arndt fondly fantasized) written a treatise on laughter, though Cicero does refer to him, here and elsewhere, as a noted wit.[58] Maybe it was an attempt to offer a backhanded compliment to the increasingly powerful Julius Caesar, whose distant relative Strabo was.[59] Or maybe the choice was rather less important than we might imagine. After all, just six years on from writing *On the Orator*, Cicero referred to this discussion in his letter to Volumnius Eutrapelus (see p. 105), mentioning the forms of wit "that I discussed through the character of *Antonius* in the second book of *On the Orator*."[60] Had he forgotten that this section was almost entirely voiced by Strabo? If so, maybe not much hung on this choice of character.[61]

There has been even more debate about the overall structure of the argument and its precise terms. At the very start of Strabo's intervention, he seems to be basing his argument on the division of *facetiae* into *cavillatio* and *dicacitas*, as the "ancients" called them—another nice instance, I would like to think, of the nostalgia characteristic of histories of laughter (see pp. 67–69). But shortly after that, when he restarts his exposition, the five basic questions about the orator's use of laughter now become the structuring principle (with a subsidiary division of wit *dicto* and *re*). No amount of modern ingenuity has been able to make the first division compatible with the second, and most critics would now agree that the opposition between *cavillatio* and *dicacitas* simply gets shelved as the new fivefold structure of the argument takes its place. In fact, maybe part of Cicero's (witty) point is to parade a shift in style over the course of Strabo's intervention—from a classification that is explicitly said to be a something of a joke[62] to a more intellectualizing, Hellenizing approach, never intended to be compatible with the other.

It is not clear, either, how the division of *facetiae* into *cavillatio* and *dicacitas* in *On the Orator* relates to the ostensibly contradictory division laid out in Cicero's later treatise *The Orator* (written in the mid-40s BCE), where he separates *sales* (witticisms) into *facetiae* and *dicacitas*.[63] Did he change the words because (as Rabbie and others have guessed) *cavillatio* was beginning to take on its later sense (which *cavil* in English still retains), of "quibble"?[64] Possibly, but the space of ten years seems a rather short time for any such linguistic shift to have been marked. In any case, that would still leave the problem of why the overarching term for wit (*facetiae*) in the earlier work was changed into one of its constituent parts in the later.[65]

This raises the yet bigger question of the exact sense of the many and various terms for wit and joking that are found in *On the Orator* and elsewhere in Roman discussions of laughter. I confidently asserted in an earlier chapter (see p. 76) that it is impossible to define precisely the differences between such words as *sal, lepos, facetia, urbanitas, dictum,* and so on—any more than we could explain the difference, if any, between a chuckle and a chortle. Was that being too pessimistic? After all, we could plausibly explain the difference between a chortle and a giggle. Does the discussion in *On the Orator* help us get closer to the differences and distinctions between these terms?

Cicero certainly offers a range of semidefinitions and carefully stressed contrasts or parallels in this treatise: *ridicula* are not all *faceta*, for example, and *frigida* can be the opposite of *salsa*, while *bona* in the phrase *bona dicta* is more or less a synonym for *salsa*.[66] This has raised the hopes of some scholars that a much more exact Roman typology of wit might be discerned, especially since it is clear that some of these terms (most notably *urbanitas*, with its whiff of urbanity in the modern sense) were becoming strongly ideologically loaded at the period Cicero when was writing—the catchwords or slogans of a particular style, whether of speech or of life.[67] Articles and even whole books have been devoted to this question, but (revealing as they are) we still remain a long way from any authoritative framework of definitions. Of course we do. It is not that these words all meant exactly the same thing. But as the different usages (of *facetiae, sal, dicacitas,* and *cavillatio*) between *On the Orator* and *The Orator* have already suggested, the contrasts and collocations that gave them meaning were unstable, provisional, and heavily dependent on context—not to mention sometimes constructed with an eye to the contrasts and collocations of an equally unstable set of Greek terms.

The word *lepos,* for example, as Krostenko amply documents, could refer in Cicero (never mind a wider range of authors) to a style of engaging wit, and it could be the result of cultured education, one of a group of desirable qualities (including *humanitas, sal,* and *suavitas*), but it could also be a proxy in Latin for the Greek *charis*—as well as the property of the uncultured *scurra* (*scurrile lepos*).[68] Quintilian likewise underlines the instability of this vocabulary when he reflects in his *Handbook* that Latin seems to have several terms for similar qualities of wit and attempts to separate them (*diducere*). Of *salsum* (salty), he has this to say: "*Salsum* we use in everyday language for *ridiculum* [laughable]. That's not what it is by definition, though anything that is *ridiculum* ought also to be *salsum.* For Cicero says that everything which is *salsum* is a feature of the Athenians, but that is not because they are particularly predisposed to laughter. And when Catullus says, 'There's not a grain of *sal* in her body,' he does not mean there is nothing *ridiculum* in her body." At which point he throws up his hands and states the blindingly obvious: "*Salsum* therefore is that which is not *insalsum* [unsalty]."[69] It's a fairly typical dead end.

But we can get further if we turn the question away from rhetoric and wit and toward the main subject of this section of *On the Orator:* that is, laughter itself. For these chapters represent a unique attempt to formulate a view of the role of laughter within public life and speaking, from a man ("new" though he may have been) at the very heart of the Roman political and social elite, and are worth considering in that particular light.

LAUGHTER AND ITS RISKS

Strabo does not linger long on the first three of his questions about laughter (what it is, where it comes from, and whether an orator should provoke it), but even the little he does have to say is more illuminating than it is usually assumed to be. The brief but varied reasons he offers for provoking laughter in the audience, from gaining goodwill to trouncing the opponent or relieving the austerity of a speech, go far beyond aggressive derision and ridicule. His other comments also point in useful directions.

On the first question, it is true that he quickly deflects the problem to Democritus, with a sideswipe at ignorant "experts," but that is not before he has succinctly characterized the nature of human laughter. He refers to it "bursting out so unexpectedly that try as we might we cannot keep it in" (a clear example of the myth of uncontrollability), and he explains how "at the same moment it takes possession of *latera, os, venas, vultum, oculos.*"[70] This is probably the most comprehensive single list we have from antiquity of the parts of the body that laughter disrupts, but it is frustratingly hard to make full sense of it. Does *latera* here mean the sides (as in the heaving of the rib cage) or, as it sometimes does, the lungs (so referring to panting)? Is *os* the mouth, the voice, or the face (or is the face ruled out because of *vultum*, "facial expression," later in the list)? And can *venas* really be referring to the blood vessels (or maybe the pulse)—or would it make better sense if, as some editors have suspected, the text actually read *genas*, "cheeks"? And how exactly are the eyes (*oculos*) involved? But in whatever way we fine-tune the interpretation, we are clearly meant to understand that laughter makes a strongly physical impact, extending well beyond the mouth. Cicero does not have a silent smile in mind, and indeed, unless we fall back on some very creative translation, smiling is not on the agenda in this discussion at all. We are talking about raising (*movere*) *laughter*.

The answer to the second question introduces a more subtle point than may at first be apparent. According to Strabo, the "locus . . . et regio" of the laughable lies "in what you might call the dishonorable or ugly." Whatever his Aristotelian influence may have been, he is suggesting something rather more complicated than the simple notion that people laugh at what is ugly. His precise claim is that "the only or the main objects of laughter are what people say to indicate or point out something dishonorable—in an honorable way."[71] In other words, laughter is provoked not by ugliness itself but—at a second-order level—by the wit of the joker who exploits the ugliness to make a joke. In fact, repeatedly in Strabo's exposition we find the joke and the joker presented as crucial intermediaries—the catalysts, if you like—between the laugher and the object of his laughter.

That is highlighted in a later passage where Strabo explains that he is moved by peevish and rather bad-tempered jokes (*stomachosa et quasi submorosa ridicula*) but not, he adds, when it is an ill-tempered person who tells them. Why not? Because in that case it is not the person's "wit" (*sal*) but his character (*natura*) that provokes the laughter.[72] Strabo's point is that laughter arises from the witty representation of the ugly, the dishonorable, or the bad tempered, not from those qualities themselves. Or at least that is how the proper kind of laughter, associated with the cultured elite, arises. In fact, much of the interest throughout this discussion lies in the methods of joking that are inappropriate—even if they reliably produce the heartiest outbursts of laughter.

Cicero is well aware that the subject of laughter—and its causes—is slippery, dependent on context, and resistant to hard-and-fast rules. He makes this point neatly when he has Strabo explain (at the beginning of his attempted classification of wit) that almost all the sources of *ridicula* can also be the source of serious thoughts (*graves sententiae*); the "only difference is that the serious [*gravitas*] derives from honorable and earnest matters, joking from those that are unseemly and, in a way, ugly."[73] In fact, he goes on, the very same words can sometimes be used both to praise and to ridicule, and he quotes a *ridiculum* of (probably) Gaius Claudius Nero, the consul of 207 BCE, aimed at a dishonest, light-fingered slave, "the only one against whom nothing in my house is locked or hidden away." In the context of the thief, this would raise a laugh, but, as Strabo insists, exactly the same could be said word for word in praise of an honest slave.[74]

But slippery as the idea of laughter is, we do find in *On the Orator* some general rules of thumb about what gets a Roman audience laughing most. By and large, verbal wit on its own is not the most effective way of raising a laugh. Double entendres, as Strabo notes twice, are liable to attract praise for their cleverness but not loud laughter: "Other kinds of joking raise bigger laughs."[75] To get more of a laugh, try combining *ambiguum* with a different type of joke. The unexpected ("when we expect one thing and another is said") is a more powerful prompt to laughter, and indeed can cause the speaker himself to crack up too: "Our own deviation [*error*] even makes us laugh ourselves." Or as he underlines later, "Our own deviation naturally amuses us. So when we have been deceived, as it were, by our own expectation, we laugh." This is the closest we ever come in the ancient world (and it is very close indeed) to a developed version of the modern incongruity theory.[76]

Sadly, however, Strabo's main example of a combination of wordplay and the unexpected is one of those cases where ancient laughter is more or less lost to us. Drawn from a farce, the joke concerns a man who has apparently taken pity on a condemned debtor whom he sees being led away. "How much is he going down for?" the observer asks (as if he were going to come up with a financial rescue passage himself). "A thousand sesterces" is the reply. Strabo then takes up the tale: "If he had gone on to say [*addidisset*] no more than 'You can take him away,' that would have belonged to the type of the laughable depending on the unexpected. But what he actually said was [*quia addidit*] 'No advance from me [*nihil addo*]—you can take him away.' So by adding a wordplay [*addito ambiguo*], another type of the laughable, he was in my opinion very witty indeed [*salsissimus*]." *Nihil addo* is probably some kind of play on the vocabulary of the Roman auction (punning on the senses of "I have no more to say" versus "I am not increasing my bid"), but how exactly it marked the man out as "very witty indeed" is not entirely clear. But with the repeated use in Strabo's account of various forms of the verb *addo*, it is hard to resist the conclusion that there is also some kind of internal joke in the Ciceronian narrative—constructing its description of verbal wit and punning in self-referentially punning terms.[77]

Puns, wordplay, and verbal quips were not without their risks. If they were obviously worked out beforehand; used indiscriminately, just for the sake of raising a laugh; or generic rather than specific, then they were the stock-in-trade not of the orator but of the *scurra*. They reeked of the commodification of laughter that was (as we shall see in chapter 8) the hallmark of the déclassé jokester. What is more, they could be counterproductive. Strabo tells a cautionary tale of a courtroom joke, making it an object lesson in why one should sometimes refrain from witticisms even when the occasion to make one presented itself. Philippus, so this story went, once asked the permission of the presiding magistrate to interrogate a witness, who happened to be tiny. The president, in a hurry, agreed: "But only if you're short." "You won't complain. It'll be a tiny interrogation." This was a laughable thing to say. But it so happened that one of the judges was even shorter, and the laughter became directed against him, so the joke seemed *scurrile*. "Jokes," Strabo explains, "that can fall on unintended targets, neat as they might be, are by definition those of a *scurra*."[78]

Strabo makes it absolutely clear that the most reliable way to raise a good laugh at Rome was not through clever puns, verbal quips, or the apposite quotation of a line of poetry. It was various forms of bodily disruption that best guaranteed a laugh. What is more likely to promote laughter (*ridiculum*) than a clown? he asks. And the clown does this with his face, with mimicry, with his voice, and by the way he uses his whole body. The point is, though, that these vulgar forms of making people laugh are almost entirely off limits for the elite orator: "Funny faces are beneath our dignity. . . . Obscenity is scarcely fitting for a gentleman's dinner party, let alone the for the Forum." The only one that gets any kind of hesitant approval is mimicry, provided that it is used "surreptitiously and in passing."[79]

In chapter 7 we shall return to the idea that mimicry was one of the central coordinates of Roman laughter (from actors to apes). But it remained on the very boundary of respectable oratorical wit. Some forms of imitation were, of course, highly to be approved: as the character of Antonius emphasizes earlier in the treatise, imitation of model orators was an important element in rhetorical training.[80] Other forms may have raised enthusiastic laughter but were in danger of crossing the line.

The marvelous story of Crassus' mimicry of his posh opponent nicely illustrates the correlation between imitation and levels of laughter (and gives a surprisingly lively picture of the presentational style of some Roman political debate). When he exclaimed, "By your noble birth, by your lineage," the listeners laughed at his "imitation of [his rival's] facial expression and accent." But when he went on, "By your statues," and extended his arm (presumably to mimic the classic pose of a Roman republican statue of an orator), "we really roared with laughter" (*vehementius risimus*).[81] Why this even stronger outburst? The logic of Strabo's account suggests two factors at work: first, the engagement of the body (rather than just the face and mouth), and second, I suspect, the reductio ad absurdum of imitation that is on display here (as Crassus the orator imitates the statue that is itself an imitation of the oratorical pose).

But the problem was that such tactics of laughter—especially if they involved "excessive imitation"—brought the orator uncomfortably close to the mime actor (*mimus*) or the professional mimic (*ethologus*). This comparison is perhaps even more loaded than that with the *scurra*. As a good deal of important recent work has explored, one of the anxieties that surrounded all oratorical performance at Rome centered on the tendentious boundary between the elite orator and the dishonorable actor (legally branded, along with prostitutes and gladiators, as *infamis*).[82] How could you draw a safe line between the powerfully persuasive performance of the expert orator and the equally persuasive, but socially abominated, performance of the *infamis* actor? Could an orator ever entirely escape the insinuation that he had more in common with an actor than he would like to admit? The question of the joking orator presents a more extreme version of that ideological dilemma. For in his capacity to make people laugh, the orator risks confusion not merely with an actor but with that particular vulgar class of actors associated with the laughter-raising mimes.

Mime actors also raised in an acute form one of the other big dilemmas in the culture of laughter at Rome: how could you distinguish the man whose wit prompted laughter from the man who was being laughed at? How could you be confident that the joker was not in fact the butt? We have already seen a version of this problem in the case of "bad-tempered jokes," when Strabo claimed to approve of those that were the result of wit but not those that were uttered by a "bad-tempered" man—with the implication that the man's natural character was in that case the butt of the joke. It is even more explicit in the case of the clown, who, Strabo makes clear, with his funny faces and so on, is the object as much as the prompt of the laughter: "He is laughed at" (*ridetur*).[83] Even if in Cicero's treatise the active sense of *ridiculus* is usually the more prominent, the passive sense ("ridiculous" in our terms) is never far away. The problem for the joking orator is that in raising a laugh, he exposes himself to be laughed *at:* laughter, in other words, risks being an own goal.

HOW AGGRESSIVE IS ROMAN ORATORICAL LAUGHTER?

The anxieties, ambivalences, and dilemmas that are so prominent in this section of *On the Orator* are strikingly different from the picture of an aggressive and relatively carefree use of laughter that has recently been extracted from the invective of Cicero's speeches. It is true that there are overlaps. Some of the quips that Strabo quotes certainly aim at the physical peculiarities of the orator's adversary (the unusual short stature of the witness, for example, or a missing eye). They also sometimes exploit the names of a particular opponent (Aulus Sempronius Musca is mocked as a "buzzer," *musca* being a word for "insect," and a man called Nobilior is ribbed as "Mobilior," or "fickle"). But Strabo highlights the dangers of these gibes just as often as their wit or cleverness: he criticizes the joke against Musca, for example, because it was spoken "just to get a laugh" (*risum quaesivit*).[84]

More generally, Strabo hedges the use of laughter in oratory with a variety of conditions and caveats: it should not be used against really serious criminals or really unfortunate individuals or those held generally in high esteem (in case it rebounds). Occasionally, he even touches on issues of restraint that modern scholarship holds to be entirely absent from the protocols of Roman oratorical laughter in theory or practice.

Corbeill, for example, considers Roman attitudes toward ridiculing personal characteristics for which the individual could not be held responsible. The Aristotelian tradition tended to exempt these from attack (it wasn't, after all, your fault if you were short). By contrast, "the Romans," Corbeill claims, "treated the condemnation of physical disadvantages quite differently. . . . A Roman located the responsibility for any deformity, regardless of its origin, solely in the person who bore that deformity."[85] But a debate about that very issue underlies one of the bantering exchanges that Strabo quotes. In this story, Crassus was in conflict with a *deformis* (ugly or deformed) opponent, who kept interrupting him. "Let's hear the pretty boy," Crassus said. When the laughter that this provoked had passed, his opponent replied, "I couldn't mold my appearance, but I could mold my talents." Crassus then retorted, to even stronger laughter, "Let's hear the eloquent speaker, then" (the joke presumably being that the man was no more eloquent than he was pretty).[86] It is true that Crassus wins the exchange, raising a good deal of laughter at his adversary's expense, but the story clearly shows that the Aristotelian question of personal responsibility was on the Roman agenda.

So how should we reconcile the picture of aggressive Roman laughter drawn from Cicero's speeches with the more theoretical discussion in *On the Orator?* Some people, no doubt, would argue that we should not try too hard. Theory and practice can diverge, even constructively (just as Cicero's philosophical views on theology are often taken to be quite separate from his day-to-day practice as a Roman priest[87]). Maybe this attempt at theorizing really was an almost independent exercise, in dialogue more with earlier traditions of Greek theorizing than with his own oratorical practice. But that approach would signally fail to take into account the strong emphasis that Cicero places throughout *On the Orator* on the specific inheritance and traditions of *Roman* oratory.

A quite different suggestion sees the apparent divergence between the treatise and the speeches from the point of view of Cicero's image and reputation. If one of the criticisms leveled against Cicero was that he never knew when to stop joking and raising laughter, that he was a *scurra* of a consul, then maybe this discussion of the role of laughter in oratory is a loaded and self-serving defense against those charges; perhaps he chose for that reason to put the section so centrally in the whole work.[88] There may be something in this view. Certainly in reading Cicero's remarks about the importance of keeping a firm boundary between the jokes of the orator and the jokes of the *scurra*, it is important not to forget that this was a boundary that he himself was often accused of transgressing. Yet there is no direct evidence at all that this long section of his essay was a response to personal criticism or an exercise in self-justification and defense, or that it was seen as such.

To turn this on its head, there is a strong argument for letting the protocols for laughter laid out in *On the Orator* nuance our view of the role and significance of the "aggressive humor" in the speeches and encourage us to see some of it as more playful than we usually assume. Some of the laughter and joking in oratory no doubt did work just as Corbeill and others have suggested. After all, even if we were to take the rules enshrined in *On the Orator* very seriously, there are no oratorical rules that are not sometimes broken (else what would be the point of the rules?). But more of the laughter than we imagine might fit the pattern that Strabo's principles suggest: that is, it was designed not only to "shatter" an opponent but to bring goodwill or to relieve the austerity of a speech and directed not at really outrageous crimes or wickedness but at relatively minor faults.

Cicero's gibes at Vatinius are instructive here. They have been taken as some of the most extreme examples of assassination by jest. As we have seen (above, p. 106), Cicero repeatedly ridiculed Vatinius' apparently disgusting appearance (in particular his facial swellings), which he made stand for Vatinius' "despicable nature" and exclusion from the communal values and good sense of the laughing crowd. Of course, we have no idea what Vatinius really looked like or how unsightly his *strumae* were (and neither did those later Roman writers who commented on them); it would certainly make a difference to how we judged the repartee to know whether the target was a gross disfigurement or just a slightly puffy face and a few warts. But it is worth noting that some ancient views presented the pattern of joking at Vatinius' expense in rather different terms from those of modern critics. Seneca, for example, refers to the way that Vatinius deflected the gibes by joking about his own appearance,[89] and some of the bons mots that Quintilian and (especially) Macrobius collected imply a relationship of much more jocular bantering between Cicero and Vatinius. On one occasion, Macrobius explains, Vatinius was ill and complained that Cicero had not been to visit him. "I wanted to come when you were consul," Cicero quipped, "but nightfall caught up with me" (one of a series of jokes about the ludicrously short terms of office of consuls under Julius Caesar). Macrobius goes on to say that Cicero was getting his revenge here, because when he had returned from exile, "brought back, he boasted, on the shoulders of the state," Vatinius had retorted, "So where did your varicose veins come from, then?"[90]

The point is that it is very hard to calibrate from the outside the aggression that comes with joking and banter, as many modern observers of the British House of Commons find—amazed to see that those who have insulted each other bitterly are, two hours later, sharing a drink in the Commons Bar. We should not assume that Cicero's jesting "invective" was always an aggressive weapon of social and political exclusion; it might also have been an interactive idiom shared between the orator and his apparent victim.[91]

QUINTILIAN'S ADVICE TO THE JOKING ORATOR

Some 150 years after Cicero wrote *On the Orator,* Quintilian composed his twelve-volume *Handbook on Oratory.* In the middle of the sixth book—much of which is devoted to how the orator might appeal to the audience's emotions (and which opens with an extraordinary account of the death of Quintilian's wife and two sons)—is a long chapter on laughter, almost as long as Strabo's diversion in Cicero's treatise. It is here that we find his comparison between Cicero and Demosthenes (see above, p. 103), his sound bite on *risus* being not far from *derisus* (p. 28), and his struggles to come up with a working definition of the word *salsum* (p. 115).[92]

Predictably enough, Cicero was one of Quintilian's major sources,[93] and there are many overlaps between the two accounts: Quintilian, for example, shares the division of wit into the categories of *dicto* (*verbo* in Quintilian) and *re,* warns against face pulling as an acceptable means of producing laughter for the elite orator, and advises his readers not to frame jokes against whole classes of people.[94] He even includes some of the same examples of jokes and quips as Cicero—though his gift for telling them certainly does not equal his model's. He rather mangles the joke about the thieving slave ("Nero said about a dreadful slave that there was no one in the house more trusted, as nothing was hidden away or locked").[95] And he seems to have missed the point of one of the better bons mots in *On the Orator.* As an example of a joke by overstatement, Strabo quotes Crassus' gibe about Gaius Memmius, the tribune of 111 BCE: "He fancies himself so exalted that when he is coming into the Forum, he ducks his head to pass under the Arch of Fabius." This turns up in Quintilian as "Cicero's remark about the very tall man: he hit his head on the Arch of Fabius."[96]

But there are significant differences too. For a start, Quintilian includes a much wider range of witty sayings than the dramatic date of *On the Orator* made possible: Cicero was restricted to jokes uttered before 91 BCE; Quintilian could cite quips from famous jokesters of later periods, including Cicero himself and the emperor Augustus. But Quintilian also drew on other discussions of laughter and related topics, including a book on "urbanity" by Domitius Marsus, to which he devotes a critical appendix (arguing, among other things, that Marsus' definition of *urbanitas* was too general),[97] and he structured his discussion under different headings, with different emphases, sometimes raising significantly different topics and anxieties, major and minor.

Quintilian makes a great deal of, for example, the analogy between wit and cookery. Cicero had hinted at this in *On the Orator*: Strabo at one point remarks that the things he is discussing amount to "seasoning" (*condimenta*) for day-to-day talk or legal cases. But Quintilian develops this into an extended analogy, linking laughter and food in a way that is an important theme in other writers (see below, pp. 148–51). Pinpointing the root of the word, he writes of *salsum* as "a simple seasoning of a speech, which is sensed by some unconscious judgment, rather like the palate. . . . For just as salt when it is sprinkled generously over food, though not in excess, brings a pleasure all of its own, so witticisms [*sales*] in speaking have something about them that gives us a thirst for listening."[98] He also puts even more emphasis than Cicero had on the gentle character of oratorical wit. "Let us never want to hurt anyone [with our joking]," he insists, "and let's have nothing to do with the idea that it is better to lose a friend than a jest."[99] We might be seeing here a chronological shift in oratorical style (from the gloves-off style of the Republic to the slightly insipid decorum of the Principate[100]), but honestly, two isolated discussions are not a strong enough foundation for any such argument.

Quintilian also introduces some striking observations not found in *On the Orator*. He claims, for example, that another characteristic of the *scurra* is that he makes jokes against himself ("one does not approve of that in an orator").[101] And he suggests that some words prompt laughter in and of themselves. "The word *stomach* [*stomachus*] has something funny about it," and so does the word *satagere* ("bustle about" or even, in the context, "overact").[102] But there are two major anxieties about the use of laughter that bulk even larger in Quintilian's discussion than in Cicero's: the first is the potential for laughter to rebound on the joker, and the second is that prompts to laughter are very often untrue.

Strabo's presentation revealed lurking worries that the orator might become, like the clown, the object of the laughter he provokes. This comes to the foreground in Quintilian's *Handbook,* which stresses on several occasions the dangerously ambiguous nature of the laughter process. Referring, for example, to Cicero's claim that laughter has its foundation "in what you might call the ugly or dishonorable," he raises the possibility that pointing the finger at such things might rebound: "When these features are pointed out in others, that's called *urbanitas;* when they rebound [*reccidunt*] on the speaker, that's called foolishness [*stultitia*]." There are even those, he observes later, who do not avoid jokes that rebound on themselves (*in ipsos reccidere*), and he proceeds to tell the story of a particularly ugly orator who made himself vulnerable by taking a sideswipe at the appearance of someone else.[103]

Quintilian also plays even more explicitly than Cicero with the different sides, active and passive, of the word *ridiculus,* with the implication that the man who raises a laugh risks becoming (in our, passive, sense) ridiculous. The starkest example is found earlier in the book, before the section dedicated to the use of laughter. Discussing the epilogues of speeches (which might sometime include wit), Quintilian as often includes a description of what to avoid. On one occasion, he explains, the prosecutor was waving in court the bloody sword with which he claimed the victim had been murdered. The other advocate pretended to be scared and hid; when he was called on to speak, he peeped out—his head still partly covered up—and asked if the man with the sword had gone. "Fecit enim risum sed ridiculus fuit" (he raised a laugh but was ridiculous).[104] Cicero might well have compared the performance to that of a mime actor.

Quintilian's concerns about truth and falsehood take us further from Cicero's themes. Cicero in fact was generally unperturbed by the lying and deception that joking could involve—as we can see in another joke about Memmius, the tribune of 111 BCE, that Strabo recounts. Crassus, he explains, once claimed in a speech that Memmius had been involved in a brawl over a girl with someone called Largus and had bitten a large chunk out of the man's arm. Not just that, but all over the town of Tarracina, where the brawl took place, the letters *LLLMM* started to appear—which Crassus claimed stood for "Lacerat Lacertum Largi Mordax Memmius" (or, as the Loeb translation nicely renders it, "Mordacious Memmius lacerates Largus' limb"). It raised a good laugh—and every word of it was made up. For Cicero, that was a fine jest, appropriate for an orator, whether it was broadly true with just a sprinkling of "fiblets" (*mendaciunculis*) or a total fabrication.[105]

It was not so for Quintilian. In a more extreme version of the traditional ancient concerns about the truth of rhetoric, he starts his section on "laughter raising" with a worry about falsehood in joking: "What brings the greatest difficulty to the subject is, first of all, that a joke [*dictum ridiculum*] is usually untrue." Although he does not often return directly to this problem, it hovers over the discussion—as when he states that "everything that is obviously made up produces laughter."[106]

This is a concern that we find elsewhere in Roman discussions of laughter in very different literary genres. One of the most memorable versions of this theme of truth versus falsehood in the production of laughter is in fact to be found in the *Fables* of Phaedrus, written in the first half of the first century CE. It is the story of a competition in front of an audience between a *scurra*, "well known for his urban wit" (*notus urbano sale*), and a peasant (*rusticus*)—as to who could do the best imitation of a pig. The *scurra* had started the show on the first day, winning loud applause for his pig noises, but the peasant challenged him to a second round on the very next day. An even bigger crowd turned up, determined to deride (*derisuros*). The *scurra* repeated his performance of the previous day, to great applause. Then the peasant came forward, pretending that he had a real pig concealed underneath his clothes—which in fact he did. He tweaked the animal's ear to make it (really) squeal, but the audience still preferred the *scurra*'s version, voting it a much better imitation of a pig than the real pig. As they threw the peasant off the stage, he produced the animal to prove to the audience what a mistake they had made.[107]

It's a dense story, made all the more complicated by the layers of simulation and dissimulation involved (even the peasant is pretending to be pretending). But the simple idea that the *scurra*, the professional jokester, could please the audience with his imitation noise better than the peasant could with his real pig is just what Quintilian would have been worried about.

SERO?

I started this chapter with a play on words that Quintilian much admired. Cicero—who had been pressed to specify at Milo's trial when Clodius had died—replied with a single (hilarious) word: *sero* (late/too late). Why did Quintilian find this response such a good joke? I am far from clear that I have the final answer to that. But the discussions of oratorical laughter in both *On the Orator* and the *Handbook* do bring us a little closer to understanding its impact on Quintilian. Various factors made this a quip of which one might especially approve. It was spontaneous and unprepared. It was a response rather than an unprovoked attack. It applied only to Clodius, rather than being a class action.

No less important, for Quintilian at least, it was true . . . unlike some of the instances of laughter and joking in the Roman imperial court that we will explore in the next chapter.

CHAPTER 6

From Emperor to Jester

LAUGHTER AND POWER

The opening pages of this book featured an encounter between an emperor and a senator in the Colosseum, with laughter—in some form—on both sides: the senator and writer, Dio Cassius, chewing on his laurel leaf to disguise the fact that he was cracking up; the emperor, Commodus, reportedly grinning in a triumphant and threatening fashion. We have also briefly glimpsed some revealing stories of the laughter and two-edged jocularity of the emperor Elagabalus (see p. 77), who was on the throne some thirty years after Commodus, from 218 to 222 CE, gleefully recounted in his fantastical biography—more fantasy than real life, it is usually reckoned.

In what is, to my knowledge, the first recorded use of the whoopee cushion in world history, his *Life* explains how Elagabalus raised a laugh as his guests were literally deflated at dinner—and his pranks are said to have included the display of hilarious lineups of eight bald or one-eyed or deaf or gouty men. In the theater, his laughter drowned out that of the rest of the audience. Other tales from the same, flagrantly unreliable source recount how he "used also in fact to joke with his slaves, even ordering them to bring him a thousand pounds in weight of spiders' webs and offering a reward," or how "when his friends became drunk, he used often to lock them up, and suddenly in the night he would send in lions and leopards and bears—tame ones—so that when they woke up at daybreak, or worse, during the night, they would find lions and leopards and bears in the room with them. And many of them died from it."[1]

The extravagant fantasies in the *Augustan History* are often more historically revealing than they appear—not simply inventions but absurd magnifications of traditional Roman concerns. We might see some of these stories of Elagabalus as inverted reflections of the anxieties that Quintilian expressed over the truth and falsehood of jokes and laughter. A chilling consequence of Roman autocracy is imagined here as the capacity of the tyrant to make his jokes come (horribly and unexpectedly) true: the tigers and so on were harmless, but the guests died anyway.[2]

It is a truism that the practice of laughter is closely bound up with power and its differentials (what social practice isn't?). The interesting question—which this chapter tries to broach—is, in what particular ways was laughter related to Roman power? We start with emperors and autocrats and move (via masters and slaves, and an extraordinarily jocular account of a chilling audience with the emperor Caligula) to reflect on the place of the joker or jester at Rome—both inside and outside the imperial court, both as a cultural stereotype and (insofar as we can glimpse it) as a character in day-to-day social reality. Several topics that we touched on in the last chapter appear again, in particular the idea of that déclassé antitype to the elite orator, the *scurra,* who is the tricky, shifting subject of the final section of this chapter. My aim is to put laughter back into our image of the imperial court and its penumbra and to highlight the part that jokers played in Roman elite culture; it turns out to be a much larger and more significant one than we tend to acknowledge.

EMPERORS GOOD AND BAD

Roman autocracy was embedded in the culture of laughter and the joke—in a pattern that stretched back well before the reign of the first emperor, Augustus.[3] It may not now be the best-known "fact" about the brutal dictator Sulla, who held brief and bloody control of the city in the 80s BCE, but in antiquity, like a number of Hellenistic tyrants and monarchs (see pp. 151, 207), he had the reputation of being an enthusiastic laughter lover. It was presumably not by chance that he was associated with precisely those jokesters whose style of jesting Cicero and Quintilian urged the orator to avoid. "He was so fond of mime actors and clowns, being very much a laughter lover," wrote the historian

Nicolaus of Damascus in the late first century BCE, "that he gave them many tracts of public land. A clear proof of the pleasure he took in these things are the satyric comedies that he wrote himself in his native language [Latin]."[4] Plutarch too picked up the tradition, explaining that the dictator "loved a joke" (*philoskōmmōn*) and at dinner was completely transformed from the austere character that he was at other times. Even just before his death (caused, in Plutarch's lurid story, by a ghastly ulceration that turned his flesh to worms), he was carousing with comics, mime actors, and impersonators.[5]

Some of the associations between autocrat and laughter are easily predictable. The basic Roman rule (which we meet again in its direct descendant, the medieval tradition of the *rex facetus*[6]) was that good and wise rulers made jokes in a benevolent way, never used laughter to humiliate, and tolerated wisecracks at their own expense. Bad rulers and tyrants, on the other hand, would violently suppress even the most innocent banter while using laughter and joking as weapons against their enemies. Anecdotes about imperial laughter illustrate these axioms time and again. Whether they are literally true or not we cannot tell, and the fact that there are examples of jokes apparently migrating from one prominent jokester to another (see pp. 105, 253n23) strongly suggests that we are dealing with cultural stereotype or traditional tales rather than fact. But they point to the bigger truth—a political lesson as much as an urban myth—that laughter helped to characterize both good and bad rulers.[7]

Dio neatly sums up one side of this in discussing Vespasian: the emperor's *civilitas* (that ideal quality of treating his people as fellow citizens, not subjects) was demonstrated by the fact that "he joked like one of the people [*dēmotikōs*] and was happy to take jokes at his own expense, and if any of the kind of slogans that are often anonymously addressed to emperors were posted up, leveling insults at him, he would post up a reply in the same vein, without being at all bothered by it."[8] Of course, *civilitas* was always something of a veneer (there was no real equality between citizens and the emperor, and especially not between the emperor and the ordinary, nonelite citizens who are often instrumental in these jokes). But it was nevertheless an important veneer in those intricate games of imperial power whose ground rules had been established under the emperor Augustus. And it is around Augustus that a large number of these anecdotes—of jokes tolerated or enjoyed—cluster.

Many of the stories of his bons mots and banter that Macrobius collected show Augustus joking with his subordinates (when, for example, someone was hesitating to offer him a petition and kept putting out and withdrawing his hand, the emperor said, "Do you think you are giving a penny [as] to an elephant?"[9]). But they also show him tolerating the quips that were aimed against him. As Macrobius has one of the characters in his *Saturnalia* remark, "In the case of Augustus, I am usually more amazed by the jokes he put up with than those he put out" (I am attempting here to capture something of the play between *pertulit*, "put up with," and *protulit*, "put out" or "uttered"). And he goes on to cite a number of examples, including a very famous joke, which we shall discover (see p. 214) has had a long afterlife, through Sigmund Freud down to Iris Murdoch, as well as a prehistory stretching back into the Roman Republic. "A barbed joke [*iocus asper*] made by some provincial became well known. There had come to Rome a man who looked very like the emperor, and he had attracted the attention of everyone. Augustus ordered the man to be brought to him, and once he had taken a look, he asked, 'Tell me, young man, was your mother ever at Rome?' 'No,' he said. But not content with leaving it at that, he added, 'But my father was, often.'" Augustus, in other words, was the kind of man who could take a joke about that bedrock of Roman patriarchal power—his own paternity.[10]

But not all the jokers were humble types. We occasionally find similar tolerance displayed toward the jocularity of the upper echelons of Roman society. In one intriguing cause célèbre of the early second century CE, jokes were used in the Senate as a vehicle for safe criticism. The story, found in a letter of Pliny, is for us a refreshing antidote to the usual image of senatorial solemnity—though Pliny himself was not amused. He was discussing the obvious, and in his view disastrous, consequence of introducing secret voting papers in senatorial elections: "I told you," he writes to his correspondent, "that you should be worried that secret ballot might lead to abuse. Well, it's already happened." Someone, he explains, at the last election had scrawled jokes (*iocularia*) and even obscenities on some ballot papers and on one had written the names of the supporters, not of the candidates; it was all intended, we might guess, as a ribald comment on the pointlessness of such procedures under autocratic rule. The loyal senators huffed and puffed and urged the ruling emperor, Trajan, to punish the culprit, who wisely lay low and was never found. The implication of Pliny's letter is that Trajan turned a blind eye and took no action.[11] If some of the more starchy observers, Pliny included, were disappointed, others would surely have congratulated the emperor on his display of *civilitas*.

"Bad" emperors too were revealed by their particular style of laughing and joking. Ancient discussions of the imperial "monsters"—from Caligula through Domitian to Elagabalus—repeatedly use laughter, and the transgression of its codes and conventions, to define and calibrate different forms of cruelty and excess, the very opposites of *civilitas*. Sometimes this was a question of an emperor not tolerating jokes made at his expense. It was said that Commodus instructed the marines, who usually looked after the huge awnings used to shade the Colosseum, to kill the people in the audience who he believed were laughing at him (no wonder Dio was worried about cracking up).[12] On other occasions it was more a question of the emperor laughing in the wrong way, in the wrong place, or at the wrong things, or making particularly sadistic (or just bad) jokes.

In the case of Claudius, his quips were decidedly feeble, or "cold" (*frigidus*): Suetonius was unimpressed by a pun on the name of a gladiator, Palumbus, which literally means "wood pigeon" (when the crowd clamored for Palumbus, Claudius promised him "if he could be caught").[13] Caligula's quips were menacing rather than cold. "At one of his more lavish banquets," Suetonius writes, "he suddenly collapsed into a fit of guffaws [*in cachinnos*]. The consuls who were reclining next to him asked him politely why he was laughing. 'Only at the idea that at one nod from me, both of you could have your throats cut instantly.'"[14] And Commodus' biographer in the *Augustan History* nicely observes that "he was also deadly in his jokes" (*in iocis quoque perniciosus*) before telling the nasty story of how the emperor put a starling on the head of a man who had a few white hairs among the black. The bird pecked at the white hairs, thinking they were worms, causing the man's scalp to fester—and presumably killing him in the end.[15]

This story echoes a theme prominent in the *Life* of Elagabalus: that the jokes of an autocrat can be literally murderous. But that is not all. In the part factual, part fantasy world of this biography, Commodus' prank also parodies a whole tradition of imperial jokes about, or against, gray hairs and baldness. One of the commonest themes in the ridicule of an emperor was the state of his head: Julius Caesar was repeatedly mocked for being bald and was said to have combed his remaining hair forward to hide his bald patch (a time-honored tactic in the circumstances, and a time-honored theme of further mockery); Domitian too (the "bald Nero") is supposed to have taken it as an insult if anyone joked about his lack of hair.[16] But this particular story of Commodus surely looks back to one of the jests of Augustus, at his daughter, Julia, collected by Macrobius. Julia was said to have worried about her gray hairs, and she took to having them plucked out by her maids. One day Augustus visited her after this had been going on. "Pretending not to notice the gray hairs on her clothes . . . he asked his daughter whether, in a few years' time, she would rather be bald or gray. When she replied, 'Personally, father, I prefer to be gray,' he told her off for the lie by saying, 'Why, then, are these women making you bald so quickly?'"[17] The contrast is clear. The wise Augustus jokingly reproves his daughter for plucking her gray hairs. The tyrant Commodus sets a bird on the head of an innocent man to do exactly that—and kills him.

Other aspects of imperial laughter are not so predictable. A different theme in this anecdotal and biographical tradition uses laughter to highlight various issues of control. Laughter in day-to-day practice was most likely as controllable for Romans as it is for us (see pp. 43–44). But one powerful Roman myth of laughter (like our own) was that as a natural irruption, it challenged the human ability to master it, and so the proper observance of the social protocols of laughter was the mark of a man (usually a man) fully in control of himself. It was one diagnostic of the faults of the emperor Claudius that he found it difficult to master his mirth. At his first attempt to give a public reading from his newly composed *History of Rome,* there was trouble from the beginning, when general laughter broke out at the sight of a very fat man breaking several benches, presumably with his sheer weight, by sitting on them. But it went from bad to worse, as the poor young prince did not manage to get through the recitation without cracking up whenever he recalled the hilarious incident. It was a telling sign of his incapacity, mental and physical.[18]

Roman protocols of control, however, operated the other way round too: the question was not simply whether the gentleman could control his laughter but whether he could control his desire to tell a joke ("to keep his *bona dicta* to himself," as Ennius' famous phrase had it; see p. 76) or resist the temptation to make jests of the wrong sort. Suetonius' two chapters on the jocularity of Vespasian nicely illustrate this. Like Dio, the biographer generally applauds this emperor's wit, and he quotes with admiration all kinds of textbook quips that would have met with the approval of Cicero or Quintilian—from the clever insertion of lines of poetry to the use of a jest to deflect hatred. (In fact, the match with the oratorical handbooks is so close that it is conceivable that their discussion of laughter lies somewhere behind these reflections of Suetonius'.) But even here the specter of the *scurra* was not far away: Vespasian's *dicacitas* could be, Suetonius admits, *scurrilis*.[19]

Yet the sharpest cutting edge of imperial laughter is seen not so much in the emperor's ability to control his own outbursts of laughing or joking as in his attempts to control those of others. One classic tyrannical attempt to prohibit laughter is supposed to have occurred under Caligula, at the death of his sister Drusilla. According to Suetonius, Caligula ruled that during the period of mourning for her, no one—on pain of death—should laugh, bathe, or dine with their family (a significant trio of "normal" social human activities, with "laughing" first in Suetonius' order). This was an obviously fruitless, not to say unenforceable, ruling and (whatever its truth) is recounted in the biography for precisely that reason. But it should also take its place with other tyrannical attempts—successful or unsuccessful, mythical or not—to dominate the forces of nature: just as Xerxes tried to bridge the Hellespont, so (more domestically) Caligula tried to conquer the natural forces of laughter among his subjects.[20]

An even more sinister aspect of imperial control was the attempt not to prevent laughing and joking but to impose them on the unwilling. Soon after describing Caligula's rules for mourning, Suetonius tells of a particularly choice piece of imperial cruelty. Caligula insisted first that a man watch the execution of his own son, then that the father come to dinner with him that very afternoon: there, with a tremendous show of affability, the emperor "pushed him to laughing and joking" (*hilaritas* and *ioci* are the Latin words). Why did the man go along with it? asks Seneca, who tells a slightly different version of the story. There is a simple answer: because he had another son.[21]

We even find a hint of a more moderate version of the imperial exaction of laughter in Suetonius' *Life of Augustus*. Toward the very end of the emperor's life, when he was staying in his villa on Capri, he still retained his generosity and jocularity: he gave presents and playfully insisted that the Greeks and Romans in his entourage swap dress and speak each other's language; indeed, "there was no kind of fun [*genus hilaritatis*] that he refrained from." But even here, and even with that most "civil" of emperors, there is a touch of menace, at least in Suetonius' description. For in those fun-filled dinner parties, Augustus not only "allowed but demanded" that his young guests show "complete freedom in joking" (*permissa, immo exacta, iocandi licentia*).[22] If laughter was a most uncontrollable bodily reaction, it was nevertheless (or perhaps for that very reason) one that emperors tried to govern, some with a lighter touch than others. To put it a different way, in the literary economy of imperial rule, the emperor's attempt to govern laughter could be a vivid political symbol of the "unnaturalness" of autocracy, even in its more gentle forms.

LAUGHTER BETWEEN HIGH AND LOW

Perhaps even more striking is the fact that these stories so often site laughter at the interface between the emperor and his nonelite subjects—ordinary Romans, provincials, or rank-and-file soldiers. For when ancient writers chose to represent the interaction between the ruler and some ordinary person or pictured him outside the palace in the people's space, they almost always did so in jocular terms. We have already seen (p. 131) Augustus tolerating a quip about his paternity from "some provincial." Even Caligula (whose tyrannical manipulation of laughter was particularly marked) is said to have put up with the banter of a Gallic shoemaker on one occasion. In Dio's words, "There was once a Gaul who caught sight of the emperor sitting on a high platform, dressed in the costume of Jupiter, and issuing oracles. The man burst out laughing. Caligula summoned him and asked, 'How do I come across to you?' And the man answered (I'm giving his exact words), 'Like a right idiot.' But he got off scot free, because he was a shoemaker. It is easier, I suppose, for people like Caligula to put up with outspokenness from ordinary people than from those of rank."[23]

But there was also the more general question of how—or in what rhetorical register—the emperor's interactions with the common people were represented. Augustus' bantering and jocular engagement with the nervous petitioner ("Do you think you are giving a penny to an elephant?") is typical. Another vivid case is the nice *iocus balnearis* (bathhouse quip) of the emperor Hadrian, who is said to have entered a set of public baths and noticed a veteran soldier rubbing his bare back against a wall. When Hadrian asked why he was doing that, the man replied that he did not own a slave to rub him down. The emperor's generous response was to present him with some slaves and the money for their upkeep (a canny recognition of the fact that slaves on their own were no free gift). But obviously the word got around, for another time, Hadrian went to the baths and found a number of old men rubbing themselves down on the walls. No slaves for them: he made them get together to rub one another down. The point of the story was to show that Hadrian was a man of the people, warmhearted, but no fool—not to mention the kind of person who would respond to a transparent scam with a jest.[24]

I am not for a moment suggesting that all relations between the Roman emperor and his subjects were "a laugh" or that there really was a consistent atmosphere of jocularity (whether relaxed or tense) when the ruler confronted ordinary Romans face-to-face. Of course, that cannot always—or even often—have been the case, and almost certainly not in the kind of unmediated exchanges that the anecdotes ask us to imagine. If Hadrian really did visit the ordinary baths, my guess is that any joking encounters he had with the great unwashed (or washed) would have been very carefully choreographed and closely policed. My point is that in Roman writing, confrontations between the ruler and individual representatives of the ruled were overwhelmingly delineated, debated, and discursively formulated in terms of laughing and joking. Literary representations, at least, used forms of laughter to facilitate communication across the political hierarchy, allowing a particular form of jocularized conversation to take place between high and low. In part this no doubt served to mask the differences of status. At the same time, laughter marked the limit of the tyrant's civility and could show him up for what he was: a tyrant (just as it could show up the subversive joker too, as subversive). Laughter, in other words, was a key operator in the discourse of Roman political power relations between emperor and subject.

So it was across other axes of power too: the discursive structures of one form of power in Roman culture and society often mapped broadly (even if details differed) onto others. For "tyrant versus subject," for example, we may read "god versus human" or "free versus slave." In these cases too, laughter could be a key signal and signifier in the operation of power—as a couple of vivid examples drawn from these other areas make clear.

Ovid often uses laughter in the *Metamorphoses* as a marker of the relationship between mortals and immortals. You do not need to read far into these poetic tales of transformation to realize that laughing in its various registers—from smug smirks through ripples of joy to triumphant cackles—was an important element in the discourse of power between human beings and the forces of the divine. On the one hand, the gods can use laughter to show their delight at their ability to change the shapes and forms of their human victims. So, for example, when he catches the elderly herdsman Battus trying to trick him, Mercury laughs as he turns the old man into a flint stone.[25] On the other hand, human laughter aimed at a god or goddess sometimes heralds the transformation of the laugher into a beast, bird, or inanimate object: the laughter is a display of human defiance, which the deity promptly punishes by the removal of human form and status. But in the more general articulation of power in the poem, this laughter also acts as a signal to the reader that the power differentials between immortal and mortal are about to be exposed or reasserted. So, for example, the servant girl Galanthis laughs when she thinks that she has tricked Juno into giving Alcmena, Hercules' mother, an easy childbirth—and is promptly turned into a weasel.[26] There is a similar pattern in the story of King Piereus' daughters, who challenge the Muses to a singing contest and lose. When they laugh at the victors, they are turned straightway into magpies.[27]

Of course, in the *Metamorphoses* the symbol of laughter is even more loaded than this, thanks to the significance of laughing as one marker of the human condition itself. In several Roman stories that focus on the interface between the human and the animal world, the loss of the ability to laugh can be a telling hint that the boundary has been transgressed (see p. 181). In Ovid's poem, the peal of laughter that emerges from some of the victims immediately before their transformation is surely meant to remind the reader that they are uttering what is, quite literally, their last laugh: as soon as Galanthis has become a weasel, she will laugh no more.[28]

More emphatically, laughter also marked the relations between master and slave. As we saw in chapter 1, many themes in Roman comedy (drawn in part from earlier Greek traditions) focused on the hierarchies of slavery and on the interaction of slaves and their owners—parading those hierarchies as both challenged and reinforced, mitigated and occluded, by joking. The idea of the clever comic slave who raised a laugh at the expense of his dim owner both subverted the power relations of slavery as an institution and, I suspect, served to legitimate them.[29] But the overriding point is that the interface between master and slave, just as between emperor and subject, was regularly framed in jocular terms.

This comes across especially starkly in a text of very different genre, and one that is much less well known, even among classicists, than Roman stage comedies: the *Life of Aesop*, an anonymous biography, in Greek, of the famous fable-writing slave. It is a puzzling, complex, composite work that probably reached its final form (or something like it) in Roman imperial Egypt of the first century CE, although its ultimate origins may well be much earlier and go back to very different areas and contexts in the classical world.[30] Flagrantly fictional (it is unlikely that any such person as Aesop ever existed, still less that he wrote the fables that go under the name[31]), it often reaches to the ideological heart of the matter—even if not to the literal truth.

Aesop cuts a "funny" figure. He is a dwarf, potbellied, snub-nosed, hunchbacked, and bandy-legged: "a walking disaster," as one modern commentator has aptly called him.[32] But despite (or because of) his appearance, he is witty, clever—and as good at cracking jokes about others as being a prompt to laughter himself for his sheer bodily peculiarities. Strikingly, at the start of the written *Life* he is also dumb, until, a couple of pages into the story in the principal version of the text, the goddess Isis gives him the faculty of speech and persuades the Muses each to give him a taste of their gifts, such as storytelling.[33] Nevertheless, as Leslie Kurke emphasizes, in the very first episode of the story, while he is still mute, Aesop manages eloquently to reveal that a couple of fellow slaves are guilty of the very crime that they are trying to pin on him: namely, eating the master's figs. He makes the pair vomit up the fruit, thus proving their guilt.[34] In the world of jests and entertainment, it was a familiar Roman paradox that—far from the verbal forms we have seen so enthusiastically recommended for the orator—silent wit and eloquence could be found in those who were, or had been, dumb (see p. 144).

Much of the rest of the *Life* is taken up with the laughing relationship between the slave and his new master, a philosopher by the name of Xanthus, who buys Aesop after he has gained the power of speech. This laughter starts from the very moment that Aesop is on display in the slave market, where Xanthus is quizzing the various slaves on sale about their qualities. "What do you know how to do?" Xanthus asks his potential living purchases. "I know how to do everything," reply two of the slaves, at which Aesop laughs (so heartily, and so badly contorting his face and baring his teeth, that he looked to Xanthus' students like "a turnip with gnashers").[35] When it comes to Aesop's turn to be quizzed about what he can do, he replies in a parodically Socratic fashion, "Nothing at all . . . because the other two boys know everything there is." That is why he had laughed (at them), exposing their foolish overconfidence in their abilities. After some more philosophical banter between Aesop and Xanthus, the philosopher decides to purchase the "walking disaster" rather than the slicker, more attractive slaves on offer—causing the slave merchant to suspect that, in making that choice, Xanthus was having a joke on his trade. "Are you wanting to make a mockery of my business?" he asks. But the tax collectors, whose job it was to collect the sales tax, found the whole transaction so ridiculous that they, in their turn, laughed and remitted the tax. Repeatedly, in other words, the insertion of (written) laughter into this story serves to mark the differentials of power, knowledge, and understanding across the hierarchies of status.[36]

And so it continues through much of the rest of the tale—until Aesop manages to secure his freedom, and in a baroque finale is forced to his death (by jumping over a cliff) at Delphi.[37] The relationship between the slave and his owner is memorably configured in bantering terms, reminiscent of those between subject and emperor. At one point, the exasperated Xanthus, who has just signally failed to answer a philosophical puzzle posed by his gardener and then hears his slave laughing, is forced to ask, "Aesop, are you just laughing [gelas] or are you taking the mickey out of me [katagelas]?" Aesop neatly extricates himself from the charge (while delivering an even sharper insult): "I'm laughing at the professor who taught you."[38]

But much of the best fun comes from the faux naïveté or willful literal-mindedness of Aesop's responses to Xanthus' instructions. This was a style of joking that Quintilian identified (and praised) in his Handbook ("Titius Maximus once stupidly asked Campatius as he left the theater whether he had been watching a play. "No, I was playing ball in the orchestra, stupid."[39]). The Life presents it as a major weapon of the slave in his bantering standoffs with his master. Typical of many exchanges is the anecdote of their visit to the baths. "Bring the oil flask and the towels," Xanthus says to Aesop as they are getting ready. Once they have arrived, Xanthus asks for the flask in order to rub himself with oil, only to discover that there is no oil inside it. "Aesop," he says, "where's the oil?" "At home," the slave quips back. "You told me to 'take the oil flask and the towels'; you didn't mention oil." Almost immediately after this, Aesop is sent home "to put lentil in the pot," and that is exactly what he does. When Xanthus gets back for supper with a group of fellow bathers, he finds that there is indeed just one lentil for supper. "Didn't you tell me to 'cook lentil' and not 'lentils'?" Aesop explains.[40] And we laugh.

The point here is not that slavery was a funny institution; it most certainly was not, any more than tyranny was. Nevertheless, in the imaginative economy of Rome—from popular theater to satiric biography—laughter and joking, with many different nuances, offered a way of representing, or occluding, the interface between slaves and their owners. Laughter stood (or was imagined to stand) at the interfaces of power.

LAUGHTER AND IMPERIAL REALITY: EMPERORS AND JESTERS

But what of social reality? In investigating the role of written laughter in the cultural world of Rome, I have insisted that these ancient accounts of laughter and joking are not necessarily true. We cannot assume that they give us a window onto laughter as we might have heard or witnessed it in the imperial court or slave household. But important as those caveats are, they do not entirely dispose of the nagging question of how far these discursive tropes related to the real-life, face-to-face confrontation between ruler and ruled. If the downstairs world of the slave kitchen is completely lost to us, can we tentatively get a little closer to the social reality of laughter upstairs in the Roman palace and in the emperor's various interactions with his subjects?

Perhaps we can. There are hints that this jocularity was not merely a written convention of imperial biographers or elite Greco-Roman historians but actually marked some of the real-life encounters in the imperial court. One extraordinary version of such banter is found in an eyewitness description by one member of a Jewish delegation from Alexandria to the emperor Caligula in 40 CE.[41] Religious and ethnic conflict was endemic in Egyptian Alexandria, and the embassy had come to put the case of the Jews of the city against the rival envoys of the Greek gentile population. The eyewitness in question was the Jewish philosopher Philo. True, this is a very "literary" piece of writing: Philo was an elite intellectual observer of Roman imperial rule whose account of his encounter with Caligula was loaded, highly crafted, and composed against a background of wider conflicts between the emperor and the Jews (focused in part around Caligula's plan to erect a statue of himself in the Temple in Jerusalem). But Philo was from outside the formal Roman hierarchies of power, from a resistant subject people—yet, in describing his meeting with the emperor, he refers to banter very similar in style to some that we have already looked at. This time we are at least seeing it from the point of view—and the pen—of the petitioner.[42]

Philo conjures up a vivid impression of both the humiliation entailed in an encounter with Caligula and its various forms of—simultaneously reassuring, puzzling, and deeply threatening—jocularity. He and his fel-

low Jewish envoys had gone to put their case to the emperor in his garden estates (*horti*) on the edge of the city of Rome. At first the emperor
seemed cavalier and decidedly hostile, and Philo complains that his
embassy was not getting a serious hearing (part of Caligula's attention
was on the inspection of the properties on his estates and possible home
improvements, not on the Alexandrian Jews).[43] The emperor's first reaction was to "grin" threateningly at them (*sesērōs*)—as Commodus had
"grinned" at the senators in the Colosseum—and to call them "god hat-
ers" (on the grounds that they did not believe that he was a god). Hearing this, the rival group of envoys from Alexandria was overjoyed: "They
waved their arms, they danced up and down, and they appealed to him
by the titles of all the gods." Some argument about whether the Jews had
offered the proper loyal sacrifices followed—while Caligula continued to
inspect the buildings and order new fixtures and fittings. At this point,
Philo appeals to another area of the culture of ancient laughter: the Jews,
he writes, were being mocked by their opponents as if they were onstage
in a mime; in fact, the whole business was "like a mime."[44]

Things then took a different turn, as Caligula demanded of the Jews,
"Why do you not eat pork?" This caused their rivals to "burst out
laughing," partly because they were amused or delighted with what the
emperor had said, partly out of flattery. For just as we saw Terence
pointing to the use of laughter as flattery in some of the exchanges in his
Eunuch (see p. 12), Philo suggests that they wanted to suck up to
Caligula by making it seem as if they thought he had spoken "with wit
and charm." On this occasion, however, the flattery may have gone too
far: their laughter was so raucous that one of the imperial guards
thought it was showing disrespect to the emperor (and we might guess
he stepped a little closer to prevent any trouble).[45]

How heartily, then, should you laugh at the emperor's jokes? There
were clearly competing views. The cautious Philo observes that unless
you were one of his close friends, it was not safe even to risk a silent
"smile" or "beam" (*meidiasai*). But if so, that is in direct contrast with
the tenor of the joking exchanges between emperor and subject that we
have seen in other literary texts, as well as with the tenor of Philo's own
account.[46] In fact, he goes on to describe another round of ostensibly
jocular bantering between Caligula and both deputations, again largely
on the subject of dietary restrictions. The Jews tried to explain that different people have different prohibitions and preferences, and one of
them intervened to point out that—never mind pork—a lot of people
did not eat lamb. That made the emperor laugh again: "Quite right," he

said, "because it's not nice." Philo considers this yet more mockery at the expense of the Jewish delegation, but in fact the emperor soon began to mellow (as Philo sees it, through the influence of God). Although his mind was still more on his new windows and rehanging some paintings, he concluded that the Jews were not so much wicked as foolish in their refusal to recognize his divinity—so he merely dismissed them, apparently reaching no judgment on the dispute between the Jews and the gentiles of Alexandria that had been put before him.[47]

This is a rich account of imperial laughter, even if it has been carefully recrafted into an overtly partisan account in the religious conflicts of the first century CE. It hints at a certain mismatch of the protocols of laughter, between the Jews and the Romans (how far is Philo [mis]reading jocularity as aggressive mockery, and does he correctly understand the regime of laughter appropriate in the imperial court?) and between the imperial guard and the Alexandrian Greeks (whose enthusiastic laughter was taken by the guard as disruptive or frankly threatening). But it certainly construes the encounter between these subordinate envoys and the emperor in more or less the same bantering terms that we have seen in literary texts of very different types and background.

Once more it is important to emphasize that we are a long way from (in Keith Thomas's words) hearing the laughter that surrounded the Roman emperor (see pp. 50–51), and in fact, in Philo's account, the imperial guardsman's objection to the laughter of the gentile delegation is a reminder of how policed any such outbursts might have been. But it also suggests that it is right to see laughter, threatening as it might be, as one important element in the real-life power relations between emperor and people—and a more audible and strident presence in Roman imperial court culture than we usually credit.

JESTERS AND CLOWNS

There are other hints of the prominence of laughter—notably in the presence of designated "laughter makers" in the imperial palace and other elite contexts. In fact, some of the pranks of Elagabalus (exaggerated as the stories in his *Life* certainly are) may not have been so very different in spirit from some of the japes and jocularity that jesters and jokers brought to Roman society, right up to (and perhaps especially among) its uppermost echelons.

The emperor's court seems to have featured a range of comics, and we know the names of some famous jesters associated with particular rulers. We have already glimpsed Sarmentus (see p. 68), a *scurra* in the circle of Maecenas and Augustus, whose jokes Quintilian references somehow (the surviving text is defective and makes no sense).[48] Gabba was another famous Augustan court jokester—whose name was still enough of a literary household word a hundred years later for Martial to compare him to Capitolinus, a prominent jester at the court of Nerva and Trajan (Martial judged Capitolinus the funnier, but on what basis—apart from a strategic preference for the living over the dead— we do not know).[49] Another might be Nero's Vatinius, whose name was an uncanny or contrived throwback to Cicero's jocular adversary (see pp. 106, 122–23).[50] But we also read of groups of jesters or other performers rather too low in laughter's pecking order to feature prominently as individuals in elite histories.

One particular group—named or nicknamed *copreae* in Latin, *kopriai* (little shits) in Greek[51]—seems to have belonged exclusively in the Roman palace or among Roman autocrats. That at least is what the usage of the terms suggests (scant as the surviving evidence is), for they only ever refer to characters in the immediate court circle.[52] Dio, for example, claims that after the death of Commodus, there was a cause célèbre about the "little shits" who survived him. In the posthumous propaganda campaign against the emperor's memory, it was said that people laughed when they were told what the nicknames of these jokesters had been but (not unlike in some modern outrages about public sector salaries) were hugely angry when they learned how much they had been paid.[53] Suetonius mentions in passing the *copreae* who used to attend Tiberius' dinner table,[54] and he tells of the nasty practical jokes they used to play on Claudius before he came to the throne.

Slow, awkward, and misshapen, Claudius was an easy target of the jests of his nephew the ruling emperor Caligula—especially as he was in the habit, so it was said, of dropping off to sleep after dinner while the party was still going on. The *copreae* used to wake him up with a whip "as if they were playing a game" (*velut per ludum*), and it was presumably these same jokesters who used to put "slippers" (*socci*) on his hands while he was snoring, so that when he stirred, he "would rub his face with them."[55] It is not entirely clear what the joke was here. *Socci* had rough bottoms, so presumably Claudius scratched his face. But was there some further significance in them? Perhaps so. *Socci* were a type of footwear sometimes associated with women or effeminate luxury, and this alone might have raised a laugh when Claudius found them on his hands—the ancient equivalent of putting diamond-studded stilettos on his hands, maybe.[56] They were also part of the kit both of comic actors (an association that could be taken to imply that the ungainly prince had become a comic spectacle) and of parasites (to whose role in laughter and at dinners I shall shortly turn).[57] But however precisely we read the joke here (and it may, of course, have operated in any number of ways), however close a reflection of real court life the report of this incident may have been, there is something undeniably reminiscent of Elagabalus' jests about the scene.[58]

These *copreae* are an intriguing but elusive group. They make the occasional appearance in accounts of Roman palace life, but we cannot trace them right down to the hard, documentary evidence of their tombstones or memorials. The funerary record of the city of Rome does, however, offer one glimpse of a curious laughter maker, from the imperial court itself—on what remains of a small, now broken commemorative plaque found just outside the city of Rome in a communal tomb for members of the imperial household.[59] It originally marked the niche for the ashes of a man who had been, as it says, a *lusor Caesaris* (a player of Caesar). His name is now missing, but those two words alone indicate that he was a slave of the emperor and that his business was some kind of entertainment. The short description that follows fills out the picture of the man and his life: "dumb eloquent [*mutus argutus*], a mimic [*imitator*] of the emperor Tiberius, the man who first discovered how to imitate barristers [*causidici*]."

What exactly this means—and in particular what it tells us about the character of his act—is not easy to fathom. It was once popularly thought that *Mutus Argutus* was the dead man's name.[60] This is extremely unlikely (for that would surely have featured in the now lost first lines of the text). But suppose it were a name—then it must certainly have been a stage sobriquet, for it is a paradoxical pairing, meaning something like "silent but sharp" or "silent but eloquent."[61] Some have suggested, not implausibly, that it should be seen as the slogan of a pantomime actor, in which case the man's act would have been a mime (in the modern sense of that word—he didn't speak).[62] But there is also a striking link here with the narrative of Aesop, who was, as we have seen, at first dumb, then powerfully eloquent, and there is perhaps a hint too at similarities in the style of banter inscribed in Aesop's *Life* and in the jesting culture of the court.

The next words of the text—"a mimic of the emperor Tiberius"—presumably indicate that he was a mimic owned by Tiberius. The slightly awkward Latin could also mean that he was a mimic whose act was to imitate Tiberius (though that would be, one imagines, a risky business).[63] But the final words of the text make clear that the highlight in his repertoire—and his own particular innovation—was mimicry of barristers. It is not, at first sight, easy to imagine the scene at Tiberius' dinner parties (assuming that is where these performances took place[64]) with our entertainer as the star turn. Did the emperor really look forward to a session of after-dinner lawyer imitations? Or did the act consist in something more like spoof declamations? We do not know. But the message of these fragmentary, fleeting, and often overlooked pieces of evidence seems clear: laughter was not only important in the discourse of imperial power but may also have been much more prominent in the social practice of the imperial court than is often assumed.

So it was too in the practice of the elite Roman household more generally. At least, there were more clowns around than we often bother to notice. Beyond various types of dinnertime comic entertainers who may or may not have been hired in,[65] we find clear cases of jesters who were permanent residents in houses of the rich. Seneca briefly discusses an intriguing example—interestingly, a woman—in one of his philosophical letters to Lucilius. He refers to the elderly Harpaste, in his own household, his wife's female clown (*fatua*), who had come to them as part of a legacy. It is a complicated reference. Seneca implies that part of Harpaste's comic character is that she is a "freak" (*prodigium*), and he reflects briefly (and archly) on prompts to laughter ("If I want to be amused by a clown, I don't have far to look: I laugh at myself"). He introduces too, as the central philosophical message of the letter, moral reflections about human folly and blindness, for Harpaste has recently gone blind but does not realize it, so keeps complaining that her room is too dark.[66] All the same, philosophical metaphor or not, it is also one clear sign that clowns could have a place in the domestic sphere of the rich.

To push this a little further—and much more speculatively—we might wonder how far the jester and jesting culture had a structural role to play in what we have come to call Roman elite "self-fashioning." If the jester was a regular presence in the domestic world of the elite, how far was the construction and self-imaging of the Roman elite male partly a process carried out in the face of, or against, the ribald, deformed, clever, joking image of the clown? Should we be seeing the clown—as Carlin Barton long ago suggested—as a distorting mirror against, or in, which the Roman saw and defined himself?[67]

I shall return to that question in the final section of this chapter, in the context of the *scurra*. But for the moment, let me suggest that this idea might help to give a different perspective on a couple of our favorite conundrums of Roman cultural and religious history. The first concerns the jesters and mimics who accompanied an elite Roman funeral, imitating, among other things, the actions of the deceased. In the funeral procession of Vespasian, for example, "Favor, a star mime actor, who wore his [Vespasian's] mask, . . . loudly asked procurators what the cost of the funeral and the procession was. When he heard it was ten million sesterces, he shouted, 'Give me a hundred thousand and chuck me in the Tiber.'" A good joke, as Suetonius reports it, on Vespasian's well-known stinginess.[68] The second are the ribald songs and scurrilous rhymes chanted apparently at the expense of the successful general at a Roman triumph. "Romans, lock up your wives. The bald adulterer's back in town" were the lyrics used at the triumph of Julius Caesar in 46 BCE, harping on that classic topic of a Roman joke—hair loss.[69]

The function of these customs has long been a puzzle. One of the commonest explanations, which economically kills both birds with one stone, is that the ribaldry or jesting in each case was "apotropaic." This word is sufficiently technical to appear to be explanatory while also being agreeably primitive—as if we were going back into the deepest wellsprings of earliest Roman tradition. How far any Roman laughter is usefully understood in these terms is debatable.[70] But it has always seemed to me that in these two cases (and in the more domestic case of the dog at the door that I looked at earlier, on pp. 58–59), the word shelves the problems rather than solves them. For one thing, it is far from clear what the laughter is supposed to be apotropaic of—what did it ward off?[71]

We might, I venture, get further if we did not think here entirely in terms of some murky area of Victorian anthropology. It is worth reflecting instead that we are witnessing in these instances other examples of the proximity between the elite Roman and the joker. Perhaps more pointedly, we are seeing, reenacted and writ large in these ceremonies, public analogues to the domestic role of jokers in the imperial court or rich mansions at Rome. At the very least, that domestic role hints that it may be less surprising than we usually assume to find jesters and jests so prominent on these ceremonial occasions. The joker accompanied the Roman at the moment of his greatest success—and to the grave. It was in the ribaldry of the jester that one version of Roman elite identity was defined and paraded.[72]

It is to further reflections on these Roman jokers—to the cultural ideology that surrounded them, the cultural connections they signaled, the problems they raised, and the prime contexts in which they were imagined to operate—that I now turn. I am moving away again from the elusive day-to-day reality of Roman social life, back toward the rather more clearly delineated structures of the Roman imaginary and its symbolic assumptions and stereotypes. I start by focusing on the figure of the parasite and the different kinds of laughter associated with the Roman dinner table—raising, in particular, issues of truth and sincerity and the way in which "laughter to order" both oiled the wheels of the Roman social hierarchy and threatened to derail them. I finish, in the final section, by reflecting more precisely on the idea of the *scurra*. Most of the time the Roman emperor still lurks in the background—though the very last character we will meet face-to-face is an early Christian martyr in a poem that turns the elite stereotype of *scurrilitas* on its head and parades the brave victim of Roman persecution as a perfect *scurra*.

DINNERTIME LAUGHTER, PARASITES, AND A SLAVE KING

I have pointed to laughter and banter between the great and the small, emperor and subject, in a wide range of contexts: from the baths through the open streets to the emperor's garden estates. But the key setting for jesters, laughter, and jocular exchanges across the hierarchies of power was that most deceptively (un)hierarchical of Roman institutions: the dinner party or banquet. It was here that Elagabalus was supposed to have deflated his whoopee cushions, it was here that "little shits" played pranks on Claudius with slippers, and it was to a dinner that Caligula invited the man whose son he had just had put to death "and pushed him to laughing and joking." There is much more to this than the simple fact that dinner was an occasion of play and fun. There was an important interrelationship between jokes and jokers, flattery and food, against the background of the markedly unequal structures of Roman dining and its representations.

It goes almost without saying that the Roman banquet was a paradoxical institution. On the one hand, it promoted equality, in the sense that eating together is one of the most powerful ways of putting all participants on an equal footing; the basic principle of commensality is that those who eat the same are the same (or, for the moment at least, can count themselves as such). On the other hand, it represented, in a particularly vivid way, the inequalities of the diners: the way the food was served, the order of serving, and the seating plan reinforced rather than undermined social hierarchies. Several Roman writers pointed disapprovingly to the practice of serving inferior guests inferior food.[73] And according to the *Augustan History,* another trick of Elagabalus' was to literalize that inequality by serving the least prestigious diners food that was not merely worse than their superiors' but entirely inedible: "To the freeloaders [*parasiti*] during the dessert course he often served food of wax or wood or ivory, sometimes pottery, occasionally marble or stone, so that everything was served to them too, but only to be looked at and made out of a different material from what he himself was eating, while they only drank through the individual courses and washed their hands as if they had eaten."[74] Part of the joke here rests on the idea of imitation and mimicry: something is pretending to be food when it is not (just as when Petronius too, in conjuring up Trimalchio's dinner party, hilariously focuses on the bluff and double bluff of food that appears somehow in disguise[75]). But the more sinister side of the joke is that it writes in stone (or wax or wood) the inequities of the imperial dinner table.

The general idea that Roman elite dining was a prime context for the display of social hierarchies (even if they were also partially hidden under the mask of commensality) is well established.[76] Less discussed has been the part that jokes and laughter played within that unequal culinary economy: from the role of the joker in exposing the differentials of power and status to the way in which the underprivileged are represented as exchanging jokes (and, along with jokes, flattery) for food.[77] It is this "culinary triangle," of laughter, flattery, and food, that is highlighted in some wonderfully self-aware snatches of ancient writing.[78]

In classical and Hellenistic Greece, just as at Rome, it was a common idea (or conceit) that a poor scrounger could earn his place at the dinner table through laughter—or, more generally, that there was a trade-off between the economy of laughter and the economy of food. We have already seen in chapter 1 the role in Terence's *Eunuch* of the "parasite," who earned his keep by laughing at the feeble jokes of his patron, whether they were funny or not. That basic principle is reflected also in the definition offered by one late antique commentator on another passage of Terence: "*Parasite* is the word for someone who eats with me or at my house, because *para* [in Greek] means 'at' and *sitos* [in Greek] means 'food.' Or else parasites are so called from obeying [*parendo*] and standing by [*assistendo*], since standing by their superiors they serve their pleasure through flattery."[79]

By suggesting different etymologies—one Greek, one Latin—this commentator points to what has been a major topic of debate: the pre-

cise relationship between Greek parasites and their Roman counterparts, particularly as they appear in the comedies of Plautus and Terence. How far was the idea essentially Hellenic, sketchily translated into
a Roman context? What adjustments or contributions came from the
Roman side? Overall, it does seem fairly clear that—whatever its Greek
origins—the figure of the parasite became naturalized at Rome and
played a part in Roman cultural debate that went beyond (even if it
remained in dialogue with) its Greek models. Cynthia Damon in particular has powerfully argued that the parasite as a cultural category
was deeply integrated into debates at Rome around that central Roman
institution patronage: or to put it more strongly, the stereotype was
developed as a negative symbolic antitype of the Roman client, combining flattery, exploitation, and humiliation.[80] It is no coincidence that in
the description of Elagabalus' discriminatory menus, it is the parasites
who were the recipients of the fake food.

Laughter is a key coordinate too. For on the one hand, the freeloader
laughed to cue, providing a reliably laughing audience for the jokes,
good or bad, of his patron. On the other, he could be expected to *produce* laughter among the other guests in return for a good meal—as we
find already in Xenophon's *Symposium* (written sometime in the first
half of the fourth century BCE), where Philip the jester arrives hungry
and more or less uninvited and makes himself welcome through mimicry and joking.[81] This idea comes over even more strongly in various
Roman comedies (whatever their precise relationship with their Greek
sources of inspiration)—where we meet a number of characters who
swap jokes for a free meal while vociferously complaining about their
lot.[82] It is a particularly vivid theme in Plautus' *Stichus*, whose most
prominent character (despite the title, which blazons the name of
another) is a parasite, the aptly named Gelasimus (Mr. Laugher, from
the Greek *gelaō*). The play is cruelly concerned with the trials of a parasite's life.[83]

Early in the drama, Gelasimus turns to the audience to try to get a
dinner out of one of them in return for a joke: "I'm selling jokes," he
says. "Come on, make a bid. Who'll say dinner? Anyone give me lunch?
. . . Was that a nod? You won't find better jokes anywhere."[84] In fact,
what he is trying, jokingly, to auction off is not only jokes but the whole
parodic paraphernalia of the parasite—including his private jokebooks,
that collection of pre-prepared wit and one-liners that had been his regular meal ticket until the dinner invitations dried up. Later in the play,
when he has abandoned the sale, we find him referring to his books in

an effort to dig out the right jokes to impress his patron ("I've consulted my books: I'm sure as I can be that I'll keep my patron with my jokes").[85] Throughout the play, various ambiguities of laughter recur, almost as a linking theme. One, as we might expect, focuses on the word *ridiculus:* the parasite is actively *ridiculus,* in the sense that he prompts laughter in others with witty gags; he is also passively *ridiculus,* in that he and his plight are repeatedly laughed at. Another aspect of ambiguity is exploited by the character of Epigonus, Gelasimus' once and possibly future patron. In addressing the parasite, he plays on Gelasimus' name, with more Latinized Greek—derived now from the Greek *katagelaō* (deride or laugh at). "I don't want you to stop being a laugher," he says at one point, "and become a laugher at me" ("Nunc ego non volo ex Gelasimo mihi fieri te Catagelasimum").[86]

There is a complex set of issues and identities at stake in the image of the parasite and the laughter he both voices and attracts. Of course, the material we have is entirely from the perspective of the elite and disapproving observer. Even if the plots of some of the comedies encourage us to imagine the world from the point of view of the underdog, the word *parasite,* like *flatterer,* remains a loaded and hostile value judgment, not a self-descriptor. That said, it is clear that one major social fault line reflected in (and exploited by) Roman literature was precisely the problematic relationship between flattery, laughter, and the supposed friendship between host and guest—or more generally between the powerful and their hangers-on. A prominent issue in the Greco-Roman ethics of social behavior was "how to tell a flatterer from a (real) friend."[87] That issue is magnified in debates that cluster around the image of the parasite—in which we see how the demands of flattery risked undercutting the sincerity of laughter and exposing the (hungry) sycophant and the vain host for what they were. What is more, the laughter of the flatterer could be hard for the host or patron to distinguish from the laughter of derision directed against himself, or accidentally rebounding onto him. The sentiments of Epigonus in the *Stichus* are, in fact, not very different from those of Xanthus that we read in the *Life of Aesop* (p. 139): "Are you laughing or taking the mickey?"

These dilemmas are cleverly captured in a letter of Seneca, who (among other verbal nuances) plays with the possible ambiguities of the word *arrideo*—which can mean not only "to laugh in response to" but also "to laugh supportively" and so also "to flatter" (see above, pp. 71–72). Seneca is discussing a tedious and foolish host, Calvius Sabinus, the consul of 26 CE, who had slaves specially trained to remember great works of literature word for word; they stood at the foot of his couch at dinner and prompted him in reciting the lines (which, even with their help, he still could not manage). It was too much for one of his subordinate guests, Satellius Quadratus, who was driven to quip about the stupidity of it all. In telling this story, Seneca links the behavior of the one who comes to eat up the food (*arrosor*), the one who comes to flatter/laugh supportively (*arrisor*), and the one who comes to quip or to laugh at their meal ticket (*derisor*)—in this case, all the same person, of course. Quadratus was, he says, "a feeder off the foolish rich and—what follows—a flatterer of them and, what is connected to both, a laugher at them."[88]

The issue of the laugher's sincerity is highlighted in a different way in a story of Dionysius II, the fourth-century BCE tyrant of Syracuse. This is preserved in Athenaeus' late second-century CE anthology and encyclopedia, *The Philosophers' Banquet,* in a section devoted entirely to anecdotes about parasites, including their excesses, playfulness, loyalties, and disloyalties.[89] Athenaeus offers a colorful range of these characters, from Cleisophus, the parasite of Philip of Macedon (who limped when the king was wounded in the leg and made a face when the king tasted bitter food, as if he also had eaten it[90]), to Andromachus of Carrhae, the parasite of Licinius Crassus (who ended up betraying his patron to the Parthians and so bringing about his defeat in the Battle of Carrhae in 53 BCE[91]). The story of Dionysius focuses directly on the problems of laughter. The tyrant challenged one of his hangers-on, Cheirisophus, who had laughed when he noticed Dionysius laughing some distance away and out of earshot. Why, he asked, was the man laughing when he could not possibly have heard what was being said?—a question that risked disrupting the implied contract between the patron and the laughing flatterer (that the flatterer must laugh when the patron does) by exposing its underlying hypocrisy. The clever flatterer replied, "I trust you that what was said was funny." He reestablished the contract, in other words (albeit in a way that not even the most gullible patron would be able to take entirely seriously).[92]

A more complicated and even more revealing example of this kind of dilemma is found in the vast *Library of History* by Diodorus—from the Roman province of Sicily (hence his now conventional name, Diodorus Siculus)—who wrote in Greek, in the first century BCE. This was a comprehensive project, tracing the history of the known world from its mythic origins to the present day.[93] In one section, which survives only in quotations in Byzantine anthologies, he discusses the origins of the slave revolts that broke out in Sicily in the second century BCE. The leader of the revolts was a slave from Apameia in Syria called Eunus, whose claims to authority over his fellow slaves rested in part on the idea that the Syrian goddess (Atargatis) directly inspired him and had made him king. According to Diodorus, his master, Antigenes, treated these claims as an amusing bit of fun, and so he proceeded to give the slave the role of jester, but with an unexpected upshot:

> As the whole thing was taken for a bit of amusement, his master Antigenes, enchanted by the hocus-pocus, used to introduce Eunus (for that was the charlatan's name) at his dinner parties and question him about his kingship and how he would treat each of those present. And when he gave a full account without any hesitation . . . laughter used to overtake the guests, and some of them, picking up some tasty morsels from the table, would present them to him, interjecting that when he became king, he should remember the kindness. But it turned out that his charlatanism really did result in kingship, and he made recompense in earnest for what he had received in jest [*en gelōti*] at the banquets.[94]

That is to say, in the carnage that really did follow, Eunus did not kill those who had fed him at the table.

This is a marvelously dense passage, which exploits and enmeshes many of the issues we have been exploring in this chapter: dining, hierarchy, joking, subverted reality, truth and falsehood, autocracy and power. It involves a slave who is treated as a jester and fed by the diners in return for his jokes. Yet the jokes turn out not to be mere fiction ("jokes as lies," as Quintilian would have seen it; pp. 125–26); they are the real plans of a slave who is claiming the status of king and patron for himself. In fact, in his role as king, he goes on to respect the patronage relationships of the dinner (joking as they may have been)—sparing the lives of those who had in their turn respected the patronage relationship by feeding him tidbits. Almost all the cultural norms of dining, patronage, and jocularity come together in this apparently simple story.

THE *SCURRA*

More than anything else, the shadow of the Roman *scurra* has stalked the pages of this book. We have seen how he represented a disreputable form of joking: vulgar, imitative, unspontaneous—though at the same time almost guaranteed to raise a laugh. We have also seen how accusations of *scurrilitas* could be used in the infighting among the Roman elite. To his enemies, Cicero was "a *scurra* of a consul," while he could criticize the jokes of others as far too like the quips of a *scurra*. There was something (as we might say) lippy or in-your-face about the *scurra;* in Roman terms, it was his *dicacitas* (lippiness) that made the emperor Vespasian appear *scurrilis* (like a *scurra*). Another good example of this style of banter (and its dangerous consequences) is found in Suetonius' story of the pointed gibe of a *scurra* against the stinginess of the emperor Tiberius. The man called out to the corpse in a passing funeral to ask it to take a message to the dead emperor Augustus that the legacies he had left to the Roman people had not been paid. He got his comeuppance: Tiberius ordered him to be put to death, but not before he had been given his money, so he could take the message to the underworld that the dues had been paid.[95]

There was also something that was—or was thought to be—characteristically Roman about the *scurra*. At least, the word was seen to be more or less untranslatable into Greek, even in antiquity. I have already suggested that it may have underlain the Greek *geloios* in Plutarch's version of Cato's quip about Cicero (see pp. 102–3). Even more strikingly, when Zeno of Sidon was talking of Socrates and wanted, presumably, to call attention to his subversive repartee, he called him "an Athenian *scurra*"—using, as Cicero (to whom we owe the reference) says, "the Latin word."[96] There was nothing in Greek, we may imagine, that would quite capture it. The marked "Romanness" of the word was part of the reason, no doubt, that Eduard Fraenkel adopted the term *Skurrilität* to refer to some distinctively Plautine (that is, non-Greek) elements in Plautus.[97]

But can we get closer than this to the character, identity, or social role of the *scurra*? That has always proved difficult.[98] We can detect all kinds of overlaps between *scurrae* and the so-called parasites of Greek and Roman comedy. It is hard, for example, not to be struck by the ready-made jokebooks of Gelasimus, which seem to fit very closely with some of the complaints of Cicero and Quintilian about the wit of the *scurra*: namely, that it was prepared in advance and that its targets were a whole class rather than an individual. Yet Gelasimus is never called *scurra*—while others in Plautus, sometimes rather smart urban types, sometimes meddling busybodies, are,[99] and so is the jester Sarmentus in Horace's *Satire*. Certainly the more or less standard translation of *scurra* as "buffoon" captures no more than part of the meaning of some of its usages.

The fact is that if we examine carefully all the people designated by this term in ancient literature, we find an apparently baffling range, from the urban flaneurs of Roman comedy through jokers and jesters in a narrower sense to Socrates or even members of the Praetorian Guard. In fact, according to the *Augustan History*, that jocular emperor Elagabalus himself was eventually murdered by *scurrae*. It is tempting to see this as a wonderfully appropriate end (a "scurrile" emperor killed by *scurrae*), but the standard assumption is that the reference here is to soldiers of the guard (with *scurra* used to reflect their city base, or "urbanity," in contrast to those troops stationed through the empire).[100]

So did the meaning of the term change over time, as Philip Corbett wondered in his essay on the *scurra*? Was there a move from an amateur to a professional sense of the term, or vice versa? Did the role of *scurra* as a social category change over the course of Roman history? Were there in fact several very different social phenomena that, for whatever reason, were lumped together under the single designation *scurra*? These are not necessarily stupid questions, but they probably miss the main point of *scurrilitas*. For not unlike *parasite* in Damon's analysis, it was hardly a simple referential term. It was, rather, a category within the imaginative economy and social policing of Roman laughter: the constructed, and shifting, antitype to the elite male jokester; the jesting transgressor of elite male values of jesting—symbiotically tied to, incomprehensible without, and always (as Cicero knew, to his cost) liable to merge with its opposite. *Scurra,* in other words, was a (negative) value judgment on the practices of laughter rather than a descriptor, a cultural constructor (and mirror) of the jocularity of the Roman elite.[101]

Or so it seems from the elite texts we have. But did the term look different from the point of view of those who did not have a stake in the elite culture of Roman laughter? Were there contexts in which it could be positively revalued, even worn as a (subversive) badge of pride? I have already regretted that we have no view of "parasites" except through the eyes of those ancient writers committed to despise them. The same is broadly true for the *scurra*—except for one precious glimpse from the fourth century CE and its religious conflicts. The glimpse in question comes from Prudentius' horribly gruesome cycle of poems *The Crowns of Martyrdom,* where we find the *scurra* reappropriated in a very different, Christian context.[102]

The second poem of the collection tells, in almost six hundred lines, the story of the martyrdom of Saint Laurence, who was roasted to death, slowly, on a gridiron in 258 CE. In a famous moment that became almost the slogan of this martyrdom (ll. 401–4), Laurence asked to be turned over just before his death, as one side was already cooked (hence, in part, his later role as the patron saint of chefs). Prudentius gives a detailed, vivid, and (presumably) highly embroidered, if not fictional, verse account of the clash between the saint and his elite pagan prosecutor. It starts with the pagan Roman demanding the wealth of the Christian church, which he believes is being concealed and not "rendered unto Caesar" (ll. 94–98). Begging for a delay, to bring out "all the precious things that Christ has" (ll. 123–24), Laurence tricks his prosecutor and parades before him the poor and the sick of Rome, as the treasures of the church. This does not go down well, and Laurence soon finds himself on the gridiron.

The style of this encounter is distinctive. Laurence is a clever, shifty, and witty character who teases the prosecutor dreadfully, and laughter plays a major role in this. Confronted with the sick and the poor as the treasures of the church, the prosecutor says, "We're being laughed at [*ridemur*]" (l. 313). He goes on to explode, "You rascal, do you think you are getting away with weaving together such great tricks with mimic mockery [*cavillo mimico*] while you act out your tale like a *scurra*? Did it seem to match your *urbanitas* to treat me with jokes [*ludicris*]? Have I been sold off to the cacklers as a bit of festival entertainment?" (ll. 317–22). At the very end of the poem, we find that those worshiping the saint not only beg him for help and tell his story but also pick up Laurence's style and "joke" (*iocantur*).[103]

Urbanitas, cavillatio, a *scurra,* and mimicry. All the old Roman terminology of jesting is on display—a testimony to its cultural longevity. In a powerful recent analysis of the poem, Catherine Conybeare focused on its jocularity, which she saw in terms of gender: that is, in terms of a conflict between the masculinity of the aggressive prosecutor and the effeminacy of a subversively witty saint.[104] But there is an even more straightforward point to be made about laughter here. For this poem of martyrdom replays that symbiotic relationship between elite Roman and jester, subverting it within a new context. The Christian writer has appropriated and revalued the role of the *scurra,* as the joking, jesting hero of the tale: the martyr as *scurra* has become the symbiotic antitype of his pagan persecutor.

Who knows if centuries earlier, long before the conflicts between "pagan" and Christian, *scurrilitas* was something in which those outside the corridors of power took pride?

CHAPTER 7

Between Human and Animal— Especially Monkeys and Asses

This book has so far featured rather few Roman women. We have glimpsed the image of the laughing prostitute (pp. 3, 80). And we have seen Augustus' daughter, Julia, as the butt of her father's good-humored banter about gray hair and baldness (pp. 132–33). According to Roman tradition, Julia was not merely on the receiving end of jokes. Alongside the anecdote about her hair plucking, Macrobius' *Saturnalia* includes a number of memorable quips that she was said to have made herself, several engaging transgressively with the moral policy of her father's regime.[1] One of the favorites for modern scholars has been her calculating approach to adultery (*flagitia,* "disgraceful behavior," as it is called here) and illegitimate births: "When those who knew of her disgraceful behavior were amazed how her sons looked like her husband Agrippa even though she gave her body for any Tom, Dick, or Harry to enjoy, she said, 'I never take on a passenger unless the ship's hold is full.'"[2]

This idea that the emperor's daughter exploited her legitimate pregnancies (when "the ship's hold is full") as an opportunity for sleeping around might be read as an outright attack on Augustus' moral legislation. Or it might be seen as banter in the risqué style of some of the emperor's own joking encounters (see p. 131). Either way, its apparently blithe self-confidence is dramatically undercut—for those who know the full story—by the fact that Julia ended up exiled for her adulteries and died a lonely death in the same year as her father.[3]

One thing that we almost entirely miss in Rome is the tradition of subversive female laughter—what we call giggling—that is a distinctive strand in modern Western culture and can be glimpsed as far back as Geoffrey Chaucer. Although in the first chapter of this book I semiseriously call Dio's stifled outburst in the Colosseum "giggles," for us that form of laughter, including its cultural and literary construction, is almost exclusively associated with women and "girls"; in its strongest form, it is, in Angela Carter's words, "the innocent glee with which women humiliate men."[4] If there was any such well-established, female alternative gelastic tradition in Roman culture, there is little reflection of it in surviving literature.[5] Unsurprisingly, perhaps, because despite its significance in women's popular culture, until recently it was a form of laughter that tended to exist outside the dominant orthodoxy, hardly figuring in male literary or cultural traditions for centuries, except to be ridiculed itself ("giggling schoolgirls"). It is not—as Carter observed of Alison's outburst at the expense of her cuckolded husband in Chaucer's "The Miller's Tale"—"a sound which is heard very often in literature."[6]

For the most part, women's laughter is carefully policed in the literary representations of the Roman world. It does not seem to represent, as a specifically gendered form, much of a threat to male egos or to male traditions of laughter and joking, or at least the rules and regulations, implicit or explicit, were intended to ensure that it did not. As on so many topics, the reflections of Ovid are notably smart here. For in the third book of the *Art of Love*—his mock instructional poem on how to catch (and keep) a partner—he parodies the norms of female laughter, in the process exposing some of the cultural fault lines in Roman gelastic conventions. He also introduces what will be the main theme of this chapter: the boundary between humans and animals, which laughter helps both to establish and to challenge. It will come as no surprise to readers familiar with the misogynistic structures of ancient thought that the laughter of women leads "naturally" on to the braying and roaring of the animal kingdom.

After two books of advice to young men—on where to hang out to make your catch (races and triumphal processions are hot spots), on being sure to remember her birthday, on playing a little hard to get, and so on—in the third book, the narrator turns to a different group of pupils. Love's mock (and mocking) "schoolmaster" now proceeds to give instructions to the female of the species. A couple of hundred lines are devoted to the care of the body, the style of the hair, and disguising your less attractive features, but then Ovid changes gear slightly. A warning to women not to laugh if they have unattractive teeth (black, too big, or crooked) launches some more general lessons in laughter. "Who would believe it?" he asks. "Girls even learn how to laugh."[7]

Well, believe it or not, he goes on to run through the main points on the syllabus of laughter. "Let the mouth," he urges, "open only so far. And keep those *lacunae* on each side small." *Lacuna* usually means "a gap" or "a hole"—but here, and only here in surviving Latin literature, it is presumably being used for what we would call a dimple.[8] How a girl could ever control her dimples is, of course, hard to imagine. But there is more complicated advice to come: "They should make sure that the bottom of the lips covers the top of the teeth, and they should not strain their sides by laughing continually but make a nice little feminine sound."

There is a good deal of characteristic Ovidian wit in this passage. Part of the joke rests on the idea that laughter could ever be the subject of instruction. "You'll never believe this," the artful teacher says. And of course we don't—but we are given the lessons all the same. Some, like the dimple regime, are more or less impossible to carry out. Others are close to incomprehensible. Commentators and translators have struggled for generations to make practical sense of "Et summos dentes ima labella tegant." "Make sure the bottom of the lips covers the top of the teeth" is certainly one possible way of rendering it; so too is "Make sure the lower lips cover the top teeth." But what could either possibly mean? "As often" one commentator despairs, ". . . Ovid's virtuoso technical display reads well, but is hard to pin down."[9] But is that not exactly Ovid's point? It is laughable to suggest, he is hinting to his readership, that you could ever learn to control the physicality of laughter. You could never follow these spuriously technical instructions; that's the joke.

Ovid concludes his advice with some warning examples of how a girl might get her laughter wrong, and this takes us almost directly to the animal kingdom. "There's one kind of girl," he writes, "who distorts her face with a frightful guffaw; there's another who you'd think was crying, when she is actually creased with laughing. Then there's one that makes a harsh noise without any charm—laughing like an ugly donkey brays as she goes round the rough millstone."[10] That comparison between woman and donkey is particularly marked in the original Latin: in a prominent play on words ("ridet / ut rudet"), the girl *ridet* (laughs) like the donkey *rudet* (brays).

That pun points us to one of the great paradoxes of laughter for Roman writers, as for later theorists. On the one hand, laughter could be seen as a defining property of the human species. Yet on the other hand, it was in laughing, in the noise produced and the facial and bodily contortions of the laugher, that human beings most closely resembled animals. The awkward point was, quite simply, that the very attribute that defined the human's humanity simultaneously made him or her one of the beasts—a braying ass, for example. Or as Simon Critchley summed it up, writing of humor rather than laughter itself, "If humour is human, then it also, curiously, marks the limit of the human."[11]

Roman writing often highlights that paradox. In Ovid's literary lessons in laughter, it is underlined not only by the pun on *ridet* and *rudet*. When, a little earlier, the poet advises the girl that she should "let the mouth open only so far," the word used for the gap between the lips opened up in laughter is *rictus:* "sint modici rictus."[12] That is a word with two principal referents: the open mouth of the human laugh and the gaping jaws of an animal. And when it refers to a laugh, it almost always suggests a contortion of the face bordering on the bestial. In Lucretius it is the grimace of death, in Suetonius the foaming mouth (*spumante rictu*) of the deformed emperor Claudius.[13] But it is Ovid in the *Metamorphoses* who exploits the word most systematically and cleverly. We have already seen (pp. 136–37) how laughter marks the power relations between gods and humans in the poem. *Rictus* is often a marker of the change of status between human and animal, which is one of the poem's main motifs. When Io, for example, is turned into a heifer, one of the signs of the transformation is that she now has a *rictus* rather than a mouth, and the *rictus* contracts (*contrahitur rictus*) when she changes back into a human.[14]

Catullus exploits a similar idea when in poem 42 ("Adeste hendecasyllabi") he focuses on the laughter of a woman who has some drafts of his poetry and refuses to give them back. Addressed to the poet's verses themselves, it is a complicated poem cast in deceptively simple terms that draw on the traditions of invective, of popular Roman rough justice, and, as has more recently been argued, of Roman comedy.[15] It also has a lot say about laughter as such. The girl who has her hands on the writing tablets (a "foul tart," *putida moecha*) thinks Catullus himself a "joke" (*iocum*), but he turns the tables on her by attacking the laughter as well as the laugher. She laughs, he writes, *moleste ac mimice:* that is, "annoyingly" and, in one literal sense, "in the style of a mime actress"— a word that, as we shall see (p. 171), is more complicated than this translation implies and goes right to the heart of one important aspect of Roman laughter culture. But more than that, she laughs "with the face of a Gallic hound," *catuli ore Gallicani*. Part of the joke must rest on the obvious pun (*catuli/Catulli*), but the image in general serves to undermine the humanity of the human laugher: the open mouth, distorted face, and no doubt bared teeth turn the woman into a beast.[16]

In the rest of this chapter I shall explore how laughter impacts on that boundary between humans and animals—highlighting other aspects of the figure of the parasite, now appearing in animal guise, and thinking harder about the roles of both mime and imitation (failed as much as successful) as key prompts to Roman laughter. I will start with "monkeys," or "apes" (shamelessly lumping all primates together interchangeably under those two popular headings[17]), and will highlight one of the notable ancient theories about laughter that these animals prompted. And I shall end with donkeys, or asses—encountering en route some famous agelasts of the Roman world, those notorious characters who were said never, or only very rarely, to have laughed. One important text will be Apuleius' *Metamorphoses,* or, as it is often now known, *The Golden Ass.* For not only does this novel explicitly focus on the boundary between man and donkey (the hero Lucius being accidentally transformed into an ass and finally, thanks to the goddess Isis, back into human form again), but one major episode in its plot is a (spoof) festival of the god Laughter (Risus).

These themes will open up another set of ideological entanglements. In the previous chapter I pointed to the connections between laughter, different forms of political and civic hierarchy, and the *convivium,* or banquet. Here the entanglement is, I should warn you, even more entangled: between laughter and mimicry, mime and the contested frontier that separates the human and animal species. That is part of the point. I want to explore the unexpected cultural connections that are exposed if you follow laughter's thread. I shall also return to that Janus-faced aspect of Roman laughter: the close links in ancient Rome between those people who make you laugh and those you laugh at.

MONKEY BUSINESS

Monkeys and apes were supposed to make Romans crack up—in a tradition of laughter that stretched back, or so they imagined, to early Greece.[18] One of the guests at the dinner party staged in Athenaeus' *The Philosophers' Banquet* refers to a story about the (semilegendary) sixth-century BCE Syrian sage Anacharsis on just this theme. Anacharsis was once at a party where jesters were brought in, and he remained solemnly unlaughing (*agelastos*). But when a monkey was brought in, then he started to laugh.[19] Why were monkeys so funny? And can the laughter that erupted around them help us understand some of the other chuckles and chortles that were said to resound around other parts of Roman culture?

Primates are good to think with. Modern science since Charles Darwin has famously debated the question of whether primates laugh, and if so, whether the physical response we might (or might not) call their "laughter" is significantly different from our own.[20] That was not, so far as we know, a concern of Greek and Roman writers, who did not use the behavior of apes to challenge the idea that only humans (plus or minus the occasional heron; see pp. 33–34) laughed. They negotiated the boundary between apes and humans in other ways, concerned not only with the similarities between primates and humans but more particularly with the imitative properties of the primates. Were they very like human beings? Or were they just pretending to be so? And what was the difference? These are questions that have intrigued recent generations too. In fact, some readers of this book (like its author) will be old enough to remember when the highlight of a visit to a zoo was the chimpanzees' tea party, in which chimps dressed up in silly human clothes sat at a table and were made to consume a human-style tea. It was a powerful prompt to reflect on what divides us from the simians.[21]

In classical Greece, monkeys—*pithēkoi*—were associated with, among other things, various forms of inauthenticity and imitation. In the first half of the fifth century BCE, Pindar used the image of the monkey to evoke deceptively persuasive speech (children, he wrote, think that apes are pretty or lovely [*kalos*], but Rhadamanthys, the judge of the underworld, is not taken in by the slander or deception associated with such creatures[22]). In later comedy and Athenian courtroom speeches, pretense—claiming, for example, rights of citizenship that you did not have—was regularly attacked as the behavior of a monkey.[23] Aristophanes, in fact, exploited for comic effect the ape's awkward place on the boundary between fraud and flattery: one of his clever coinages, the word *pithēkismos* (monkeying around or monkey business), captures the ideas of both mimicry or pretense and fawning or toadying.[24] And he was not the only writer to do so. In a short surviving fragment of another fifth-century BCE comic dramatist, Phrynichus, four men are each compared to a monkey: one a coward, one a flatterer, and one an illegitimate, so spurious, citizen, or an imposter (the last comparison is sadly lost).[25]

Writers of the Roman world inherited and developed all these themes. But the closeness between the Latin words *simia* (monkey) and *similis* (like or similar)—and the tempting, though incorrect, idea that one derived from the other—gave an added edge to many Roman explorations of the mimetic properties of the monkey.[26] Puns on the two words go back at least as far as the poet Ennius, whose tag "simia quam similis turpissima bestia nobis"—or "the simian, how similar that ugly creature is to us"—is quoted by Cicero.[27] And in many different contexts, apes and monkeys became bywords for mimicry.

The Roman comic theater found in the figure of the monkey a powerful symbol of its own mimetic tricks. Plautus in particular packed his plays with monkey names (Simia, Pithecium, and so on), monkey dreams, even monkey bites,[28] and this simian conceit was visualized in a curious statuette, almost certainly of Roman date, that depicts a comic actor with an ape's head in place of a theatrical mask (see fig. 3).[29] Horace too, with Ennius surely somewhere at the back of his mind, could refer to a secondhand, imitative poet as "a monkey."[30] And Aelian's confidence—in the late second or early third century CE—that mimicry was the defining property of this particular animal fits well with the Roman cultural landscape. "The monkey is the most imitative creature," as he explained, "and every bodily action that you teach it, it will learn exactly, so as to be able to show it off. Certainly, it will dance if it has learned how and will play the pipes if you teach it." He later observed that the animal's habits of imitation could be the death of it (or at least lead to its capture). Monkey hunters in India would put their shoes on in sight of their prey, then leave out some more pairs for the animals to copy their actions—the trick was that the monkeys' shoes were attached to snares.[31]

Various images discovered at Pompeii turn on the monkey's notorious mimicry of human beings.[32] One statuette depicted some kind of ape dressed in a Phrygian cap and clutching a dagger.[33] A curious painting from one of the grandest houses in the town shows a boy with a monkey that is dressed in a tunic and (presumably) all ready to show off its imitative skills (see fig. 4).[34] But most striking of all is a painted frieze that caricatures the founding heroes of Rome. It includes an image of Romulus and (in a much better state of preservation) one of the escape of Aeneas, with his father and son, from Troy. All these human characters are represented as strange crossbred apes, with outsize penises, tails, and dog heads (see fig. 5).[35] There has been considerable debate on what the exact joke was here. Some have seen a learned visual pun (the nearby island of Pithecusae [Monkey Island] was also known as Aenaria, which many Romans thought meant "Aeneas island"—so the picture conflates the two).[36] Others have detected "comic resistance" to the Romanization of Pompeii and to the Augustan exploitation of the legends of early Rome.[37] But whatever precise reading we give to these images, they point at least to the comic interchangeability of monkeys and mythical heroes; monkeys could even play the role of Rome's founding fathers—for a laugh.

But what exactly was it that made apes such a prompt to laughter? We would be deceiving ourselves if we thought we could explain why any particular Roman cracked up when they caught sight of a monkey (let alone of an Aeneas in ape form). But a series of anecdotes and moralizing discussions in Roman literature takes us closer to understanding the shifting relationships between "monkey business" and laughter. These stories point to the importance of mimicry and flattery and also to the edgy intersection between the human and the animal.

At one level, as Aristophanes' coinage implies, the monkey could be seen as the bestial equivalent of the human parasite—the freeloading guest who traded flattery and laughter for a meal. This is exactly what Plutarch suggests in his essay *How to Tell a Flatterer from a Friend*. "Do you see the monkey?" he asks at one point. "He can't guard your house, like a dog can; he can't carry loads like a horse; he can't plough the land like oxen. So he endures abuse and buffoonery and puts up with practical jokes, offering himself as an instrument of laughter. That's just like the flatterer."[38] The monkey, in other words, is nature's version of human culture's "flatterer-cum-clown." That is what Phaedrus hints too when he makes one of his fables turn on an encounter between a tyrant and a flatterer, and from the animal kingdom chooses a lion to stand for the tyrant and an ape for the flatterer.[39] It is also a point that the story of Anacharsis underlines. For when he was asked to explain why the monkey had made him laugh when the jesters had not, the sage replied that a monkey was laughable (*geloios*) "by nature but a man only by practice."[40]

Another major factor must be the imitative side of the monkey. We have already seen (p. 119) how Roman orators could be almost guaranteed to raise a laugh—vulgar as it might be—by mimicking their opponents in voice and stance, and we shall shortly look at aggressively imitative forms of comic performance staged purely for laughs. Part of the hilarity that apes and monkeys prompted certainly went back to their mimicry of human beings. But one or two anecdotes hint at something a little more complicated than mimicry pure and simple. They suggest that what was particularly laughable about these primates was their position on the very boundary between human and animal—and the precariousness of their attempts to imitate human beings. To put it another way, some of the loudest laughter accompanied their *failed* attempts at imitation, which exposed the mimicry for what it was.

These ideas underlie a story told by Lucian, the second-century CE satirist and essayist. It features an Egyptian king who had taught a troupe of monkeys to do a Pyrrhic dance, which they did very expertly, dressed up in masks and purple robes—until, Lucian writes, one of the spectators threw some nuts into the show. At that moment, monkeys became monkeys again, forgot the dance, threw off their fancy dress, and fought for the nuts. And the spectators laughed.[41]

Lucian is using this story to make a particular point in the course of a gleefully satiric philosophical debate. The monkeys are like those hypocrites who purport to despise wealth and advocate the sharing of property. . . until one of their friends is in trouble and needs some cash, or there's some gold and silver on offer. Then they reveal their true nature. But Lucian offers insights too into the working of laughter. Who caused the laughter, and how? There turn out to be two different prompts here. On the one hand, there is the man who threw in the nuts (explicitly described by Lucian as *asteios*—the Greek equivalent of the Latin *urbanus*, "cleverly witty"). On the other hand, there are the monkeys themselves. In their case, it is their inability to sustain their human role— their recrossing of the boundary between ape and man—that provokes the hilarity.

A different nuance—pointing to different pressure points along the fuzzy dividing lines between ape and man—is found in an anecdote in Strabo's *Geography*, in his discussion of North Africa. For a brief moment, a laugh interrupts the sober, scientific narrative. Writing in the early first century CE, Strabo is drawing on an account by the Stoic philosopher and intellectual Posidonius, who lived about a hundred years earlier. As he sailed along the African coastline, Posidonius caught sight of a colony of wild monkeys in a forest, some living in the trees, some on the ground, some nursing their young, and some that made him laugh: these were the ones with heavy udders, the bald ones, and those with obvious disfigurements.[42] These monkeys were not, of course, actively imitating anyone; they were just being monkeys. In that way, the story serves to remind us that "imitation" rests as much in the observer's perception of similarity as in any intentional mimicry. The joke here is that

Posidonius laughs at those features that he would have laughed at if the animals had been human beings (we have already seen baldness as a surefire prompt to laughter in the Roman world; pp. 51, 132–33, 146). It is a further suggestion that some of the laughter about ancient monkeys stems from the ambiguity of their position on the boundary between the human and animal kingdoms—or at least our perception of it (in other words, the joke's probably also on Posidonius, and us).

All these anecdotes offer telling hints about the connections between primates and human laughter, but only hints, not attempts to face head on the basic question of why people laughed at monkeys. There was, however, one writer of the Roman Empire—the physician Galen—who did face that question directly, in an extraordinary few paragraphs of reflection in which he not only tried to explain what is funny about the ape but also came close to using the ape's example to reflect back onto human practice and to explain why human clowns (or comic artists) make us laugh. Buried in a long medical treatise, *On the Usefulness of Parts of the Body,* this brave ancient discussion of laughter has not received the attention it deserves.

I gave a brief preview of Galen's reflections in chapter 2, summarizing his idea that monkeys and apes operate, as we would put it, as "caricatures" of the human being. "We laugh particularly," he wrote, "at those imitations that preserve an accurate likeness in most of their parts but are completely wrong in the most important ones." And he refers to the example of the ape's "hands," which are similar to human hands—but for the thumbs, which are not opposed to the fingers and so are not only useless but "utterly laughable" (*pantē geloios*). But this is only one part of a longer discussion that raises further issues about how visual joking works.

Two passages in this treatise are particularly important. The first, which includes the discussion of the ape's "hands," has more to say both about the animal's capacity for imitation and about the practice of human artists who try to raise a laugh. For Galen—in a way that echoes the story about the monkeys and the nuts—the basic point about the primates is that they are bad imitators rather than good ones. Pindar's famous quotation about children finding monkeys "beautiful" reminds us, he explains, that "this creature is a laughable [*geloion*] toy for children at play, for it tries to mimic all human actions but fails in these laughably [*epi to geloion*]. Have you not seen an ape trying to play the pipes and dance and write and everything else a human being does correctly? What ever did you think? Did you think he handled it all just like us, or laughably [*geloiōs*]? . . . As for its whole body, my argument as it goes on will show that it is a laughable [*geloion*] imitation of a human being."[43] He continues by suggesting that there is an analogue here for the procedures of the comic artist: "If a painter or a sculptor, when he was depicting [*mimoumenos*] the hands of a human, was going to make an intentional error for a laugh [*epi to geloion*], he would make exactly the kind of error that we see in apes." Later in the treatise, Galen returns to the apes in summing up his overriding principle that the character of the parts of the body matches the character of the soul:

> For the ape, as has already been stated, being an animal laughable [*geloios*] in its soul and an inferior [*pros to cheiron*] imitator,[44] nature has clad in a body to correspond. In fact, the whole framework of the bones in its legs is put together in such a way that it cannot stand up nice and erect, and it has muscles in the back of its legs that are utterly laughable [*geloiotatous*] and incompatible with its structure. It is for this reason that it cannot stand safely and perfectly erect. But just like a human being stands and walks and runs with a limp when he is raising a laugh [*gelōtopoiōn*] and mocking [*skōptōn*] another of the species who is lame, that's just how an ape uses its legs.[45]

There are all kinds of problems with this discussion, enterprising as it is. Galen moves rather too effortlessly among different versions of imitation: from the simplest sense of "likeness" through active "imitation" to an artist's "caricature." But he makes a radical (in ancient terms) attempt to explain why the ape's mimetic properties make it so laughable. In Galen's view, while the creature may ape the human (to pick up for a moment on our own language of monkey mimetics) and seem very like the human in particular respects, it never fully crosses the boundary that divides it from our species, and that's what makes us laugh.

It is, however, all the more significant a discussion because Galen draws a parallel between the laughter caused by monkeys and apes and that caused by various human "laughter makers." This is one of a tiny number of ancient attempts explicitly to reflect on how some visual images can make people laugh.[46] In the last passage I quoted, Galen links the naturally awkward movements of the monkey with the mimetic, histrionic movements of the man who raises a laugh by mocking the lame—as if, to reverse the question, the laughable nature of the ape could help to explain why we laugh at the human mimic or clown. To push this a little further than Galen does, he comes close to seeing not just the monkey as a jester but the jester as a monkey. This is, in a way, another variant on the idea that the monkey is laughable "by nature but a man only by practice."

These monkey themes set the scene for the rest of this chapter, which looks next at human mimes and mimics and closes with Apuleius' version of crossing species boundaries. In between, I return to the example of Anacharsis, who spent most of the party *agelastos* (unlaughing), and to the question of what could get a nonlaugher to laugh—which involves similar issues of mimicry and the dividing line between animals and humans.

MIME, MIMICRY, AND MIMESIS

Monkeys stood better than any other creature for the connection between mimicry and laughter. But they were not the only mimics in the Roman world to signal laughter. Hovering over the Roman orator as he was tempted to raise a laugh with a wicked impersonation of his opponent was the specter of the Roman mime and its actors. There was at Rome an ambivalent relationship between the practice of oratory and the practice of the stage in general: orators could, and did, learn tricks of the trade from skilled actors, but nonetheless actors were definitely at the other end of the social, political, and cultural hierarchy from Cicero and his like; according to the axioms of Roman power, which partly correlated status with the ownership of one's own words, an actor was condemned to be only a mouthpiece of the scripts of others.[47] There was no such ambivalence about mime. The mime actor (*mimus*), like the *scurra*, was a dreadful antitype of the elite orator. Mime was the one ancient theatrical genre most firmly associated with laughter, but to suggest that in raising a laugh a Roman orator was playing his part in a Roman mime amounted to an insinuation that he was quite beyond the pale. So why were mimes so laughable—and so unacceptable? What was their role in the "laughterhood" of Rome?

Mime is a contested genre in modern scholarship. We know much less about Roman mimes than we would like to. We tend to speculate with misplaced confidence on what we don't know—while sometimes overlooking some of the obvious things we do. There is general agreement that whatever its debt to an earlier Greek tradition, mime was a particularly important medium in Rome, influencing all kinds of literary production, from Horace through Latin love elegy to Petronius ("the missing link in Roman literary history," as Elaine Fantham once dubbed it).[48] There is agreement too that mime was one of the few ancient theatrical genres that featured women as performers, and both male and female actors had speaking parts—this was not mime in our (silent) sense of the term.[49] After that, things become murkier.

It is sometimes assumed that there was a fairly clear distinction between mime and "pantomime"—a performance (again quite unlike the modern genre of the same name) normally consisting of silent dancers accompanied by singers. But in practice, ancient writers blurred the distinction; like the learned diners in Macrobius' *Saturnalia,* they slipped easily between talk of mime and talk of pantomime (see pp. 78–79).[50] It is also commonly said that, in sharp contrast to performers in other major theatrical genres of antiquity, mime actors performed without masks. That may be so, but it is a claim that rests largely on one passage of Cicero's *On the Orator*—where the character of Strabo asks, "What could be more *ridiculus* than a *sannio*? But he produces laughter [*ridetur*, "is laughed at"] with his face, his expression, his voice, in fact with his whole body. I can say that this is funny [*salsum*] yet not in a way that I would want an orator to be, but like a mime actor."[51]

The modern interpretation rests on the idea that if the face is a prompt to laughter, the character concerned cannot have been wearing a mask (for that would have hidden the face). But this passage does not say that. It refers to the face and expression of some kind of clown (*sannio*) and compares his general style of laughter production with that of a mime actor.[52] In any case, a funny expression might actually be the expression of a mask—especially as we have a strong hint in Tertullian of a tradition of masked mime ("The image of your god covers his foul and notorious head," he writes of what seems very likely to be a mime actor).[53] Perhaps we are seeking uniformity where none is to be found.

For the rest, there is a wide range of conflicting and incompatible testimony on the nature of Roman mime, onto which it is hard to impose much convincing order. Roman writers sometimes strongly associate mimes with low life, suggesting that performances took place in front of common crowds on the street, but other times they refer to mimes put on in the residences of the elite and in front of some very upmarket fans of the genre.[54] They sometimes imply that mimes were improvised, off-the-cuff performances, though our knowledge of mime comes mostly from what survives of crafted literary versions, including those written by the well-to-do (so it is said) Laberius, who was notoriously asked by Julius Caesar to act in one of his own mimes (insult or flattery?).[55] Sometimes our sources suggest that the plots were drawn from everyday life and were by and large bawdy to boot; that is certainly what the genteel characters of the *Saturnalia* assumed (see p. 78), and plenty of the surviving fragments on papyrus focus on adultery stories, farts, and the "lower bodily stratum" in its limited varieties.[56] But other mime plots were clearly mythological, even if they ended up as lusty parodies rather than straight renderings (such as Laberius' *Anna Peranna* or the versions of Virgil's *Eclogues* performed by well-known mime stars).[57]

It is not hard to see why some scholars have rather desperately resorted to constructing a chronological development (whether a shift in the character and audience of the mimes from popular to elite culture, or alternatively an ever-increasing scale of bawdiness—"lewder as time went on," as one critic recently put it[58]). Nor is it hard to see why others have suggested that mime was something of a catchall category that embraced "any kind of theatrical spectacle that did not belong to masked tragic and comic drama."[59] The idea that the ancient *mime* could be as loose a term as the modern *farce* is an attractive one, and it conveniently accommodates the otherwise awkwardly conflicting evidence. But even so, it tends to sidestep (or not take seriously enough) those two things that we know for sure about mime: its whole point was to make people laugh, and it was a strikingly imitative genre.

There can be no doubt that mime and laughter went together, and for that reason alone, mime deserves its share of the limelight in this book. Where we have met it in earlier chapters, it has always been as a laughter raiser (for better or worse, vulgar or not). This connection can be documented time and again. It is emphasized, for example, in some of the memorial verses composed to commemorate notable actors or authors in the genre. Philistion, an early imperial mime writer, is written up in a verse that proclaims how "he made the mournful lives of men to mix with laughter." A similar message is conveyed in the memorial to the mime actor Vitalis, who is said to have "unleashed laughter in sad hearts."[60] And as late as the sixth century CE, the Sophist Choricius of Gaza defends the power of mimes against Christian critics of the genre by praising their restorative and laughter-provoking power and—interestingly, taking another view of laughter's role on the species boundary—argues that laughter was in fact a property shared by humans and the gods.[61]

Why, then, was mime so powerful a producer of laughter? Again, the reason that any individual laughed at any individual performance is lost to us; answers might range from some carnivalesque pleasure in bums and farts to the simple fact that everyone else in the audience was splitting their sides. But in the discussions of mimes in our elite authors, the key factor links laughter and—as the very name suggests—the imitative nature of the genre. This went far beyond the more general (and philosophically controversial) questions of mimesis that underlay all theatrical representation; the hilarity of the mime was linked to its specific practices of mimicry.[62]

It remains debatable how far ancient actors in the major theatrical genres of tragedy and comedy "acted" in our terms. There are some hints that, as time went on, various forms of impersonation gradually became more important in mainstream ancient drama, with greater stress on, for example, realistic characterization of language and accent— even from behind a stylized mask.[63] All the same, imitation of this kind was never taken to be a defining feature of the tragic or comic theater as it was of the various performance traditions that go under the heading of *mime*. Cicero and Quintilian both point to the aggressive mimicry of this genre. The anecdote about the (panto)mimes in Macrobius also centers on the realistic imitation of the mad Hercules, although the audience misread it (see p. 79).[64] And those ancient scholars who attempted to define the essence of mime (for modern scholars are not the first to try to impose order on the tricky complexities of classical culture) repeatedly emphasized its imitative qualities. For example, Diomedes, a fourth-century grammarian, writes of its "imitation of different forms of speech," its "bawdy imitation of lewd words and deeds," and how it was named for its mimetic properties ("as if it were the only genre that used imitation, although other forms of literature [*poemata*] do likewise, but it alone, as if by some particular prerogative, claimed rights over what was common property"); along similar lines and at roughly the same date, Evanthius refers to mime's "everyday imitation of common things and trivial people."[65]

We cannot write this off merely as a grammarians' solution, resorting to etymology ("mimes are mimetic") as a convenient means of explanation. For Cicero, Quintilian, and Macrobius insist that the mime actors' mimicry was instrumental in the production of laughter. The audience laughed at the imitation and pretense of these actors, which was not far from saying—by easy shorthand and slippage—that the audience laughed *at* the actors themselves (if they didn't, the mime would fail). It was this aspect, as much as the whiff of low life, that determined the orator's fear of being mistaken for a *mimus*. That would mean he had failed the challenge confronting the elite public speaker: how to provoke laughter (as a *ridiculus*) without simultaneously becoming its butt (*ridiculus* in the other sense).

This is a simple set of connections between laughter and mimicry and mime but one that can enrich our understanding of some famous passages of Roman literature. I have already highlighted (p. 159) one particular line in Catullus' poem on the verses he wants given back: the tart who is hanging onto his poetry tablets laughs, he writes, *mimice ac moleste*. I glossed this provisionally as "in the style of a mime actress," and that is generally the sense that most translators of the poem now give. For Guy Lee, this was the "odious actressy laugh" of the whore; for John Godwin, the woman was "laughing like an actress"; for Peter Whigham, she was "like a stage tart." Commentators too take broadly this line, with Kenneth Quinn reducing the image to that of a pouting ancient equivalent of a modern cinema starlet.[66] Some of this may underlie Catullus' invective; it seems likely that there was laughter on (as we would say) both sides of the curtain at a mime, and it is not unreasonable to suppose that mime actors and actresses had a distinctive, perhaps lewd, laugh—though hardly, I think, a starlet's pout. But Catullus' gibe is edgier than that. Almost impossible as it is to translate, it parades the idea of vulgar, bodily, laughable imitation on the part of the thieving whore. It may also point to the fact that if the girl is to be seen in a mimic guise, then—as much as she is cackling "like a stage tart"—we too are laughing *at her*. And that, of course, is exactly what the poem itself is doing.

Some of these issues also underlie the so-called Quartilla episode, near the beginning of what survives of Petronius' first-century CE novel, *Satyricon*. Modern critics have intensely discussed this story—partly because there are so many gaps in the text we have that it is an intriguing challenge to explain exactly what happens and in what order.[67] But it is clear enough that, as the surviving story opens in the standard version, the narrator and the antiheroes of the novel receive a visit in their lodgings from an attendant of Quartilla, a priestess of the phallic god Priapus. She announces the imminent arrival of her mistress—who is coming to call on the men in response to their earlier disruption of Priapus' holy rites. When the priestess arrives shortly after, she sheds a stream of histrionic tears about the sacrilege committed, then embarks on a full-on orgy—many of whose details are (maybe happily) lost in the lacunae of the text as it has come down to us.

As most critics have observed, laughter is a recurring element in this episode (and Maria Plaza has rightly pointed to many of the tricky interpretative difficulties it raises in the narration—in terms of who is laughing at whom and whose laughter we treat as authoritative[68]). But there is, for my concerns in this chapter, a particularly relevant outburst immediately before the scripted orgy starts. Just as Quartilla moves from her crocodile tears to the preparations for the sexual party, the women laugh in a terrifying way—and then everything resounds *mimico risu*.[69] The same issues of translation come up again. We find, in various modern versions, "stagy laughter," "farcical laughter," "rire théâtral," and the "laughter of the low stage."[70] But once again, that is only part of the point. As Costas Panayotakis and others have clearly shown, this section of the *Satyricon* is constructed around the themes and conventions of mime—and mimetic plots.[71] This might indeed suggest that Quartilla and her attendant laugh in a "stagy" way, with all the ideas of pretense that might entail, or that they laugh with the bawdy vulgarity of mime actors.

Yet the explicit phrase *mimico risu* encourages us to focus more directly on the connections and associations of mime and on the wider "economy" of laughter in these performances—as it involves both actors and audience. It is an economy that Petronius here both exploits and inverts. Quartilla's mime show ought to have raised some hearty chuckles from its audience, for that is the nature and purpose of mime. In fact, the reaction of the audience in the text—by which I mean the narrator and his friends—is dazed astonishment. Partly the butts of the joke, partly nonlaughing spectators, they can only exchange glances. They do not laugh at all. In a way, this is a subversion of the genre. Petronius is not simply drawing on mime but also upsetting its very conventions, destabilizing the assumed relationship between actors and audience and hinting at further questions about who exactly is laughing at whom.[72]

DEATH BY LAUGHTER—AND SOME AGELASTIC TRADITIONS

There were even wider—and sometime dangerous—implications in Roman connections between different forms of imitation and laughter. One of these is starkly illustrated in an anecdote preserved in Festus' second-century CE dictionary, *On the Meaning of Words*.[73] Under the entry for *Pictor* (painter), we read of the death of the famous fifth-century BCE artist Zeuxis: "The painter Zeuxis died from laughing when he was laughing immoderately at a picture of an old woman that he himself had painted. Why the story was related at this point by Verrius when his purpose was to write about the meaning of words, I really do not understand—and when he also quoted some not particularly clever anonymous lines of poetry about the same thing: 'What limit is he going to set on his laughter, then, / Unless he wants to end up like that painter who died laughing?'"[74] This story was to have a notable afterlife in a self-portrait by Rembrandt, painted in his old age. It shows the artist laughing, and in the background is an apparently ugly figure. The significance of this scene has often puzzled critics. Is this, for example, Rembrandt as Democritus? Almost certainly it is not. For the secondary figure in the background seems clearly female, and if so, this must surely be Rembrandt as Zeuxis—facing his end, with a specifically painterly reference (see fig. 6).[75]

I am not concerned here with the truth of the story (it is first attested centuries after the death of Zeuxis, and even assuming that the reference in Festus to the Augustan writer Verrius Flaccus is correct, we have no idea what his source might have been). Nor am I concerned with the physiological possibility of death through laughter—a well-known urban legend in both ancient and modern culture. My question is simply why would we imagine that Zeuxis would find a painting of an elderly lady so laughable? And so very laughable that it killed him?

We might think in terms of mainstream ancient misogyny (and of the despised cultural category of the crone). What else are old women fit for, except to be laughed at? What would an artist do who had made an image of a crone, except laugh at it? Are old women deadly, even in the laughter they provoke? Misogyny of this sort may well be part of it, but there is more to this story of laughter than that.[76]

Whatever Zeuxis' paintings really looked like (they are all lost), later descriptions and discussions, largely of Roman date, focused on their imitative quality. This is most clearly seen in the famous, and much analyzed, story of the mimetic competition between Zeuxis and his rival Parrhasius recounted by Pliny the Elder: Zeuxis painted a bunch of grapes so lifelike that it deceived the birds (who came to peck at them), but it did not secure his victory, because Parrhasius created an image that deceived even Zeuxis (he painted a curtain, which Zeuxis tried to pull back).[77] The anecdote in Festus about the painting of the old woman is another—so far unrecognized—story on the same theme, suggesting an even more challenging aspect of Zeuxis' mimetic prowess and another aspect of the laughable properties of Roman imitation. Here it is surely Zeuxis' own imitation that he finds so hilarious—and it kills him. It is hard not to imagine that Rembrandt knew exactly what he was doing when he re-created himself in the guise of Zeuxis.

This story of Zeuxis leads us in various directions. It points us, obviously, to other ancient examples of those killed by their own laughter. But it also gestures in a different direction, toward the nonlaughers, the agelasts, in the classical world—for one memorable anecdote provides a link between a group of unfortunate victims of their own laughter and a notorious Roman who had supposedly never laughed in his whole life. This offers us a glimpse of a scene so funny in ancient terms that it could either produce laughter powerful enough to kill or produce a chuckle in a man whose trademark was that he never cracked up. It is a memorable scene that will also bring us back, in the final section of this chapter, to the borderline between human and animal—but this time with asses and donkeys as the focus of attention.

The history and culture of laughter are necessarily bound up with those who do not laugh. The story of laughter should not leave out those who do not get the joke. Yet agelasts rarely get much cultural attention (and indeed are peculiarly difficult to study), except at the moment when they too break down and something finally elicits laughter from them. One of the most powerful motifs in the European fairy tale is the "princess who would not laugh" and the (usually) erotic origins and consequences of her first hilarious outburst.[78] And the famous classical Greek story of how the goddess Demeter, grieving for the loss of Persephone, was induced to laugh when Baubo lifted her skirts and exposed her genitals has been as intensely discussed by modern feminist literary critics as by classicists.[79] In addition to Athenaeus' brief account of the sage Anacharsis, who cracked up only at the sight of a monkey, there is a wide range of stories from the Roman period (even if often focusing on characters from the Greek past) that concern much more determined, long-term, or sometimes involuntary agelasts and explain what finally got them chortling and with what consequences.

One of these offers a different perspective on the links between laughter and imitation.[80] This tale is again from Athenaeus but drawn (and maybe adapted) from a multivolume history of Delos by one Semus—now lost apart from some short quotations and dated, only by guesswork, any time between the third century BCE and the mid- or late second century CE.[81] It concerns a man called Parmeniscus of Metapontum, who had been to consult the oracle of Trophonius in Boeotia. One feature of this particular oracle was that people temporarily lost their ability to laugh after the consultation,[82] but unusually, the loss seemed to be permanent in Parmeniscus' case—forcing him to seek the advice of the Delphic oracle. The Pythia gave an apparently encouraging response: "You ask me about laughter soothing [*meilichoiou*], unsoothed one [*ameiliche*]; mother at home will give it to you—honor her greatly."[83] But going home to his mother did not restore Parmeniscus' laughter as he had hoped. Later—and still unable to laugh—he happened to be in Delos and visited the temple of Leto, Apollo's mother, "thinking that her statue would be something remarkable to look at. But when he saw that it was just a shapeless piece of wood, he unexpectedly laughed. And seeing the meaning of the god's oracle and freed from his affliction, he honored the goddess greatly."

We have very little idea of what elements of historical truth, if any, are embedded in this suspiciously classic tale of the oracle's riddling opacity and the consultant's misinterpretation (Parmeniscus failed to spot that it was Apollo's mother who was meant).[84] We do not know if Parmeniscus was a bona fide historical character or at what date the events were supposed to have taken place.[85] But strictly factual or not, the story offers some important reflections on ancient laughter and on ancient religious ideology—as Julia Kindt has recently argued in a detailed analysis of Parmeniscus' adventures.[86]

For Kindt, the point of the story turns on the understanding of religious images, on different modes of religious viewing, and on the relationship between anthropomorphic statues of the gods and alternative forms of divine images, such as Leto's statue—aniconic, less naturalistic versions capturing the essence of the deity in a plank of wood or a barely worked stone. It is certainly true that without any knowledge of those two complementary and competing modes of representation in ancient religious culture (the iconic versus the aniconic), it would be hard to make much sense of the story. But Kindt goes on to suggest that the real essence of the story is a lesson in the rules of visuality, as Parmeniscus comes to appreciate "the complexities of divine representation"—and demonstrates his appreciation in the changing quality of his laughter, which "becomes more self-reflective."[87]

I rather doubt it. So far as I can see, those "complexities" are no more than the context and peg for Parmeniscus' most important lesson: namely, how to interpret the words of the oracle correctly. And there is no hint in the story of any change of quality in the laughter: Parmeniscus "unexpectedly laughed."[88] The important issue is much simpler than Kindt implies: Why did Parmeniscus laugh?

Partly, the laughter follows from the defeat of expectations and the incongruity of the statue. In fact the word *paradoxōs* (unexpectedly) probably suggests this: it was not simply that Parmeniscus laughed when he did not expect to; he also laughed at the unexpected. But there is an underlying issue of imitation here too. In Athenaeus' account, what finally dispelled Parmeniscus' inability to laugh was the sight of a statue that was, in his view, a very poor imitation of what it was pretending to be. This is, in other words, another example of how mimesis and, more specifically, the boundaries of successful imitation were linked to the production of laughter. At the same time, it is another clear case of the double-sidedness of laughter and the laughable in the Roman world. For the logic of the story is that this block of wood could seem ridiculous (in our sense) as an image of Leto, but it simultaneously embodied the power to *make* someone laugh (and in this case, that was the power of the goddess and not ridiculous at all).

Parmeniscus was an unwilling agelast, but others—throughout Greek and Roman culture—were much more active refuseniks in matters of laughter.[89] The most notorious nonlaugher in the Roman world was Marcus Licinius Crassus, who lived in the late second century BCE and was the grandfather of the more famous Crassus who died fighting the Parthians at the Battle of Carrhae in 53 BCE. According to Cicero, the satirist Lucilius, who was Crassus senior's contemporary, first nick-named him *Agelastos* (in Greek), and writers from Cicero to Saint Jerome regularly take him as one extreme case of a Roman who hated laughter. As Pliny the Elder summed it up, "People say that Crassus, the grandfather of the Crassus killed in Parthia, never laughed, and for that reason was called Agelastus."[90]

But Pliny was overstating the case. For the point that most Roman writers stress is that Crassus had indeed laughed—just once in his life ("But that one exception did not prevent him being called *agelastos,*" as Cicero insists). What was it that caused Crassus to crack up on that one occasion? The only explanation we have comes from Jerome, again referring back to Lucilius. It was the saying "Thistles are like lettuce to the lips of a donkey"—or perhaps, we should imagine, it was the sight of a donkey eating thistles and the (presumably) common proverb that such a sight evoked.[91] For the story of Crassus is very close to a couple of others that writers in the Roman Empire told of notable characters catching sight of a donkey consuming something unexpected—and dying of the laughter this produced.

Death by laughter is a vivid image (and a common cliché) in many cultures, from the casual hyperbole of the phrase "They just died of laughter" (an idiom that we saw with the blustering soldier of Terence's

Eunuch, pp. 10, 14) to the curious stories of people reputed to have literally passed away laughing. We could add to Zeuxis many modern examples, from the novelist Anthony Trollope, who is said to have fallen into a coma after laughing uncontrollably at a reading of a comic novel, to the bricklayer from Kings Lynn who died in 1975 after thirty minutes of hysterics at a television comedy show, *The Goodies*.[92] Two particular ancient characters—the Stoic philosopher Chrysippus and the Greek comic poet Philemon (both of the third century BCE)—provide a striking match for Crassus. For they were said to have died laughing when they saw a donkey eating figs and drinking wine.

Valerius Maximus, in a section on notable deaths in his anthology *Memorable Deeds and Sayings*, has this to say of the death of Philemon: "Philemon was carried off by the force of excessive laughter. Some figs had been prepared for him and placed in his sight. When a donkey started eating them, he called to his slave to chase the animal off. But the slave didn't arrive till they were all eaten. 'Since you've been so slow,' he said, 'you might as well now give the donkey some wine [*merum*, unmixed wine].' And he followed up this witty quip with such a bout of breathless cackling [*cachinnorum*] that he crushed his feeble old windpipe with the all the rough panting."[93] Much the same was told by Diogenes Laertius about the death of Chrysippus (including the detail about the unmixed wine).[94]

There are all kinds of puzzles and intriguing details in these stories. For a start, "what happened when the donkey ate the figs" looks exactly like one of those free-floating anecdotes that get attached to any number of people, and (as we shall soon see) there are hints that the donkey story, even without its fatal consequences, was part of a wider popular joking tradition. But it may be significant that the same town, Soli in Cilicia, was supposed to be the original home of both Philemon and Chrysippus. Is this, perhaps, a story that had a specific association with that particular place or that gets shifted between different native sons? If so, what would the implications be? The details of the narrative raise curious questions too. Why figs? Is the fact that the Greek word *sukon/ suka* (fig/s) was occasionally used for genitalia part of what makes the story so laughable?[95] And why the stress on unmixed wine? In the ancient world, to drink wine that was not mixed with water was usually the mark of the uncivilized or the bestial. Diogenes Laertius' account of Chrysippus also includes an alternative version of his cause of death: drinking unmixed wine. So should we see a connection between that and what was fed to the donkey?[96]

Many loose ends remain. Yet it is clear that there is a common theme running through these stories of the fatal power of laughter and the story of Crassus' single laugh (sharply brought into focus in Tertullian's passing reference to Crassus—where the violence of his unprecedented laugh actually killed the agelast[97]). The prompt for each of these peculiarly powerful forms of laughter is the blurring of the (alimentary) boundaries between the human being and the donkey: the quip that made Crassus laugh reformulated donkey diet in human terms; the cue to laughter that finished off Chrysippus and Philemon was a donkey literally crossing the boundary between animal and human diet. As with the monkeys, that edgy dividing line between beast and man was one on which laughter particularly flourished.[98]

That boundary is of course precisely what is at issue in Apuleius' second-century CE novel *Metamorphoses* (or *The Golden Ass*), which tells the story of the transformation of a man into a donkey—and in which Risus (Laughter) reaches the status of a god. It is to a couple of the specifically gelastic aspects of that novel that we now turn, in this chapter's final section, starting with one episode that acts out in a more complicated way that scene of the donkey stealing human food.

MAKING AN ASS OF YOURSELF

The main lines of Apuleius' plot are well known.[99] The story is told through the mouth of Lucius, a well-born young man of Greek origin, who in the third of the novel's eleven books is turned into a donkey (or ass).[100] This was a mistaken transformation, needless to say. Lucius was trying out the magic potions of the mistress of the house in which he was a guest, with the help of her slave girl. His idea was to experiment with the ointment that would turn him into a bird—but the girl mixed up the jars, and he ended up as a donkey. Most of the novel is the story of Lucius' adventures as an animal, or rather as a human being trapped in an animal's body—an apt symbol of the (ludicrous) transgression of the dividing line between man and beast. In the last book, he is returned to human form under the auspices of the Egyptian goddess Isis, and the story ends with him being enrolled as an official of her consort Osiris by the god himself.[101]

Almost certainly this plot was not wholly the creation of Apuleius. Another, much shorter and simpler version is preserved with the works of Lucian, under the title *Lucius, or The Ass,* but the precise relationship—chronological and otherwise—between it and Apuleius' novel is not known.[102] Nor is it certain how either of them related to another work, now lost but described by the Byzantine patriarch Photios in the ninth century as "Lucius of Patrai's several books of *Metamorphoses*."[103] But whatever the exact relationship between these texts, and whatever the innovations of Apuleius may have been,[104] there is one vivid incident found in both surviving versions of the story that is a strikingly close parallel for the tale of the donkey, the sight of whose eating and drinking is supposed to have killed off Chrysippus and Philemon.[105]

To follow Apuleius' account (overall very similar to the shorter version), near the end of his adventures as an animal, Lucius the donkey came into the possession of two brothers, both slaves: one a confectioner, one a cook. Every evening they used to bring home the rich leftovers from their work and spread them out on their table for supper before going off to the baths to freshen up. And every evening, while they were away, the donkey would nip in to gobble up some of the delicacies, "for I was not so stupid or such a real ass that I would leave that delicious spread and dine on the horribly rough hay."[106] Eventually, as the donkey ate more and more of the best goodies, the brothers noticed the disappearances and suspected each other of stealing the food (in fact, one—presciently, in a way—accused the other of an "inhuman" crime[107]). But soon enough they noticed that the donkey was getting fatter, though it was apparently not eating its hay. Suspicions aroused, they spied on him one evening and broke down in laughter when they saw what was going on—so loudly that their boss heard, came to take a peek, and split his sides too. In fact, he was so delighted with what he had seen that he invited the donkey to a proper dinner, with human food and drink and everyone reclining on couches in the standard human way. Here the animal played the part of the joking parasite—and was even referred to by the master as "my parasite."[108] The guests were consumed with laughter.

Like almost every story in Apuleius, this is much more complicated than it might at first sight appear. At this point in the narrative, the donkey is very close to his final retransformation back into his human form, and his human dietary indulgence here, as well as his role as *parasitus*, or even "friend" (*contubernalis, sodalis*), is partly to be read as moving toward that.[109] This is also a sophisticated literary parody. As Régine May has shown, the pair of food workers in this story are carefully modeled on cooks as they appear in Plautus' comedies, and they serve up decidedly Roman-style food. But whereas cooks in Plautus are characteristically those who pinch the nibbles, this pair is resolutely honest—and it is their donkey who is doing the thieving.[110]

But my interest is in the links with the other donkey stories. It is obvious that the basic point of this extended gag is very similar to that of those other anecdotes: the ass that usurps food intended for human beings causes outrageous laughter. True, no one dies in the stories of the donkey and the food workers, but both versions stress the violence of the laughter provoked by the sight of the animal consuming the men's food (the master in Apuleius, for example, laughed "till his belly hurt," *adusque intestinorum dolorem;* the Greek account likewise refers repeatedly to the power of the laughter evoked[111]). There is, however, a clear hint that the account of Apuleius is even more closely related to the point and the plot of those anecdotes of death by laughter. He knew some of those particular stories, or he was familiar with the popular joking theme of the "dining donkey," of which they are the surviving traces—and he was directly exploiting it.[112]

Broadly similar as they are, there is in fact one significant difference in detail between the two surviving versions of this episode in Lucius' story.[113] In the shorter one, when the donkey is finally in company at the proper dinner table, someone suggests that he have a glass of wine—diluted ("'This ass will drink some wine too, if someone will dilute it and give it to him.' The master gave those orders, and I drank what was brought").[114] In Apuleius, by contrast, we find exactly the same insistence on unmixed wine as in the stories of Chrysippus and Philemon. One of the guests at the donkey's dinner party (a *scurrula,* a joker) says, "Give our friend here a drop of unmixed wine [*merum*]." The master agrees. "Supporting the suggestion, he said, 'That's not a stupid joke, you rascal, for likely as not this friend of ours is really keen on a glass of *mulsum* too.'" *Mulsum* was another form of unwatered wine, mixed only with honey—and that is what "our friend" the donkey was given.[115]

The implication of this stress on undiluted wine remains puzzling, but it is a marked link between *The Metamorphoses* and those other stories of uncontrollable or deathly laughter. In a characteristically clever literary or cultural parody, Apuleius is complicating the simplest form of the anecdote of the donkey diet—by speaking through the "voice" of the animal but also by prizing apart the different viewpoints on the story and on the laughter so often prompted by the confusion between human and beast. The characters in this novel laugh at the donkey eating like a human being; the readers laugh because they know that the donkey is actually human anyway. Laughter can be shared even when we are laughing "at" different things; there is a tricky relationship, Apuleius reminds us, between laughter within and outside the text.

That is only one brief episode in Apuleius' sometimes frustrating and delightfully complicated novel, which has attracted an enormous amount of recent critical attention. Some of this attention stems from the influence of Jack Winkler's classic study of the novel, *Auctor & Actor: A Narratological Reading of Apuleius' "The Golden Ass,"* which appeared in 1985. Winkler brilliantly focused on the narratological complexities of the text and on the hermeneutic games it revels in playing with the reader and with the slippery voice of the narrator. As his title (which has become something of a mantra in the field of classics) signals, there is a shifting and uncertain relationship between the role of the narrator as author (*auctor*) and the role of the narrator as character in the book (*actor*). It is sometimes rather too easy to forget that Winkler was not the first critic to stress the sophistication of Apuleius' text (against those who deemed it appallingly messy and inconsistent).[116] But *Auctor & Actor* did kick-start a new wave of Apuleian scholarship, which celebrated the cleverness and intricacies of the novel and its artful engagement with earlier literature.

This sophistication extends to the use of laughter within the text. In the short version of the story ascribed to Lucian, laughter appears as a simple diagnostic consistent with the standard ancient position that only humans could laugh. That is to say, Lucius laughs before his transformation from human shape but never as an ass. As soon as he has been turned into an ass, in fact, the narrator remarks that his laugh has turned into a bray (*onkēthmos*).[117] In Apuleius' novel, laughter (largely by others, at the donkey) is woven throughout the plot, and the question of who is laughing at whom—and why—is one part of the hermeneutic riddling of the text. I want to conclude this chapter by looking harder at the most striking role for laughter in the structure of the novel, the festival of the god Risus (Laughter), in which Lucius is a reluctant participant immediately before his accidental transformation into an animal. This is the original context for the words *auctor et actor,* and in that context we find a rather different sense for the now famous phrase.[118]

The basic plot of the episode is again fairly simple, though this time it is found in Apuleius alone. It starts one night early in the novel, when Lucius, still in his human form, is at a drunken dinner with relatives in the town where he is staying (Hypata in Thessaly). They happen to mention that on the next day they will be celebrating one of their annual festivals, *sollemnis dies.*[119] It is a nice pun on the Latin *sollemnis* (both "regular established ritual" and "solemn" in our sense). For the god to be honored is Laughter, who will be propitiated with an appropriately "merry and jolly ritual."

That festival, however, almost instantly seems to be forgotten, as the story takes a different turn. For things start to go very wrong after dinner, when Lucius gets back to the house where he is staying—only to discover three men trying to break in. He ends up killing the lot. In the morning he is arrested for murder and taken to the forum to be tried. The puzzling thing is that every one of the spectators is laughing[120]—and there are so many of them that the case has to be transferred to the theater. There Lucius makes a speech in his defense, fearing the worst, until finally the magistrates insist that he uncover the corpses of the three men he has killed, to take stock of his crime. When he eventually does so, he discovers that they are not corpses at all but three wineskins that he gashed to pieces in his drunken state, thinking they were robbers.[121] Laughter breaks out even more, and so fiercely that some of the audience, doubled up, have to "press on their stomachs to ease the pain."

Lucius is perplexed and upset, and it does not assuage him very much then to be told by the magistrates that this is the festival of Laughter— which always blossoms with some new ingenuity. In this case, that ingenuity had been the joke on Lucius and his mock trial. In order to escape further laughter ("which I myself had created"[122]), he goes off to the baths before meeting up with the slave girl—who within a few pages will have accidentally contrived his metamorphosis into a donkey.

It is a memorable episode, and it so caught the imagination of Federico Fellini that he transposed a version of it into his film adaptation of Petronius' *Satyricon*. It has also caught the imagination of generations of classicists, who have tried to explain what this strange festival is all about and what it is doing in Apuleius' plot. There have been a number of overoptimistic attempts to suggest that it has definite links to real religious rituals and a real god of laughter (for which there is no reliable evidence at all) or, rather more plausibly, to link the proceedings evoked here to more general structures of ancient religious thought and practice (notably the scapegoat ritual—with Lucius playing the part of the scapegoat[123]). Others have seen it in more specifically textual terms, as a metaliterary device pointing to the comic genre of the novel as a whole, and recently it has been argued that the episode is based on a Roman mime.[124]

This (literary) festival of Risus has, however, even more important implications for our understanding of how ancient laughter works, both inside and outside this novel. Several critics have pointed to the parallels (or reversals) between this gelastic episode, which immediately precedes Lucius' transformation into a donkey, and the gelastic episode we have just examined, with the cooks and their master, which immediately precedes his return to human form. In both instances, Lucius is the object of laughter, but whereas at the festival of Risus he is ashamed and humiliated, at the dinner he feels increasingly pleased by the laughter that greets him.[125] Apuleius is surely exploiting the role of laughter in marking that fragile boundary between man and beast.

Beyond this, the episode also points to the ambiguities of laughter more generally. That is partly a question of terminology (for the reader, one of the jokes of the festival of Risus is the foregrounding of *cachinnare* as much as *ridere*[126]) and partly the old conundrum of how we explain laughter's causes (the narrative of the ritual proceedings is built around Lucius' puzzlement at what the laughter is all about). But it is the slogan *auctor et actor*—which Winkler used to highlight the edgy relationship in the novel between Lucius as narrator and Lucius as character in the plot—that offers the sharpest reflection on laughter (sharper even than Winkler acknowledged). For here we find a particularly memorable summing-up of that recurrent theme in ancient reflections of laughter: the ambivalence between laughter's producer and laughter's butt.

The phrase is used by the magistrates of Hypata when they reassure Lucius that his whole ordeal has been part of the festival of Risus. After they have explained their annual celebration of divine Laughter, they insist that Lucius is now under the god's protection: "That god will accompany the man who is *auctorem et actorem suum,* lovingly and with his blessing, everywhere he goes, and he will never let you feel grief in your heart, and he will constantly brighten your expression with serene pleasure."[127]

What do these magistrates mean by "the god accompanying his [*suum,* that is 'his own'] *auctorem et actorem*"? They are certainly not referring to Winkler's idea of the tricky relationship between narrator and character or between "the authorization of a text's meaning and the credibility of ego-narrative."[128] However insightful his reading is— and, of course, this optimistic prophecy uttered just before Lucius is miserably transformed into an ass is just one example of what he had in mind—the magistrates' words in their original context mean something quite different. Alexander Kirichenko, in arguing for the link between this episode and mime, has focused particularly on the word *actorem.* That, for him, is precisely what Lucius was in this scene: a mime actor.[129] But we should not overlook the explicit link (underlined by *suum*) to Laughter itself, divine or not: Lucius is being cast as the producer and agent of Laughter. In other words, through the voice of the magistrates, explaining to this man-about-to-be-ass the nature of this pseudogod, we find again a lesson about the dual aspect of laughter and the close connection between its active producer (*auctor*) and its vehicle, agent, or, as we would say, butt (*actor*).[130]

As the words of Lucius himself underline, when he reflects shortly afterward on the laughter "which I myself had created" (*quem ipse fabricaveram*), there is a fine line between the person who makes you laugh and the one you laugh at. Lucius is both.

CHAPTER 8

The Laughter Lover

An egghead [*scholastikos*] and a bald man and a barber were
making a journey together and camping out in a lonely place.
They arranged for each of them to stay awake in turn for
four hours and guard the luggage. When it fell to the barber
to keep watch first, wanting to pass the time, he shaved the
head of the *scholastikos* and, when his shift was done, woke
him up. The *scholastikos* rubbed his head as he came to and
found himself hairless. "What a right idiot the barber is," he
said. "He's gone all wrong and woken up the bald man
instead of me."[1]

This is number 56 in the ancient collection of some 265 jokes that goes
under the title *Philogelos,* or "Laughter lover."[2] Written in decidedly
unstylish Greek, the collection is usually dated to the later Roman Empire
(the fourth or fifth century CE is the favorite guess) and includes a wide
range of gags—from jokes about ridiculous misers ("Heard the one about
the mean old man who made himself the heir in his own will?") to quips
on bad breath ("How does a man with bad breath commit suicide? He
puts a bag over his head and asphyxiates himself!") and comic warnings
about cheap honey ("I wouldn't even be selling it, the salesman eventually admitted, if that mouse hadn't gone and died in it").[3]

The joke about the egghead, the bald man, and the barber is one of
the longest in the collection and gives some of the most detailed narrative context (the journey, the risks to the luggage, the boredom of keeping watch, and so on). In it we meet again one of the favorite figures of
fun at Rome: the baldy (pp. 51, 132–33, 146). And we are introduced
for the first time to another major character in the repertoire of ancient
joking, the *scholastikos* (provisionally translated "egghead"), who
takes the lead in almost half the jokes in the *Philogelos*. His place here,

in a trio with the barber and the baldy, echoes all those modern gags that start with similar threesomes: "An Englishman, a Scotsman, and an Irishman went into bar . . ." It is an echo that probably helps to explain why the joke is a favorite with many modern readers of the *Philogelos:* it really does seem to slip easily into that particular comic convention of our era.[4] But not all readers since antiquity have been so amused. Samuel Johnson, publishing one of the earliest English translations of a selection of these gags, struggled to make sense of the punch line here and blamed the manuscript copyists for the obscurity.[5]

There are jokes that still seem bad to us, *frigidi,* as the Romans might have said (see pp. 56, 132). In exploring the *Philogelos* in greater detail, I shall have cause to wonder once more just how much ingenuity is required, or legitimate, in getting (or forcing) ancient gags to provoke a modern chuckle. But I shall also look at some basic questions about this collection. Who might have compiled it, and when? What was it for, and what are the jokes *about*? There can be no doubt that the jokes in the *Philogelos* were intended to make readers or listeners laugh; that is clear from the title alone—"Laughter lover." But what can such a collection of jokes, or of laughter themes, tell us about the society that produced or transmitted them, its priorities, anxieties, and concerns? What role did the *Philogelos* play in the "laughterhood" of Rome? More than that, what was the purpose (and the history) of a jokebook of this kind? I shall argue that in classical antiquity, the jokebook was characteristically, if not exclusively, Roman. And at the end, I will come close to suggesting—though I will stop just short—that the joke as we understand it was a Roman invention.

CONSTRUCTING THE "LAUGHTER LOVER"

The text of the *Philogelos*—funny, intriguing, sometimes disappointing—is more complicated than it might at first seem. The fact is that the book we know as the "Laughter lover" never existed in the ancient world, certainly not in the form in which we now read it. Our printed texts go back to half a dozen or so medieval and later manuscripts, which preserve a series of overlapping but not identical jokes. Most of these are shared among several manuscripts (and the title *Philogelos* is included in several), but no two of them have exactly the same selection. The most complete manuscript version, dating to the eleventh century, is found as part of a much longer anthology of ancient and biblical literature (including popular tales and fables). It contains 260 of the *Phi-*

logelos jokes, although there are several instances where the same joke, almost word for word, appears twice. The shortest and earliest version, in a tenth-century manuscript, forms the final element of a larger collection of "light literature"[6] (including a Greek translation of an Arabic version of a group of Indian fables). The end of this manuscript is lost. There would once certainly have been more jokes, but only seven survive. The first of these occurs in no other manuscript of the collection; the remaining six are found in others—but in a completely different order. This pattern of survival, loss, disruption, and repetition explains my intentional vagueness ("some 265") about the total number of jokes we are dealing with.[7]

The modern printed *Philogelos* is constructed by amalgamating these different manuscript versions. In a sense, we could say that of all classical literature that has "survived": each play of Euripides, each book of Tacitus is a modern scholarly reconstruction from the different, sometimes contradictory manuscript versions that have come down to us. But the *Philogelos* is a particularly extreme case of that. Despite great scholarly expertise and ingenuity in trying to understand and see behind the many-stranded manuscript tradition that confronts us, we have no clear idea what the original archetype was like. The one thing of which we can be most confident is that it was not identical to our printed text. We do not even know whether it is appropriate to think in terms of a single archetype for a collection of jokes—which, like traditional collections of recipes, gardening tips, or workout routines, might always exist in multiple, slightly different versions (even if they claim to go back to some semimythical originator or compiler, such as Mrs. Beeton, the Roman Apicius, or, for that matter, Jane Fonda).

There is at least one hint that the versions of "the *Philogelos*" were even more diverse than they might appear. At one point in his *Histories* (*Chiliades*), the twelfth-century Byzantine scholar John Tzetzes quotes a joke that he attributes to the "Laughter lover"; it is a punning quip about a sick man trying to get rid of an unwelcome guest.[8] Not only is this not found in any of the surviving manuscripts (or in modern printed editions), but Tzetzes treats *Philogelos,* or "Laughter lover," not as the title of the collection but as its author: as he puts it, "Philogelos wrote this somewhere in his book." Maybe Tzetzes was simply confused or misremembering.[9] Or maybe there was another collection of jokes in circulation whose author or compiler went under the name of Philogelos. After all, "Laughter lover" would be an entirely appropriate pen name for a man behind a book of gags.[10]

But to complicate the picture even more, we find other names firmly associated with the *Philogelos,* whether as authors or anthologizers. Our most complete manuscript ascribes the collection to "Hierokles and Philagrios, the *grammatikos*" (maybe "grammarian," maybe "teacher," maybe "scholar"); some others, which include smaller selections of jokes, name only "Hierokles." We have no idea who these men were—despite some desperate modern attempts, on the basis of no evidence at all apart from the name, to pin the collection onto some (probably humorless) fifth-century CE pagan philosopher from Alexandria.[11] The Byzantine dictionary-cum-encyclopedia known as the *Suda* (a repository of recondite information as revealing, and misleading, as Pliny's *Natural History*) offers a very different story. There we read that the *Philogelos* was the work of one Philistion—the name, as we have seen (p. 169), of a famous early imperial mime writer and possibly the pen name (or stage name) of many more. The *Suda* adds the tantalizing detail that the book was dedicated to a man named Koureus or to a man from Kourion in Cyprus or was the kind of book you would take to the barbershop (*koureus*)—the lumpy Greek and uncertain manuscript readings are more or less compatible with each translation.[12] We have no idea which of these is correct or how to interpret the information (there is no sign of any such dedication in any of the surviving manuscripts, so is the *Suda* referring to another work of the same name?). If it were the case that a barbershop is mentioned, that might link the *Philogelos* to that hot spot of ancient popular culture: the place where ordinary men went to get shaved and trimmed and have a chuckle.[13]

The most economical way of resolving all this conflicting evidence is to imagine a fluid tradition underlying the collection—one that grows and develops while parading different authors and popular gurus as its founding fathers. The *Philogelos,* in other words, was not a single authored work but a generic title for a set of texts with strong similarities but no fixed archetype or orthodoxy; it was a fluid tradition, constantly adjusted and adapted, shortened or expanded, in new versions and compilations.

The contours of geography and chronology within the collection certainly suggest a mixed origin. For the jokes refer to a wide range of places and cultures across the Greco-Roman Mediterranean. We meet characters from the Greek-speaking cities of Abdera, Kyme, and Sidon, but there are also passing references to Rome, the river Rhine, and Sicily.[14] Of the only four personal names mentioned—deities and mythical heroes apart—two are Greek ("Drakontides" and "Demeas," a name common in Greek comedy) and two are Roman ("Scribonia" and "Lollianus").[15] And although the jokes are transmitted in Greek, several of the gags are set against an explicitly Roman cultural background, from currency (denarii) to the ceremonies celebrating the thousandth anniversary of Rome itself.[16]

The anniversary joke provides the only precisely datable reference in the *Philogelos*. ("A *scholastikos*, at the festival that took place in Rome at the millennium [21 April 248 CE], saw a defeated athlete in tears and wanted to cheer him up. 'Don't be upset,' he said. 'At the next millennial games, you'll be the winner.'")[17] But it is generally thought, on the basis of the language, that the text as we have it is a couple of centuries later than that—although there are also jokes in our collection that go back considerably earlier than the third century CE or at least point to earlier characters and events.[18] Some of them are found, in a more or less identical form, in Plutarch, who wrote at the turn of the first and second centuries CE. For example, one notable joke in the *Philogelos* about a chatty barber ("A witty guy was asked by a chatty barber, 'How would you like me to cut your hair?' 'In silence' came the reply") crops up in Plutarch's *Sayings of Kings and Commanders,* where it is ascribed to the fifth-century BCE king Archelaus of Macedon,[19] and Plutarch uses another—about (not) lending a scraper in a bathhouse to people who may have turned up without one—to illustrate a usefully jocular method of refusing those who ask you for favors.[20]

Behind a few of the other gags, we can even detect a veiled reference to famous characters of the late Roman Republic or early empire. "Scribonia," whose opulent tomb is the subject of one joke (it was in "a very unhealthy place"), may perhaps be the first wife of the emperor Augustus.[21] But there can be no doubt that a story about the notoriously philistine Mummius, who destroyed the city of Corinth in 146 BCE, underlies another of the jokes, even though it has been anonymized (under the rubric of a generic egghead): "A *scholastikos* taking some old master paintings from Corinth and loading them onto transport ships said to the captains, 'If you lose these, I'll want new ones to replace them.'"[22] There is a hint of the original target in the mention of Corinth. But the hidden reference to Mummius is made absolutely clear from a parallel passage in Velleius Paterculus' *History of Rome,* where a version of exactly the same quip is quoted to illustrate the general's proverbial boorishness. No one who knew the first thing about antiques would think that you could possibly replace them on a deal of "new for old."[23] How any of these earlier jokes found their way into the *Philogelos* in this diluted form—by way of lost literary sources or that convenient scholarly standby "oral tradition"?—we can only speculate.

The search for an original text, an original author, and even an originary date (beyond a vague "Roman") for the *Philogelos* is almost certainly futile. We can, however, detect some basic principles of order, classification, and structure that underpin our collection and define its overall form. First, almost all the jokes concern a type of subject, not a named individual: the egghead, the man from Abdera, the witty guy, the man (or occasionally woman) with bad breath, the cowardly boxer, and so on. In most of them, the very first word identifies the type in question (*scholastikos, Abderitēs,* or whatever) and introduces a joke of usually no more than a few lines (sometimes less). The equivalent modern idiom would probably be "Heard the one about the Abderite?"

The main manuscripts divide the jokes up, fairly systematically, according to these types, as do the modern printed texts (while adding to the end, for want of anywhere else for them to go, a small collection of stragglers from divergent manuscripts, so disrupting the basic scheme[24]). The first 103 in our text have as their hero or antihero the *scholastikos*—a word that has proved a challenge for translators and interpreters. There is almost certainly a connection between this figure and a stock character from the ancient comic stage (in fact, the only *scholastikos* to be given a personal name in the *Philogelos* is the very "stagy" Demeas). But according to Plutarch, the young Cicero too—on his return to Rome after study in Greece—was teased for being a "Greek and *scholastikos*." So is it "absent-minded professor," "numbskull," or (as I have been using, with some hesitation) "egghead"? None of these quite gets it.[25]

The essential point is that the *scholastikos* is someone who is foolish by reason of his learning, who applies the strictest of logic to reach the most ridiculous conclusions, and who represents the reductio ad absurdum (literally) of academic cleverness. False analogy is his most besetting sin, as in this classic case of advice given by an "egghead doctor": "'Doctor' says the patient, 'whenever I get up from my sleep, for half an hour I feel dizzy, and then I'm all right.' And the doctor says, 'Get up half an hour later.'"[26] Yet what gives some of these jokes an added edge is that the *scholastikos* is not simply stupid. Sometimes we end up feeling that his apparent errors are more correct than they seem or point to some more interesting truth. When the rich *scholastikos* refuses to bury his *small* son in front of a *large* crowd, he is absolutely right: the mourners have come only to ingratiate themselves with the father.[27] And when the healthy egghead avoids meeting his doctor in the street, as he feels embarrassed not to have been ill for such a long time, he is both being an idiot and pointing up the oddity of our relationship with a man whose livelihood depends on our misfortune.[28]

After the *scholastikos,* two jokes follow on misers, then later in the collection we find a run of fourteen jokes on witty guys, thirteen on grumpy men (*duskoloi*), ten on simpletons, and so on. But second only to the eggheads as the most prominent type figures are the citizens of three particular towns of the Roman Empire in the eastern Mediterranean: Abdera, Sidon, and Kyme. With some sixty entries between them, we read in joke after joke of their hilarious (though occasionally—as with the egghead—*pointed*) idiocy. "A man from Kyme," for example, "was swimming when it began to rain, so he dived down deep so as not to get wet," or "A man from Abdera, seeing a eunuch chatting with a woman, asked someone else if it was the eunuch's wife. When the man observed that a eunuch couldn't have a wife, he said, 'It's his daughter, then.'"[29]

Exactly why these particular peoples and places became such focuses of laughter we cannot hope to know, and it is perhaps dangerous to make a simple comparison with the modern ethnic joke (the English cracking gags at the expense of the Irish or the French at the expense of the Belgians, for example[30]). But they do give us another glimpse into the cultural geography of Roman laughter (see pp. 51–52). In fact, in the case of two of the three towns, there are clear snatches of evidence to suggest that the jokes of the *Philogelos* reflect a wider tradition of jocularity—about them or at their expense.

The geographer Strabo, for example, refers to the people of Kyme being "ridiculed for their stupidity"; this was partly, he writes, because three hundred years after the foundation of their town they "gave away" their customs dues and even before that had not used them to the state's profit—so that people said it had taken them a long time to realize that they were living by the sea.[31] Abdera was even more strongly connected with laughing and joking. One obvious focus was the story of Democritus, the famous Abderite philosopher, who would not stop laughing (see pp. 92–94). But the connection went deeper than that. For Martial, the town was a byword for stupidity, while Cicero could use the phrase "It's Abdera here" to refer to the topsy-turvy folly of senatorial business at Rome.[32] It was not only the compilers of the *Philogelos* who saw these towns and their dumb inhabitants as good for a laugh.

There are, however, minor but significant differences in the rhetoric of these jokes about Abdera, Kyme, and Sidon that allow us a precious insight into the various sources and joking styles that must lie somewhere behind the *Philogelos*. It is true that most of the jokes turn out to be fairly interchangeable across the collection: although the type characters are quite distinct, the mininarratives and punch lines appear to migrate easily among those different types. A joke about an egghead with stolen property ("A *scholastikos* who had bought some stolen clothes smeared them with pitch so they wouldn't be recognized") is repeated more or less verbatim as a joke about a man from Kyme,[33] and gags on the theme of whether a liter of wine measures the same as a liter of oil or water are found in different variants attached to both eggheads and a *grammatikos* (teacher) from Sidon.[34] But this general interchangeability should not disguise the ways in which the jokes devoted to each of those three places are in some—often overlooked—respects quite distinct.

First, there is a clear contrast between the Abderite and the Sidonian jokes. Abderites almost always appear as just that: "a man from Abdera," with no further definition. Sidonians are always qualified by a trade, a profession, or some similar description. Whatever the quip ("'Lend me a knife as far as Smyrna'; 'I don't have a knife that stretches that far'"[35]), it is always tied to some "Sidonian fisherman," "Sidonian centurion," and so on—or, in the example just quoted, a "Sidonian butcher." The jokes about the people of Kyme are different again. To be sure, this group includes many that would slip easily into other categories or are even almost exact doublets of others in the wider collection. But there are a number that stick out from the general run: they are specifically concerned with the dysfunctional political community of the town or with its political institutions and magistrates—in a way, strikingly reminiscent of Strabo's quip about the harbor dues. So, for example: "When the people of Kyme were fortifying their town, one of the citizens, called Lollianus, built two parts of the defenses at his own expense. When the enemy were threatening, the Kymeans, angry [at Lollianus' actions], agreed that no one but Lollianus should stand guard over his stretch of wall." That is to say, in their resentment at the intrusion of individual patronage into their community relations, the Kymeans respond with a literal-mindedness that is bound to be self-destructive: if he built it on his own, he can defend it on his own![36]

What explains these differences in style? Presumably, behind the collection of gags that we now have (or have reconstructed) there lay earlier traditions and smaller-scale compilations, with their own subtly different themes, clichés, and idioms of joking, creating their own comic expectations.[37] A "Sidonian joke" would not be complete without a trade or profession. If a joke about Kyme was promised, you would already half-expect to be laughing at political folly. Tiny example as this is, it offers a rare glimpse into the implicit rules of ancient joking—into what might make an ancient joke sound right.[38]

Of course, whether any ancient Roman ever did sit down to read or listen to anything resembling our *Philogelos*—to have a chuckle at a dozen jokes about Sidonians, one after another, let alone at more than a hundred *scholastikos* gags end to end—is highly debatable. It all depends on what we think the text, or its ancestors, might have been *for*. The correct answer to that question is almost certainly beyond us (and the use and function might, in any case, have changed over the history and prehistory of our text). But different assumptions about its origin, purpose, and social level lead to very different interpretations and judgments about the collection as a whole, which it is useful to expose.

It could be that all or part of the text we have was some real-life version of those jokebooks that were the tools of the trade of the Roman comic parasite, with their own walk-on part as props in Roman comedy (see pp. 149–50, 202–3). If so, then no one would ever have listened to these jokes in the form in which we read them, one after another. Any such collection would have been used as an aide-mémoire for the jokester, who would have selected from it and embroidered at will. Hence, perhaps, the unadorned, rather telegraphic form of most of the gags (which I have tried to reproduce in my translations): these were bare skeletons of jokes, onto which the live jester was supposed to put the comic flesh.

It is also possible (and perfectly compatible with the idea of a jokester's handbook) that we have in the *Philogelos* something approaching a popular tradition of laughter, lying partly outside the elite protocols and idioms that have necessarily been the subject of most of my case studies so far. That would fit nicely with the possible reference in the *Suda* to the "barbershop" (if only we could be confident of that interpretation). It would also reflect the wider medieval manuscript tradition, which tends to group versions of our text with popular fable and "light literature." And it might help explain the prominence of the *scholastikos* among the jokes: a pointed example of the little people making fun of the useless learning of their "betters."

Yet it would be hard to disprove the entirely contrary idea that, whatever the deeper sources of this text, the form of "our" *Philogelos* owes most not to some bona fide popular tradition (much as we would love that to be the case) but to some late antique academic systematizer. If we leave aside the dubious reference to the "barbershop," we might equally well be dealing with the work of some study-bound, second-rate clone of Macrobius, who in the academic world of the late empire set himself the task of collecting and classifying what made people laugh. The jokes on *scholastikoi* might then have a more subtle and interesting part to play. It is worth remembering that in modern cultures, jokes about learning tend to come not from those who are unlearned but from countercultural subgroups among the learned (students and dissident radicals or off-duty, partying professors). Maybe it was similar in antiquity too. In fact, I have a sneaking suspicion that there would have been no one in ancient Rome who loved jokes about eggheads more than the eggheads themselves.[39]

Leaving all those possibilities in play (and that is where they must necessarily stay), I want to turn to think more specifically about the character of these 260-something jokes in the *Philogelos* and their underlying themes and preoccupations. In what ways might they have prompted laughter? And if we look beyond the type figures that give our version of the book its formal structure, what are the jokes actually about? For whatever their origins, this is the biggest assemblage of Roman jokes that we have. Are they merely a series of witty pot shots against men with bad breath, eggheads, and the dim denizens of Kyme? Or is the "Laughter lover" pointing us to some bigger issues, concerns, and fault lines in Roman culture?

GETTING THE JOKE

The jokes in the *Philogelos,* though mostly only a few lines long, come in a variety of recognizable styles. Some reflect the themes of fable, stage comedy, or epigram, others the spirit of mime (though we find very little of mime's bawdiness; this is in general a very clean collection).[40] Many of the gags turn on puns and wordplay.[41] Some work by conjuring up a striking visual image ("A *scholastikos* bought a house and peeking out of its window asked passersby if it suited him"—as if, we must imagine, he was trying on his house like he might have tried on a cloak).[42] One, at least, appears to match the observation of Cicero (see p. 112) that simply inserting some unexpectedly apposite quotation from poetry could be funny (in the *Philogelos* an actor pursued by two women—one with bad breath, the other with dreadful body odor—quotes a line from tragedy that neatly captures his dilemma).[43]

A number of them can still raise a laugh, even if they may need a helping hand from modern translations. Most of the English versions of the *scholastikos*, for example—whether "egghead," "numbskull," or "absent-minded professor"—are chosen precisely because they are part of the idiom of modern comedy and predispose us to a chuckle. Other jokes now seem decidedly less funny. That must sometimes be because of the almost unbridgeable gap between some of antiquity's conventions of joking and our own. Crucifixion, for example, does not have a big part in the modern comic repertoire. So the joke in the *Philogelos* about the man from Abdera who saw a runner being crucified and quipped, "He's no longer running, but flying," is likely to leave us cold—and uncomfortable.[44]

Scholarly ingenuity and expertise can sometimes rescue others or at least provide some excuse for the apparent lack of any funny point. The various editors of the Greek text of the *Philogelos* have on occasion blamed sloppy medieval copyists for missing out the punch line. So, for example, Roger Dawe, when confronted with a joke that simply reads, "An egghead, wanting to catch a mouse that was all the time gnawing at his books, sat down in the dark crunching meat . . . ," decided that someone, in the process of transmission, must have failed to finish the gag (for surely it was better than that).[45] Other critics have scoured the texts to unearth hidden puns in an attempt to recover the funny points we have missed (much like Fontaine's project with Plautus; see p. 56).

A typical example is the very first joke in the modern collection: "An egghead asked a silversmith to make a lamp. When the smith asked how big he should make it, the egghead replied, 'For eight people.'"[46] Maybe it is a good enough gag as it stands: the *scholastikos* confuses the conventions of measurement, for lamps are not sold according to the number of people they will illuminate (even though, from another perspective, that might not be such a bad way of doing it). But a clever recent study, convinced that on that standard interpretation it must be "one of the least funny items in this . . . book," has claimed that we have simply missed the puns. The Greek word for "lamp" (*luknos*) is also the word for a fish, and *poieō* (make) is very occasionally attested in the sense of "prepare" (as in food or cooking). So maybe this is really a smart wordplay on lamps and fishes, on making and cooking. "How big do you want the lamp/fish?" Enough for eight.[47]

Or maybe not.[48] Satisfying as this—and other ingenious modern reconstructions of these jokes[49]—may be, we have to beware of that old pitfall of pouring too much energy into making them funny for us. In fact, it would be a fair assumption that some of the jokes in this collection were feeble anyway and not likely to raise a laugh even among an ancient audience. It is not merely that jokebooks, to fill their pages, tend to include bad jokes alongside the good, for the sad truth is that there are never quite as many sparkling ones as you need. It is also, more fundamentally, that the cultural coordinates of joking make bad and good jokes symbiotic and inseparable. We need the bad jokes to appreciate the good; they provide the necessary chorus line behind those that really will make us chuckle.

Among this chorus line in the *Philogelos* I would count one rather flat little story of a "simpleton" apprentice (presumably to a barber–cum–nail cutter). "A simpleton apprentice, told by his master to cut a gentleman's nails, started to weep. When the client asked why, he said, 'I'm scared, that's why I'm crying. For I'm going to hurt you, and you'll get sore fingers, and the master will beat me.'"[50] Likewise an even shorter tale of a "meanie" in the fuller's workshop: "A meanie went into a fullery and, not wanting to pee, died."[51] There must be some connection here with the use of urine in the fulling and laundry industry in Rome. Possibly (and this is the best explanation I can offer) the mean man was so keen not to give his valuable urine to the fuller for free that he retained it until his bladder burst and he died.[52]

Of course, some of these may have raised more laughs in the telling than they do on the page. Suppose that the jokes as recorded in the *Philogelos* were always intended as telegraphic summaries, to be embroidered and given comic color by the jester; then any performance might have added the kind of circumstantial detail that the bare one-liner of the meanie in the fullery seems desperately to need. (What exactly detained him, for example? Why didn't he just leave the fullery to have a pee?) We can only guess at the relationship between the text and the telling. But in general, I have little doubt that we go against the grain of this or any such collection if we demand that all its jokes be *good* jokes—whether by ancient or modern standards.

VIEWING THE WORLD AWRY

Good or not, jokes have plenty to tell us about Roman culture. Whether they prompted loud chortles, modest sniggers, or blank bemusement, they offer a sideways glance into ancient puzzles, problems, and debates that can otherwise remain hidden from us.

It is almost a truism (and one that I have exploited in this book) that laughter is a marker of areas of disruption and anxiety, whether social, cultural, or psychic. We have seen, for example, how Roman laughter negotiated the contested boundaries of power and status—between animals and humans, emperors and subjects. And the simple calculation that roughly 15 percent of the jokes in the *Philogelos* in some way concern death (from coffins to suicide or inheritance[53]) is probably enough to encourage some amateur Freudian theorizing in us all.

In thinking more widely, however, about the cultural implications of the jokes in the *Philogelos,* I have again found Simon Critchley's discussion of joking and laughter particularly helpful. For Critchley, jokes and (in his terms) "humour" operate in part as distancing devices, inviting us to view the world awry. Jokes are appealing because they help us to see our lives and assumptions "as if we had just landed from another planet" and to "relativize the categories" that we usually take for granted. "The comedian is the anthropologist of our humdrum everyday lives" and turns those of us who see the point of the joke—those who *get* it—into domestic anthropologists too. In the process of laughing, we are not only freed from "common sense"; we also recognize the misrepresentations, shortcuts, and occlusions that common sense rests on. For Critchley, in other words, jokes are as much heuristic, intellectual devices as windows into the wellsprings of our unconscious.[54]

We have already seen some aspects of this domestic anthropology. When we laughed at the *scholastikos* dodging his doctor because he had not been ill for a long time (pp. 190–91), we were at the same time recognizing the strangeness of our relationship with a man whose prosperity depends on our sickness. Likewise there are a number of jokes in the *Philogelos* that focus on the peculiar status of dreams and their relationship to waking reality. For example, "Someone met a *scholastikos* and said, 'My learned sir, I saw you in a dream.' 'Good god,' he replied, 'I was so busy I didn't notice you'" (or, in a slightly different variant, "'You're lying,' he said. 'I was in the country'").[55] Another egghead "dreamed that he trod on a nail and so bandaged his foot. An egghead friend asked the reason and, when he learned, said, 'We deserve to be called idiots. Why on earth did you go to bed without your shoes on?'" Much the same point is made in the joke about the cowardly hunter who dreamed he was chased by a bear, so bought some hounds and had them sleep next to him.[56]

Of course, many Romans would have had a more pressing interest in their dreams than modern dreamers have, seeing them as much more directly prophetic or diagnostic than any recent psychoanalytic theory would allow.[57] It is perhaps for that reason that the questions posed in these jokes turn out to be more acute than their simple comic form might suggest. There is more under the spotlight here than the general relationship between dream life and the waking world. Readers or audience are being prompted to reflect on the relative temporalities of dreams and everyday life, on the relationship between the dreamer and the other people who appear in the dream (what effect does our dreaming about someone else have on them?), and on the ability of the waking world to impact on the sleeping (can we be so sure that the hounds by the bedside will not keep the dream bears off?). In Critchley's terms, these gags—"like small anthropological essays"—acted to estrange ancient readers or listeners from their unreflective, commonsense assumptions on the nature of dreaming. The reward for the laugher would be the pleasure of reflecting differently on the problems of the dreamworld and of exploiting the capacity of the joke to expose the nagging puzzles normally hidden or brushed aside. Exactly where, for example, does a dream take place?

Other jokes in the collection, found across the various categories into which it is usually divided, seek to raise a laugh by challenging conventions of Roman social or cultural life that were even more fundamental. A few target the rules of succession, the orthodox ordering of family life, and the taboos that surrounded it. These expose the slippery relativity of the categories "father" and "son." So, for example, "A *scholastikos* got up one night and into bed with his grandmother. Taking a beating for it from his father, he said, 'Hey, you—it's been such a long time that you've been screwing my mother without getting a beating from me, are you angry that you found me just once on top of your mother?'"[58] The question is: How can rules and prohibitions acknowledge the shifting categories of family relations? In this joke, the consequence of the son resting his case on the law of nature—that everyone's father is someone else's son—is sexual mayhem. But in another gag, it is precisely that point that saves the day, as well as a baby's life. For there the story is that a young *scholastikos* has had a child by a slave, and his father suggests killing it (a fairly typical "solution" to unwanted children in the ancient world). The son's response? "Put your own children in their graves first, before you talk of getting rid of mine."[59]

A rather more unexpected convention held up for particular scrutiny in the *Philogelos* is that of number. We might have predicted that the rules and discontents of family and sexual life would have been obvious targets for a Roman jokester; we would not, I think, have imagined that the conventional symbols of number and their relationship to "real" quantity would have been an even more prominent theme. Yet repeatedly we find jokes pointing to and playing with what we might call numerical tropes. In their simplest form—and for a modern readership, we must admit, it's not particularly funny—these rest on that old joking standby: the confusion of signifier and signified. So an egghead on a ship that was in danger of sinking, carrying with him a written debt bond for "one and a half million," decided to lighten its load simply by erasing the five hundred thousand. Whereas the other passengers had thrown their luggage overboard, the *scholastikos* proudly announces that he has reduced the weight of the ship (and, of course, at the same time the burden of his debt) just by rubbing out the 5.[60]

Much the same point underlies another, at first sight very different, gag. "A *scholastikos* was going away, and a friend asked him, 'Please buy me two slave boys, each fifteen years old.' He replied, 'OK, and if I can't find the pair, I'll buy you one thirty-year-old.'" Though we might be tempted to see sex as the main theme here (and indeed I have heard a few sexist modern jokes weighing up the virtues of two twenty-year-old women against one forty-year-old), the bottom line is surely number and the gap between numerical symbol and bodily reality. To spell it out (beyond an ounce of remaining humor): although two fifteens certainly do make thirty, one thirty-year-old slave is no substitute for two fifteen-year-olds. And with that comes a glimpse of the shifting, unstable conventions of number and counting, for, after all, one two-pound bag of flour would have been as good as two one-pound bags.[61]

Variants on this theme are found throughout the collection, playing space, size, time, and value against the symbols of number in subtly different ways. The subjects of these jokes range from the man from Kyme who broke into the house of a money lender to recover the most expensive IOU (and so took away the heaviest file) to the "Sidonian egghead" with a country estate who—wanting to make it nearer town—simply removed seven of the milestones along the route; from the *scholastikos* who wondered if the ladder had as many rungs going down as going up to the doctor from Kyme who charged half as much for treating a tertian fever (with a three-day recurrence) as a semitertian (with an alternate day recurrence).[62] This is another striking case where the repeated, underlying themes of joking give us an unexpected glimpse into some of the embedded debates, uncertainties, and contestations of the Roman world: here, how arithmetic works and how on earth to understand what a number is.

Those uncertainties notably extend to personal identity. One deceptively simple question—"How do I know who I am?"—leaves its vivid mark on the *Philogelos*. The gag about the *scholastikos,* the bald man, and the barber that launched this chapter revolves around exactly that issue (how do I tell the difference between "me" and "someone else"? Is it just a hair's breadth?). So do many others, including some of the most memorable in the collection. They repeatedly ask where authority and the rights of authentication in questions of personal identity lie. One short version goes like this: "A *scholastikos* bumped into some friend of his and said, 'I heard that you had died.' He replied, 'But you can see I'm alive.' And the *scholastikos* came back, 'But the person who told me was far more trustworthy than you.'"[63]

That is essentially the same point that we find in a rather more complex joke tagged to "a grumpy man" who wanted to avoid an unwelcome visitor who had come to call on him at home. "Someone was looking for a grumpy man. But he answered, 'I'm not here.' When the visitor laughed and said, 'You're lying—I hear your voice,' he replied, 'You scoundrel, if my slave had spoken, you would have believed him. Don't I seem to you more trustworthy than him?'"[64] This is, in fact, one of those jokes in the *Philogelos* with a venerable history stretching back centuries. Cicero quotes a similar though longer anecdote in *On the Orator*.[65] It is set in the second century BCE and features the Roman poet Ennius and Scipio Nasica, a leading member of one of republican Rome's grandest families. This story starts with Nasica calling on Ennius, only to find a maid who explains that Ennius is out. Despite her assurances, Nasica is convinced that she is just speaking to order and that Ennius really is at home. A few days later, the roles are reversed: "When Ennius had gone to call on Nasica and was asking for him at the door, Nasica cried out that he was not at home. 'What?' said Ennius. 'Don't I recognize your voice?' 'What a nerve you have,' retorted Nasica. 'When I was looking for you, I believed your maid when she said that you weren't at home. Don't you trust me myself?'"

There are some significant differences between the two versions. This is another case where the *Philogelos* includes an anonymized version of a joke elsewhere attributed to famous historical characters (see pp. 189–90). The main moral of the story is different too: in *On the Orator,* the apparently offending line is Nasica's clever way of teaching Ennius a lesson; in the joke collection, it is simply a crass piece of deception on the part of the grumpy man. But issues of identity and authority run through both, nuanced as they are by issues of status and slavery. In the simpler version of the *Philogelos*, the main question is whom you can trust to vouch for someone or for their presence or absence. The joking paradox points to the fact that it is impossible for anyone to vouch for their own absence.

Several other jokes touch on these and similar themes. "Was it you or your twin brother who died?" asks an egghead when he meets the survivor in the street. Another egghead decides to give his baby his own name, "and I'll just do without one." What, in other words, is the relationship between naming and selfhood? At an embalmer's studio, a man from Kyme tries to identify the dead body of his father through his distinguishing feature: that is, his cough. How far, this joke asks, does identity—and its markers—survive death? How funny is it that the affliction, which presumably defined the old man and eventually killed him, turns out to be no use at all in identifying him among a load of other look-alike corpses?[66]

Whatever the precise social origin of the *Philogelos,* its variants, and its predecessors—whether we imagine it coming fresh from the barbershop or crafted on the library desk—laughter here is pointing us to the debates and anxieties that must have bulked large in a world where formal proofs of identity were minimal: no passports, no government-issued ID, not much in the way of birth certificates or any of those other forms of documentation that we now take for granted as the means of proving who we are.[67] In the Roman world, identity was a problem: people must have gone to ground, reinvented and renamed themselves, pretended to be who they were not, or failed to convince even their closest family that they really were who they claimed to be. The domestic anthropology of these jokes presumably raised a laugh (or hoped to) by exposing to a Roman audience the very nature of their day-to-day uncertainties about the self. When that egghead woke up, rubbed his head, and wondered if he had suddenly turned into the bald man, he was gesturing—hilariously, maybe—to shared anxieties about who in fact was who. Just as the story of the man who wanted to keep the dogs by his bed, to frighten off the dream bears, chimed with all kinds of Roman questions about the status of what you "saw" when you were asleep.

ROMAN JOKEBOOKS

The *Philogelos* is the only Roman jokebook to survive. Modern (re)-construction though it is, it certainly descends from a joke collection, or more likely collections, assembled, configured, and reconfigured in the Roman Empire. Whatever the point or the funny side of its individual gags, the *Philogelos* as a whole raises questions about the genre of the jokebook. Where and when did such anthologies originate? What do they imply about the status of jokes and joking? What hangs on the apparently simple fact that jokes could become the object of collecting and classification?

We have already come across references to various collections that may have been similar in some ways to the *Philogelos*. Different compilers gathered together the wit and wisdom of Cicero in several volumes. These presumably provided the raw material for Macrobius' chapters on Cicero's jokes, and collections of the same kind may well have been the ultimate source of the numerous wisecracks of Augustus and Julia also quoted in the *Saturnalia* (see pp. 77–78, 104–5, 130–31, 156). In fact, anthologies of witty sayings coined by notable individuals were clearly part of the stock-in-trade of ancient literary production. There are surviving examples in the various collections of *apophthegmata* compiled by Plutarch (*Sayings of Kings and Commanders, Sayings of the Spartans,* and *Sayings of the Spartan Women*) and clear traces of them in such works as Lucian's *Life* of the second-century CE philosopher Demonax, which largely consists of a list of his witty or moral sayings (often referred to as *chreiai*)—presumably drawn from some earlier anthology.[68] And there were once many more, now known only from the occasional quotation or brief reference. Julius Caesar, for example, was supposed to have compiled his own *Dicta Collectanea* (Collected Sayings), reputedly suppressed after his death by Augustus.[69]

Wit may well have been the hallmark of these collections. But whatever their superficial similarities to the *Philogelos*, they are crucially different in one major respect. They are all, as the title *Dicta* or *Apophthegmata* suggests, compilations of sayings of particular named individuals, which remain explicitly tied to their originators—even if there were sometimes competing claims about who exactly had coined which bon mot. In that sense, they are as close to the traditions of biography as to the traditions of joking.[70] They stand clearly apart from the unattributed, decontextualized, generalized jokes of the *Philogelos*.

To these, the closest parallel may possibly be found in the 150 volumes of *Ineptiae* (Trifles), later called *Ioci* (Jokes), put together by an imperial librarian named Melissus in the reign of Augustus. But although it was obviously a vast compendium of wit, we do not have the faintest clue of its focus or organizational principles. It too might have been organized biographically, as a series of witty sayings by great men and a few women.[71] Clearer parallels, albeit fictional, are the jokebooks that formed a distinctive part of the professional equipment of parasites in

Roman comedy (see pp. 149–50). In Plautus' *Stichus* we find the unfortunate Gelasimus trying to learn up jokes from his *libri* (books)—which at one point earlier in the play he had tried to auction off to the audience in return for dinner (a classic case of a desperate man selling his sole means of support just to get his next meal).[72] Saturio, the parasite in the *Persa* (*The Persian*), perhaps has a better idea of the value of his books. He sees their jokes as a potential dowry for his daughter: "Look, I've got a whole cartful of books. . . . Six hundred of the jokes in them will be yours for your dowry."[73]

Whatever their real-life models may have been, Plautus' jokebooks were ultimately a figment of his imagination, and he never quotes any of their (imaginary) gags. The terms he uses to describe them—*verba, dicta, logi, cavillationes,* and so forth—could mean almost anything across the whole repertoire of wit, joking, and banter. But the logic of the comic plot demands that these quips were multipurpose, brought out and adapted for any occasion when the parasite might want to raise a laugh; it demands that they were generic rather than specific jokes. It is for that reason that some modern readers of the *Philogelos* have been keen to see that collection as the closest we have to the practical aide-mémoire of an ancient jester.

That is, however, to miss a more important signal that Gelasimus, Saturio, and their joking equipment offer. For despite the close, formal relationship between Roman comedy and its Greek comic ancestors, there is no indication at all that parasites in Greek comedy came onstage carrying their jokebooks or that jokebooks ever acted as props in the Greek comic repertoire. None of the surviving traces of those plays gives any hint of them. Arguments from silence are, of course, always perilous. But the evidence we have (and there are, as we shall see, other pointers in the same direction) suggests that jokebooks of this type, whether on or off the stage, were something characteristically Roman. To return to some of the big themes I broached in chapter 4, the jokebook—in contrast to compendia of witty maxims or sayings attached to named characters—may be one of those features that help us prize apart a little the "laughterhood" of Rome from that of Greece.

This is not the usual story. Scholars have normally assumed that there must have been such general joke anthologies in the ancient Greek world and massaged fragments of evidence to fit. Robert Maltby, for example, has taken Saturio's reference to "Athenian" and "Sicilian" jokes among those that might make up his daughter's dowry ("They'll be all Athenian; you won't get a single Sicilian") as proof of Athenian and Sicilian traditions of jokebooks.[74] But that is to miss the point. Saturio was surely referring casually to the stereotypical hierarchy of jesting in the Roman world, with "Attic salt" coming out on top, Sicilian wit a little way behind (see p. 94). Only really tip-top jokes were to be included in the dowry—even Sicilian ones wouldn't be quite good enough.

To others, the surviving titles of classical and Hellenistic Greek anthologies of wit and humor have suggested a literary tradition very much in the style of the *Philogelos*. But that too is very hard to sustain when we look at what little we can reconstruct of the books beyond their titles. At first sight, for example, we might expect Aristodemus' collection—*Geloia Apomnēmoneumata* ("Funny Stories" or "Humorous Memoirs")—to contain a mixed bag of jokes, not simply the sayings of particular individuals. Maybe it did. But the few quotations preserved from it in Athenaeus (and that is all we have) suggest something closer to named, authored bons mots.[75]

Even the supposed remains of a genuine Hellenistic jokebook—now often hailed as a single precious survival of the genre—hardly stand up to much scrutiny. The traces of text on this very ragged third-century BCE papyrus are frankly scant. They seem to indicate a series of one-line comments or questions grouped under various headings. *Eis purron* is the only heading to survive complete, but editors have disagreed whether this means "to (or against) a redhead" or "to (or against) Pyrrhos" (as a proper name, with a capital *P*). They have also disagreed about the status of the one-liners set beneath the headings. In the case of *eis purron*, so far as we can decipher the wording, these seem to take the form of "You do not have a face [*prosōpon*], but . . . ," repeated with different and equally puzzling insertions following the *but*: "the evening sun," for example, "the coals of the fire," and so on.[76] It is down almost entirely to the efforts of Rudolf Kassel that it is has become known as a jokebook, for he bravely tried to connect some of its idioms with the banter of the *scurrae* in Horace's *Satire* on the journey to Brundisium (see p. 68) and other Latin comic forms.[77] Unsurprisingly, other critics have thought differently, detecting instead the remains of an anthology of epigrams or even some kind of physiognomical text.[78] The fact is that the papyrus is far too fragmentary to yield any certain conclusion—except that there is nothing, beyond some possible scheme of classification by type of character, to link it with the kind of material we find in the *Philogelos*.

We can never state with complete confidence that any particular cultural form or literary genre did not exist in either the Greek or the

Roman world (in fact, some of the jokes in the *Philogelos* pointedly remind us how tricky it is to authenticate absence). The literary culture of classical and Hellenistic Greece certainly spawned collections of all sorts (including witty maxims, epigrams, riddles, and sayings), and we could debate endlessly where the boundary lay between one type and another, what their various functions were, and what might count as a book of "jokes." But all the indications are that jokebooks, of the kind we have been exploring in this chapter, were not a significant part of the classical Greek landscape; they were much more commonly a Roman product (whether of the Latin world of Plautus or the wider, mixed culture of the Roman imperial Mediterranean). If so, our next, and final, question must be: what does that imply about the role, status, and function of the Roman joke? To put it another way, what difference does it make to the idea of joking that a joke could become a free-floating "collectible"?

THE ROMAN JOKE?

There could be no such thing as the world's (or even the Western world's) first joke. Any claim about where "the joke" began quickly collapses under questions of definition. What distinguishes jokes from all the other verbal ways of provoking laughter? Does a witty epigram, a fable, or a pun count as a joke? If laughter is as old as humanity, can we possibly imagine a time in the history of human communication when language was not used to raise a laugh?

Yet when Gelasimus comes onstage and threatens to sell his jokes and his jokebooks in exchange for a good dinner, we are in a distinctive and recognizable world of joking. Jokes here are commodities of a sort. Even though the scene is itself meant to be a joke, Gelasimus' gags are deemed to have a value. They are objects that play a role in a system of exchange. They have an existence independent of the individual jokester; in Saturio's case, they can even be bequeathed down the generations. They are also objects with their own history; in fact, we saw in Thraso's joke about the young Rhodian in Terence's *Eunuch* (pp. 13, 90–91) that a joke's history could be part of its point and part of what prompted a laugh. For all its Roman comic coloring, there is something familiar to us about this. In the modern world also, jokes are often part of a system of exchange. We *swap* jokes. We tell them competitively. For us too, they can be commodities with a genealogy and a value. Some people even make their living by selling wisecracks to radio and television.

There is much less sign of that sort of commodification in the world of classical and Hellenistic Greece. Of course, there were all kinds of ways in which language and literature of that period raised a laugh; there were many sharp and funny sayings attributed to famous figures, from statesmen to philosophers; and there were various times when a joke was expected (the idea of a freeloader getting a dinner by playing the jester was not a Roman invention). There are also occasional hints of a more generalized, anonymized style of gag that is reminiscent of the *Philogelos*. The closest we come is in Aristophanes' comedy *Wasps*, where, in the rumpus at the end of the play, old Philocleon tries unsuccessfully to calm things down in what he has been told is a gentlemanly and sophisticated way—by telling a "Sybarite story": "A man from Sybaris fell out of his chariot and somehow smashed his head very badly. For in fact he wasn't a skilled driver. Then a friend of his stood over him and said, 'People should pursue whatever trade they know.'"[79] Sybarite stories are a curious subgenre of ancient moralizing wit, focusing on the supposed stupidity of the inhabitants of the South Italian city of Sybaris, which proverbially—before its destruction in the late sixth century BCE—had been far too rich for its own good. The stories are known mainly from snatches of quotations in writers of Roman date and are usually grouped with fable—as they are by Aristophanes himself earlier in the play ("something funny from Aesop or a Sybarite story"). The anonymous stupid Sybarite cannot help but recall those dumb inhabitants of Abdera, Kyme, and Sidon in the *Philogelos*.[80]

In classical and Hellenistic Greece, however, jokes do not seem to have been treated as collectible commodities in quite the way they were in Rome or in the Roman world. That difference is nicely captured in a story about King Philip of Macedon reported by Athenaeus in his extraordinary multivolume encyclopedia-cum-anthology of literature and culture, *The Philosophers' Banquet*. Written in Greek by a man from the Roman province of Egypt around the turn of the second and third centuries CE, this pretends to be the script of a dinner party hosted by a wealthy Roman patron and featuring a number of learned discussants who exchanged quotations and a dazzling (and sometimes, let's be honest, tedious) brand of academic chitchat. Jokes and joking were among Athenaeus' themes, and I have already taken advantage of some of the offbeat material he preserves, including the curious story of Parmeniscus and his inability to laugh (see pp. 174–76). One character at this party—a Roman by the name of Ulpian—has a particularly revealing tale to tell about Philip attempting to buy some jokes.[81]

Ulpian explains that in Athens in the fourth century BCE, there was a group of witty men who used to meet in a sanctuary just outside the city. Known as The Sixty, from their number, they had a particular skill (*sophia*) in raising a laugh. When Philip heard of the group, he offered a large amount of cash in exchange for their gags (*geloia*): "He sent them a talent of silver, so that they would write their jokes down and send them to him."[82] This story has often been used as another piece of evidence for the existence of joke collections in fourth-century Greece (this group of jokesters was just "the sort who might have transformed their oral repertory into written jokebooks," as one critic has written).[83] And so it might at first sight appear.

It is only in the course of writing this chapter that I have come to realize that the story—and its underlying moral—much more likely points in the opposite direction. Although the summary that Athenaeus offers is very brief, it is closely followed by anecdotes relating to the fondness for laughter of a couple of notoriously unpleasant autocrats (Demetrius Poliorcetes and Sulla). In the original Athenian context, the story of The Sixty was almost certainly seen not as a positive instance of an enterprising spirit of literary collecting but as a negative example of transgressive, autocratic commodification: Philip, the rich and powerful monarch, wrongly thought he could buy the wit of The Sixty in convenient, take-away, paper form (whether or not they sent the jokes to him we are not told[84]).

The Roman world was different. To put it at its starkest, the commodification of joking (into jokes swapped, handed down, collected, or bought and sold) was not some sign of the transgressive will of an autocrat; it seems much more like a Roman cultural norm. That is the implication not just of the banter of Gelasimus and his fellow Roman comic parasites or of the idiom of the *Philogelos*. The striking disparity of vocabulary between Latin and Greek that I stressed in chapter 4 nudges us in the same direction. Latin has an extremely—almost needlessly— rich range of words for a joke, whereas the Greek language seems to prioritize the vocabulary of laughing and laughter, with *geloion* and *skōmma* (to which we might possibly add *chreia*) rather overstretched in doing their duty as the words for gags of various types.

It would be dangerously oversimplifying to draw sharp and fixed contrasts between the joking cultures of "Greece" and "Rome" from these telling hints. Yet it would also be irresponsibly unimaginative to remain blind to the different cultural coordinates of jokes and joking that they suggest: in particular, the idea that in the Roman world, the joke not only operated as a mode of interaction but existed as a cultural object or a commodity in its own right (or as a noun rather than a verb). The most risk-averse scholar might see this in terms of a difference in emphasis, complicated maybe by the patterns of evidence and its survival. The boldest would be tempted to make much more radical claims, locating the origins of "the joke," as we now understand it, within Roman culture and seeing it—far outstripping bridge building and roads—as one of the most important bequests of the Romans to the history of the West. As I reach the end of this book, rather like a comic as the show comes to its close, I am inclined to boldness.

But whatever line we choose to take, the question of how exactly to account for the particular character of the joke in the Roman world remains puzzling. And it takes us back to all those issues of how we might write a history of laughter, including its changes over time (and place), that I raised in chapter 3. Various factors seem relevant here. We could point to the nature of Roman rhetorical theory and practice and the way it reified different forms of speech. We could focus on the social relations that Roman comedy represents between Gelasimus and his patrons (whether onstage or in the audience). How far was the idea of a joke as a commodity connected to the notoriously sharp-edged transactional relations in the Roman world between patron and client, rich and poor? Was it in that context that joking became defined as an object of exchange (as much as a mode of cultural interaction)? We might also, more cynically, reflect that it was one of the hallmarks of imperial Rome's domination to commodify culture—whether that of the rest of the Mediterranean or its own. Everything in the Roman Empire had a price. Just as the imperial conquerors did in their purchase, confiscation, replication, exchange, classification, and valuation of works of art, so too they did with wit, jokes, and joking. No surprise, then, that "the King Philip model" became one powerful strand in the "laughterhood" of Rome.

All those factors may have a part to play. But as always, it is well worth paying careful attention to what the inhabitants of the Roman Empire themselves had to say—and, in this case, to return finally to Athenaeus. Just before he tells of Philip's interest in The Sixty, Ulpian is already dealing with the subject of jokes, and he broaches the question (crazy as it may seem to us now) of who invented "the joke." His main text is a few lines from a play (*The Madness of Old Men*) by a fourth-century BCE comic dramatist, Anaxandrides: "Rhadamanthys and Palamedes had the idea of making the person who comes to the dinner party without any contribution [*asymbolos*] tell jokes." We know little or nothing about the context of this remark in the play, which does not survive beyond scattered quotations and references. But particularly revealing for the history of laughter is the way in which Ulpian introduces and constructively misinterprets the lines he quotes: "In *The Madness of Old Men*," he says, "Anaxandrides claims that Rhadamanthys and Palamedes were the inventors [*heuretai*] of jokes."[85] That is not what Anaxandrides wrote at all: so far as we know, he merely said that these two mythic figures were the first to have the bright idea of getting freeloaders at dinner to pay for their food with laughter.

These few lines encapsulate a lot more about Greek and Roman laughter than it might appear. Athenaeus, writing in the late second century CE, has—unconsciously perhaps—reinterpreted Anaxandrides' claims about a social practice (the role of a parasite at dinner) into claims about jokes themselves. Indeed, most modern writers have followed Athenaeus in suggesting that Anaxandrides attributed the invention of *geloia* (jokes) to Rhadamanthys and Palamedes, two well-known inventors and intellectuals in the Greek mythological tradition.[86] Anaxandrides did nothing of the kind. In fact, this deceptively simple passage marks the shift I have been suggesting from the *practice of joking* to the commodified *joke*. The fourth-century Greek dramatist was talking about the former, but the Roman-period author assumes the latter—reflecting the status of the joke in his world, as an object of study and theorizing in its own right, as an object with its own value and history, as an object that could be invented or discovered.

That is the sense in which we might conclude that it was indeed "the Romans" who invented "the joke."[87]

Afterword

Toward the end of my time at Berkeley, I had a long coffee break in the Free Speech Movement Café on campus with Erich Gruen, a renowned Berkeley ancient historian whose work I have read, debated, and sometimes disagreed with since I was an undergraduate in the 1970s.

We reflected on the themes of my Sather Lectures and on the distinctive features, sometimes strangeness, of Roman laughter. We talked about many of the topics that I have now written up in this book: the place of laughter on the boundary between human and animal, emperor and subject, gods and men; the absence of smiling as a cultural signifier; the range of (to us) weird Roman speculations on where the origins of laughter might lie. How could we imagine a world in which the lips, rather than the soles of the feet, might be thought the most ticklish zone of the human body? Could we ever see the funny side of a casual joke about crucifixion? Did we really believe that there were some chemical substances in the ancient world—or, for that matter, magical springs— that made people giggle? Besides, what would a history of ancient (or later) laughter look like, and how would Roman laughter fit into that?

Erich's approach was characteristically against the grain. For him, he said, the surprising thing about Roman laughter was not its strangeness. To be sure, it could sometimes seem puzzling, even incomprehensible, in many of the ways that I had pointed out. But no less striking was the simple fact that two thousand years later, in a radically different world, we could still laugh at some of the gags that apparently had made the

Romans crack up. Wasn't the big problem, he asked, the *comprehensibility* of Roman laughter, not the reverse?

We talked on for a while, wondering what might explain our capacity to get the Roman joke, or at least to get some Roman jokes. It would obviously be dangerous to set one's face entirely against the universals of neuroscience. The prompts to laughter in the human brain may in some ways transcend cultural difference. It would be equally dangerous to be blind to those patterns in world folklore that—however we explain it—throw up very similar themes and story lines in popular tales, fables, and sayings across the globe. In fact, there are traditional Arabic jokes with a striking resemblance to some of those in the *Philogelos*.[1] Yet most of what I had talked about through the lectures suggested that by and large, cultural differences in the practice of laughter trump whatever cultural or biological universals it might be reassuring to fall back on.

Over the five years since that conversation, I have become increasingly convinced that the reason we can laugh along with the ancient Romans is because it is from them that—in part at least—we have learned *how* to laugh and what to laugh *at*. I still think that there is an element of suggestibility in the chuckles that some gags in the *Philogelos* can produce in a modern audience (we laugh because we are determined to, and because it is funny in itself to laugh at jokes that have been around for two millennia—and anyway, they are translated and told with the idiom of modern jokes in mind). But there is more to it than that.

However tentative the claim that the Romans invented the joke must always remain (and, of course, I meant it to some extent as a provocation), one thing is absolutely certain: those wits and scholars from the Renaissance on who helped to define the main contours of European laughter culture with their learned debates and hugely popular collections of jokes and "merry tales" looked directly back to ancient Rome as ancestor and inspiration. Cicero's *On the Orator* provided them not only with the closest thing they had to a theory of laughter but also with a collection of wisecracks that could be taken over—as they stood or redressed in modern clothing—into their own anthologies of *facetiae*, and there was Macrobius' *Saturnalia* to be raided as well, where the bons mots of Cicero himself could be found.[2] By the eighteenth century, parts of the *Philogelos* were also widely available. In fact, the great Cambridge classicist Richard Porson (1759–1808) is commonly said to have planned to write a scholarly edition of the best-known jokebook of that period, *Joe Miller's Jests,* in order to show that every single joke in it was descended from the ancient "Laughter lover." He would have been wrong—but not as wrong as you might think.[3]

Of course, there have been all kinds of other influences on modern laughter. It would be ridiculous to claim an unadulterated line of descent from the Roman culture of laughter to our own, and no less ridiculous to imagine a single homogenous culture of modern Western laughter anyway, whether across or within linguistic and ethnic boundaries (the long tradition of Jewish joking is one other tradition among many). And, of course, the raids that our ancestors made on classical joke collections were highly selective. Erudite Renaissance humanists and eighteenth-century jokesters must have found some of what they read in their ancient sources as baffling as we do, sometimes more so; as we've already seen (p. 186), Dr. Johnson struggled to get the one about the egghead, the bald man, and the barber. Nonetheless, the jokes that they selected, retold, adapted, and handed down from those Roman models are built into the foundations of our modern idioms of joking, stand-up, and comic one-liners. So it's hardly surprising that we still laugh at them—or that they should demand (and deserve) the kind of attention I have given to them, and to the wider "laughterhood" of Rome, in the course of this book.

In fact, we still retell Roman jokes almost word for word—knowingly or, more often, unknowingly.

One of the quips attributed to Enoch Powell—a notorious twentieth-century politician, sardonic wit, and expert classicist—is his reply to a chatty barber. "How should I cut your hair, sir?" "In silence" was Powell's answer. This circulates widely in collections of modern humor and repartee and gains grudging admiration even from those who detest Powell's politics. My guess is that Powell was well aware that he had borrowed his clever retort from the joke about the chatty barber in the *Philogelos,* or alternatively from the same quip recounted by Plutarch and attributed to King Archelaus of Macedon (p. 189). I wouldn't even be surprised if for Powell, part of the joke was that he knew exactly where it came from and those who repeated it with such admiration clearly didn't.[4]

Other classical jokes can be even more deeply buried in our culture. It was pure serendipity that for bedside reading during the first weeks of my stay in Berkeley I had chosen Iris Murdoch's novel *The Sea, the Sea.* It's a classic Murdoch tale of angst and sexual intrigue among the privileged classes, featuring in this instance a retired actor, Charles Arrowby, who hopes (vainly) to escape his difficult metropolitan entanglements by moving to a cottage on the coast. Almost halfway through the novel, he spends a drunken evening with his friend and rival Peregrine, who is keen to stay up drinking all night. "Don't go," he pleads, as Charles finally makes a move. "I'll tell you Freud's favourite joke, if I can remember it. The king meets his double and says, 'Did your mother work in the palace?' and the double says, 'No, but my father did.' Ha ha ha, that's a good joke!" He then drunkenly repeats it, thinking that Charles hasn't seen the point: ". . . for Christ's sake, don't go, there's another bottle. 'No, but my father did'!"[5]

Whether or not this was Freud's favorite joke, we haven't a clue. But Freud certainly used it as an example in his own book on jokes. There it is a member of the royal family on tour in the provinces who "noticed a man in the crowd who bore a striking resemblance to his own exalted person. He beckoned to him and asked: 'Was your mother at one time in service in the Palace?'—'No, your Highness,' was the reply, 'but my father was.'"[6] Murdoch's joke jumped off the page at me. Of course it did: I'd been reading it that very day in the library. But neither Murdoch nor Freud seems to have spotted that "Freud's favourite joke" went back almost two thousand years. Macrobius quoted it as a great example of how patiently Augustus put up with quips told at his expense (see pp. 130–31, 252n10). And Valerius Maximus quotes a very similar snatch of banter describing an encounter between a Roman governor of Sicily and an ordinary resident in the province who was his spitting image. The governor was amazed at the likeness, "since his father had never been to the province. 'But my father went to Rome,' the look-alike pointed out."

The old ones, as they say, really are the best.

Cambridge
1 December 2013

Acknowledgments

I arrived at UC Berkeley in September 2008 with a mess of ideas about laughter in my head and absolutely nothing on paper. I am enormously grateful to all the classicists and ancient historians there (faculty and graduate students) for giving me the support and confidence to pull that mess together—and for making me feel so at home. I shall never forget clothes shopping with Leslie Kurke, touring the local wineries and having my first American Thanksgiving with Andy Stewart and Darlis, learning about the mysteries of election "propositions" with Kathy McCarthy, and reconnecting with Ron Stroud after more than thirty years. The graduates took me under their wing and were determined that I should miss nothing of the excitement of a U.S. presidential campaign. It is good now to bump into so many of them at conferences in different parts of the world and find them going from strength to strength. They are a great advertisement for Berkeley.

In the long process of turning the lectures into this book, I have had generous help from colleagues in Cambridge and elsewhere, who have read parts of the draft and answered queries of all kinds: Colin Annis, Franco Basso, James Clackson, Roy Gibson, Ingo Gildenhard, Simon Goldhill, Richard Hunter, Val Knight, Ismene Lada-Richards, Robin Osborne, Michael Reeve, Malcolm Schofield, Ruth Scurr, Michael Silk, Caterina Turroni, Gloria Tyler, Carrie Vout, Andrew Wallace-Hadrill, Tim Whitmarsh. Joyce Reynolds has read and commented on the whole manuscript (I feel very privileged to be approaching my sixtieth birthday and still able to discuss my work with my old undergraduate teacher!).

Many other people have also contributed to the project. Debbie Whittaker chased up endless references and used her unusually sharp eyes to get the bibliography under control. Lyn Bailey and the staff of the Classics Faculty Library in Cambridge went far beyond the call of duty in helping me find books and check references in the final stages. My contacts at UC Press (especially Cindy Fulton and Eric Schmidt) have been a pleasure to work with, as has Juliana Froggatt, a great copy editor. The learned commenters on my blog (http://timesonline.type-pad.com/dons_life/) have chipped in with all kinds of sharp suggestions, from bibliography to joke interpretations; one even spotted that my subtitle was a clear, if unconscious, echo of Adam Phillips's great book, *On Kissing, Tickling, and Being Bored.*

Special thanks must go to my fellow students of ancient laughter: To Stephen Halliwell, who read and discussed two key chapters with me (and boosted my confidence when it was flagging), and to Catherine Conybeare, who did likewise and kindly shared a preliminary version of her new book, *The Laughter of Sarah* (which coincidentally arrived on my desk in printed form just as I was writing my afterword). And above all to Peter Stothard, who came to the rescue on several occasions when I was feeling defeated by what I was trying to write; he had a wonderful knack of seeing my point, and how it could most effectively be put, better than I did myself.

My family, Robin, Zoe, and Raphael, have helped in all the ways that families do, and more—including (in Raphael's case) the filial duty of helping to check references and translations. They deserve a bit of a break from *Laughter in Ancient Rome.*

Texts and Abbreviations

In the notes, I have followed the conventions of *L'Année philologique* for abbreviating the titles of periodicals. For titles of ancient works, I have given a fairly full version or used the abbreviations of the *Oxford Classical Dictionary* (third edition). In a few cases where it is standard practice and there can be no confusion (e.g., Catullus or Livy), my references omit the title entirely. All translations, unless otherwise indicated, are my own. I have used standard editions of ancient texts—Oxford Classical Texts, Teubners, or recent Loebs—but have pointed to different manuscript readings where significant. For modern works with a potentially misleading discrepancy between the date of the edition I have cited and the date of first publication, I have indicated both, in this form: Hobbes 1996 [1651].

Other abbreviations are as follows:

AE	*L'Année épigraphique: Revue des publications épigraphiques relatives à l'antiquité romaine.* Paris, 1888–.
AL	*Anthologia Latina*, ed. A. Riese et al. Leipzig, 1894–1926.
Anec. Graeca	*Anecdota Graeca*, ed. I. Bekker. Berlin, 1814–21.
AP	*Anthologia Palatina*, in *The Greek Anthology*, Loeb Classical Library, ed. W. R. Paton. London, 1916–18.

CGL	*Corpus Glossariorum Latinorum,* ed. G. Goetz et al. Leipzig, 1888–1923.
CIL	*Corpus Inscriptionum Latinarum.* Berlin, 1863–.
DK	*Die Fragmente der Vorsokratiker griechisch und deutsch,* 11th ed., ed. H. Diels and W. Kranz. Zurich and Berlin, 1964.
GCN	*Groningen Colloquia on the Novel.* Groningen, 1988–.
GLK	*Grammatici Latini,* ed. H. Keil. Leipzig, 1855–80.
IDelos	*Inscriptions de Délos.* Paris, 1923–.
ILS	*Inscriptiones Latinae Selectae,* ed. H. Dessau. Berlin, 1892–1916.
Jacoby, *FGrHist*	*Die Fragmente der griechischen Historiker.* Berlin, Leiden, 1923–.
L&S	*A Latin Dictionary,* ed. C. T. Lewis and C. Short. Oxford, 1879.
LGPN	*A Lexicon of Greek Personal Names,* ed. P. M. Fraser et al. Oxford, 1987–.
LIMC	*Lexicon Iconographicum Mythologiae Classicae.* Zurich, 1981–.
New Pauly	*Brill's New Pauly,* ed. H. Cancik, H. Schneider, and M. Landfester, English trans. ed. C. Salazar and F. G. Gentry. Leiden, 2002–10.
OLD	*Oxford Latin Dictionary,* ed. P. Glare. Oxford, 1982 (rev. 2012).
PLM	*Poetae Latini Minores,* ed. A. Baehrens. Leipzig, 1879–83 (rev. F. Vollmer).
P.Oxy.	*Oxyrhynchus Papyri.* Egypt Exploration Society. London, 1898–.
PPM	*Pompei, pitture e mosaici,* ed. G. Pugliese Carratelli. Rome, 1990–99.
Rerum memorandarum Lib.	F. Petrarca, *Rerum memorandarum Libri,* ed. G. Billanovich. Florence, 1945.
ROL	*Remains of Old Latin,* Loeb Classical Library, ed. E. H. Warmington. London and Cambridge, MA, 1935–40.

Notes

PREFACE

1. The poem is titled "Invocation of Laughter" (1909): ". . . O laugh out laugheringly / O, belaughable laughterhood—the laughter of laughering laughers . . ." This translation is from www.russianpoetry.net, a project of Northwestern University's Department of Slavic Languages and Literatures. It is also featured in Parvulescu 2010, 1–4.

1. INTRODUCING ROMAN LAUGHTER

1. Dio 73(72).18–21 gives a full account of these spectacles (20.2 notes the plans to fire into the crowd, in imitation of Hercules' attack on the Stymphalian birds); Hopkins and Beard 2005, 106–18, describes the arrangement of the audience and conventions of the proceedings (including on this occasion).

2. Herodian 1.15.

3. Dio 73(72).21.

4. On his name, see Roxan 1985, no. 133; Gowing 1990. Dio was probably a few years under forty at the time, hence my *young*.

5. Dio 73(72).23 (the timetable of composition); Millar 1964, 1–40.

6. Dio 73(72).21.

7. Carter 1992, 190. This essay is a wonderful attempt to redefine the "giggle" as a mechanism of female power (rather than as the trivializing laughter of "girls" and a sign of their powerlessness). See further p. 157.

8. *Anec. Graeca* 1.271. The erotics of κιχλίζειν and its association with prostitutes are clear in the numerous examples collected in Halliwell 2008, 491. But it is a more complicated word (and sound) than is often acknowledged; see, for example, Herodas 7.123, which describes it as "louder than a horse"—hardly a

"giggle" in our terms (despite the onomatopoeia). Jeffrey Henderson 1991, 147, points to other (erotic) associations.

9. The Greek insistently repeats the words: κἂν συχνοὶ παραχρῆμα ἐπ᾿ αὐτῷ γελάσαντες ἀπηλλάγησαν τῷ ξίφει (γέλως γὰρ ἡμᾶς ἀλλ᾿ οὐ λύπη ἔλαβεν), εἰ μὴ δάφνης φύλλα, ἃ ἐκ τοῦ στεφάνου εἶχον, αὐτός τε διέτραγον καὶ τοὺς ἄλλους τοὺς πλησίον μου καθημένους διατραγεῖν ἔπεισα, ἵν᾿ ἐν τῇ τοῦ στόματος συνεχεῖ κινήσει τὸν τοῦ γελᾶν ἔλεγχον ἀποκρυψώμεθα (Dio 73[72].21.2). In alluding (with no details) to a story of laughter defying all attempts to restrain it, Aristotle (*Eth. Nic.* 7.7, 1150b11) writes of people "bursting out in a flood of laughter" (τὸν γέλωτα ἀθρόον ἐκκαγχάζουσιν).

10. Dio 9.39. Dionysius of Halicarnassus' account of the same incident (*Ant. Rom.* 19.5) also features Tarentine laughter and shit, but it is the bad Greek, rather than the funny clothes, of the ambassadors that provokes the mirth. For a further example of Dio, as an eyewitness, using laughter as a response to the bathos of imperial power, see 74(73).16.

11. Despite the brave optimism of J.R. Clarke (2003; 2007, 109–32), who attempts to exploit visual images to access the world of "ordinary" people's laughter; see further above, pp. 57–59.

12. Hopkins 1983, 17 (my italics).

13. Critchley 2005, 79.

14. It is hard to capture elegantly in English the potential slippage between something or someone who is laughable in the sense of "capable of raising a laugh" and something or someone who is laughable in the sense of "ridiculous." Where it seems particularly important, I highlight the issue with a hyphen: *laugh-able*. The more pronounced ambiguity in the Latin *ridiculus* is discussed on pp. 102–3, 125.

15. τὴν δὲ κεφαλὴν τὴν ἑαυτοῦ σεσηρὼς ἐκίνησεν (Dio 73[72].21.2). The word is discussed by Halliwell 2008, 521, 533nn12–13.

16. Suetonius, *Calig.* 27; Seneca, *De ira* 2.33; discussed on p. 134.

17. These paragraphs touch on a view of laughter commonly associated with Mikhail Bakhtin; see further pp. 59–62. Critchley 2005 offers a brisk critique of Bakhtin, on which I draw here, and, in so doing, usefully headlines Slavoj Žižek's critique of Umberto Eco's *The Name of the Rose* (with its strident claims that totalitarianism offers no place for laughter) and Žižek's (semiserious) arguments that Eastern-bloc totalitarianism was anyway itself always "a joke"; see especially Žižek 1989, 28–30. Semiserious or not, Žižek encourages us to think of a much more diverse engagement between laughter and political power.

18. A wall painting from the Villa San Marco at Stabiae captures this scene (Barbet and Miniero 1999, vol. 1, 211–12; vol. 2, plate 12.4), and Dio's reference to Hercules and the Stymphalian birds (see above, n. 1) suggests that the emperor's antics were seen in mythic terms. But maybe we should not press this too far; the truth is that the canonical image of Perseus with the head of Medusa held high in one hand and sword in the other is in large part a creation of the Renaissance (with Benvenuto Cellini's statue from the Piazza della Signoria in Florence a key inspiration).

19. For example, Hopkins 1983, 16–17; Dunkle 2008, 241.

20. We should be alert to (at least) two senses of the English phrase *laugh at*. In the weaker sense, "What are you laughing at?" is more or less synonymous with "Why are you laughing?" ("I'm laughing at the jokes"). In the stronger sense, it represents something more aggressive ("I'm laughing at Commodus"). This is not unlike the range of the Latin "Quid rides?" (as in the passage of Terence discussed on pp. 11, 14).

21. For Romans laughing at the bald, see pp. 51, 132–33, 146.

22. The complexities of Dio's account are well noted by Hekster 2002, 154–55.

23. The precise details of the history of Roman games (*ludi*) and the development of theatrical performances within them are complex, and in part obscure; see F.H. Bernstein 1998; F.H. Bernstein 2011; Beard, North, and Price 1998, vol. 1, 40–41, 66–67; vol. 2, 137–44. Manuwald 2011, 41–55, reviews the festival contexts of theatrical performances.

24. Beacham 1991, 56—85 (on stages and staging); Manuwald 2011, 55–68 (Temple of the Great Mother, 57); Goldberg 1998 (specifically on the Temple of the Great Mother and comic performances of the second century BCE).

25. Hunter 1985 is a sane introduction; Marshall 2006 includes an up-to-date discussion of masks (126–58); with Manuwald 2011, 79–80. For masks, or not, in mime, see above, p. 168.

26. We rely here on the possibly unreliable account of Suetonius, *Poet., Terence* 2 (and we must assume that the "repeat performance" refers to the first production).

27. Barsby 1999 and Brothers 2000 are helpful discussions of the play as a whole.

28. Another manuscript version of the *didascalia* ascribes the first performance to the Ludi Romani (Barsby 1999, 78)—which would (sadly) rule out any direct connection between the representation of the eunuch in the play and the original performance context. The cult of Magna Mater was a complex amalgam, parading both Roman and disconcertingly foreign elements (such as castration); on these representational and other complexities, see Beard 1996.

29. Gnatho himself had already paraded that insincerity a couple of hundred lines earlier (249–50), in a double entendre on his life as a sponger, discussed on pp. 71–72.

30. My translation of this line ("Dolet dictum inprudenti adulescenti et libero," 430) follows Donatus' commentary and those more recent critics and translators (such as Barsby [1999, 164]) who see Gnatho flattering Thraso, by offering (mock) sympathy for the young Rhodian.

31. *TH.* una in convivio / erat hic, quem dico, Rhodius adulescentulus. / forte habui scortum: coepit ad id adludere / et me inridere. "quid ais" inquam homini "inpudens? / lepu' tute's, pulpamentum quaeris?" *GN.* hahahae. *TH.* quid est? *GN.* facete lepide laute nil supra. / tuomne, obsecro te, hoc dictum erat? vetu' credidi. *TH.* audieras? *GN.* saepe, et fertur in primis. *TH.* meumst. *GN.* dolet dictum inprudenti adulescenti et libero. *PA.* at te di perdant! *GN.* quid ille quaeso? *TH.* perditus: / risu omnes qui aderant emoriri. denique / metuebant omnes iam me. *GN.* haud iniuria.

32. *TH.* ego hinc abeo: tu istanc opperire. *PA.* haud convenit / una ire cum amica imperatorem in via. *TH.* quid tibi ego multa dicam? domini similis es. *GN.*

hahahae. *TH.* quid rides? *GN.* istuc quod dixti modo; / et illud de Rhodio dictum quom in mentem venit.

33. Donatus on *Eun.* 426; see also Eugraphius on *Eun.* 497.

34. *GLK* 6.447.7 (Marius Plotius Sacerdos); see also 1.419.7 (Diomedes, "hahahe"), 3.91.3–4 (Priscian, "ha ha hae"), 4.255.31 ([Probus], "hahahae"), 6.204.23 (Maximus Victorinus, "haha"). The minor textual variants in the manuscript tradition do not alter the main point (or sound). The recognition of laughter sounds in Greek texts is complicated by the fact that the simple substitution of a smooth for a rough, aspirated breathing turns a *ha ha ha* into an *ah ah ah!* Possible instances of laughter scripted in Greek comedy are discussed (and largely rejected) by Kidd 2011, with full reference to earlier bibliography, back to late antique and medieval critics who saw the problems that the presence or absence of aspiration caused.

35. One enterprising seventeenth-century systematizer, "un astrologue Italien, nommé l'Abbé Damascene," attempted to classify the variants in these sounds and relate them to the different temperaments, *hi hi hi* indicating melancholics, *he he he* cholerics, *ha ha ha* phlegmatics, and *ho ho ho* hotheads; cited in *Dictionnaire universel françois et latin*, vol. 5 (Paris, 1743), 1081. Kidd 2011, while acknowledging some version of *ha ha ha* as a possible means of representing laughter in Greek, points also to such variants as αἰβοιβοῖ and ἰῂῦ.

36. From Johnson's *Life of Cowley*, first published in a collected edition of 1779–81 (see now, conveniently, Lonsdale 2009, 33); it is an exaggeration because Johnson is referring to not only the *sound* but also the *cause* of laughter (a universalizing claim that this book will dispute).

37. Fraenkel 1922, 43–45 (2007, 32–35) offers the most significant variant interpretation—"You are a hare: you go after tasty food" (or in its weaker form "Du suchst dir *pulpamentum* wie ein Hase," "You look for *pulpamentum* like a hare")—which Fantham 1972, 80, follows but Wright 1974, 25–27, convincingly rejects.

38. Barsby 1999, 163. I stress "Donatus' text," as the version of his commentary that has come down to us is a very mixed tradition, including Donatus' own discussion and his compendium of earlier scholarship on the play as well as later additions and glosses incorporated in the process of transmission (Barsby 2000; Victor 2013, 353–58).

39. "Vel quod a physicis dicatur incerti sexus esse," Donatus, *Eun.* 426. Frangoulidis 1994 shows more generally how the themes of the exchanges between Thraso and Gnatho look forward to later scenes in the play.

40. Cicero, *De or.* 2.217; see p. 28.

41. Freud 1960 [1905]; his analysis in terms of "displacement" (86–93) seems particularly relevant here. The idea of incongruity is characteristic of (among others) the "General Theory of Verbal Humor" (GTVH), as developed in Attardo and Raskin 1991 and Attardo 1994. They stress, in a much more nuanced way than my crude summary suggests, how the *sequence* of interpretative dilemmas and their resolution construct a joke.

42. On Freud and the physicality of laughter, see pp. 38–39, 40.

43. SHA, *Carus, Carinus, Numerianus* 13.3–5.

44. For possibly older Greek antecedents, see pp. 90–91.

45. See p. 4.

46. Festus, p. 228L; Diogenes Laertius 7.185. See pp. 176–78 for further examples and discussion.

47. Interestingly, Donatus (*Eun.* 497) sees Thraso's question ("What are you laughing at?") and the whole exchange in terms of the soldier's desire to elicit flattery for his wit from the sponger (as at 427). Although the commentary reflects on the point of Parmeno's joke and its exaggeration of Thraso's status (495), it does not canvas this as a possible prompt for Gnatho's *hahahae*.

48. Goldhill 2006 discusses these issues well; Bakhtin 1986, 135, by contrast, claims (at least in relation to carnival laughter) that "laughter only unites" (see further pp. 60–62). Billig's stress on laughter and "unlaughter" (2005, 175–99) is also useful here.

49. Sharrock 2009, 163–249, discusses other aspects of "tired old jokes" (with a nice analysis of this particular exchange at 164–65). In general, recent discussions of laughter, ancient or modern, have tended to underplay its learned, practiced, or habitual aspects.

50. This idea of the self-reflexivity of laughter is a major theme throughout Halliwell 2008.

51. I have taken all these examples from good recent translations of *The Eunuch*: Radice 1976, Brothers 2000, and Barsby 2001. A particularly rich selection of laughter insertions (from *with a smile* to *digging him in the ribs*) can be found in the Loeb translation of Plautus, Nixon 1916–38.

52. A vague "dozen or so" because emendation can add to the total: Plautus, *Poen.* 768, *Pseud.* 946, 1052, *Truculentus* 209, and conjectured at *Mil.* 1073; Terence, *An.* 754, *Haut.* 886, *Hec.* 862, *Phorm.* 411, as well as *Eun.* 426, 497. The fragment of Ennius is quoted by Varro, *Ling.* 7.93 (= Ennius, frag. 370 Jocelyn; *ROL1*, Ennius, unassigned fragments 399); the mention of a shield has encouraged the (unnecessary) assumption that the original context was tragic. I have not included in my total here nine instances of scripted laughter (*hahahe*) in the *Querolus,* an anonymous version of Plautus' *Aulularia* probably composed in the early fifth century CE, nor the glosses of grammarians. But they would not point to any significantly different conclusion.

53. Other instances imply other emotions: for example, disbelief at Plautus, *Pseud.* 946, or relief at *Truculentus* 209—which, together with *Pseud.* 1052, encouraged Enk (1953, vol. 2, 57–58) and others to reinterpret the *(ha)hahae* as merely an exhalation, the Latin equivalent of "phew," a classic scholarly attempt to normalize Roman laughter.

54. This was widely reported in the British media: e.g., the *Daily Mail* (www.dailymail.co.uk/news/article-1085403/Jim-Bowen-brings-worlds-oldest-joke-book-London-stage—reveals-ancestor-Monty-Pythons-Dead-Parrot.html) and the BBC (http://news.bbc.co.uk/2/hi/7725079.stm).

2. QUESTIONS OF LAUGHTER, ANCIENT AND MODERN

1. *De or.* 2.235; the words are put in the mouth of the lead character in this part of the dialogue, Julius Caesar Strabo. I am lightly paraphrasing "Strabo"'s list of questions: "Quid sit ipse risus, quo pacto concitetur, ubi sit, quo modo

exsistat atque ita repente erumpat, ut eum cupientes tenere nequeamus, et quo modo simul latera, os, venas, oculos, vultum occupet?" (The text is uncertain: did Cicero imagine laughter taking over the blood vessels, *venas*, or cheeks, *genas*? See p. 116.) Quintilian (*Inst.* 6.3.7) follows Cicero's disavowal: "I do not think the origin of laughter has been satisfactorily explained by anyone— though many have tried" ("Neque enim ab ullo satis explicari puto, licet multi temptaverint, unde risus"). For Cicero the jokester, see pp. 100–105.

2. *De motibus dubiis* 4 (erections), 10.4–5 (laughter), with Nutton 2011, 349.

3. Pliny, *HN*, praef. 17, proclaims the array of facts; for his encyclopedic project in general, see Murphy 2004; Doody 2010.

4. 7.2, 7.72. See pp. 35, 83–84.

5. 11.198.

6. 11.205 ("sunt qui putent adimi simul risum homini intemperantiamque eius constare lienis magnitudine"). Pliny may be referring to removal (as he notes here that an animal can continue to live if its spleen is removed because of a wound), but elsewhere (23.27) he refers to drugs that reduce the size of the spleen. Serenus Sammonicus (*PLM* 21.426–30) and Isidore (*Etym.* 11.1.127) agreed with, or followed, Pliny in stressing the role of the spleen in laughter.

7. 7.79–80.

8. 24.164. For the identification with cannabis, see André 1972, 150: "Très certainement le chanvre indien (*Cannabis indica*, variété *de C. sativa* L)"; "crowfoot" is the suggestion of *L&S*, the *OLD* being more guarded with "a plant yielding a hallucinatory drug."

9. 31.19; Ramsay 1897, 407–8. For the springs on the Fortunate Islands, see Pomponius Mela 3.102.

10. 11.198. For the Greek tradition of such laughter, see Aristotle, *Part. an.* 3.10, 673a10–12, and Hippocrates, *Epid.* 5.95. How far this was clearly or systematically distinguished from the tradition, attested even earlier, of the "sardonic smile" or grimace of pain is a moot point; see Halliwell 2008, 93n100, 315.

11. Praef. 17; the first book of the *HN* consists entirely of a list of contents of books 2 to 37, with the authorities consulted for each.

12. 31.19 ("Theophrastus Marsyae fontem in Phrygia ad Celaenarum oppidum saxa egerere"). Usually assumed to be derived from Theophrastus' lost work *De aquis*; see Fortenbaugh et al. 1992, 394–95 (= *Physics*, no. 219).

13. Aristotle, *Part. an.* 3.10, 673a1–12.

14. *De usu part.* 1.22 (Helmreich) = 1, pp. 80–81 (Kuhn); discussed further above, pp. 165–67. For issues of Galen's dissection and his views on the homology between animal and human, see Hankinson 1997.

15. *Mor.* 634a–b (= *Quaest. conviv.* 2.1.11–12).

16. *De or.* 2.236 ("Haec enim ridentur vel sola vel maxime, quae notant et designant turpitudinem aliquam non turpiter"); Quintilian, *Inst.* 6.3.7.

17. *De or.* 2.242 (mimicry), 2.252 ("pulling faces," *oris depravatio*), 2.255 (the unexpected), 2.281 ("incongruous"); for further discussion of Cicero and incongruity, see p. 117. See also Quintilian, *Inst.* 6.3.6–112; like Cicero, Quintilian (6.3.7) stresses the different ways that laughter is stimulated, from words to action and touch.

18. *De or.* 2.217: "'Ego vero' inquit 'omni de re facilius puto esse ab homine non inurbano, quam de ipsis facetiis disputari.'" It is even closer to the modern cliché if we emend the text (as many have) to read *facetius* for *facilius* ("more wittily than wit itself").

19. Though, conceivably, in opting for "crowfoot" *L&S* had in mind *Ranunculus sardous* (the "Sardinian buttercup" or "laughing parsley"), a member of the crowfoot family that is said (by, e.g., Pausanias 10.17.13, though not by Pliny, *HN* 25.172–74) to produce a sardonic grin.

20. Fried et al. 1998.

21. Plato (*Resp.* 5.452d–e, and *Phlb.* 49b–50e) expresses a view of laughter as derisory; in general, as Halliwell 2008, 276–302, makes clear, Plato has much more to say about laughter than is usually recognized.

22. One influential recent source of this is Skinner 2004, which, as its title hints, explicitly equates Aristotle with "the classical theory of laughter" and has telling references throughout to "Aristotle's theory" (141) or even "Aristotelian theory in its most blinkered form" (153). See also Skinner 2001 and 2002 for similar, though not identical, versions of the argument. Other references to Aristotle as a systematic theorist, or to one or both of his two main laughter "theories," include Morreall 1983, 5; Le Goff 1997, 43; Critchley 2002, 25; Taylor 2005, 1. Billig 2005, 38–39, is a rare discordant view, describing Plato and Aristotle as offering "scattered observations" rather than "theories."

23. The classic attempt to find the Greek sources of Cicero's account of laughter in *De or.* 2 is Arndt 1904, esp. 25–40, identifying Demetrius of Phaleron as the principal influence. Greek sources also play a major part in the discussion of Cicero in Grant 1924, 71–158. More recently, along similar lines, Freudenburg claimed, "It is quite clear that the Hellenistic handbook writers on rhetoric, followed by Cicero, made no significant advance upon Aristotle's theory of the liberal jest" (1993, 58). "The liberal jest" is the hallmark of the witty gentleman (*eutrapelos*); see above, p. 32.

24. To parody Whitehead 1979 [1929], 39, with its famous claim that the "European philosophical tradition . . . consists of a series of footnotes to Plato."

25. For example, McMahon 1917; Cantarella 1975.

26. Eco 1983. Not all critics have admired *The Name of the Rose*. For Žižek (1989, 27–28), "there is something wrong with this book" ("*spaghetti* structuralism" as he nastily calls it) and its views on laughter. Laughter, in Žižek's worldview, is not simply "liberating" or "anti-totalitarian" (his words) at all, but often "part of the game" of totalitarianism.

27. Skinner 2008 (my italics). Classicists have been known to write in similar, if slightly less confident, terms; see, for example, Freudenburg 1993, 56.

28. Janko 1984, revisited by Janko 2001. Now in the de Coislin collection in the Bibliothèque Nationale (hence its modern name), the *Tractatus* was once part of a monastery library on Mount Athos. The sections most directly concerned with laughter are 5–6; some of their observations are very close to those found in a preface to manuscripts of Aristophanes and clearly belong to the same tradition—whatever that is.

29. Eloquent are, for example, Arnott 1985 (nicely summarizing, at 305, the much earlier conclusion of Bernays 1853, to the effect that the *Tractatus* was "a

miserable compilation by a pedantic ignoramus"); Silk 2000, 44 ("Janko's rewarding study . . . tends to evade its striking mediocrity"). Nesselrath (1990, 102–61) carefully argues against a direct Aristotelian connection but produces Theophrastus out of his hat. Halliwell 2013 (reviewing Watson 2012) is a succinct denunciation of the *Tractatus*.

30. Silk 2000, 44.

31. I owe much here to the view of Aristotle's theory of tragedy in Silk 2001. Note especially 176: "Aristotle's theory (indeed, his treatise [*Poetics*] as a whole), nevertheless, enjoys the reputation of a coherent argument, and not merely a series of brilliant, but loosely connected, *aperçus*. What is responsible for this? The answer, I suggest, is not the findings of Aristotle's scholarly interpreters (whose very public disagreements about this, that and the other point of doctrine tell their own story), but rather the constructive—or constructional—use made of Aristotle in post-Aristotelian theories of tragedy (and/or other serious drama), for which Aristotle's theory of tragedy is a given, and for which it is characteristically constructed as a *coherent* given." Although I would probably lay more responsibility at the door of Aristotle's modern "scholarly interpreters" (as Silk himself does in the footnote to this passage), the role of Renaissance historians and modern "laughter theorists" (from the Renaissance on) seems to me crucial in the retrospective construction of "the Aristotelian theory of laughter" too. For an even more trenchant view of the general incoherence of the *Poetics*, see Steiner 1996: "As I listen, endlessly, to debates on the *Poetics* . . . I am prepared to wager that the young man who took notes at Aristotle's lecture was sitting very near the door on a very noisy day" (545n5).

32. A "theory of laughter" would also imply the definition of laughter as an independent field of inquiry. Despite a range of (lost) treatises "on the laughable" (περὶ τοῦ γελοίου) and despite intense ancient speculation on many aspects of laughter, it is not clear that laughter was ever so defined in antiquity; see Billig 2005, 38–39. The distinction drawn here between "ideas (or even theories) about" and a "theory of" is a crucial one, and my choice of expression throughout this book will reflect that importance.

33. *Eth. Nic.* 4.8, 1127b34–1128b9, a passage that has prompted very different reactions from critics: subtle and sophisticated for Halliwell 2008, esp. 307–22; muddled ("it slides from tautology to tautology") for Goldhill 1995, 19. Halliwell 2008, 307–31, provides a useful point of departure, with bibliography, for all the passages I discuss here.

34. *Part. an.* 3.10, 673a6–8: τοῦ δὲ γαργαλίζεσθαι μόνον ἄνθρωπον αἴτιον ἥ τε λεπτότης τοῦ δέρματος καὶ τὸ μόνον γελᾶν τῶν ζῴων ἄνθρωπον (not *De Anima* 3.10 as Bakhtin 1968, 68, has it). See further Labarrière 2000 (which does not, for me, rescue the passage from the charge of circularity).

35. *Eth. Nic.* 4.8, 1128a30; earlier in the passage (1128a4–7), Aristotle characterizes "buffoons" as those who do not avoid giving pain to the butts of their jokes (τὸν σκωπτόμενον). Much modern criticism of Aristotle's view on comedy has focused on his attitude to Aristophanic Old Comedy and the personal attacks on individuals it contains (see, for example, Halliwell 1986, 266–276, esp. 273, which critiques that focus; M. Heath 1989); this may not be unrelated to his views on laughter, but it is not my concern here.

36. *Poet.* 5, 1449a32–37: μίμησις φαυλοτέρων μέν, οὐ μέντοι κατὰ πᾶσαν κακίαν, ἀλλὰ τοῦ αἰσχροῦ ἐστι τὸ γελοῖον μόριον. τὸ γὰρ γελοῖόν ἐστιν ἁμάρτημά τι καὶ αἶσχος ἀνώδυνον καὶ οὐ φθαρτικόν, οἷον εὐθὺς τὸ γελοῖον πρόσωπον αἰσχρόν τι καὶ διεστραμμένον ἄνευ ὀδύνης.

37. *Rh.* 2.12, 1389b10–12: καὶ φιλογέλωτες, διὸ καὶ φιλευτράπελοι· ἡ γὰρ εὐτραπελία πεπαιδευμένη ὕβρις ἐστίν. Note that Aristotle does not say that "wit" is the *only* way that those who are fond of laughter demonstrate this fondness—rather that those who are fond of laughter will also be witty.

38. The very nature of theater raises one problem about the location of the potential pain. The tacit assumption seems to be that the pain would be that of the actors in their comic masks, at whom the audience laughs. But why would they, whose job it was to provoke laughter, have been liable to *pain* in the face of it? A similar point is made, in relation to Aristophanes, by Sommerstein 2009, 112.

39. Goldhill 1995, 19; the issue is made even more loaded by the fact that the *Nichomachean Ethics* itself is addressed to the πεπαιδευμένος (*Eth. Nich.* 1.3, 1094b22–25).

40. Exactly how far Aristotle is presenting laughter as derisive in this passage is debatable. It depends in part on how far you imagine that his τὸ γελοῖον carries the derisive sense of the Greek word καταγελᾶν ("to laugh down" or "scoff at"). It is certainly true that Aristotle in the *Poetics* appears to offer a genealogy of comedy from aggressive satire, but the implications of this for laughter as a whole are less clear. Malcolm Schofield has usefully suggested to me that we might see the Aristotelian witty gentleman as a "tease" who gently makes fun of someone's faults, in such a way as to give pleasure rather than pain—complicated by the fact (as Aristotle notes in *Eth. Nic.* 4.8, 1128a27–8) that people vary in what they find pleasurable or painful.

41. As is well known, the image of laughter in Greek literature is much more varied, nuanced, and (sometimes) gentle than derision. One classic example is the parental laughter of Hector and Andromache (Homer, *Il.* 6.471) when baby Astyanax takes fright at the sight of the plume of his father's helmet.

42. *Rh.* 1.11, 1371b34–35; the words are bracketed in, for example, Kassel 1976, following Spengel 1867—and the exclusion tentatively supported by Fortenbaugh 2000, 340. Fortenbaugh 2000, with 2002, 120–126, provides a useful discussion of the topic.

43. David, *In Isagogen* 204.15–16: "Other animals too are capable of laughter, as Aristotle says in the *History of Animals* about the heron" (ἔστι καὶ ἄλλα ζῷα γελαστικά, ὥσπερ ἱστορεῖ ὁ Ἀριστοτέλης ἐν τῇ Περὶ ζῴων περὶ τοῦ ἐρωδιοῦ). How exactly we are to explain this claim (mistake, misremembering, or subsequent loss of the relevant passage of Aristotle) is unclear.

44. Porphyry, *Isagoge* 4 (κἂν γὰρ μὴ γελᾷ ἀεί, ἀλλὰ γελαστικὸν λέγεται οὐ τῷ ἀεὶ γελᾶν ἀλλὰ τῷ πεφυκέναι), trans. Barnes 2003. Other writers of Roman imperial date to make this claim include Quintilian, *Inst.* 5.10.58; Clement, *Paedagogus* 2.5. The fact that in the second century CE, Lucian (*Vit auct.* 26) explicitly associates this claim with a character representing Peripatetic philosophy may, but does not necessarily, mean that it originated with Aristotle or his immediate successors (there were plenty of "Peripatetic philosophers" in the Roman Empire). See further, Barnes 2003, 208–9n22.

45. Ménager 1995, 7–41 (on the history of this idea from antiquity to the Renaissance); Screech 1997, 1–5. On Jesus, see Le Goff 1992. In the canonical gospels of the New Testament, Jesus never laughs; he does so repeatedly in the fragmentary Gnostic "Gospel of Judas" (see Pagels and King 2007, 128, arguing that his laughter always introduces the correction of an error).

46. Physiology of laughter: Pliny, *HN* 11.198; Aristotle, *Part. an.* 3.10, 673a1–12; babies: Pliny, *HN* 7.2, 7.72; Aristotle, *Hist. an.* 9.10, 587b5–7. On Zoroaster, see Herrenschmidt 2000; Hambartsumian 2001.

47. In the context of his discussion of metaphor at *Rh.* 3.11, 1412a19–b32 (often wrongly cited, for obvious reasons, as *Rh.* 3.2; see, for example, Morreall 1983, 131).

48. Leeman, Pinkster, and Rabbie 1989, 190–204, offers the most recent detailed discussion of the possible sources (arguing for a mixture of Greek and Roman); 188–89 discusses *cavillatio, dicacitas,* and *facetiae.* Fantham 2004, 186–208 (quotation on 189), with Corbeill 1996, 21–22nn13–14, a sharp, up-to-date account.

49. Halliwell 2008 is especially good on philosophical views of laughter: esp. 271–76 (Pythagoreanism), 276–302 (Platonic Socrates), 302–7 (Stoicism), 343–71 (Democritus), 372–87 (Cynicism).

50. I am referring here to Stein 2006 (the use of slapstick in a hookworm eradication campaign); Janus 2009 (the scripted laughter in Joyce interrupts the traditionally "silent reading" of the novels); Lavin and Maynard 2001 (comparing survey centers where interviewers are "prohibited" from laughing in the course of an interview with those where they are not); Kawakami et al. 2007 (drawing distinctions between and dating the occurrence of spontaneous vs. social laughter in infants).

51. Chesterfield 1774, vol. 1, 326–32, esp. 328 (letter of 9 March 1748), reprinted in D. Roberts 1992, 70–74, esp. 72; see further above, pp. 60, 66–67.

52. W. Lewis et al. 1914, 31 ("We only want Tragedy if it can clench its side-muscles like hand on it's [*sic*] belly, and bring to the surface a laugh like a bomb"); Cixous 1976 ("She's beautiful and she's laughing," 885; "rhythm that laughs you," 882). The essays of Baudelaire 1981 [1855] and Bataille 1997 [1944] have been influential in many of the most radical approaches to laughter. The rich tradition of laughter in feminist writing, from fiction to psychoanalysis, is a major theme of Parvulescu 2010, esp. 101–18, to which Lessing 1962 (a feminist novel, in which laughter is a major player) would be an important addition (see, briefly, Scurr 2003). For a different strand of modern feminist use of laughter (in relation to a Latin text), see above, pp. 84–85.

53. Morreall 1983, 4–37; Critchley 2002, 2–3; more skeptically, Halliwell 2008, 11. Lippitt 1994; 1995a; and 1995b offer a clear, critical introduction to each theory in turn.

54. Hobbes 1969 [1640], 42; *Sudden Glory* is the title of Sanders 1995.

55. Ludovici 1932, 98–103; Gruner 1978, 43; R.A. Martin 2007, 44–47 (a useful summary). Quotation: Rapp 1951, 21.

56. *Rh.* 3.11, 1412a31.

57. Kant 1952 [1790], 196–203, quotation on 199; Bergson 1911, esp. 12–38; Raskin 1985; Attardo and Raskin 1991; Attardo 1994 (put into a

classical perspective by N. Lowe 2007, 1–12). For those unfamiliar with the old English joke about the door, it plays on the aural ambiguity between the noun *jar* (a storage vessel, often of glass) and the adjective/adverb *ajar* (meaning "slightly open").

58. Deckers and Kizer 1974; Deckers and Kizer 1975; Nerhardt 1976; Deckers 1993; with a useful overview in R. A. Martin 2007, 68–70. The question of whether the subjects in this case may (also) be laughing *at* the experimenters is rarely raised!

59. Spencer 1860.

60. *Phil.* 2.39: explaining that as the army camp was "full of care" (*plena curae*), the jokes served "to relax their minds" (*animis relaxantur*—the verb can indicate a release from pressure)—though I may be trying to push this too far, when Cicero is thinking much more generally of the role of joking as a break from the cares of war. Corbeill 1996, 185–89, discusses the jokes made on this occasion.

61. Freud 1960 [1905] ("The hearer of the joke laughs with the quota of psychical energy which has become free through the lifting of the inhibitory cathexis," 201). Experimental psychology does not confirm what Freud's argument seems to imply: that the more repressed you are, the more you will laugh at a dirty joke (Morreall 1983, 32).

62. M. Smith 2008 rightly criticizes the preoccupation of most laughter theorists with uncontrollable laughter. Ruch and Eckman 2001 is typical in its classification of outbursts of laughter into "spontaneous" on the one hand and "contrived" or "fake" on the other (the terms themselves are a giveaway). The recent neurological work of Sophie Scott and her colleagues has been much more interested in "social" as well as uncontrollable laughter, tracing differences and similarities in the response of the brain to laughter of different types. See, for example, McGettigan et al. 2013; S. Scott 2013.

63. Scruton in Scruton and Jones 1982 offers useful observations about the range of and exclusions from modern studies of laughter ("It is not laughter, but laughter at or about something, that interests the philosopher," 198); likewise Parvulescu 2010, 3–4 ("Most 'theories of laughter' are not concerned with laughter").

64. Morreall 1983, 30, points to the difficulty in Freud's view of the conversion of psychic into physical energy, as does, rather more elegantly, Cioffi 1998, 264–304, in his discussion of Wittgenstein's critique of Freud ("Imagine a world in which, like ours, people laughed at jokes, but unlike ours did not know what that were laughing at until they discovered the unconscious energic processes hypothesised by Freud," 277). Richlin 1992a, 72, sums up some of the basic problems with the Freudian account succinctly: "That the pleasure consists in relief, in the released pressure of a lifted inhibition, does not describe the feeling of a laugh very well." Earlier generations of modern laughter theorists were more concerned to link the physical "symptoms" of laughter to its cause: Laurence Joubert, for example, traces laughter to a physical reaction of the heart, contracting and expanding in response to conflicting emotions of joy and sorrow (Joubert 1980 [1579], 44–45). Gatrell 2006, 162–67, traces the eighteenth-century reaction against such physical explanations.

65. See, for example, Gruner 1997, 131–46 (in which a groan in response to a pun is an admission of defeat). Note Baudelaire's pointed dismissal of the theory as a whole: "Laughter, so they say, comes from superiority. I should not be surprised if, in face of this discovery, the physiologist himself were to burst out laughing at the thought of his own superiority" (1981 [1855], 145). On the general problems with all-encompassing theories of "amusement," see Scruton in Scruton and Jones 1982, 202.

66. Freud 1960 [1905], 248–54. Perhaps the most problematic aspect of this very problematic argument is Freud's claim that *in the process of ideation* more energy is expended on a large movement than on a small one.

67. Berger 1997, 29–30 (incongruity); Sanders 1995, 249. Quotation: Bergson 1911, 18.

68. Morreall 1983, 16 (incongruity)—though Morreall adds, "Because it [the incongruity theory] did not fit in with the superiority theory of his *Poetics* and *Nichomachean Ethics*, he never developed it"; Atkinson 1993, 17–18 (relief).

69. Hobbes 1996 [1651], 43; Skinner 2001, 445–46; Skinner 2002, 175–76; Skinner 2004, 162–64.

70. Richlin 1992a, 60 (psychosocial dynamics); Goldhill 2006, 84 (not knowing what we are laughing at); Corbeill 1996, 4–5 (tendentious vs. innocent).

71. Le Goff 1997, 46–47, briefly discusses the question of how far laughter can be reduced "to a single phenomenon."

72. Douglas 1971, 389. Embedded in her remarks is also the assumption, standard at least since Bergson (1911, 12), that laughter is essentially social, that you cannot laugh alone (hence the canned laughter on television programs). For Pliny, see above, p. 25. I say *probably* because in some circumstances and in some cultures, belching too can straddle the divide of nature and culture and be taken as meaningful. The other action to which Pliny refers in this passage, spitting, is different again: this is always communication, and not a natural bodily eruption.

73. Aristotle, [*Pr.*] 35.7, 965a18–22, though the next passage of this compilation (almost certainly put together in Peripatetic circles over a long period from the third century BCE on) claims that people are ticklish only in the armpits. Joubert 1980 [1579], 86, identifies the skin between the toes as a prime site for tickling.

74. Provine 2000, 99–127; R. A. Martin 2007, 173–76. One much disputed theory of tickling—the so-called Darwin-Hecker hypothesis—suggests that there is much more in common between tickling and humor than is usually allowed: both produce laughter by very similar neural processes involving the same region of the brain (Darwin 1872, 201–2; Panksepp 2000, but see C. R. Harris and Christenfeld 1997; C. R. Harris and Alvarado 2005).

75. In my experience, one particularly sadistic version involves contriving an excuse to remove a child from the room—when s/he returns, all the other children are uproariously laughing. Soon enough the returner will join in the laughter, and at that point s/he faces increasingly aggressive questions from the others on what s/he is laughing at—until tears are the result.

76. Lautréamont 1965 [1869], 5.

77. Nietzsche 2002 [1886], 174–75; 1990 [1886], 218.

78. Douglas 1971, 387.

79. Turnbull 1961 (quotation on 45); the mountain people (the Ik) are the subject of Turnbull 1973. Ballard 2006 and Boyer 1989 offer critiques of Turnbull's general approach to the Pygmies. "Subjective, judgmental and naïve" are the words of Fox 2001 (referring specifically to Turnbull's treatment of the Ik).

80. On Chesterfield, see pp. 36, 60, 66–67.

81. For example, Catullus 64.284; Lucretius 1.8. The etymology of *ridere* is uncertain, but the Greek γελᾶν (laugh) may have a root in the idea of brightness and luster, and it is not inconceivable (though unlikely) that the poets are making a scholarly allusion to that in their usage. On γελᾶν, see Halliwell 2008, 13n33, 523, for a sensible discussion, with bibliography.

82. Darwin 1872, 120–21, 132–37, 198–212; with Davila-Ross et al. 2011 (as just one example of up-to-the-minute investigations of ape laughter). Dogs: Douglas 1971. Rats: Panksepp and Burgdorf 1999; Panksepp 2000.

83. Panksepp and Burgdorf 1999, 231, briefly discusses the opposition.

84. Scruton in Scruton and Jones 1982, 199.

3. THE HISTORY OF LAUGHTER

1. Herzen's remark (2012 [1858], 68) is quoted by, among others, Bakhtin 1968, 59; Halliwell 2008, vii; and Le Goff 1997, 41.

2. Le Goff 1997, 41, usefully highlights this distinction between protocol and practice.

3. Published as Thomas 1977. In French, the work of Jacques Le Goff has been similarly programmatic; see Le Goff 1989. Thomas's original talk was given as the Neale Lecture in English History at University College London on 3 December 1976. He started by suggesting that Sir John Neale, in whose honor the series had been founded, would have thought laughter an "ill-defined and even unhistorical" topic of research. The idea that one's predecessors or more senior colleagues would disapprove of the subject is something of a cliché among historians of laughter. Saint-Denis (1965, 9) complained that his university authorities had found the topic so distasteful that they refused even to publish a summary of his course of lectures—"Le rire des Latins"—in their *Revue des Cours et Conférences*; even in the 1990s, Verberckmoes 1999, ix, said much the same.

4. Plutarch, *Mor.* 633c (= *Quaest. conviv.* 2.1.9). Cicero, *De or.* 2.246, likewise puts a joke against a *luscus* (a man blind in one eye) in the category of the "scurrilous"; predictably, the emperor Elagabalus (SHA, *Heliog.* 29.3) enjoyed making a joke of all kinds of people with bodily "peculiarities," from the fat to the bald and the *lusci* (see p. 77). Plutarch's protocols might suggest that the joking songs of Caesar's soldiers (Suet., *Iul.* 51) should be seen as relatively good humored.

5. Dio Chrysostom, *Or.* 32.1 (ἐπειδὴ παίζοντες ἀεὶ διατελεῖτε καὶ οὐ προσέχοντες καὶ παιδιᾶς μὲν καὶ ἡδονῆς καὶ γέλωτος, ὡς εἰπεῖν, οὐδέποτε ἀπορεῖτε), 32.56 ("as if you'd been hitting the bottle"—ἐοίκατε κραιπαλῶσιν).

6. Tacitus, *Germ.* 19. This passage already hints at some of the complexities in understanding the sense of the apparently simple word *ridet*, which I will explore in more detail. "Laughs off"—in the sense of "takes as a joke"—seems attractive here and accords with the phrase that follows (*nec corrumpere et corrumpi saeculum vocatur*, "and to corrupt or be corrupted is not put down to 'the times we live in'"). But as many recent critics have emphasized (for example, Richlin 1992a), "ridicule" in traditional Roman culture could be a powerful weapon against deviance. My hunch is that Tacitus is being (as often) even smarter than he seems and is querying not merely contemporary Roman corruption but some of the most traditional mechanisms (here ridicule) through which Rome had policed its morality. (But see above, pp. 105–8, 120–23, on the tendency of modern scholarship to overemphasize the aggressive, policing functions of Roman laughter.)

7. Twain 1889, 28–29.

8. Leeman, Pinkster, and Rabbie 1989, 259.

9. Murgia 1991, esp. 184–93.

10. *Inst.* 6.3.100, the Latin text of D. A. Russell in the Loeb Classical Library (similar to that printed in the Teubner text, ed. L. Radermacher).

11. "Hopelessly ungrammatical" because *mentiri* is a deponent verb, used in the passive voice, whereas *mentis* is an active form. There is a little more logic to some of these changes than I have perhaps made it appear: *mentis,* for example, might be a (not unparalleled) manuscript conflation of an original *me*[*n*] *ex te metiris.*

12. Murgia 1991, 184–87, includes further and fuller arguments for his changes.

13. The impossible *obicientibus arbore* demands some change. Murgia would reasonably claim that it is easier to see how his version (*barbare*) rather than the more usual *obicienti atrociora* could have been corrupted into the garbled text of the manuscript (*arbore*). But he has not convinced other textual critics (for example Russell, whose Loeb text of 2001 notes but does not follow Murgia). Murgia's emendation of the main joke entails other changes to earlier sentences. The phrase "Umis quoque uti belle datur" introduces the story in the manuscripts of Quintilian. *Umis* makes no sense whatsoever. It is usually emended to "Contumeliis quoque . . ." ("Insults also can be neatly used"—"I suppose this emendation must be right," Winterbottom 1970, 112); Murgia suggests "Verbis quoque . . ." ("Words/quips also can be neatly used").

14. Fontaine 2010.

15. On one occasion, for example, he claims that Varro (*Ling.* 9.106) already in the first century BCE was working from a faulty text of Plautus that had missed the joke (Fontaine 2010, 29); if so, there are interesting implications for the transmission of jokes within the Roman world itself. But it may not be so. Even assuming that Fontaine's reading is the correct version of what Plautus wrote, Varro's text—as Fontaine concedes—may have been "fixed" by a later editor to bring it into line with what by then had become the standard reading.

16. *Rud.* 527–28; Fontaine 2010, 121–23. He goes on to suggest a pun elsewhere in the play on the word *algor* (cold), as if it were a verbal form meaning "to gather seaweed." Sharrock 2011 discusses this particular suggestion and Fontaine's overall approach.

17. The telling phrase of C.W. Marshall, on the jacket of Fontaine 2010.

18. In arguing in this way, I am not unaware of the strand of research (stretching back to Darwin 1872) that claims there are natural physiological facial expressions of emotion—a strand that some art historians have recently exploited. David Freedberg, for example, has drawn on the research of Paul Ekman and others to argue for clearly identifiable expressions in works of art (see Freedberg 2007), yet as he himself admits, problems and controversies remain, and it is certainly not enough to assert, as he does (33–34), "A comparison of the terrible images shown on Al-Jazeera of Margaret Hassan immediately prior to her execution in 2004 and earlier photographs of her smiling leaves one with no doubt at all about the possibility of identifying constants of emotional expression. The fear and the cheerfulness are instantly and indisputably identifiable as such." Here I would stress only that, even if we were to accept a "natural" relationship between expression and emotion, an artistic representation is a very different matter—while in any case, laughter is not itself an emotion or even necessarily the product of emotion (or, as Parvulescu 2010, esp. 6–9, would have it, "a passion").

19. Quotations from Stewart 2008; Goldhill 2008; Cohen 2008; R.D. Griffith 2008.

20. For example, M. Robertson 1975, vol. 1, 101–2, and Trumble 2004, 14–15, see it as a form of animation; Giuliani 1986, 105–6, combines animation with beauty (at the start of a more complex discussion that includes the Gorgon's "grimace," 105–12); Yalouris 1986 canvasses the idea of aristocratic contentment. On smiling in general, see above, pp. 73–76.

21. The best survey of these debates is Halliwell 2008, 530–52, which also discusses ancient descriptions (including some of the Roman period) of art that refer to laughs and smiles (notably several in [the older and younger] Philostratus' ecphrases of painting: e.g., Philostratus mai., *Imag.* 1.19.6, 2.2.2, 2.2.5; Philostratus min., *Imag.* 2.2, 2.3). The theoretical implications of the Gorgon's expression are central to Cixous 1976 (see above, pp. 36–37).

22. Trumble 2004, l–liii; quotation from Wallace Collection 1928, 128. Schneider 2004 discusses medieval images of laughter, including the famous sculpture of the Last Judgment at Bamberg Cathedral, with Jesus between the Blessed and the Damned. This account makes clear what a fine line there is between the ecstatic smiles of the Blessed and the grimaces of the Damned. The *Mona Lisa* offers another puzzle, debated by Freud, John Ruskin, Bernard Berenson, and many others; reviewed by Trumble 2004, 22–29. So too, as Le Goff points out (1997, 48–49), do images of the story of Isaac. Though laughter is fundamental to that story (and the name *Isaac* means "laughter"), "if one looks at representations . . . one finds no attempt to represent the laughter."

23. J.R. Clarke 2007.

24. J.R. Clarke 2007, 53–57. It is tempting to link this (as Clarke does) with the laughter headlined by Petronius, *Sat.* 29, even though the coordinates are rather different. There a man falls down in astonishment at seeing a lifelike painting of a dog at the entrance to Trimalchio's house, and his friends laugh at him (not at the dog!); the passage is minutely analyzed by Plaza 2000, 94–103. As a further example of a funny double take, Clarke offers (52) the story of the

contest in illusionism between the painters Zeuxis and Parrhasius (Pliny, *HN* 35.65–66); though laughter is not explicitly mentioned here, it does link with another story of Zeuxis, which I discuss on pp. 72–73.

25. The idea of laughter as apotropaic is a major theme in Clarke's book (esp. 63–81). In my view (see, e.g., Beard 2007, 248, and above, p. 146), this term explains much less than many scholars like to think and raises more problems than it solves. Do we really imagine that the entranceway to the bijou House of the Tragic Poet was a place of liminality haunted by the evil eye?

26. Ling 2009, 510.

27. Thomas 1977, 77 (my italics). Likewise Le Goff 1997, 40 ("Attitudes to laughter, the ways in which it is practised, its objects and its forms are not constant but changing. . . . As a cultural and social phenomenon, laughter must have a history"); Gatrell 2006, 5 ("Studying laughter can take us to the heart of a generation's shifting attitudes, sensibilities and anxieties").

28. Chesterfield 1774, vol. 1, 328 (letter of 9 March 1748); reprinted in D. Roberts 1992, 72.

29. He references in particular the French version of Elias 1978—whose original German text, *Über den Prozess der Zivilisation* (1939), had not yet been translated into English. It is no coincidence that one of Elias's essays, left unfinished and unpublished at his death, was on laughter; it is discussed by Parvulescu 2010, 24–26.

30. All quotations from Thomas 1977.

31. Bakhtin 1968.

32. Pan'kov 2001.

33. Le Goff 1997, 51, rightly stresses that Bakhtin was only the most famous of a large group of Soviet scholars working on laughter in the mid-twentieth century; see also (in German translation) Lichačëv and Pančenko 1991.

34. Even some of Bakhtin's warmest admirers concede this. See, for example, Stallybrass and White 1986, 10: "It is difficult to disentangle the generous but willed idealism from the descriptively accurate in passages like these. Bakhtin constantly shifts between prescriptive and descriptive categories in his work."

35. Gatrell 2006, 178 (chapter title).

36. This chronology is sketched in the first chapter of Bakhtin 1968, 59–144; quotations on 72, 107, 119.

37. Burke 1988, 85 (reviewing four books heavily dependent on Bakhtinian analysis, including Stallybrass and White 1986, and briefly surveying the reception of Bakhtin in the West). For the enthusiastic adoption of Bakhtin by some critics of classical literature and art, see, for example, Moellendorff 1995; Branham 2002; J. R. Clarke 2007, 7–9; and below, nn. 46–47.

38. Pan'kov 2001, 47.

39. Critiques (or critical developments) of aspects of Bakhtin's treatment of carnival run into thousands. I have found particularly useful Davis 1975, 97–123, and Stallybrass and White 1986, esp. 6–19 (on the simultaneously radical and conservative aspects of carnival), with Chartier 1987 (on the discourse of nostalgia in the culture of carnival); Le Roy Ladurie 1979 (on carnival's violence); M. A. Bernstein 1992, 34–58 (on its potential savagery, with important reflections on earlier, Nietzschean models of carnival and their

ambivalence); J. C. Scott 1990, 72, 172–82 (stressing the *apparent* acquiescence of the people in the elite script of carnival); Greenblatt 2007, 77–104 (on the relationship between Rabelais's text and "real" laughter); Silk, Gildenhard, and Barrow 2014, 121–24 (from a classical starting point).

40. Gatrell 2006, 161.

41. For a brief introduction to the festival and a review of the literary evidence, see D'Agostino 1969; Scullard 1981; Graf 1992, 14–21 (on the etiology and the ritual).

42. Frazer 1913, 306–411; Nietzsche 1986 [1878], 213; Nietzsche 2002 [1886], 114. M. A. Bernstein 1992, 34–35, emphasizes the underlying pessimism of Nietzsche's account. Frazer was predictably most concerned with drawing a connection between the "Saturnalian king" and his motley crew of dead, divine, and priestly kings. This connection was, he believed, supported by the puzzling *Acts of Saint Dasius,* which claims (in what is probably a Christian fantasy) that the Saturnalian king in a military garrison on the Danube c. 300 CE was killed at the end of his thirty-day "rule." See Cumont 1897; Musurillo 1972, 272–75; Versnel 1993, 210–27.

43. Bakhtin 1968, quotations on 7, 138, 70, 14. Bakhtin's stronger claim of a literally unbroken continuity between the Saturnalia and medieval carnival (8) has generally been viewed more suspiciously (Nauta 2002, 180).

44. Versnel 1993, 136–227, reflects many of these claims (from a partially Bakhtinian perspective); "exuberant gorgings . . ." is his phrase (147), echoed in Minois 2000 ("les orgies des saturnales," 65). See also Bettini 1991, 99–115; Champlin 2003, 150–51 (at the Saturnalia "within the miniature republic of the household, slaves might act as magistrates and judges," 150); Dolansky 2011 (495: "Normative codes of behavior were reversed, with masters waiting upon slaves who enjoyed the right to drink to excess and chide their masters").

45. There is no firm evidence for the precise dating of the *Apocolocyntosis.* Nauta (1987, 78–84) lays out the arguments and inferences (such as they are) that might point to a specifically Saturnalian date as an introduction to his Saturnalian reading of the text (focusing on laughter and the inversion of norms). Branham 2005 discusses at length Bakhtin's stress on "Menippean satire"—the genre of the *Apocolocyntosis.*

46. Gowers 2005, 60, puts both *Sat.* 2.3 (Damasippus) and *Sat.* 2.7 (Davus) in a Saturnalian frame ("The topsy-turvy festival of the Saturnalia . . . allows two speakers . . . freedom of speech . . . to remove the smug mask Horace manufactured in Book 1"). Sharland 2010, 261–316, is a particularly hard-line Bakhtinian reading of the Saturnalia and a hard-line Saturnalian reading of *Sat.* 2.7. See, e.g., 266: "True to the customs of the Carnival, and its predecessor the Saturnalia, a lowly character (in this case, Davus) has been elevated to the position of 'king' figure, and is allowed to 'reign' temporarily'; 268: "Through its inversions and reversals, Carnival (and Saturnalia) characteristically juxtaposed opposites, matched incompatibles, and joined odd couples."

47. The classic discussion of comedy as an inversionary Saturnalian genre is Segal 1968 (e.g., 8–9, 32–33), though its inspiration is more Frazer (8) than Bakhtin; the position is reiterated in Segal 2001, 149 (in which Bakhtin has a walk-on part on 8). For other carnivalesque readings, see, for example, Bettini

1981, 9–24; Gowers 1993, 69–74 (a more subtle connection between the textual banquets of Plautine comedy, carnivalesque consumption, and the Saturnalia). Other students of Roman comedy have been dubious about a carnivalesque or Bakhtinian reading, or about some aspects of it: for example, Manuwald 2011, 149; McCarthy 2000, 17–18, esp. n. 26 (deploying Bakhtinian theory but questioning its social "optimism").

48. Part of the Saturnalian spirit is captured in the illustration accompanying the month of December in the fourth-century CE Calendar of Philocalus, which shows a man, wearing tunic and cape, standing beside a gaming table—with some game (of the edible sort) hanging up behind him. Stern 1953, 283–86, with *planches* 13 and 19.2.

49. There was feasting and drinking, yes, but no evidence of gross bingeing in the style of carnival. Not surprisingly, it is hard from the scanty material we have to get a clear idea of levels of consumption: Seneca, *Ep.* 18 (a curmudgeonly letter on how far the philosophical elite should join in the Saturnalia), talks vaguely of *luxuria* and of dining *hilarius* (in a jollier fashion); Aulus Gellius 2.24.3 refers to sumptuary laws covering the occasion (but sumptuary legislation is no guide to levels of real excess); SHA, *Alex. Sev.* 37.6 suggests that this particularly mean emperor splashed out on just a pheasant for Saturnalia. Gowers 1993, 69–74 stresses the consumption of pork as a carnival dish. Exactly how drunk Cato's slaves would have got on the rations he prescribed for the Saturnalia (*Agr.* 57) is anyone's guess. Assuming the text is correct, he suggests that the most generous ration for a month's wine amounted to just under a liter a day per head. Additionally, slaves should be allowed an extra ten liters on the Saturnalia and Compitalia (separately or combined is unclear). Ten liters of modern-strength wine consumed on a single day would indeed suggest Bakhtinian excess, but we are probably dealing with wine of lower strength, and it might not have amounted to much more than double rations if consumed over the duration of both festivals.

50. *Apoc* 4.3; the emperor's dying words are reported as "O dear I think I've shat [*concacavi*] myself."

51. Of course, the *Saturnalia* is a self-consciously elite work, full of wit, upper-class jokes, and ludic learning, embedded in one version of the academic culture of the fifth century CE. But its wit is in fact not so different from the style of Saturnalian wit we find elsewhere. For references to riddles and puns, see *AL* 286; Aulus Gellius 18.2, 18.13.

52. Macrobius, *Sat.* 1.12.7, 1.24.23.

53. Seneca, *Ep.* 47.14, contra Champlin 2003, 150, which relies on almost certainly faulty modern punctuation. Contra Versnel 1993, 149, Dio 60.19 refers to slaves adopting not the "roles of their masters" but the "*clothes* of their masters."

54. Tacitus, *Ann.* 13.15; discussed by Champlin (2003, 150–53) in the context of his wider claims that there was a "Saturnalian style" to the reign as a whole. Tacitus certainly is suggesting that having Nero on the throne was like being ruled by "Saturnalicius rex."

55. Accius *apud* Macrobius, *Sat.* 1.7.36–37 (= *ROL*2, Accius, *Annales* 2–7): the masters prepare the meal, but it is eaten together; Macrobius, *Sat.* 1.11.1;

SHA, *Verus* 7.5 (slaves and masters eating together, at Saturnalia and other festivals); Macrobius, *Sat.* 1.7.26 (*licentia*). Note also the slogan on the Calendar of Philocalus (see n. 48), "Now, slave, you can play/gamble with your master." Bakhtin and many modern accounts tend to use the ideas of inversion and equality interchangeably, but in fact they represent two crucially different forms of festal transgression.

56. Pliny's famous account of not spoiling his household's fun at the Saturnalia (*Ep.* 2.17.24) oozes paternalism. (A casual reference of his to the Saturnalia in *Ep.* 8.7 no doubt reflects traditions of Saturnalian free speech, but I am not convinced that it should be seen in quite the inversionary terms that Marchesi 2008, 102–17, imagines.)

57. Fairer 2003, 2.

58. See above, n. 28. Chesterfield's advice is often assumed (by, e.g., Morreall 1983, 87) to be fairly typical of eighteenth-century preoccupations with the control of laughter. True, it is not unparalleled; see, for example, the advice of Pitt senior to his son (W. S. Taylor and Pringle 1838–40, vol. 1, 79). But as Gatrell (2006, 163–65, 170, 176) makes clear, Chesterfield's published views were extreme and, in any case, represented an insistence on the control of laughter that can be found at other periods. Chesterfield was also more complicated than he is given credit for—a renowned wit, of (by the standards of the day) grotesque appearance, and celebrated prankster (see Dickie 2011, 87).

59. Thomas 1977. His tactic (as his choice of words indicates: "lingers," "among the common people," "continued in villages," etc.) is to reconcile the differences by implying that more isolated regions or those below the elite took longer to adopt the new protocols.

60. A phrase supposedly uttered by Queen Victoria but as historically perilous as Lord Chesterfield's advice, for even more reasons: it is not clear that Victoria ever said this or—if she did—in response to what. Vasey 1875 is a truly thoroughgoing, much less well-known, and sometimes hilarious agelastic treatise. "The conclusion is unavoidable, that the absurd habit of laughing is entirely occasioned by the unnatural and false associations which have been forced upon us in early life" (58) gives a flavor.

61. This theme runs throughout Chartier 1987.

62. Much recent work on eighteenth-century laughter and other forms of "sensibility" is alert to this nexus of complexity. In addition to Gatrell 2006 and Dickie 2011, Klein 1994 is an illuminating study. There are, of course, subtle variations on these generalizations. As Ruth Scurr alerted me, the laughter of the French revolutionaries was defined as more innocent than the contrived and vicious laughter of the royal court (see, for example, Leon 2009, 74–99). Some modern celebrations of the relaxation of comic censorship in print and onstage might seem to point in the opposite direction, but the celebration of the freedom of public expression of coarseness is different from the celebration of increasing coarseness itself.

63. *Fam.* 9.15. This is, in fact, a more puzzling passage than my quotations suggest. If the text as we have it is broadly correct (which it may well not be), Cicero included his home region of Latium among the foreign influences. But as Shackleton Bailey (1977, 350) asks, "How can Cicero of Arpinum equate

Latium with *peregrinitas?*" The overall sense is clear, though the details are irrecoverable. As we shall see in the next chapter, Cicero's rhetorical treatises are more equivocal about the propriety of old-fashioned *festivitas.*

64. Livy 7.2; Horace, *Epist.* 2.1.139–55. The passage of Livy—which offers a brief, multistage account of the origins and development of dramatic festivals at Rome—has been intensely debated (on its meaning, sources, and reliability); for a review, see Oakley 1997, 40–58. In the third stage, the performers are said to give up uttering crude compositions akin to *Fescenninus versus* (presumably the jesting banter characteristic of Livy's second stage). Horace's genealogy envisages the rustics bantering until the *Fescennina licentia* became so nasty that it had to be controlled by law. For the disputed etymology of *Fescennine*—from the name of an Etruscan town or from *fascinum*—see Oakley 1997, 59–60.

65. Gowers 2005; Gowers 2012, 182–86, 199–204 (with review of earlier work); Oliensis 1998, 29.

66. The title of the second chapter of Saint-Denis 1965; the first reflects a similar style: "Jovialité rustique et vinaigre italien." See also Minois 2000, 71: "Le Latin, paysan caustique."

67. Macrobius attributes some *Fescennini* to the emperor Augustus (*Sat.* 2.4.21); otherwise, as Oakley (1997, 60) rightly insists, the only institutional context attested in the late Republic and early empire is the wedding ritual (Hersch 2010, 151–56); whether or not the term should be applied also to the ribald, joking verses sung at a Roman triumph—as Graf (2005, 201–2), along with many others, implies—is far less clear.

68. Conybeare 2013 is a major study of laughter focused on biblical and theological texts, Jewish and Christian, to which readers frustrated by my limitations are warmly directed!

4. ROMAN LAUGHTER IN LATIN AND GREEK

1. The *OLD,* for example, offers "to smile at, upon or in response to" for *arridere/adridere* and "to laugh at, mock, make fun of" for *irridere; ridere* with a dative suggests "to laugh as a sign of goodwill." The etymology of *ridere* is obscure, despite occasional attempts to relate it to the Sanskrit for "to be shy" or to the Boeotian form κριδδέμεν (a variant of γελᾶν, "laugh").

2. Ovid, *Ars am.* 2.201; Terence, *Ad.* 864; Horace, *Ars P.* 101.

3. Silius Italicus 1.398; another decidedly sinister use of *arridere* (Seneca, *Controv.* 9.2.6) is discussed on pp. 79–80. It most likely indicates mocking laughter at Cicero, *De or.* 2.262.

4. *Eun.* 249–50; Priscian in *GLK* 3.351.11 (= *Inst.* 18.274). Most modern translators and critics who have rightly focused on this passage (e.g., Damon 1997, 81; Fontaine 2010, 13–14) have also missed the full nuance, whichever way they choose to translate *adridere.*

5. Martial, *Epigram.* 6.44: "omnibus adrides, dicteria dicis in omnis: / sic te convivam posses placere putas" (ll. 3–4, as the manuscripts have it); the typical sting in the tail turns out to be the man's fondness for oral sex. For the emendation, see Shackleton Bailey 1978 (quotation on 279, my emphasis—and he goes

on: "Since that compound does not take a dative in classical Latin, *omnibus* must become *omnis*"); this reading is now incorporated in his Teubner edition of 1990 and repeated in the Loeb Classical Library edition of 1993. For critical discussion of the emendation and Shackleton Bailey's interpretation of the poem, see Grewing 1997, 314; Nauta 2002, 176–77.

6. Catullus 39, passim; Tacitus, *Ann.* 4.60 (a more sinister context).

7. Ovid, *Ars am.* 3.283 (advising girls not to display *immodici rictus* while laughing); Lucretius 5.1064 (of dogs); see further p. 159.

8. Nonius Marcellus 742 (Lindsay): "non risu tantum sed et de sono vehementiore vetustas dici voluit."

9. *Verr.* 2.3.62. That at least is Cicero's highly colored presentation of the scene (he admits that Apronius' uproar is only extrapolated from his laughter at the trial).

10. Persius 1.12; see 1.116–18 for an explicit comparison with Horace.

11. Catullus 13.5; Suetonius, *Vesp.* 5.2; Lucretius 4.1176.

12. Nonius Marcellus 742 (Lindsay) quoting Accius (= *ROL2*, Accius, *Tragoediae* 577) on the pounding of the ocean—the text is not entirely certain, and on another reading *cachinnare* could refer to the screeching of a seabird; Catullus 31.14 (of the ripples of Lake Garda), 64.273 ("leviter sonant plangore cachinni"). There is a curious set of relations here with aspects of the Greek laughter lexicon. Γελᾶν, in Greek, is commonly used for the behavior of the sea. *Cachinnare* matches (even if it is not directly derived from) the Greek καχάζειν, which does not appear to be used metaphorically for the sound of water, though the very similar Greek word καχλάζειν (with a lambda) is a regular term for "splashing." It is tempting to think that this pairing lies somewhere behind Catullus' play with *cachinnare* (or perhaps καχάζειν and καχλάζειν are not as separate as modern lexicography likes to make them).

13. M. Clarke 2005 is a useful recent review of relevant material stressing the unfamiliarity of the Greek semantics of "smiling": see also Lateiner 1995, 193–95; Levine 1982; Levine 1984. For the stress on the face: Sappho 1.14; *Hom. Hymn* 10.2–3 (note that, very unusually, Homer, *Il.* 15.101–2, has Hera laughing "with her lips").

14. Halliwell 2008, 524, part of a longer, careful discussion (520–29) of Greek laughter terminology and its physical referents, though apart from this appendix, μειδιῶ has hardly a mention in the book.

15. For example, Virgil, *Aen.* 1.254 (see also Homer, *Il.* 15.47); Servius Auct. (ad loc.) quotes a parallel passage from Ennius, which uses *ridere* rather than *subridere*: Ennius, *Ann.* 450–51 (*ROL*) = 457–58 (Vahlen).

16. Catullus 39. In Kaster 1980, 238–40, the key examples are *Sat.* 1.4.4, 1.11.2 (quoted), 3.10.5, 7.7.8, 7.9.10, and 7.14.5 (translated accordingly in his edition of Macrobius for the Loeb Classical Library), but note also 1.2.10 (involving the whole face) and 7.3.15 (accompanying an apparent insult), neither of which quite match. Kaster is, I suspect, too keen to find smiles in both Macrobius and the texts he uses for comparison. He refers, for example, to the smiles of Cicero's dialogues "as an instrument of amused debate and rejoinder," but the Ciceronian passages he cites refer explicitly to a variety of "laughing" (*ridens, adridens*, etc.). I am relieved that König 2012, 215–26, has

(independently) similar reservations over details in Kaster's argument on smiling, although for different reasons.

17. Catullus 39.16; Ovid, *Ars am.* 2.49; Ovid, *Met.* 8.197; Livy 35.49.7; Quintilian, *Inst.* 6.1.38 (*renidentis* a plausible emendation for the manuscript *residentis*).

18. Apuleius, *Met.* 3.12; Valerius Flaccus 4.359; Tacitus, *Ann.* 4.60.2.

19. 1.2.10.

20. This is obviously made more complicated by the fact that *os, oris* (occasionally used with *renideo,* as at Ovid, *Met.* 8.197) could refer to the face or the mouth.

21. I am thinking here of the work of such scholars as Paul Ekman (1992; 1999) and that discussed in ch. 3, n. 18. I hope that by this point in the book I do not need to explain why I do not follow such a universalist path.

22. Chesterfield 1890, 177–79 (letter of 12 December 1765, to his godson), reprinted in D. Roberts 1992, 342–43: "The vulgar often laugh but never smile; whereas, well-bred people often smile, but seldom laugh." Similar sentiments are expressed in Chesterfield 1774, vol. 1, 328 (letter of 9 March 1748), reprinted in D. Roberts 1992, 72.

23. "Kissing," Jones's (as yet) unpublished paper given at Columbia University in 2002, also points to the ancients' careful calibration of different styles of kissing.

24. Le Goff 1997, 48 ("I wonder whether smiling is not one of the creations of the Middle Ages"); see also Trumble 2004, 89.

25. Plutarch, *Caes.* 4; Edwards 1993, 63.

26. The survival of so much Roman writing on oratory—some of which is concerned with how or whether to make the listener laugh (on which see pp. 107–20, 123–26)—may exaggerate the apparent preponderance of joking terms over laughter terms, but there is no reason to imagine that the whole imbalance should be ascribed to this.

27. A piece of popular wisdom rejected by Quintilian: "Potius amicum quam dictum perdendi" (6.3.28). It is possibly echoed by Horace, *Sat.* 1.4.34–35 (but different versions of the text and its punctuation give a significantly different sense; see Gowers 2012, 161), and by Seneca, *Controv.* 2.4.13. There are some echoes in modern sloganizing too, but the point is always reversed: "It's better to lose a jest than a friend."

28. Cicero, *De or.* 2.222 (= Ennius, frag. 167 Jocelyn; *ROL*1, Ennius, unassigned fragments 405–6).

29. "Cato," *Disticha.*, prol.: "Miserum noli irridere" (likewise "Neminem riseris").

30. Sonnabend 2002, 214–21, offers a brisk summary of scholarship on these lives; A. Cameron 2011, 743–82, is a fuller and more recent discussion (though underplaying, as most critics do, some of the work's importance, whatever its fictionality: "trivial . . . product," 781). The collection was probably produced in the late fourth century CE.

31. SHA, *Heliog.* 32.7, 29.3 ("ut de his omnibus risus citaret"), 25.2.

32. *Sat.* 2.1.15–2.2.16.

33. 2.3.1–2.5.9; on the style of these jokes and Macrobius' possible sources, see pp. 104–5, 130–31, 202.

34. 2.2.16 (*antiqua festivitas*); 2.4.21 (Augustus' "Fescennines"); see pp. 68–69.

35. 2.2.10, 2.2.12–13. On Evangelus and Servius, see Kaster 1980, 222–29.

36. *Sat.* 2.6.6–2.7.19 (avoidance of *lascivia*, 2.7.1); for mime's bawdy character in general, see pp. 168–69, 170.

37. *AP* 7.155; *PLM*3, 245–46; see further above, p. 169.

38. 2.7.16 (on the blurring of mime and pantomime here, see pp. 168, 170).

39. For an overview, see Bonner 1949; Bloomer 2007; Gunderson 2003, 1–25 (a more theorized account). Spawforth 2012, 73–81, considers the interface between Greek and Roman traditions.

40. *Controv.* 9.2.

41. Principally, Livy 39.42–43; Valerius Maximus 2.9.3; Cicero, *Sen.* 42. Briscoe 2008, 358–59, reviews the variants.

42. On the law in this case, see Bonner 1949, 108–9.

43. 9.2.9, 9.2.11.

44. Drunkenness: 9.2.3; slippers: 9.2.25; *ioci*: 9.2.1; *iocari*: 9.2.9–10; laughter: 9.2.6.

45. For the erotics of laughter, see pp. 3, 157–59. Halliwell 2008, 491, collects a wide range of instances (in Greek) of sexualized laughter, from the classical to the early Christian period.

46. Another example of (sexualized) laughter as a transgressive irruption into the public official sphere is found in the trial of Maximus, the (likely fictionalized) Roman prefect of Egypt (*P.Oxy.* 471). The "transcription" of the prosecution speech focuses on Maximus' relationship with a young boy, whom he included in his official business. One specific accusation is that the boy used to laugh in the midst of Maximus' clients. See Vout 2007, 140–50 (but note that the text does not claim that the boy was laughing "in the face of his clients," 148; the point is that he was *laughing* in the sphere of serious, official business).

47. *Controv.* 9.2.7.

48. *Ars am.* 3.279–90 (discussed on pp. 157–59).

49. *Aeneid* 4.128; discussed by Konstan 1986, careful to acknowledge the problem of reading this as a smile ("the smile, or perhaps it is a laugh," 18). Though intended for high school students, Gildenhard 2012, 138–39, offers a concise paragraph summing up the main interpretative problems of Venus' laugh.

50. *Ars P.* 1–5 ("Humano capiti cervicem pictor equinam iungere si velit . . . risum teneatis?"). The passage is more puzzling than it seems, for the laughable incongruities are in fact standard themes in Roman painting; see Frischer 1991, 74–85; Oliensis 1998, 199–202.

51. Coleiro 1979, 222–29, reviews the main suggestions; more briefly, Coleman 1977, 150–52.

52. Du Quesnay 1977, 37, is unusual in arguing that the singular "parent" here is the father.

53. "Enigmatic" is the euphemism of Nisbet 1978, 70, for the final four lines of the *Eclogue.*

54. The text has been a matter of dispute since the Renaissance at least, with both Politian and Scaliger advocating what is now the standard reading against the manuscripts, largely on the basis of the parallel passage in Quintilian (*Inst.*

9.3.8). Just to add to the complexity, the manuscript versions of Quintilian do in fact include the same version of these lines as the Virgilian manuscripts, but Quintilian's use of this passage as an example of a plural relative (*qui*) attached to a singular referent (*hunc*) makes it clear that he had in mind a different text, more or less as modern editors have it. The issues are reviewed by Coleman 1977, 148–49; Clausen 1994, 144 (from which I take the word *natural*). Note, however, some remaining support for the manuscript reading: for example, F. della Corte 1985, 80.

55. The quotation is from Clausen 1994, 144 (my emphasis); similarly R.D. Williams 1976, 119; Norden 1958, 63 ("*Ridere* c. acc. heisst überall sonst 'jemanden auslachen', nicht 'ihm zulachen'"). Both Perret 1970, 55, and Nisbet 1978, 77n135, see that this is far too sweeping and cite many counterexamples, including Ovid, *Ars am.* 1.87.

56. Pliny *NH*, 7.2, 7.72 (see p. 25), with Norden 1958, 65–67; Nisbet 1978, 70. This modern tradition of seeing the baby's *risus* as similar to that of Zoroaster goes back principally to Crusius 1896, 551–53.

57. See, for example, Perret 1970, 55 ("Il ne peut s'agir du sourire de la mère à l'enfant"); the different versions are briefly reviewed by R.D. Williams 1976, 120, and Coleman 1977, 148.

58. Nisbet 1978, 70; words such as *tenderness* and *intimacy* (Putnam, 1970, 162; Alpers 1979, 173) recur in these discussions.

59. Whatever the sentimentality, Nisbet is one of the very few translators to stick firmly to the word *laugh* rather than *smile* (translations in 2007 reprint of Nisbet 1978).

60. Catullus 61.209–13 ("Torquatus volo parvulus / matris e gremio suae / porrigens teneras manus / dulce rideat ad patrem / semihiante labello"). Modern critics are divided on whether this is merely a close epithalamic parallel (a vague back-reference for Virgil) or a direct source (e.g., Putnam 1970, 163: "borrowed"). Hardie 2012, 216–18, reviews the more general links between this *Eclogue* and Catullus 61 and 64. We should note that there is no hint of divinity in the laughter of Catullus 61 and that the divinity implied in Theocritus, *Id.* 17.121–34, a possible inspiration for the final line of the *Eclogue*, has nothing to do with any laughing baby.

61. Bataille 1997, 60. He continues, "All of a sudden, *what controlled the child falls into its field*. This isn't an authorization but a fusion. It's not a question of welcoming the triumph of man over deteriorated forms, but of intimacy communicated throughout. Essentially the laugh comes from *communication*" (italics in the original).

62. Parvulescu 2010, 161–62, rightly detects echoes of Virgil in Kristeva's treatment of the laughter exchanged between mother and child (esp. Kristeva 1980, 271–94).

63. Warner 1998, 348.

64. It is striking that hardly any classical treatment of this text references its role in modern theory—nor, it must be admitted, vice versa. In fact, there is some sorry mangling of the Latin in the nonclassical discussions; for example, "Incipe, puer parvo" in the first printing of Warner 1992 (348; later corrected), introducing yet another ungrammatical scribal error into a complex text.

65. The bibliography on constructing identity and on cultural change in the Greco-Roman world is now immense. In addition to other works cited in the following notes, significant contributions include Millett 1990; Woolf 1994; Goldhill 2001; Dench 2005; Mattingly 2011.

66. *Epist.* 2.1.156 ("Graecia capta ferum victorem cepit"). As Wallace-Hadrill 2008, 24–25, points out, modern scholars rarely quote the very different view of Ovid, *Fast.* 3.101–2, whose language alludes to Horace.

67. For examples, see Van Dommelen 1997; Hill 2001, 14, (constellation); Webster 2001, 217–23 (hybridity and creolization); Wallace-Hadrill 2008, 27–28 (bilingualism); Le Roux 2004, 301 (crossbreeding, *métissage*). The influence (and terminology) of such theoretical and comparative studies as Bhabha 1994, esp. 112–16 (for "hybridity"), and Hannerz 1987 is clear.

68. Wallace-Hadrill 2008. The clearest summary of the arguments is at 17–27, which also offers a punchy critique of some of the currently favorite metaphors while opting instead for the model of bilingualism (and also for a model of Greco-Roman cultural interaction based on the diastolic and systolic phases in the operation of the human heart). Wallace-Hadrill 1998 offers a brisk earlier version of his linguistic (code-switching) analogy.

69. Some sensible reflections on the shared traditions of laughter between elite and nonelite are found in Horsfall 1996, 110–11 (though Horsfall is overall more confident than many about our ability to access Roman "popular culture").

70. Again, there is a vast bibliography. Significant contributions among the new wave of studies of Greek literature and culture in the empire include Swain 1996 (reflecting on "how the Greek elite used language to constitute themselves as a culturally and politically superior group," 409); Whitmarsh 2001 (the question is "how 'the literary' is employed to construct Greek identity in relationship to the Greek past and the Roman present," 1–2); Spawforth 2012 ("Where Greek culture was concerned, an 'imperial style of signalled incorporation' made clear the 'pure' brand of Hellenism that the ruling power sought to uphold as morally acceptable to the Romans," 271). Konstan and Saïd 2006 includes a particularly useful range of essays.

71. Goldhill 2001; Woolf 1994 (the phrase is also used as the title of Woolf 1998, which focuses on Gaul).

72. Fraenkel 1922 (the English translation, Fraenkel 2007, reviews the impact of the book, on xi–xxii). From a more strictly historical perspective, the work of Erich Gruen has been particularly influential here; see, for example, Gruen 1990, 124–57.

73. Christenson 2000, 45–55; Beard 2007, 253–56.

74. Terence, *Eun.* 1–45; with Barsby 1999, 13–19; Brothers 2000, 20–26. Terence's Thraso derives from Menander's Bias. But the matter is complicated by the fact that there is a character named Gnatho in Menander's *The Toady* and another, Strouthias, who seems to be (from the fragments that remain) the inspiration for part of the portrayal of Terence's Gnatho. Perhaps Terence conflated the two, keeping Gnatho's name, or perhaps the same character went under two different names in Menander's play. See further Brown 1992, 98–99; Pernerstorfer 2006, 45–50 (for the arguments that a single character was called by two different names). Pernerstorfer 2009 attempts a major reconstruction of

the play, reprising the conclusions of the earlier article; for another, succinct, attempt to summarize the plot, see Gomme and Sandbach 1973, 420–22.

75. Menander, *Kolax* frag. 3 (= Plutarch, *Mor.* 57a = *Quomodo adulator* 13): γελῶ τὸ πρὸς τὸν Κύπριον ἐννοούμενος. Plutarch does not mention the title of the play but does name two of its characters. See Gomme and Sandbach 1973, 432; Pernerstorfer 2009, 112–13. Lefèvre 2003, 97–98, is almost alone (and unconvincing) in believing that these words "have nothing to do with Terence."

76. Gomme and Sandbach 1973, 432; Brown 1992, 94; Pernerstorfer 2009, 113.

77. Wallace-Hadrill 2008 (lamps: 390–91); Spawforth 2012 (cultural comportment: 36–58).

78. Halliwell 2008, 343–46, 351–71 (with 332–34, clearly summarizes the evidence and impact—including Beckett 1938, 168). McGrath (1997, vol. 1, 101–6; vol. 2, 52–57, 58–61) offers useful discussions of several of Rubens's versions of Democritus. For Heraclitus, see Halliwell 2008, 346–51.

79. *De or.* 2.235. He assumes Democritus' expertise in laughter, not necessarily that Democritus is known as a laugher.

80. "Laughing Mouth" (Γελασῖνος) is Aelian's term (*VH* 4.20); Halliwell 2008, 351, 369 (for "patron saint"); Juvenal 10.33–34; see also Horace, *Epist.* 2.1.194–96.

81. Hippocrates, [*Ep.*] 10–23 (with text and translation in W. D. Smith 1990). Hankinson 2000 and Halliwell 2008, 360–63, offer clear introductions.

82. [*Ep.*] 10.1 (ὁ δὲ πάντα γελᾷ).

83. [*Ep.*] 17.5 (ἐγὼ δὲ ἕνα γελῶ τὸν ἄνθρωπον).

84. The only reference to laughter in a (possibly) authentic surviving fragment of Democritus is 68B107a DK, which states that one should not laugh at the misfortune of others. The earliest explicit reference to Democritus being a renowned laugher himself (rather than an expert) is Horace, *Epist.* 2.1.194–96.

85. Plutarch, *Lyc.* 25 (statue); *Agis and Cleom.* 30 (shrine); Halliwell 2008, 44–49, offers a brief survey of the evidence for Spartan laughter.

86. Plutarch, *Lyc.* 12, 14.

87. Plutarch, *Mor.* 217c = *Apophthegmata Lac.*, Androcleidas.

88. A temptation not resisted by David 1989.

89. The Roman-period reconstruction of (and investment in) primitive Sparta is a theme in Spawforth 2012 (e.g., on the traditions of the *sussitia*, 86–100). In part, this tradition was no doubt the Spartans' own way of claiming a distinctive identity (happy to provide theme-park reenactments of primitive rituals); in part, it was a literary/discursive phenomenon, as writers of Roman date created a distinctive vision of the Spartan past.

90. Cordero 2000, 228, reviews the possibilities. They suggest that the tradition may go back to the third century, but "rien ne le prouve."

91. Plutarch, *Lyc.* 25, cites the Hellenistic historian Sosibios (Jacoby, *FGrHist* 595F19).

92. Chesterfield 1774, vol. 1, 262–63 (letter of 3 April 1747).

93. Cicero, *De or.* 2.217, sums it up; Plautus, *Pers.* 392–95, is a comic version of the hierarchy.

94. Plutarch, *Mor.* 854c = *Comp. Ar. & Men.* 4. The cultural complexity is nicely signaled by the fact that Plutarch here not only Hellenizes a Roman term to talk about the Greek dramatist Menander but goes on to compare Menander's "salt" to the salt of the sea from which Aphrodite was born. The reference at Plato, *Symp.* 177b, is almost certainly literally to salt rather to than wit.

5. THE ORATOR

1. Quintilian, *Inst.* 6.3.47–49. The force of the pun relies on the particular similarity between *quoque* and the vocative case of *coquus* (*coque*), so "I will vote for you *too*" is heard as "I will vote for you, *cook*," jokingly rubbing in the man's humble origins. The second pun was at the expense of a man who had been flogged in his youth by his father: the father was *constantissimus* (completely steadfast), the son *varius* ("vacillating" or "multicolored," i.e., black and blue).

2. Quintilian, *Inst.* 6.3.49. The background and outcome of the trial are discussed by Mitchell 1991, 198–201; Riggsby 1999, 112–19; Steel 2005, 116–31. In pondering this pun, I have canvassed other possible linguistic resonances (with *sericus*, meaning "silk," *sero*, "to bolt or bar," and *sero*, "to join or contrive") but without finding any plausible or pointed result.

3. Rawson 1975, xv; Simon Goldhill, interviewed by an Australian newspaper (*The Australian*, 24 September 2008) about his ideal ancient dinner party companions, chose Sappho, Hypatia, Aristophanes, Alcibiades, and Phryne, as "that would be more fun than Augustus, Caesar, Jesus, St Paul and Cicero." I am not so sure.

4. Brugnola 1896 is a nice monument to Cicero "the jokester," very much in the ancient tradition.

5. Plutarch, *Cic.* 1 (chickpea), 24 (self-importance), 27 (jokes—ἕνεκα τοῦ γελοίου). Against the man with ugly daughters, he quoted a line of some tragic drama ("It was against the will of Phoebus Apollo that he sired children"). The joke against Faustus Sulla (son of the dictator) rested on a double entendre. He had fallen into debt and issued notices (προέγραψε) advertising his property for sale; Cicero quipped that he preferred the son's notices to the father's (Sulla senior had issued notices with lists of those to be put to death—the word προγράφω, or *proscribo* in Latin, refers to both kinds of notice).

6. Plutarch, *Cic.* 38.

7. Though written in the form of a speech, this was never actually delivered and most likely was always intended for written circulation only; Ramsey 2003, 155–59.

8. Cicero, *Phil.* 2.39–40.

9. The possibility (or difficulty) of laughter in times of trouble is a common theme in Cicero's letters: *Att.* 7.5.5 (SB 128); *Fam.* 2.4.1 (SB 48), 2.12.1 (SB 95), 2.16.7 (SB 154), 15.18.1 (SB 213).

10. *Comp. Dem. & Cic.* 1.

11. *Comp. Dem. & Cic.* 1 (also quoted at Plutarch, *Cat. Min.* 21); on possible senses of λαμπρός, see Krostenko 2001, 67–68.

12. "Funny": Rabbie 2007, 207; "comedian": Krostenko 2001, 224. Dugan 2005, 108, offers "amusing." The Loeb Classical Library version of *Cat. Min.*

21 runs "What a droll fellow our consul is," and of *Comp. Dem. & Cic.* 1, "What a funny man we have for a consul."

13. *Inst.* 6.3.1–5.

14. Macrobius, *Sat.* 2.3.10, 7.3.8; Seneca, *Controv.* 7.3.9. The repartee starts with a gibe by Cicero against Laberius, who had just been given equestrian rank by Caesar and was trying to take his seat in the designated equestrian area—when everyone sat close together so as not to let him in. Cicero quips, "I would have let you in except that I am cramped in my seat" (the implication being that elite rows had become full of any riffraff promoted by Caesar). Laberius retorts, "How strange, given that you usually sit on two seats" (a dig at Cicero's vacillations of support between Caesar and Pompey). Seneca makes the parallel absolutely explicit: "Both men speak very wittily, but neither man has any sense of boundary in this area."

15. *Sat.* 2.1.12 (a phrase here ascribed to Vatinius); with Cicero, *Fam.* 9.20.1 (SB 193), implying that his friend Paetus had called Cicero *scurra veles* (a "light-armed *scurra*," "the *scurra* of the troop"), presumably in friendly banter.

16. Other, in my view less likely, suggestions for Cato's original words include *facetus* or *lepidus* (Leeman 1963, 61, 398n100; Krostenko 2001, 225); the quip would then point to the "overaestheticized" implications of those terms, incompatible with the masculine traditions of public speaking and office holding.

17. *Inst.* 6.3.5. Macrobius, *Sat.* 2.1.12 notes that some people suspected that Tiro himself had made up some of the jokes.

18. *Fam.* 15.21.2 (SB 207).

19. Macrobius, *Sat.* 2.3.3.

20. Macrobius, *Sat.* 2.3.7. This is a subtler pun than it at first seems, as Ingo Gildenhard has helped me appreciate, playing on the conflict between military preparations and those for a dinner party (see Brugnola 1896, 33–34). As I have translated it, the joke consists in Cicero displacing the life and death issues of civil war by turning to the trivial business of when you should arrive at a dinner party, but the military reading surely remains latent, with *nihil . . . paratum* also referring to the general lack of preparation of the Pompeians ("Look who's talking: the state of preparation in this camp is pathetic"). Corbeill's reading (1996, 186) produces a more *frigidus* point: "You've arrived late in the day" . . . "But not too late, as you have nothing ready."

21. It was Petrarch in the fourteenth century who established Cicero as a jester for the humanists (*Rerum memorandarum Lib.* 2.37, 2.39, 2.68), with further discussion in Bowen 1998.

22. *Fam.* 7.32.1–2 (SB 113). The name (or perhaps it is the nickname) of the correspondent points to the artful wit of this letter, which is as much a joke itself as a comment on the treatment of Cicero's *bona dicta*; see further Hutchinson 1998, 173–74; Fitzgerald 2000, 97; Krostenko 2001, 223 (which gives the passage a rather different stress—that Cicero is happy to be credited with the jokes of others, provided they are good ones). Note Cicero's claim elsewhere that Caesar would be able to recognize which quips were bona fide Ciceronian: *Fam.* 9.16.3–4 (SB 190).

23. Quintilian, *Inst.* 6.3.77; Macrobius, *Sat.* 2.4.16 (Vatinius, in order to show that he had recovered from his gout, boasted that he was now walking

two miles a day [in Macrobius, only one]. The retort is: "Yes, I'm not surprised; the days are getting a bit longer"). The slippage and migration of jokes is discussed by Laurence and Paterson 1999, 191–94.

24. Among studies earlier than those I discuss here, note Haury 1955 (focused particularly on irony); Geffcken 1973 (on comic aspects of *Pro Caelio*), now with Leigh 2004; Saint-Denis 1965, 111–61 (focusing especially on *Pro Caelio, In Verrem,* and *De oratore*).

25. *Att.* 1.18.1 (SB 18)—he can neither joke nor sigh. Hutchinson 1998, 172–99 (quotes on 177); see also Griffin 1995.

26. Richlin 1992a. For the rhetoric of invective and the main coordinates of sexual humor, see 57–104.

27. Freud 1960 [1905], 132–62 (quote on 147); Richlin 1992a, 59–60.

28. Corbeill 1996 (quotes on 5, 6, 53); on the persuasive or reassuring function of jokes and laughter, see also Richlin 1992a, 60 (again drawing on, and developing, a Freudian perspective).

29. Reflected in, for example, Connolly 2007, 61–62; Vasaly 2013, 148–49. Another important strand of work, with a strongly linguistic emphasis, is found in Krostenko 2001 (though his focus on "social performance" offers in many ways a complementary approach to the construction of identity through wit, laughter, and their terminologies). It is important to stress that what sets this "new orthodoxy" apart from some apparently similar earlier approaches (focusing on derision and humorous invective) is the constructive social function (one sense of *controlling* in Corbeill's title) it ascribes to laughter.

30. *Inst.* 6.3.7.

31. The expression of Fantham 2004, 186.

32. In particular, shorter sections in *Orat.* 87–90 and *Off.* 1.103–4.

33. Guérin 2011, 151, rightly refers to the provocation of laughter as "une zone de risque"; for Richlin 1992a, 13, it is the use of obscenity rather than the ambivalence of laughter that makes courtroom joking a risky proposition.

34. The first certain reference to *De Oratore* is in a letter to Atticus of November 55 (when the work is finished enough to suggest that Atticus copy it), *Att.* 4.13.2 (SB 87).

35. All recent work on this text is underpinned by the five-volume commentary of Harm Pinkster and others, which appeared between 1981 and 2008 (the relevant volume for the discussion of laughter in book 2 is Leeman, Pinkster, and Rabbie 1989), and it can be assumed to be a major reference point in what follows. This edition has largely replaced the earlier commentary of A. S. Wilkins, published between 1879 and 1892 (the relevant volume being Wilkins 1890). The best up-to-date translation, with introduction, is May and Wisse 2001; Fantham 2004 is an illuminating guide to the text and its literary, cultural, and historical significance.

36. At *De or.* 1.28, the participants agree to "imitate Socrates as he appears in the *Phaedrus* of Plato" and to sit down under a plane tree for their discussion; see Fantham 2004, 49–77. Although they are, in our terms, oratorical experts, they are keen to distinguish themselves from professional Greek experts (e.g., *De or.* 1.104).

37. May and Wisse, 2001, 14–15, succinctly introduces the characters; Fantham 2004, 26–48, discusses Crassus and Antonius in detail. Cicero adopts the Platonic device of setting his dialogue just before the death of the lead character (Socrates in Plato's *Phaedo* and *Crito*); here all the characters but one (Cotta) were dead by the end of 87 BCE. The year 91 BCE might be seen a loaded choice: only the year before, Crassus, as censor, had expelled the *Latini magistri* (Latin teachers of rhetoric) from Rome (*De or.* 3.93; Suetonius, *Rhet.* 1).

38. *Fam.* 1.9.23 (SB 20). Aristotle's dialogues are almost entirely lost, but they certainly featured much less cut and thrust, and longer expository speeches by the participants. Cicero may also have had in mind Aristotelian content as well as form.

39. See, e.g., R. E. Jones 1939, 319–20; Dugan 2005, 76.

40. In addition to the works already cited, notable recent interventions, often with a particular focus on the section on laughter, include Gunderson 2000, 187–222 ("Love"); Krostenko 2001, 202–32; Dugan 2005, 75–171; Guérin 2011.

41. *De or.* 2.216–90. In addition to the commentaries noted above, Monaco 1974 offers a text, an Italian translation, and extensive notes on this section of the work alone; Graf 1997, 29–32, offers a succinct discussion.

42. *De or.* 2.234. This image is taken up again at the end of the section (2.290).

43. *De or.* 2.217, 2.231, 2.239.

44. *De or.* 2.216.

45. *De or.* 2.235.

46. Leeman, Pinkster, and Rabbie 1989, 188–204; Rabbie 2007, 212–15 (a revised, less "speculative," English version). The earlier tradition is represented by Grant 1924, 71–87, 100–131 (drawing on Arndt 1904). To be fair, it did admit a few Ciceronian additions to or deviations from Greek precedents ("Sed iam abscedere videtur Cicero a fontibus Graecis ac suum tenere cursum," Arndt 1904, 36, in relation to *De or.* 2.268.), but the default position was that everything went back to a lost Greek source unless there was overwhelming evidence to the contrary. The old view is still assumed in some popular writing on the subject (such as Morreall 1983, 16) and is more or less revived wholesale by Watson 2012, 215–23, in yet another attempt to pin the *Tractatus Coislinianus* (see above, p. 31) to Aristotle.

47. *De or.* 2.217; see also 2.288. These Greek books do not survive; see p. 34.

48. *De or,* 2.216 (*suavis*), 2.236 (*locus . . . et regio*)—though Corbeill 1996, 21–22, nuances the parallels between Aristotelian and Ciceronian terminology.

49. There is an unresolved controversy (conveniently summarized by Fantham 2004, 163–64) around the availability in antiquity of some of the works of Aristotle, and so to which ones Cicero could have had direct access.

50. Leeman, Pinkster, and Rabbie 1989, 188–89.

51. As argued, for example, by Monaco 1974, 29, in relation to the Memmius story of *De or.* 2.283.

52. *De or.* 2.2.

53. See p. 54 for the textual confusion between *locus* and *iocus*.

54. These *veteres* could be in theory either Greek or Roman (as Pinkster, Leeman, and Rabbie 1989, 214, makes clear). But the strongly Latin character of the terms makes the latter much more likely, although no doubt versed in Greek theory.

55. It is an even smarter exchange than it might appear. As A.S. Wilkins 1890, 113, and Leeman, Pinkster, and Rabbie 1989, 216, clearly document, "bark" (*latrare*) was a word used for shrill speakers. Krostenko 2001, 214–15, points to Cicero's use of the word *venustus* for "spur-of-the-moment" humor of this kind.

56. Guérin 2011, 271–303, discusses these two antitypes in detail, though suggesting an oversystematic, rigid distinction between the two (the *scurra* is the antitype of oratorical *dicacitas,* the *mimus* of oratorical *cavillatio*). Grant 1924, 88–96, offers a convenient collection of sources. See further above, pp. 152–55, 167–70.

57. The Latin is hard to pin down: "In re est item ridiculum, quod ex quadam depravata imitatione sumi solet; ut idem Crassus: 'Per tuam nobilitatem, per vestram familiam.' Quid aliud fuit, in quo contio rideret, nisi illa vultus et vocis imitatio? 'Per tuas statuas,' vero cum dixit, et extento bracchio paulum etiam de gestu addidit, vehementius risimus." I follow Monaco 1974, 124, here in seeing this as laughter generated by the mimicry (*depravata imitatione*), with the imitation of the statue (*extento bracchio*) prompting the most raucous chuckles. Leeman, Pinkster, and Rabbie 1989, 248, argues that the joke rests on the unexpected addition (*aprosdokēton*) of "per tuas statuas" after "per tuam nobilitatem, per vestram familiam" and that the extended arm is a reference to the position of a man taking an oath. But this interpretation hardly delivers on the mimicry that Cicero emphasizes. See further, p. 119.

58. *De or.* 2.216; *Off.* 1.108. Dugan 2005, 105, puts the strongest recent case for seeing Cicero's choice of Strabo ("whose public persona and oratorical style provoked suspicions that were similar to those which he himself incited") as significant.

59. Zinn 1960, 43.

60. *Fam.* 7.32.2 (SB 113).

61. Ingo Gildenhard has suggested to me that the name is significant: at the very least there is something a bit joking in having the disquisition on joking delivered by a man whose name means "squinter." And just suppose we were to imagine that "Strabo" was a stock comic character; then we might also imagine a running metaliterary joke in the criticism of mime.

62. *De or.* 2.218 ("leve nomen habet utraque res").

63. *Or.* 87.

64. Leeman, Pinkster, and Rabbie 1989, 189, followed by Fantham 2004, 189.

65. Inevitably, the influence of earlier Greek terminology has been sought here. Kroll 1913, 87, for example, sees the Peripatetic terms *charis/gelōs* behind *facetiae/dicacitas* (though in this case even Grant [1924, 103–18] is unconvinced and finds no exact Greek equivalent for the pairing).

66. *De or.* 2.251 (*ridicula/faceta*), 2.260 (*frigida/salsa*), 2.222 (*bona dicta/salsa*).

67. Grant 1924, 100–131, while acknowledging the difficulties, attempts a series of systematic definitions; likewise Leeman, Pinkster, and Rabbie 1989, 183–88 ("Einige Differenzierung zwischen dem Gebrauch der verschiedenen Termini ist . . . möglich, wobei aber Grant . . . manchmal zu weit gegangen ist," 183), and Guérin 2011, 145–303. Krostenko 2001 offers a highly technical sociolinguistic study of many of these key terms, emphasizing their mutability. Ramage 1973 attempts to track ideas of *urbanitas* throughout Roman history. Fitzgerald 1995, 87–113, is the clearest introduction to the issues.

68. Krostenko 2001, 207–14.

69. *Inst.* 6.3.18–19: "Salsum in consuetudine pro ridiculo tantum accipimus: natura non utique hoc est, quamquam et ridicula esse oporteat salsa. Nam et Cicero omne quod salsum sit ait esse Atticorum non quia sunt maxime ad risum compositi, et Catullus, cum dicit, 'Nulla est in corpore mica salis,' non hoc dicit, nihil in corpore eius esse ridiculum. Salsum igitur erit quod non erit insulsum." This passage reveals some of the acute difficulties in translating, let alone in making precise sense of, Roman discussions of wit and its terminology. In the first sentence, is Quintilian saying that *salsa* ought also to be *ridicula,* or that *ridicula* ought also to be *salsa?* The position of the *et* strongly suggests the former, but the explanations that follow (after *nam*) make the latter almost certain. And what is the sense of *ridiculum?* Modern translators render Quintilian's comment on Catullus as "He does not mean there is nothing ridiculous in her body" (D. Russell in the Loeb Classical Library) or "Non c'è niente di ridicolo" (Monaco 1967). It makes perfect sense in English (or Italian), but it ignores the other, active Latin sense of *ridiculum*—to make you laugh. Catullus could well be saying (as some modern commentators agree; see, e.g., Quinn 1970, 424) "there is not a spark of wit" in her. Throughout the passage there is an instability between the active and the passive sense of these words (as in *ad risum compositi*). Matters are further confused by the fact that Cicero (*De or.* 2.251) attempts (tendentiously maybe) to distinguish the *salsum* of the orator and the mime actor.

70. *De or.* 2.235. For the reading of *venas* or *genas*, see Leeman, Pinkster, and Rabbie 1989, 238.

71. *De or.* 2.236.

72. *De or.* 2.279.

73. *De or.* 2.248.

74. *De or.* 2.248.

75. *De or.* 2.254.

76. *De or.* 2.255, 2.260; see also p. 28.

77. *De or.* 2.255 (for the financial sense, see Plautus, *Rud.* 1327).

78. *De or.* 2.245.

79. *De or.* 2.252.

80. *De or.* 2.90–92; though there are dangers even in this kind of imitation, as Antonius points out (you have to make sure that you copy the most important features of the model, not merely those that are easy to imitate).

81. *De or.* 2.242.

82. See, e.g., Edwards 1993, 98–136 (see 117–19 for the comparison of actors and orators). Dupont 2000 is a subtle discussion of the interrelationships

between Roman oratory and theater, as is, more briefly, Fantham 2002 (drawing particularly on Quintilian, *Inst.* 11.3). See further above, p. 167.

83. *De or.* 2.251.

84. *De or.* 2.247, 2.256.

85. Corbeill 1996, 26.

86. *De or.* 2.262.

87. One classic statement of this "brain-balkanisation" is Feeney 1998, esp. 14–21.

88. Krostenko 2001, 223–25; Dugan 2005, 105–6.

89. Seneca, *Constant.* 17. Vatinius is here dubbed (like Cicero) a *scurra*—but also *venustus* and *dicax*. "He used to joke about his own feet and scarred neck; in this way he escaped the wit [*urbanitas*] of his enemies—who outnumbered his deformities—and particularly Cicero's."

90. Macrobius, *Sat.* 2.3.5. Relations between Cicero and Vatinius were more complicated than the terms of simple enmity in which they are often painted. Cicero defended Vatinius in 54 BCE. Even if this was largely under pressure from Caesar and Pompey (see his lengthy explanation in *Fam.* 1.9 [SB 20]), there are later clear signs of cordiality, in, e.g., *Att.* 11.5.4 (SB 216); *Fam.* 5.9–11 (SB 255–59).

91. "Interactive" (as Ingo Gildenhard encourages me to say) is key here, and a feature lost from the necessarily nondialogic character of the speeches as circulated in written form. One might be tempted to say that the aggressive humor is a feature more of the written versions than of the original oratorical scene; that, in writing, invective has replaced the dialogic banter that is so central to the picture of joking in *De Oratore*.

92. *Inst.* 6.3 (with Monaco 1967, including Italian translation and notes); Fernández López 2007 is a brief introduction to the work as a whole.

93. Cicero's account is explicitly referenced at, for example, *Inst.* 6.3.8 (*De or.* 2.236), 6.3.42 (*Orat.* 87).

94. *Inst.* 6.3.23 (*verbo/re*), 6.3.26 and 29 (funny faces), 6.3.34 (classes of people).

95. *Inst.* 6.3.50.

96. *De or.* 2.267; *Inst.* 6.3.67.

97. *Inst.* 6.3.102–12.

98. *De or.* 2.271 (see also 2.227); *Inst.* 6.3.19.

99. *Inst.* 6.3.28.

100. As suggested in another context (see pp. 131, 252n11) by Sherwin-White 1966, 305.

101. *Inst.* 6.3.82. See above, n. 89, for a *scurra*, Vatinius, who apparently told jokes on himself to his advantage.

102. *Inst.* 6.3.112, 6.3.54 ("est enim dictum per se urbanum 'satagere'"). Martial, *Epigram.* 4.55.27–29, suggests that foreign place-names could be funny too.

103. *Inst.* 6.3.8, 6.3.32.

104. *Inst.* 6.1.48.

105. *De or.* 2.240–41.

106. *Inst.* 6.3.6, 6.3.70 ("ridiculum est autem omne quod aperte fingitur").

107. Phaedrus, *Fabulae* 5.5; see also John Henderson 2001, 119–28. Here, as Henderson observes (224n70), the phrase *urbanus sal* signals Roman "show biz."

6. FROM EMPEROR TO JESTER

1. SHA, *Heliog.* 26.6, 25.1.

2. Variations on this theme are found in other ancient reflections on the autocrat's relationship to laughter and joking—in, for example, the story of the young Julius Caesar's encounter with the pirates. In captivity, Caesar joked with the pirates that when he was free, he would crucify them, which is what he did. Suetonius (*Iul.* 4; see also 74) underlines the point: he really carried out "what he had often threatened them as a joke" ("quod saepe illis minatus inter iocum fuerat"). The message is that in different ways, the jokes of the powerful could turn out to have a greater truth-value than you might want.

3. Laurence and Paterson 1999 is an important introductory study on the whole theme of emperors and jokes.

4. Nicolaus' *Historiae* does not survive complete; this passage is quoted by Athenaeus, *Deipnosophistae* 6.261c = Jacoby, *FGrHist* 90F75. Nicolaus was writing in Greek, hence the stress on "native language."

5. Plutarch, *Sull.* 2, 36.

6. Succinctly characterized by Le Goff 1993, 26; in a slightly later period, Bowen 1984.

7. See further Laurence and Paterson 1999, 191–94; SHA, *Avid. Cass.* 2.5–6, a late antique reflection on such migration. In what follows, I hope it goes without saying that "Augustus quipped" is shorthand for "Augustus is said to have quipped."

8. Dio 65(66).11.

9. *Sat.* 2.4.3; quoted by Quintilian, *Inst.* 6.3.59, as an example of raising a laugh by *similitudo*, or comparison. Other examples of friendly imperial jocularity include Suetonius, *Tit.* 3.2 ("cum amanuensibus suis per ludum iocumque certantem"); SHA, *Hadr.* 20.8.

10. *Sat.* 2.4.19–20. Roughly the same quip is told by Valerius Maximus (9.14 ext. 3), made to a republican governor of Sicily.

11. *Ep.* 4.25 (picking up a story from *Ep.* 3.20). The overall sense of the anecdote is clear, but there are some difficulties in the details. One crucial (and awkward) sentence is "Quid hunc putamus domi facere, qui in tanta re tam serio tempore tam scurriliter ludat, qui denique omnino in senatu dicax et urbanus et bellus est?" I have translated this, in common with others, as "What do we imagine that the kind of man who plays around just like a *scurra* in such a weighty matter and at such a serious moment does at home—when he is so sarcastic, facetious, such a sharp talker even in the Senate?" This would imply that Pliny sees the Senate as no place for the *dicacitas,* etc., that Cicero admired (and for Sherwin-White 1966, 305, is an illustration of a shift in the culture of wit). But I have wondered if it might rather mean "What do you imagine the man does at home who plays around just like a *scurra* in such a weighty matter and at such a serious moment yet in the Senate is a wonderfully witty, elegant, and smart speaker?"—implying approval of *dicacitas,* etc.

12. SHA, *Comm.* 15.6. See also Suetonius, *Cal.* 27.4 (a writer of "Atellan farces" burned alive in the amphitheater by Caligula for a dodgy pun, "ob ambigui ioci versiculum").

13. *Claud.* 21.5.

14. Suetonius, *Cal.* 32.3. Suetonius, *Cal.* 33, repeats a similar quip ("among his various jokes," when he was smooching around the neck of his wife or mistress, he would say, "What a lovely neck—off it could come just as soon as I give the word").

15. SHA, *Comm.* 10.4.

16. Suetonius, *Iul.* 45.2; Suetonius, *Dom.* 18.2; Juvenal 4.38 (*calvus Nero*). Emperors also joked about the baldness of others; Caligula famously, and nastily, ordered a line of prisoners to be executed "from bald head to bald head" (Suetonius, *Cal.* 27.1; Dio 59.22.3); see also SHA, *Heliog.* 29.3 (see p. 77).

17. *Sat.* 2.5.7.

18. Suetonius, *Claud.* 41.1 ("ne sedato quidem tumultu temperare potuit, quin ex intervallo subinde facti reminisceretur cachinnosque revocaret").

19. *Vesp.* 22–23 (compare, for example, Cicero, *De or.* 2.236, 2.257). The specter of inappropriate wit also hovered over the emperor Augustus. We might, for example, wonder how far the adverse side of the mime was to be seen in his last words as reported by Suetonius (*Aug.* 99.1): Had he played his part well, he asked, in the *mime* of life?

20. Suetonius, *Cal.* 24.2; the classic account of Xerxes at the Hellespont is Herodotus 7.33–35.

21. Suetonius, *Cal.* 27.4; Seneca, *De ira* 2.33.3–5 (without specific reference to laughter).

22. *Aug.* 98. Wallace-Hadrill 2008, 38–41, discusses other aspects of this passage.

23. Dio 59.26.8–9. A story told of Hadrian, as of other rulers, focuses on his encounter with an ordinary woman he passed on a journey and points in a similar direction. In Dio's account (69.6.3). she tries to waylay him with a request, but he brushes her off, saying that he does not have time. Her retort, however, turns him in his tracks: "Don't be emperor, then." The simple idea was that the emperor ought to have time for the humble and that the humble could answer back. This is discussed (with the parallels) by Millar 1977, 3–4.

24. SHA, *Hadr.* 17.6–7.

25. *Met.* 2.676–707. Barchiesi 2005, 295, compares this with the encounter between Athena and Odysseus at Homer, *Od.* 13.287, where Athena is said to "smile" (μειδιᾶν). He admits that it "develops very differently" ("lo sviluppo sarà ben diverso")—so differently, I would suggest, that it points to the very different significance of *ridere* and μειδιᾶν.

26. *Met.* 9.306–23.

27. *Met.* 5.662–78. As Stephen Halliwell has suggested to me, there is a similarity between the sound of some of these creatures and human laughter, or it is easy enough to imagine one; for hearing the sound of crows (in the same family as magpies) as laughter, see Halliwell 2008, 3.

28. Unsurprisingly, Ovid's work is a treasure chest of clever comments and reflections on and around laughter both human and divine. We shall focus on

some more of these in the next chapter (see pp. 157–59). For more on divine laughter (as well as the misfit between the Greek μειδιᾶν and the Latin vocabulary of laughter), see Ovid, *Fast.* 4.5–6, with the parallels in Ennius and Lucretius noted by Fantham (1998, 91), though she treats *ridere* here as unproblematically "smile.".

29. The "clever slave" of comedy is usefully discussed by Fitzgerald 2000, 10–11, 24–26, 44–47, and McCarthy 2000, esp. 211–13.

30. The most convenient edition of this text is Perry 1952, 35–208 (from which I take my references, with G and W indicating the different manuscript versions). For a translation, see Lloyd Daly in Hansen 1998, 111–62; Jouanno 2006. The complexities of the manuscript and papyrological tradition and the questions of cultural background are summarized succinctly by Hopkins 1993 (esp. 11) and in greater detail by Kurke 2011, 1–49 (including an excellent review of the secondary literature). In general, Kurke is more inclined than I am to identify earlier Greek traditions in the *Life* rather than to stress the Roman surface detail (such as monetary denominations; see *Vita Aesopi* W 24, 27); Pelliccia 2012 also resists Kurke's intention to "frog-march the evidence backward" (40).

31. Note the carefully agnostic comments of Kurke 2011, 13 (citing further references to the ongoing debate on the "real existence" of Aesop).

32. Hopkins 1993, 13; *Vita Aesopi* G 1; *Vita Aesopi* W 1.

33. *Vita Aesopi* G 7 (in W 7, the goddess concerned is Tyche).

34. *Vita Aesopi* G 2–3; W 2–3, with Kurke 2011, 191–92. Kurke also points to other cultural roles of mutism in this text: for example, as a signal of social exclusion (162–63) or an analogue of fabular speech (201). Figs are also prominent in various laughter stories discussed above, p. 177.

35. *Vita Aesopi* G 24; W 24 (with reference to the "turnip" not in G).

36. *Vita Aesopi* G 25–27; W 25–27.

37. Freedom: *Vita Aesopi* G 90; W 90; death at Delphi: G 140–42; W 140–42. Kurke 2011, 53–94, fully discusses the critique of Delphic authority that the story implies.

38. *Vita Aesopi* G 36; W 36.

39. *Inst.* 6.3.71. The original Latin does not quite say "stupid" at the end, as in the English idiom of such gags, but it very nearly does: "Stulte interrogaverat exeuntem de theatro Campatium Titius Maximus an spectasset. Fecit Campatius dubitationem eius stultiorem dicendo: '<non> sed in orchestra pila lusi.'"

40. Baths: *Vita Aesopi* G 38; lentil(s): G 39–41; W 39–41.

41. Philo, *Leg.* 349–67.

42. Smallwood 1970, 3–50, discusses the historical background and the literary tradition of the *Legatio*. Conybeare 2013, 28–39, discusses the stress on laughter in Philo's philosophical and theological works.

43. Stackelberg 2009, 135–40, explores the physical context of the meeting between the emperor and the envoys.

44. *Leg.* 349–59; mime: 359 (καὶ γὰρ τὸ πρᾶγμα μιμεία τις ἦν). Smallwood 1970, 321–22, collects other references, in Philo and elsewhere, to the mocking of Jews being compared to mime, though she is carried away by the idea that some ancient figurines that *may* represent mime actors possibly have a

distinctively Jewish physiognomy. The vocabulary at 351 and 368 also signals this episode as "theatrical" in a more general sense.

45. *Leg.* 361: πάλιν πρὸς τὴν πεῦσιν γέλως ἐκ τῶν ἀντιδίκων κατερράγη τοσοῦτος, τῇ μὲν ἡδομένων τῇ δὲ καὶ ἐπιτηδευόντων ἕνεκα κολακείας ὑπὲρ τοῦ τὸ λεχθὲν δοκεῖν σὺν εὐτραπελίᾳ καὶ χάριτι εἰρῆσθαι, ὥς τινα τῶν ἑπομένων αὐτῷ θεραπόντων ἀγανακτεῖν ἐπὶ τῷ καταφρονητικῶς ἔχειν αὐτοκράτορος.

46. *Leg.* 361. As Smallwood 1970, 322, puts it, if this was the rule, "Dio and Suetonius know nothing of this."

47. *Leg.* 362–67.

48. *Inst.* 6.3.58 (the standard modern text simply draws from Horace's account in *Sat.* 1.5 to fill the obvious gap in what has survived of Quintilian).

49. Martial, *Epigram.* 1.101. Plutarch, *Mor.* 760a (= *Amat.* 16), recounts a joking encounter between Gabba (called a γελωτοποιός) and Maecenas; see also Quintilian, *Inst.* 6.3.27, 6.3.80 (6.3.62 may also refer to Gabba).

50. Tacitus, *Ann.* 15.34: "Vatinius inter foedissima eius aulae ostenta fuit, sutrinae tabernae alumnus, corpore detorto, facetiis scurrilibus."

51. The sense of *copreae* might be rather "found on the dung heap" (from κοπρία, "dung heap"), but I have been unable to resist "little shits."

52. I include in this the "courts" of rivals or enemies; Dio (in a speech of Octavian) refers to the table companions of Antony and Cleopatra being called κοπρίαι (Dio 50.28.5).

53. Dio 74(73).6.

54. *Tib.* 61.6.

55. Suetonius, *Claud.* 8.

56. Pliny, *HN* 37.17; Seneca, *Ben.* 2.12.1. Caligula was said to wear them— see Suetonius, *Cal.* 52: "socco muliebri."

57. *Soccus* could, in fact, be used as a metonym for comedy, as *cothurnus* (buskin) was for tragedy; see Horace, *Epist.* 2.1.174; Ovid, *Rem. am.* 376. For a parasite's *soccus,* see Plautus, *Persa* 124.

58. I am aware that there may seem to be something risky about assuming that Suetonius' account is much closer than that of the SHA to the reality of court life. But it's not too risky. Suetonius had inside experience of the Roman palace (Wallace-Hadrill 1983, 73–96), and the use of the term *copreae* in different contexts and writers implies a recognizable referent. It is, as I have been suggesting, another case where these late imperial biographies hit the spirit if not the fact of Roman imperial life.

59. *CIL* 6.4886 (= *ILS* 5225): ". . .] Caesaris lusor / mutus argutus imitator / Ti. Caesaris Augusti qui / primum invenit causidicos imitari." The fullest and most acute recent discussion is Purcell 1999 (who, however, prints the text as "mutus et argutus").

60. Wallis 1853, 79–80.

61. *Argutus* on its own is a term that is more generally associated with the repartee of the Roman wit or jokester; see, for example, Plautus, *Truculentus* 491–96.

62. Garelli 2007, 251; a late antique glossary defines a female pantomime actress as "omnium artium lusor" (*CGL* 5.380.42); Petronius, *Sat.* 68, has perhaps a similar household "imitator."

63. Laes 2011, 470, evades the problem by punctuating differently, to read "Mute and bright imitator. Of the household of Tiberius." But the isolated phrase "Of the household of Tiberius" is very awkward, even by the standards of this awkward Latin.

64. Purcell 1999, 182–83, reviews various possible settings (including public performance), but the repeated stress on the emperor in this text strongly suggests that we are dealing principally with a court entertainer.

65. See, for example, Pliny, *Ep.* 3.1.9, 9.17; with further references and discussion in C.P. Jones 1991 and Dunbabin 2008.

66. *Ep.* 50 (esp. 2). Pliny, *Ep.* 5.19, also concerns a resident household comedian; similarly, Petronius, *Sat.* 68 (n62).

67. Barton 1993, esp. 107–8 ("What did the Romans see in the mirror of deformity?") and 141 (Seneca's Harpaste as a "freakish avatar" of the elite philosopher). This is an extremely powerful discussion (also linking the mimes I will be treating in the next chapter); in general, however, Barton stresses the roles of derision and monstrosity more strongly than I think plausible.

68. *Vesp.* 19.2.

69. Suetonius, *Iul.* 51. See also Suetonius, *Iul.* 49.4; Dio 43.20; and the discussion in Beard 2007, 247–49.

70. The clearest ancient example of laughter presented in these terms is found in the Greek story of Baubo, who exposes her genitals and makes the mourning Demeter laugh; it is explicitly called apotropaic by, for example, Zeitlin 1982 (145). For further references and brief discussion, see above, p. 174.

71. The "evil eye" is far too catchall a solution to be useful; see further Beard 2007, 248.

72. Barton 1993, 140, briefly discusses Vespasian's funeral (though not the triumph)—seeing the joker along these lines, as "the monstrous double" of the emperor.

73. For example, Juvenal 5; Martial, *Epigram.* 2.43, 3.60, 4.85; Pliny, *Ep.* 2.6. Gowers 1993, 211–19, discusses the ideology and the practice of such inequalities.

74. SHA, *Heliog.* 25.9.

75. Petronius, *Sat.* 49, raises all kinds of questions about food and deception. Apicius' "*patina* of anchovy without anchovy" is a more mundane case (4.2.12).

76. D'Arms 1990 is a useful overview of the general paradoxes of equality and inequality of the *convivium;* further aspects are discussed by Barton 1993, 109–12; Roller 2001, 135–46; Roller 2006 (for the hierarchies implied by posture), esp. 19–22, 85–88, 130–36.

77. The most acute discussions of this particular area include Roller 2001, 146–54 (focusing on verbal exchanges witty and otherwise at the dinner party), and Damon 1997, an important study that lies in the background of much of my exploration in the pages that follow.

78. I am borrowing here Lévi-Strauss's famous phrase, for which see Lévi-Strauss 1997 [1965].

79. Schlee 1893, 98.18–21.

80. Damon 1997, 1–19, is a good introduction, with further bibliography, to some of the main debates about parasites; 23–36 sketches the main characteristics of the figure; 252–55 summarizes her key conclusions on the "sites of discomfort" (255) in the institution of patronage. Other useful recent discussions of different aspects of the parasite, and his cultural origins, include Nesselrath 1985, 88–121; J.C.B. Lowe 1989; Brown 1992; J. Wilkins 2000, 71–86; Tylawsky 2002; König 2012, 242–65.

81. Xenophon, *Symp.* 1.11–16, and, for example, 2.14, 2.20–23, 4.50. Halliwell 2008, 139–54, is a sharp discussion of different modes of laughter throughout this work, rightly stressing the role of mimicry and questioning quite how uninvited we should imagine Philip to be (143–55). Huss 1999, 104–6, lists numerous close—or not so close—ancient parallels.

82. Damon 1997, 37–101, reviews these plays. Maltby 1999 discusses four particular characters (from Plautus' *Menaechmi, Captivi, Persa,* and *Stichus*). How far we are meant to identify significantly different types in this repertoire of characters—to distinguish, say, the "parasite" from the "flatterer"—is anything but certain; I have not here attempted to delineate any precise calibration of these hungry, flattering jokesters.

83. Arnott 1972 remains one of the best, most sympathetic introductions to the play—and to the role of its parasite.

84. *Stich.* 221–24: "logos ridiculos vendo. age licemini. / qui cena poscit? ecqui poscit prandio? / . . . ehem, adnuistin? nemo meliores dabit." *Logi* is a loan word whose Greek associations may have remained strong (see also ll. 383, 393), but later in the play (l. 400) the Latin *dicta* is used as an exact equivalent for these jokes.

85. *Stich.* 454–55: "Libros inspexi; tam confido quam potis, me meum optenturum regem ridiculis logis." For the role of jokebooks, see above, pp. 201–5.

86. *Ridiculus: Stich.* 171–77 (whose precise order is uncertain), 389. *Catagelasimus: Stich.* 630 (the slightly awkward translation brings out the point). Ritschl 1868, 411, asserts that *ridiculus* never holds a passive sense in this period ("non sit is qui risum movet invitus, sed qui iocis et facetiis risum dedita opera captat"), a view widely followed (by, e.g., Maltby 1999). This seems to me highly implausible and—by missing the subtlety signaled in l. 630—reduces the *Stichus* to the uninteresting play it has been taken to be. (See the damning comments on it summarized by Arnott 1972, 54.) Bettini 2000 reaches similar conclusions on Gelasimus to my own, by a different route (see esp. 474); Sommerstein 2009, despite an apparent zeal to oversystematize laughter in Aristophanes, also points to some of these ambivalences.

87. It provides, for example, the main subject of a long essay by Plutarch: *Mor.* 48e–74e (= *Quomodo adulator*).

88. Seneca, *Ep.* 27.5–7: "Habebat ad pedes hos [servos], a quibus subinde cum peteret versus quos referret, saepe in medio verbo excidebat. Suasit illi Satellius Quadratus, stultorum divitum arrosor et, quod sequitur, arrisor et, quod duobus his adiunctum est, derisor, ut grammaticos haberet analectas." Satellius' quip (that he should have "scholars to gather up the bits") appears to work by pushing further the idea of the commodification of knowledge and its relation to the slave

economy: *analecta* was the title of the slave whose job it was to pick up crumbs around the dinner table, here imagined as scholars picking up the dropped crumbs of the host's quotations. Roller 2001, 148–49, briefly discusses the passage, linking the three terms rather differently. Similar connections underlie a clever (but usually overlooked) pun in Juvenal 5. This poem sends up a dysfunctional dinner party where a client puts up with the humiliation of his status, to the scorn of the satirist. Toward the end, we learn what scraps the client is to be served, in contrast to the lavish food of his host. They include *semesum leporem*—or "half-eaten hare," as the commentaries explain (from *lepus, leporis*). But, of course, that *leporem* could also come from a word we noted in the last chapter among the vocabulary of joking: that is *lepos, leporis* (wit or joking). So on the client's menu may be half-eaten hare, but it could also be a half-eaten joke. A nice illustration of the overlap between laughter and hierarchical banquets!

89. Athenaeus, *Deipnosophistae* 6.234c–262a; sympathetically discussed by Whitmarsh 2000, with reference to the wider Greek (prose) tradition of parasites and flatters.

90. 6.248d–f.

91. 6.252d.

92. 6.249e.

93. Green 2006, 1–47, is a clear introduction to the work (though Green's interests focus on Diodorus' account of the fifth century BCE); Stylianou 1998, 1–139 (specifically on the early fourth century BCE), has greater detail.

94. Diodorus Siculus 34/5.2.8–9. Sources for the Sicilian slave revolts and brief discussion can be found conveniently in Shaw 2001.

95. Suetonius, *Tib.* 57.2.

96. *Nat. D.* 1.93: "Latino verbo utens scurram Atticum fuisse dicebat." The passage has caused critics considerable trouble (see, for example, Dyck 2003, 177), but the basic point (often missed) is that it almost certainly exposes an untranslatable difference between the Greek and the Roman idiom of laughter (while paradoxically seeing Socrates in distinctively Roman terms). I say *almost certainly* because (as Stephen Halliwell reminds me) if Zeno was addressing an audience including Romans (such as Cicero), he may have adjusted his vocabulary accordingly.

97. Fraenkel 1922 (pinpointed in Fraenkel 2007, xiii).

98. Corbett 1986 collects many of the wide-ranging citations, but he struggles (probably fruitlessly, as I shall suggest) to impose any clear explanatory structure on the sometimes bafflingly varied usages of the word *scurra* (and his efforts certainly did not impress Don Fowler: "It is almost a model of how not to go about an investigation of this kind" [1987, 90]). By far the sharpest discussions I know are Barton 1993, for which the *scurra* is part of the repertoire of elite antitypes in Rome; Habinek 2005, 182–85, stressing the *scurra* as a category of anxiety.

99. See, for example, Plautus, *Trin.* 199–211; *Curc.* 296–97 (assuming the *servi* of the *scurrae* are like their masters); *Most.* 15–16.

100. SHA, *Heliog.* 33.7; Corbett 1986, 73.

101. On this view, the wide range of usages of the term reflects the range of boundaries that could be laid, in different places, between the proper and improper practice of laughter at Rome—hardly now recoverable.

102. Palmer 1989 and M. Roberts 1993 give useful overviews of these poems.

103. Conybeare 2002, 197–98, explains how critics have tried to get rid of the word *iocantur,* which has an impeccable manuscript tradition.

104. Conybeare 2002.

7. BETWEEN HUMAN AND ANIMAL—ESPECIALLY MONKEYS AND ASSES

1. Macrobius, *Sat.* 2.5.

2. *Sat.* 2.5.9.

3. Julia's jokes are the subject of Long 2000 (especially the Macrobian context) and Richlin 1992b (with a discussion of her life). The text signals, without explicitly mentioning, Julia's fate: the account is tied to her "thirty-eighth year" (2.5.2), that is 2 BCE, the year of her exile to Pandateria. The different phases of her exile, in conditions of varying severity, are reviewed by Fantham 2006, 89–91.

4. Carter 1992, 190.

5. I am referring here not just to moments when a woman laughs (or women laugh) at a man (or men) but when she laughs, in a gendered role, as a woman, at a man (which is what, in its powerful and positive valuation, the giggle signifies). Halliwell's prostitutes (2008, 491) and most uses of κιχλίζειν do not quite match this, though Theocritus, *Id.* 11.77–78 (girls giggling at the unfortunate Polyphemus), comes close; in Latin, Horace, *Carm.* 1.9.22, is rather further away.

6. Carter 1992, 189 (she continues on 190: "To reproduce this giggle, a man must identify with a woman rather than with another man and perceive some aspects of male desire as foolish").

7. *Ars am.* 3.279–90 ("Quis credat? Discunt etiam ridere puellae," 281). Martial, *Epigram.* 2.41, explicitly looks over his shoulder at Ovid (the Paelignian poet) in ridiculing Maximina, a girl with three black teeth: "Ride si sapis, o puella, ride / Paelignus, puto, dixerat poeta." The quotation "Ride . . ." is probably a loose allusion to this passage of *Ars Amatoria* rather than taken from a lost Ovidian poem; see Cristante 1990; C. Williams 2004, 150–51.

8. Gibson 2003, 211, lists various passages in Latin where *lacuna* is used for other types of "bodily hollows." Martial, *Epigram.* 7.25.6, uses *gelasinus* (a transliteration from the Greek) for "dimple." But in general, dimples are not major players in Roman literary culture.

9. Gibson 2003, 212.

10. I follow the reading and punctuation of Gibson 2003, 60 (with 212–13)—"est quae perverso distorqueat ora cachinno; / risu concussa est altera, flere putes; / illa sonat raucum quiddam atque inamabile: ridet / ut rudet a scabra turpis asella mola" (ll. 287–90)—though none of the uncertainties affect the main point of my argument here.

11. Critchley 2002, 29. Critchley's observations in this section (25–38) have influenced some of the main themes of this chapter, in particular his stress on the role of humor at and across the boundaries between the human and the

animal ("Humour explores what it means to be human by moving back and forth across the frontier that separates humanity from animality, thereby making it unstable," 29). As I hope to show, Roman writing strikingly foreshadows this major point.

12. *Ars am.* 3.283.

13. Lucretius 6.1195; Suetonius, *Claud.* 30.

14. *Met.* 1.640 (where *rictus* is a convincing emendation for the manuscript *ripas*), 1.741. This is a repeated image in the poem: see, for example, 2.481 (the beautiful face of Callisto deformed by a *lato rictu* on her transformation into a bear), 13.568 (Hecuba on the cusp of transformation into a dog "rictuque in verba parato latravit"). The thirteenth-century pseudo-Ovidian *De Vetula* picks up the animality of the *rictus:* "Rictus ei, non risus inest, et sacrificari / Deberet certe potius quam sacrificare" (2.148–49); a *rictus* belongs to the sacrificial animal, not the human sacrificer. See also Miller 2010, 15, 150.

15. The poem is discussed as a literary play on the traditions of *flagitatio* by Fraenkel 1961; Selden 2007, 524–27. Goldberg 2000; 2005, 108–13, stress its comic legacy.

16. Translators and critics differ on the precise point of comparison between the dog and the woman. Most take it, as I have, to refer to the facial distortion; a few stress instead the sound of yelping, taking *os* as "mouth" rather than "face": "with the noisome yap of a Gallic hound," as Selden renders it (2007, 525). For the *rictus* of dogs and possible points of comparison with human laughter, see Lucretius 5.1063–66; Plautus, *Capt.* 485–86; Apuleius, *Apol.* 6 (discussed by Tilg 2008, 113–15).

17. For this popular usage—eliding the different species and subspecies, the tailed and the tailless, the chimps, baboons, gorillas, and other simians —I must apologize to primatologists. Scientists (modern and ancient) identify a wide variety of different characteristics and crucial distinctions. In particular, monkeys and apes belong to different scientific families (apes being hominoids; monkeys being either Cercopithecidae, Cebidae, or Callitrichidae). But these technical distinctions do not significantly impact on day-to-day debates and representations.

18. The title of this section is borrowed from Connors 2004; it was too good to miss (and is not wholly unparalleled in antiquity: see n. 24).

19. Athenaeus, *Deipnosophistae* 14.613d.

20. See pp. 46–47 for "laughing" primates (and "laughing" rats).

21. Connors 2004 is the most up-to-date and sophisticated study of Roman ideas of apes (summing up, on 179, their perennial fascination: "Our human shape is replicated in them but also [from one point of view] distorted: wild, hairy, they meet our gaze across an unbridgeable divide between human and animal, nature and culture"). McDermott 1935; 1936; 1938 are still useful points of reference. All these provide an important background to the rest of this section. For "ape lore" in later periods and the cultural construction of modern primatology, see Janson 1952; Haraway 1989; De Waal 2001. Although chimpanzees' tea parties may be a thing of the past, the use of primates higher up the cultural food chain is alive and well: see, e.g., Self 1997, a satiric novel in which human beings have been changed into chimpanzees.

22. Pindar, *Pyth.* 2.72–75. I am skating over some of the difficulties of this "critic-bedevilled sentence," on which see C. Carey 1981, 49–55 (quote on 49).

23. In addition to McDermott 1935 and 1938, Demont 1997 and Lissarrague 1997 assemble and discuss a wide range of classical Greek references to the habits of monkeys; for those in comedy in particular, see Lilja 1980. As these studies show, the stereotype of the monkey in classical Greece is not restricted to imitation and deception but also includes, for example, ugliness, low birth, and ferocity.

24. Aristophanes, *Eq.* 887–90. The context is some political banter in which two rivals are trying to bribe Dēmos, the personification of the Athenian people, with a cloak. The repartee shows that the reference to the monkey signals both mimicry ("No, I'm only copying your ways, as a man at a drinking party might when he borrows another man's slippers to go and have a crap") and flattery or bribery ("You're not going to out-toady me"). Sommerstein 1981, 93, 191, misses some of the point, which is seen by Neil 1901, 127, and Demont 1997, 466. *Suda*, s.v. πιθηκισμοῖς περιελαύνεις, points explicitly to the various possible significances of "monkey business" here: trickery, flattery, and imitation.

25. Phrynichus, frag. 21 (Kassel and Austin). The best guess is that the final "monkey" would have been a sycophant (see also Demosthenes, *De cor.* 242; Aristophanes, *Ach.* 904–7).

26. Summed up briskly at Connors 2004, 183–84, 189. Isidore, *Etym.* 12.2.30, refers to the etymology but insists that it is false. The Greek pairing of πίθηκος (monkey) and πιθανός (persuasive) could open up other related possibilities, puns, and associations.

27. Cicero, *Nat D.* 1.97 (Ennius, *Satir.* frag 69 [Vahlen] = *ROL*2 Ennius, *Satir.* 23). The pun works despite (or because of) the fact that the first *i* in *similis* is short, in *simia* long. Other examples of such wordplay include Ovid, *Met.* 14.91–98; Martial, *Epigram.* 7.87.4; Phaedrus, *Fabulae* 4.13.

28. Connors 2004, 189–99, 202; briefly, hitting the nail on the head, John Henderson 1999, 34.

29. Lissarrague 1997, 469.

30. *Sat.* 1.10.18; with Gowers 2012, 316–17.

31. Aelian, *NA* 5.26 (see also 6.10); for the snares, see 17.25 (with Diodorus Siculus 17.90.1–3—though in a nice inversion of teaching and learning, Diodorus claims that the monkeys taught the hunters this trick). It is noteworthy that Aristotle's main discussion of apes and monkeys (*HA* 2.8–9, 502a16–b26) does not stress their capacity for mimicry.

32. A. King 2002, 433–34, reviews the representations of monkeys, etc., at Pompeii and includes a brief discussion of those I refer to here; McDermott 1938, 159–324, is a comprehensive catalogue of images of simians in all media from the classical and preclassical Mediterranean world.

33. M. Della Corte 1954, 210n498 (it is now lost).

34. From the House of the Dioscuri (6.9.6–7); see *PPM* 4.976, no. 225. It is not impossible that there were such performing monkeys in Pompeii, as the discovery there of a simian skeleton hints (Bailey et al. 1999).

35. Often the image of the escape of Aeneas is discussed alone, but de Vos 1991, 113–17, makes clear the link between it and the image of Romulus;

followed by J. R. Clarke 2007, 151–52. For dog-headed baboons (*cynocephali*), see McDermott 1938, 4–13, 35–46.

36. Brendel 1953.

37. McDermott 1938, 278–80; J. R. Clarke 2007, 153–54 ("comic resistance"). Cèbe 1966, 369–70, lists further explanations.

38. Plutarch, *Mor.* 64e (= *Quomodo adulator* 23). Plutarch elsewhere—*Mor.* 60c (= *Quomodo adulator* 18)—casts the mythical simian Cercopes as flatterers, again eliding monkey, laughter, and flattery. Hercules carried off this mischievous pair of creatures, upside down, hanging over his shoulder, after they tried to steal his weapons. In the longest, late version of the story (ps.-Nonnus, *Comm. in IV Orationes Gregorii Naz.* 4.39, of the sixth century CE; with Nimmo Smith 2001, 29–30), they start to discuss his "black arse"—and Hercules bursts out laughing and lets them off. For the complex tradition of the Cercopes (who in some versions gave the name to Pithecusae, modern Ischia), see Marconi 2007, 150–59; note also Woodford 1992; Kirkpatrick and Dunn 2002, 35–37; Connors 2004, 185–88.

39. Phaedrus, *Fabulae* 4.14; acutely discussed by John Henderson 2001, 180–86. The text survives largely in a medieval paraphrase.

40. Athenaeus, *Deipnosophistae* 14.613d.

41. Lucian, *Piscator* 36; the anecdote is included as a fable in Perry's collection (1952, 504, no. 463).

42. Strabo, *Geographica* 17.3.4 (= Posidonius, frag. 245. [Kidd]).

43. *De usu part.* 1.22 (Helmreich) = 1, pp. 80–81 (Kuhn).

44. I am half tempted to see this phrase also proleptically; that is, "the ape imitates for the worse."

45. *De usu part.* 3.16 (Helmreich) = 3, pp. 264–65 (Kuhn).

46. Horace, *Ars P.* 1–5, might (almost) count as another.

47. For further discussion, see pp. 119–20.

48. Fantham 1988. The influence of mime on particular authors and genres is discussed by, for example, McKeown 1979; Wiseman 1985, 28–30, 192–94; Panayotakis 1995, xii–xxv (summarizing the main theme of the book).

49. The modern literature on Roman mime is now very large. Panayotakis 2010, 1–32, is a useful résumé with copious bibliography; Bonaria 1955–56 collects fragments and *testimonia;* some of Webb 2008, 95–138, is relevant to earlier periods of the Roman Empire. On women, see Webb 2002; Panayotakis 2006.

50. The essays in E. Hall and Wyles 2008 give a good coverage of the debates about ancient pantomime. A standard list of the features supposed to distinguish ancient mime from pantomime is summarized by Hall 2008, 24. But Wiseman 2008 draws attention to the overlap between the two. As Panayotakis crisply sums it up, "The boundaries demarcating mime from pantomime were not always as clear as some scholars, seeking to impose order on inherently diverse and contradictory source materials, have liked to imagine" (2008, 185).

51. *De or.* 2.251 (". . . non ut eius modi oratorem esse velim, sed ut mimum").

52. Marshall 2006, 7, and Manuwald 2011, 183, offer the standard view; Panayotakis 2010, 5–6, is more cautious. Hunter 2002, 204–5, discusses the character of the *sannio*.

53. Tertullian, *Apol.* 15.3. Plautus, *Truculentus* 594, suggests that masks did not necessarily preclude the idea of facial expression; however, Athenaeus, *Deipnosophistae* 10.452f, is rather better evidence for an unmasked tradition in mime. Richter 1913 chooses (overconfidently) to identify grotesque figurines as mime actors because they have no masks.

54. Note that according to Servius (see below, n. 57), even Cicero—whatever his expressed disdain—went to watch the mime actress Cytheris.

55. Macrobius, *Sat.* 2.7.1–5; with Barton 1993, 143–44, who sees the story of Laberius as part of Rome's "physics of envy."

56. The most extreme case is the so-called Chariton mime (*P.Oxy* 413; Cunningham 1987, app. no. 6; the date is uncertain but sometime before the 200s CE, which is the date of the papyrus).

57. Aulus Gellius 16.7.10 refers to the vulgar vocabulary of *Anna Peranna*; Panayotakis 2008, 190–97, discusses Virgilian renderings in mime, e.g., Servius ad *Ecl.* 6.11—the particular performer is elsewhere (Cicero, *Phil* 2.20) called a *mima*. Panayotakis imagines the performances were relatively straight. I wonder . . . I am likewise more skeptical than most about how far we can hope to identify precise roles for those known as "first mime," "second mime," etc.

58. Walton 2007, 292.

59. Panayotakis 2010, 1; Fantham 1988, 154 ("Best defined negatively. Whatever did not fit the generic categories of tragedy or comedy, Atellane or the Italian togate comedy, was mime").

60. Philistion: *AP* 7.155 (there are numerous scattered references to "Philistion" in the context of mime—e.g., Martial, *Epigram.* 2.41.15; Ammianus Marcellinus 30.4.21; Cassiodorus, *Var.* 4.51; it may have been a common stage or pen name); Vitalis: *PLM* 3.245–46.

61. For example, Choricius, *Apologia mim.* 31–32 (at the mimes, Dionysos takes pity on human beings and is "so generous . . . as to prompt laughter of every kind"), 93 ("Humanity shares two things with the divine: reason [or speech] and laughter"). For a clear recent review of this text (with earlier bibliography), see Malineau 2005; Choricius is important to Webb's (2008, 95–138) discussion; Bowersock 2006, 61–62, notes similar gelastic themes in contemporary Syriac defenses of mimes.

62. The close link between mimicry and Roman laughter is emphasized by Dupont 1985, 298–99 (in the context of a wider discussion of mime, 296–306), which likewise distinguishes these aggressive forms of imitation from mimesis more generally.

63. Csapo 2002 reviews some of the main issues and includes a good discussion of Aristotle's anecdote about the fifth-century actor Callippides (*Poet.* 26, 1461b34–35), attacked for being a "monkey." As Csapo rightly insists, the criticism did not rest on the fact that he acted with "exaggerated gestures"; his crime was not overacting in our sense but rather "imitating actions that are best not imitated at all" (128), including, in Aristotle's words, those of "the inferior" and of "lower-class women" (*Poet.* 26, 1462a9–10). Csapo draws a clear and useful distinction between this mimicry and more general issues of tragic mimesis.

64. Note also the mimicry implied by Suetonius, *Cal.* 57.4—discussed in terms of the (imitative) roles of the different actors in the mime company by

Kirichenko 2010, 57; our lawyer imitator (see p. 144) might fit under this general heading too.

65. *GLK* 1.491.13–19; Evanthius, *Excerpta de comoedia* (Wessner) 4.1.

66. Lee 1990, 43; Godwin 1999, 67; Whigham 1966, 100; Quinn 1970, 217 ("The *mimae* were the cinema stars of the ancient world. . . . Her pout looks like a dog showing its teeth").

67. On the overall articulation of the full plot of the novel (of which only a small section survives), see Schmeling 2011, xxii–xxv; Sullivan 1968, 45–53, discusses the (irresolvable) problems of the ordering of this particular section.

68. Plaza 2000, 73–83.

69. *Sat.* 18.7–19.1 ("Complosis deinde manibus in tantum risum effusa est ut timeremus. . . . Omnia mimico risu exsonuerant").

70. Branham and Kinney 1996, 17 ("stagy"); Walsh 1996, 14 ("low stage"); "farcical" is M. Heseltine's version in the Loeb Classical Library (27); "théâtral" is A. Ernout's in the Budé (15).

71. Panayotakis 1994 stresses the resonances of the figure of Quartilla with mime acting ("like an *archimima* in her own production of a mimic play," 326), though sometimes pushes the exact parallels too far (even rewriting the episode as a mimic script on 329–30); largely reprised in Panayotakis 1995, 38–51. Other studies also point to the general influence of mimes, here and elsewhere, in the novel. See, e.g., Schmeling 2011, 55 (with earlier bibliography).

72. I am here developing some of the implications of Plaza's discussion of the episode (2000, esp. 77–79), including her interest in the "inversion of social and literary norms."

73. It is a text with a complicated history: Festus was drawing on the work of the Augustan scholar Verrius Flaccus, but part of Festus' dictionary is now known only through a summary by an eighth-century scholar, Paul the Deacon. And that is only part of the text's vicissitudes—which are a major theme of the essays in Glinister and Woods 2007.

74. Festus, s.v. "Pictor Zeuxis," p. 228L. My translation glosses over some of the predictable textual confusions.

75. Golahny 2003, 199–205, clearly justifying the identification of the scene.

76. For a brief collection of misogynistic themes on old women in Roman culture, see Parkin 2003, 86–87.

77. Pliny *HN* 35.65–66 (the second part of the passage tells the story of Zeuxis' dissatisfaction with his own lifelike rendering of a child). Discussions include Elsner 1995, 16–17; Morales 1996, 184–88; S. Carey 2003, 109–11.

78. Warner 1994, 149–50.

79. The scattered ancient evidence to Baubo (and her relation to the similar figure of Iambe) is collected and discussed from a classical perspective in, for example, H. King 1986; Olender 1990; O'Higgins 2001, 132–42. For modern feminist explorations, see Cixous and Clément 1986, 32–34; Warner 1994, 150–52. See also ch. 6, n. 70.

80. Athenaeus, *Deipnosophistae* 14.614a–b.

81. Jacoby, *FGrHist*, no. 396 (the story in question is F10). No surviving quotations from Semus are found in authors earlier than the late second century CE; how long before that he wrote is frankly impossible to be certain.

82. In addition to this story, see Pausanias 9.39.13 and, more explicitly, *Suda*, s.v. εἰς Τροφωνίου μεμάντευται.

83. My translation tries to capture the verbal echoes of the oracle's response: promising soothing laughter for the "unsoothed" Parmeniscus.

84. "Mothers" in literary oracular responses were never what they seemed: in another famous example, "kissing your mother" turned out to mean kissing the earth (Livy 1.56).

85. It is often assumed (by, e.g., Rutherford 2000, 138–39) that this Parmeniscus was identical with the Pythagorean philosopher "Parmiscus" of Metapontum listed in a third-century CE treatise by Iamblichus (*De vita Pythag.* 267, p. 185 (Nauck), emended to "Parmeniscus") and perhaps also with the Parmiscus whose dedication at the sanctuary of Leto is recorded on an inscribed temple inventory of 156/5 BCE (*IDelos* 1417A, col. 1, 109–11). Maybe, or maybe not. The passing reference to a Pythagorean Parmeniscus in Diogenes Laertius (*Vitae* 9.20) does not clinch it either; as *LGPN* makes very clear, Parmeniscus and its cognates are commonly attested Greek personal names.

86. Kindt 2012, 36–54, based on Kindt 2010.

87. Kindt 2012, 49: "Parmeniscus' laughter, we may assume, changes in quality as it becomes self-reflective. It starts off as a naïve and unreflected response to the apparent crudeness of divine form and turns into an astonished appreciation of the complexities of divine representation as Parmeniscus grasps the meaning of the oracle." Kindt 2010, 259, is more tentative ("we may suspect" rather than "assume").

88. παραδόξως ἐγέλασεν gives absolutely no hint of any change.

89. Halliwell 2008, 38–40, provides a useful collection of Greek agelasts (though some of this laughter avoidance is not attested before the Roman period; see, e.g., Plutarch. *Per.* 5).

90. Cicero, *Fin.* 5.92; Jerome, *Ep.* 7.5; Pliny, *HN* 7.79. Other references include Fronto, *Ad M. Antoninum de eloquentia* (van den Hout) 2.20; Ammianus Marcellinus 26.9.11.

91. In Jerome's letter (*Ep.* 7), the focus is not so much on Crassus himself but on the proverb: ". . . secundum illud quoque, de quo semel in vita Crassum ait risisse Lucilius: 'similem habent labra lactucam asino carduos comedente.'" The idea of the donkey eating thistles as a visual spectacle, lying behind the popular saying, is clearly suggested in one of Babrius' collection of fables (133): a fox spots a donkey eating thistles and asks him how he can eat such spiky food with his soft tongue.

92. N.J. Hall 1983, 1035–39 (a less lurid version of the Trollope story than is often told). There is always the temptation to track down some medical cause, as in the case of the Kings Lynn bricklayer: see www.bbc.co.uk/news/uk-england-18542377.

93. Valerius Maximus, 9.12, ext. 6.

94. Diogenes Laertius, *Vitae* 7.185.

95. For the obscene associations of figs, see Jeffrey Henderson 1991, 23, 118, 135. Is it relevant that it was figs that Aesop made his thieving fellow slaves vomit up (see above, p. 138)?

96. Diogenes Laertius, *Vitae* 7.184.

97. Tertullian, *De anim.* 52.3.

98. The curious text known as the *Testamentum Porcelli* (The piglet's last will and testament) provides another example here. Jerome stresses that it was well known to get people cracking up, *cachinnare,* rather than *ridere* (*Contra Rufinum* 1.17).

99. The subtitle of Schlam 1992 has inspired this section's title.

100. My terminology on donkeys is not quite so loose as that on monkeys, but I recommend M. Griffith 2006 to anyone wanting precise information on the varieties of ancient (especially Greek) equids and their cultural resonances.

101. The essays collected in Harrison 1999 offer a good conspectus of recent Anglophone approaches to the *Metamorphoses,* from what is now a vast bibliography. Fick-Michel 1991, 395–430, assembles references to laughter in the novel; Schlam 1992, 40–44, is a briefer critical résumé.

102. It is generally agreed that this cannot be the second-century CE satirist Lucian; Mason 1999a, 104–5, sums up the arguments. In what follows, I will usually call the work Lucianic.

103. Photios, *Bib. Cod.* 129. The problems in getting to the bottom of what Photios is saying are laid out as clearly and sharply as anywhere in Winkler 1985, 252–56; see also Mason 1999a, 103–4.

104. The usual modern assumption is that the lost work of Lucius of Patrai is the earliest, but there has been endless learned conjecture (and plenty of false certainty) about the precise relationships of the various versions (summed up well by Mason 1999b), in particular which sections of Apuleius' novel were his own invention and which derived from Lucius of Patrai. The wildly different conclusions on the extent of Apuleian originality reached (on the basis of minute philological dissection of the text) by Bianco 1971 and van Thiel 1971 are instructive (as well as dispiriting); Walsh 1974 clearly summarizes their differences.

105. Apuleius, *Met.* 10.13–17; ps.-Lucian, *Onos* 46–48.

106. *Met.* 10.13. I wonder if we should detect here a nod toward the saying about the donkey and the thistles.

107. "Ne humanum quidem": *Met.* 10.14. As Zimmerman 2000, 214, observes, "The ironical play with *humanum* becomes more complex when one considers that it is his very *sensus humanus* . . . that makes the ass steal human food."

108. *Met.* 10.16.

109. J.R. Heath 1982 discusses the role of human nutrition in Apuleius (though not focusing on this passage in particular); for the presentation of the ass as a (human) friend, see *Met.* 10.16, 10.17.

110. R. May 1998; 2006, 300–302.

111. *Met.* 10.16; *Onos* 47 (τοσοῦτον γελῶσιν, πολὺν γέλωτα, etc.).

112. Apuleius could not possibly have read the work of the third-century Diogenes Laertius, though Valerius Maximus was writing at least a century earlier. But my claim does not depend on whether Apuleius was familiar with these precise texts (and indeed there are no verbal echoes between the Latin versions of Valerius and Apuleius, and Apuleius in any case offers a different account of Philemon's death, in *Florida* 16). The implication of what I have shown so far is that the "dining donkey" story was a well-known popular joke

in the Roman world—and that common knowledge underpins my discussion of Apuleius' use of it here.

113. I do not see other significant differences between the two accounts that are relevant to my arguments on the culture of laughter. Zimmerman 2000, 229–30, contrasts the donkey's reaction in each text to being laughed at when first caught eating: pleasure in Apuleius (10.16), shame and embarrassment in ps.-Lucian (47). But pleasure very soon returns in the Lucianic account, as Zimmerman allows.

114. *Onos* 47.

115. *Met.* 10.16.

116. Bakhtin (1981 [1937–38]) underlined the polyphonic aspects of the novel in an essay first published half a century earlier.

117. *Onos* 10 (before transformation), 15 (braying), 55 (for the implication of laughter after his return to human shape).

118. *Met.* 2.31–3.13.

119. *Met* 2.31.

120. *Met* 3.2 ("nemo prorsum qui non risu dirumperetur aderat").

121. The story of the "murder" and the revelation of what "really" happened is, of course, more complicated than I am making it seem; for its literary precedents and the confrontation between reality and illusion staged here, see Milanezi 1992; Bajoni 1998; R. May 2006, 195–98.

122. *Met.* 3.13.

123. He is in fact called "victim" (*victimam*) at *Met.* 3.2.

124. D. S. Robertson 1919 casts around for real-life ancient ritual parallels (involving the leading of a scapegoat around town); partly followed by James 1987, 87–90. Habinek 1990, 53–55, stresses the (structural) role of Lucius as scapegoat. Kirichenko 2010, 36–39, 45–58, identifies mimic elements (comparing the *risus mimicus* of Petronius). R. May 2006, 182–207, the best introduction to the episode and previous scholarship on it, points to its theatricality and metaliterary aspects.

125. R. May 2006, 190–92; Zimmerman 2000, 25–26, 225–26 (for verbal echoes in the description of laughter between the two episodes).

126. *Cachinnus: Met.* 3.7 (with Van der Paardt 1971, 67; Krabbe 1989, 162–63).

127. *Met.* 3.11: "Iste deus auctorem et actorem suum propitius ubique comitabitur amanter, nec umquam patietur ut ex animo doleas, sed frontem tuam serena venustate laetabit assidue." Or so it reads if we accept an early twentieth-century emendation of the manuscript tradition. *Auctorem et actorem* is Vollgraff's conjecture (1904, 253) for the unsatisfactory or incomprehensible manuscript reading: whether *auctorem* with the meaningless *et torem* written into the interlinear space above, or the alternative and feeble *auctorem et tutorem*. It is generally now accepted that *auctorem et actorem* is correct, but given the phrase's celebrity status, it is worth remembering that this is (only) a conjecture. Tatum 2006 discusses Vollgraff's conjecture, plus the background of the phrase in earlier Latin, at length, leading to (in my view) difficult conclusions on Apuleius' links with Cicero, though La Bua 2013 takes a similarly Ciceronian direction in the discussion of Lucius' mock trial.

128. Winkler 1985, 13.

129. Kirichenko 2010, 58, also stressing the contrast between the *actor* as "passive" ("Lucius improvises in accordance with a pre-ordained storyline") and the *auctor* as auctorial/authorial (he "creatively co-authors the entire performance"); see above, pp. 119–20, 167, on the role of actors as "only mouthpieces of the scripts of others."

130. Schlam 1992 picks up the ambiguity here, with a slightly different emphasis from mine: "In an ironic sense the promise offered by the magistrates turns out to be true. Laughter does accompany the Ass, but he is the wretched object at which others laugh, often maliciously" (43).

8. THE LAUGHTER LOVER

1. Σχολαστικὸς καὶ φαλακρὸς καὶ κουρεὺς συνοδεύοντες καὶ ἔν τινι ἐρημίᾳ μείναντες συνέθεντο πρὸς τέσσαρας ὥρας ἀγρυπνῆσαι καὶ τὰ σκεύη ἕκαστος τηρῆσαι. ὡς δὲ ἔλαχε τῷ κουρεῖ πρώτῳ φυλάξαι, μετεωρισθῆναι θέλων τὸν σχολαστικὸν καθεύδοντα ἔξυρεν καὶ τῶν ὡρῶν πληρωθεισῶν διύπνισεν. ὁ δὲ σχολαστικὸς ψήχων ὡς ἀπὸ ὕπνου τὴν κεφαλὴν καὶ εὑρὼν ἑαυτὸν ψιλόν· Μέγα κάθαρμα, φησίν, ὁ κουρεύς· πλανηθεὶς γὰρ ἀντ' ἐμοῦ τὸν φαλακρὸν ἐξύπνισεν. Different manuscripts of the text (see pp. 186–87) include a shorter and slightly differently worded version of this joke, with the same point.

2. I cite the jokes from the edition of A. Thierfelder (1968), which is in general to be preferred to the more recent Teubner edition of R.D. Dawe (2000), on which see the important and wide-ranging review Jennings 2001. The *Philogelos* has been the subject of several recent studies (on both its textual tradition and—rather less often—its cultural significance). Note especially Thierfelder 1968; Baldwin 1983 (though the translations are sometimes misleading); Andreassi 2004 (the best modern introduction)—all these underlie what follows and are cited only to draw attention to particularly significant discussion or to indicate disagreement. Brief cultural explorations include Winkler 1985, 160–65; Bremmer 1997, 16–18; Hansen 1998, 272–75; Schulten 2002. In addition, there are several more or less popular modern translations, along the lines of "the world's oldest jokebook": for example, Cataudella 1971, 89–154 (with a useful scholarly introduction); Löwe 1981; Zucker 2008; Crompton 2010.

3. These three examples are based on 104, 231, and 173 (I confess that my paraphrases here have adjusted the ancient jokes to familiar modern comic idioms).

4. This is not, in other words, a case of creative translation from the Greek into modern comic clichés. Note, however, this is the only joke in the collection to start in this way; the trio of characters was not in general the cliché of ancient joking that it is of modern.

5. Johnson 1741, 479. His translation runs: "The Sage fell to scratching his Head, and finding no Hair, abused the Barber for not calling the Philosopher in his Turn, for do not you know, says he, that I, who am the bald Man, was to have been called up last." It is a useful example of the varied responses that jokes get as they travel through time.

6. Wilson 1996, 212.

7. Thierfelder 1968, 129–46, is the clearest account of the whole manuscript tradition; note also Perry 1943. Rochefort 1950 discusses the full contents of the main manuscript (A = Par. Sup. Gr. 690). The first joke (now 265) in the earliest manuscript (G = Cryptoferratensis A 33) has a point similar to that of two others in the full collection but is significantly different in language and detail. "A *scholastikos* was asked how many pints the jar held and answered: 'Do you mean of wine or water?'" Compare number 92, which has a *scholastikos* ask his father how much a three-pint (πεντακότυλος) vessel holds, and 136, which has a teacher from Sidon ask a pupil (though the text is uncertain) how much a three-pint vessel holds—"Do you mean wine or oil?" he replies.

8. Tzetzes, *Chil.* 8.969–73 (Leone).

9. It may be significant that Tzetzes elsewhere tells a very similar joke, which he ascribes to a "story" or "fable"; see *Epistulae* 50 (Leone).

10. These possibilities and more are explored by Baldwin 1986; Andreassi 2004, 63–65. We should bear in mind that book titles and their authors can, and do, blur; *Mrs. Beeton* refers to both book and author, as in many cases does *Livy* (and there was likewise confusion in the medieval world over whether *Suda* was the title of an encyclopedia or the name of its compiler).

11. On the Alexandrian Hierokles and other homonyms, see Andreassi 2004, 28–29. The dual authorship between Hierokles and Philagrios given by the longer manuscript selections, in contrast to the shorter selections ascribed to Hierokles alone, has predictably launched theories about originally separate works of Hierokles and Philagrios that were at some point combined—a combination that might (or might not) explain some of the complexity of the manuscript tradition (intricately discussed by Thierfelder 1968, 129–202, with diagram on 202).

12. *Suda* Φ 364 (Adler); the text as printed there runs οὗτός [Philistion] ἐστιν ὁ γράψας τὸν Φιλόγελων, ἤγουν τὸ βιβλίον τὸ φερόμενον εἰς τὸν Κουρέα (but a minor textual emendation, or even just the substitution of a lowercase for an uppercase K, would produce very different senses). For further possible links with Philistion, see Cataudella 1971, xxv; Reich 1903, 454–75 (which trusts the *Suda*'s attribution).

13. *New Pauly*, s.v. "Philogelos"; Bremmer 1997, 16, with 25n32. On the culture of barbershops, see S. Lewis 1995 (a survey of Greek material); Polybius 3.20; Plutarch, *Mor.* 508f–509c (= *De garr.* 13).

14. Abdera: 110–27; Kyme: 154–82; Sidon: 128–39; Rome: 62; Rhine: 83; Sicily: 192.

15. Drakontides: 170; Demeas: 102; Scribonia: 73; Lollianus: 162.

16. Denarii: 86, 124, 198, 213, 224, 225; anniversary: 62. Other Latinizing forms in the Greek (in, e.g., 135, 138) may also point to the cultural background, as well as reflect early Byzantine Greek usage.

17. 62. Other hints of a possibly third-century CE context have been squeezed from the text: the use of *myriads* as a unit of currency in 80 and 97, and in 76 the possible reference to the temple of Serapis in Alexandria (the destruction of that Serapeum in 391 would give a terminus ante quem for the origin of the joke—but Alexandria is not actually mentioned!); see Thierfelder 1968, 224 (noting that the joke implies "going up" [ἀνελθόντι] to the temple— for the Alexandrian Serapeum was on a hill).

18. "It is generally thought" sidesteps many divergent views. Robert 1968, 289, is unusual in using the reference to the millennial celebrations to pinpoint (more or less) the principal date of composition; Rapp 1950–51, 318, by contrast, considers many of the jokes to be at least in the dress of the ninth or tenth century.

19. 148; Plutarch, *Mor.* 177a (= *Regum et Imperatorum Apophth.*, Archelaus, 2); *Mor.* 509a (= *De garr.* 13).

20. 150; Plutarch, *Mor.* 534b (= *De Vitioso Pudore* 14). For other parallels, see 206 (with Athenaeus, *Deipnosophistae* 8.350b; Diogenes Laertius, *Vitae* 1.104); 264 (with Plutarch, *Mor.* 178f [= *Regum et Imperatorum Apophth.*, Philip, 24]); Valerius Maximus, 6.2 ext. 1; Stobaeus, *Anthologium* 3.13.49 (attributing the story to "Serenus").

21. 73. On the possible identification, see Thierfelder 1968, 224. The funny idea of people objecting to the unhealthy siting of tombs (which could not harm those already dead) is also the theme of 26.

22. 78: Σχολαστικὸς εἰκόνας ἀρχαῖα ζωγραφήματα ἐχούσας ἀπὸ Κορίνθου λαβὼν καὶ εἰς ναῦς ἐμβαλὼν τοῖς ναυκλήροις εἶπεν· Ἐὰν ταύτας ἀπολέσητε, καινὰς ὑμᾶς ἀπαιτήσω. Andreassi 2004, 71–80, is a good discussion of the processes of anonymization of these jokes: "Dallo 'storico' al 'tipico' (e viceversa . . .)" (71).

23. Velleius Paterculus 1.13.4 (ending with the punch line ". . . iuberet praedici conducentibus, si eas perdidissent, novas eos reddituros"). We should add to this pair 193, which reprises a joke told by Cicero (*De or.* 2.276) about the poet Ennius and Scipio Nasica (discussed on p. 200).

24. This is why some of the final few jokes return to the theme of the *scholastikos*, otherwise found in the first half of the book, and the first joke in the earliest manuscript, unattested elsewhere, is relegated to the final entry in the modern text, number 265.

25. The best discussion of the *scholastikos*, stressing the connections with comic performance, is Winkler 1985, 160–65, with Andreassi 2004, 43–51 (including a review of modern translations), and Kirichenko 2010, 11–16. The character is a leitmotiv of Conte 1997 (though not specifically as he appears in the *Philogelos*). I have borrowed *egghead* from Baldwin 1983.

26. 3: Σχολαστικῷ τις ἰατρῷ προσελθὼν εἶπεν· Ἰατρέ, ὅταν ἀναστῶ ἐκ τοῦ ὕπνου, ἡμιώριον ἐσκότωμαι καὶ εἶθ' οὕτως ἀποκαθίσταμαι. καὶ ὁ ἰατρός· Μετὰ τὸ ἡμιώριον ἐγείρου.

27. 40; some manuscript versions do not include the detail of the father's status, so making only the humorous contrast between the small boy and the large crowd.

28. 6; with 253, a briefer version. 174 ("A man from Kyme") is on a similar theme, and 27 inverts the point.

29. 164: Κυμαῖος ἐν τῷ κολυμβᾶν βροχῆς γενομένης διὰ τὸ μὴ βραχῆναι εἰς τὸ βάθος κατέδυ; 115: Ἀβδηρίτης εὐνοῦχον ἰδὼν γυναικὶ ὁμιλοῦντα ἠρώτα ἄλλον, εἰ ἄρα γυνὴ αὐτοῦ ἐστι. τοῦ δὲ εἰπόντος εὐνοῦχον γυναῖκα ἔχειν μὴ δύνασθαι ἔφη· Οὐκοῦν θυγάτηρ αὐτοῦ ἐστιν. The first of these jokes points nicely to the different status of water when in a pool or when falling from the sky: we don't, after all, think of swimming as "getting wet."

30. The origins of these modern traditions of joking in national(ist) geopolitics set them clearly apart from the ancient traditions, despite superficial simi-

larities often noted (by, for example, Toner 2009, 98). The cities of the *Philogelos* are more internal than foreign objects of jocularity. And the jokes are probably closer to the English "disgusted-of-Tunbridge Wells" style of quip, where Tunbridge Wells stands for a town whose inhabitants are caricatured as elderly, conservative, and out of touch with modernity (and always writing to newspapers to express their "disgust").

31. Strabo, *Geographica* 13.3.6; briefly discussed by Purcell 2005, 207–8 (which appears to find the passage, in detail, as puzzling as I do). This similar anecdote definitely referring to the city in Asia Minor makes it virtually certain that the jokes on Kyme in the *Philogelos* are not referring to either of the other ancient towns that could be spelled in the same way (in Euboea or our Cumae, in South Italy).

32. Martial, *Epigram.* 10.25 (see also Juvenal 10.50); Cicero, *Att.* 4.17.3 (SB 91), with 7.7.4 (SB 130). See also Machon, frag. 11, 119–33 (Gow); Lucian, *Hist. conscr.* 1.

33. 35; 158.

34. See above, n. 7. Occasionally too the type characters might be combined, as in 131, which concerns a Sidonian *scholastikos*.

35. 137 (essentially the same joke as 99).

36. 162: Κυμαίων <τὴν> πόλιν τειχιζόντων εἰς τῶν πολιτῶν Λολλιανὸς καλούμενος δύο κορτίνας ἰδίοις ἐτείχισεν ἀναλώμασι. πολεμίων δὲ ἐπιστάντων ὀργισθέντες οἱ Κυμαῖοι συνεφώνησαν, ἵνα τὸ Λολλιανοῦ τεῖχος μηδεὶς φυλάξῃ ἀλλ' ἐκεῖνος μόνος.

37. Parts of the *Philogelos* show signs of an internal logic or significant ordering within the division into type characters: 25, 26, and 27, for example, are a trio concerning death; 52 is a neat inversion of the preceding joke. It is, of course, impossible to be sure whether such patterns are to be put down to the compilers or to whatever source text they might have been using.

38. There is a trace of another standard joke line in the *scholastikos* group: on three occasions (15, 43, 52), just before the punch line (and as if to signal it), the egghead says words to the effect of "What an idiot I am," "No wonder they call us idiots" (μωροὶ καλούμεθα, μωροὶ νομιζόμεθα, μωρός εἰμι).

39. West (1992, 268) comes close to suggesting an academic function for the book when she writes, "But it seems worth raising the question whether it was really intended as a joke book, or whether it embodies an attempt at a motif-index, compiled, perhaps, to assist an analysis of various forms of wit and humour."

40. Andreassi 2004, 37–43, reviews the various connections with other genres. Jokes with a probable link to fable include 142 and 180 (see also Andreassi 2006, on the "greedy man" [λιμόξηρος] in the *Philogelos* and the *Life of Aesop*). Kirichenko 2010, 11–16, discusses mimic themes in the *scholastikos* jokes. Floridi 2012 discusses links between the *Philogelos* and scoptic epigram; for specific points of comparison, see, e.g., 97 and *AP* 11.170; 235 and *AP* 11.241. The few sexual jokes in the collection include 45 (see above, p. 198), 244, 245, 251. Whether this reflects the character of the *Philogelos* from its earliest phases or is the result of medieval bowdlerization, we do not know.

41. E.g., 4, 135, 184, 189.

42. 14; the vocabulary and metaphors suggest the influence of comic performance and/or mime (see Aristophanes, *Thesm.* 797; Herodas, *Mimiambi* 2.15).

43. 239: "Οἴμοι, τί δράσω; δυσὶ κακοῖς μερίζομαι" ("Alas, what shall I do? I am torn between two evils").

44. 121: οὐκέτι τρέχει, ἀλλὰ πέτεται. There are links with *AP* 11.208; see Floridi 2012, 652–53. But the epigram is simpler, resting only on a play between running (to dinner) and flying.

45. 8: Σχολαστικὸς θέλων πιάσαι μῦν συνεχῶς τὰ βιβλία αὐτοῦ τρώγοντα κρέας δακὼν ἐν τῇ σκοτίᾳ ἐκάθισεν . . . "Sententiam non completam esse monuit Dawe" is the comment in his Teubner edition. Others have not been so despondent. Perhaps the joke is that the *scholastikos* was pretending to be a cat (so Thierfelder 1968, 205).

46. Σχολαστικὸς ἀργυροκόπῳ ἐπέταξε λύχνον ποιῆσαι. τοῦ δὲ ἐξετάσαντος, πηλίκον ποιήσει, ἀπεκρίνατο· Ὡς πρὸς ὀκτὼ ἀνθρώπους.

47. Felice 2013.

48. To be honest, I find this interpretation slightly puzzling. For—to think it through in finer detail than the joke probably deserves—the *scholastikos* can hardly have mistaken the silversmith for a fish seller in the first place. Are we to imagine that he is the clever exploiter of the pun by replying to the silversmith's question with an answer that exposes the double meaning? Nor am I convinced that the "very occasional" usage is enough to give ποιέω a clear resonance of food preparation; so far as I can see, we are dealing with one passage from the Septuagint (Genesis 18:7).

49. Different kinds of ingenuity are on display in Thiel 1972 (emendation of the text of 237, accepted and elaborated in Dawe's Teubner text); Morgan 1981 (attempting to restore sense to 216 by translating κυβερνήτης as "governor" rather than "steersman"); Rougé 1987 (elucidating some of the nautical and navigational terminology); Lucaszewicz 1989 (emending the text of 76 to produce a joke about the *scholastikos'* slave relations).

50. 200: Ἀφυὴς μαθητὴς ὑπὸ τοῦ ἐπιστάτου κελευσθεὶς ὀνυχίσαι οἰκοδεσπότην ἐδάκρυσε. τοῦ δὲ τὴν αἰτίαν ἐρωτήσαντος ἔφη· Φοβοῦμαι καὶ κλαίω· μέλλω γὰρ τραυματίσαι σε, καὶ παρωνυχίδας ποιήσεις, καὶ τύψει με ὁ ἐπιστάτης. Thierfelder (1968, 261–62) does his best, pointing to links with the previous joke and to the logical confusion of the simpleton's complaint; Baldwin's mistranslation (1983, 38) does not help. The joke does, however, serve to remind us of the difficulties (and pain) of nail trimming in antiquity.

51. 214: Φθονερὸς εἰς γναφεῖον εἰσελθὼν καὶ μὴ θέλων οὐρῆσαι ἀπέθανεν.

52. For an up-to-date (and rather less lurid than usual) view of the use of urine in the fulling industry, see Flohr and Wilson 2011, 150–54; Flohr 2013, 103–4, 170–71 (though without reference to this joke). I have been helped with this joke by some careful comments by Istvan Bodnar on an earlier podcast version of these ideas. Even so, some problems remain—including my translation *meanie,* implying niggardly (so not wanting to give his urine away for free). That is not the most obvious sense of the Greek φθονερὸς, which more usually (as in the other jokes in this category) suggests spitefulness.

53. These include jokes on parricides: 13, 152; the death of a slave: 18; misunderstanding about or disputed death: 22, 29, 70; inheritance: 24, 104, 139, 229; tombs: 26, 73; funerals: 38, 40, 123, 154, 247; coffins: 50, 97; infanticide,

57; the death of a son: 69, 77; suicide: 112, 231; crucifixion: 121; condemnation to death: 168; sudden death: 214; the death of a wife: 227.

54. Critchley 2002, 65–66, partly drawing on Mary Douglas's famous essay on jokes (1968) and crisply encapsulating approaches that underlie other, more specific contributions to joke studies (see, for example, Kerman 1980, discussing "light-bulb" gags in broadly similar terms). It is striking that some jokes in the *Philogelos* explicitly make issues of relativism (or the failure to understand the nature of a different perspective) the topic of joking: see, for example, 49, in which a *scholastikos,* looking at the moon, asks his father if other cities have moons like theirs.

55. 5: Σχολαστικῷ τις ἀπαντήσας ἔφη· Κύριε σχολαστικέ, καθ' ὕπνους σε εἶδον. ὁ δέ· Μὰ τοὺς θεούς, εἶπεν, ἀσχολῶν οὐ προσέσχον; the alternative version is 102.

56. 15: Σχολαστικὸς καθ' ὕπνους ἧλον πεπατηκέναι δόξας τὸν πόδα περιέδησεν. ἑταῖρος δὲ αὐτοῦ πυθόμενος τὴν αἰτίαν καὶ γνούς· Δικαίως, ἔφη, μωροὶ καλούμεθα. διὰ τί γὰρ ἀνυπόδητος κοιμᾶσαι; 207 (see also 124, 243). The theme of dreaming versus reality is also found in scoptic epigrams; see Floridi 2012, 643.

57. W. V. Harris 2009 is an important survey; Harris-McCoy 2012, 1–41, is a useful introduction to the dream interpretations of Artemidorus.

58. 45: Σχολαστικὸς νυκτὸς ἐπανέστη τῇ μάμμῃ αὐτοῦ. πληγὰς δὲ διὰ τοῦτο ὑπὸ τοῦ πατρὸς λαβών· Σύ, εἶπεν, τοσοῦτος χρόνος ἐστὶν ἐξ οὗ τὴν μητέρα μου ὀχεύεις, μηδὲν ὑπ' ἐμοῦ παθών, καὶ νῦν ὀργίζῃ ἐπὶ τῇ μητρί σου ἅπαξ με εὑρών. Baldwin 1983, 65, detects the influence of mime.

59. 57: Πρῶτον, ἔφη, σὺ τὰ τέκνα σου κατόρυξον, καὶ οὕτως ἐμοὶ συμβούλευε τὸν ἐμὸν ἀνελεῖν.

60. 80: Σχολαστικοῦ πλέοντος ἐκινδύνευεν ὑπὸ χειμῶνος τὸ πλοῖον. τῶν δὲ συμπλεόντων ἀπορριπτούντων ἐκ τῶν σκευῶν, ἵνα κουφισθῇ τὸ πλοῖον, κἀκείνῳ τὸ αὐτὸ ποιεῖν παραινούντων, ὁ δὲ ἔχων χειρόγραφον ἑκατὸν πεντήκοντα μυριάδων, τὰς πεντήκοντα ἀπαλείψας· Ἴδε, φησίν, ὅσοις χρήμασιν ἐπεκούφισα τὴν ναῦν. Rougé 1987, 10–11, sees the point of this most clearly.

61. 12: Σχολαστικῷ ἀποδημοῦντι φίλος αὐτοῦ ἔλεγεν· Ἀξιῶ σε δύο παῖδας ἀγοράσαι μοι, ἑκ<άτερον> πεντεκαίδεκα ἐτῶν. ὁ δὲ εἶπεν· Ἐὰν τοιούτους μὴ εὕρω, ἀγοράσω σοι ἕνα τριάκοντα ἐτῶν. I include the sexual reading in deference to my graduate class at Berkeley, who had no doubt at all that that was the sense.

62. IOU: 161; country estate: 131 (a doublet of 60; Baldwin 1983's translation is misleading); ladder rungs: 93; tertian fever: 175a. Others jokes on related themes include 3, 62, 71, 84, 196, and the gags about wine and water in n. 7.

63. 22: Σχολαστικὸς ἀπαντήσας τινὶ φίλῳ αὐτοῦ εἶπεν· Ἤκουσα, ὅτι ἀπέθανες. ὁ δὲ ἀπεκρίνατο· Ἀλλ' ὁρᾷς με ζῶντα. καὶ ὁ σχολαστικός· Καὶ μὴν ὁ εἰπών μοι κατὰ πολὺ σοῦ ἀξιοπιστότερος ἦν.

64. 193: Δύσκολόν τις ἐζήτει. ὁ δὲ ἀπεκρίνατο· Οὐκ εἰμὶ ὧδε. τοῦ δὲ γελάσαντος καὶ εἰπόντος· Ψεύδῃ· τῆς γὰρ φωνῆς σου ἀκούω—εἶπεν· Ὦ κάθαρμα, εἰ μὲν ὁ δοῦλός μου εἶπεν, εἶχες ἂν αὐτῷ πιστεῦσαι· ἐγὼ δέ σοι οὐ φαίνομαι ἀξιοπιστότερος ἐκείνου εἶναι;

65. *De or.* 2.276.

66. Twin: 29; baby's name: 95; corpse: 171.

67. Proofs of identity and status, including birth certificates, were not nonexistent in the Roman world; they were presumably commoner where issues of

status and privilege were at stake and in some parts of the empire more than others (though how far the pattern of their survival reflects the original distribution is unclear). Schulz 1942; 1943 remain useful surveys of the evidence. Wallace-Hadrill 2011, 144–45, briefly discusses a case in Herculaneum where an individual's birth details remained obscure (as I strongly suspect must have been the norm).

68. Lucian, *Demon.* 12–62. Schlapbach 2010, esp. 258–60, offers a sophisticated reading of the relationship between these witty sayings and Lucian's construction of the written life of Demonax. Modern usage of the ancient terms *apophthegmata* and *chreiai* tends to imply too clear a division between the two categories: the former being "clever sayings," the latter more specifically "moral maxims" or witty parodies of such. In practice, the categories merge, as they also do with proverbs and riddles. On the interchangeability, see McClure 2003, esp. 274.

69. Suetonius, *Aug.* 56. It was apparently a juvenile collection by the dictator and presumably consisted of his own *dicta* (though that is not explicitly stated), or why would Augustus have wanted to keep it under wraps?

70. Such compilations as Plutarch's *Sayings of the Spartans* are also classified according to speaker, even if the book as a whole adds up to a portrait of cultural or ethnic character.

71. Suetonius, *Gram.* 21. The title probably militates against a compilation of sayings, but it does clinch the issue; the collection of Aristodemus (see p. 204) seems to have been much more biographical than its title would suggest.

72. *Stich.* 454–55, 221–24.

73. *Persa* 392–94: "Librorum eccillum habeo plenum soracum / . . . / dabuntur dotis tibi inde sescenti logi."

74. Maltby 1999, referring to *Persa* 395 ("atque Attici omnes; nullum Siculum acceperis"). We might compare Gow's confidence that Machon's *Chreiai* could well have been "a valuable vademecum" for an ancient jester, similar to "a modern book of jokes from which a public speaker or raconteur . . . can refresh his memory or replenish his repertoire" (1965, 24). As Kurke 2002 makes clear, whatever this puzzling text was, it certainly was not that.

75. It is hard to get much sense of the work (and its date is, in any case, a matter of guesswork: second century BCE or later, but how much later?). The quotations in Athenaeus are all jokes attached to named individuals—kings, gluttons, parasites, and prostitutes; see, e.g., 6.244f (giving the terminus post quem), 6.246d–e, 8.345b–c, 13.585a. They may have some resemblance to the types of the *Philogelos*, but how close a resemblance I am not sure.

76. The text is found most conveniently in Siegmann 1956, 27–37, which discusses in detail the different readings and interpretations up to that date. Almost everything about this text is contested. It is unclear, for example, whether *Pyrrhos*—if thought of as a proper name—is a "real" name or a nickname (such as *Ginger*). The only other more or less comprehensible heading, though much restored, appears to be εἰ[ς] φα[λ]ακρόν (few letters are entirely clear, and again there has been debate on whether it refers to a bald man or is some form of proper name).

77. Kassel 1956. This view is accepted by, e.g., Maltby 1999; Andreassi 2004, 22–23 ("ha convincentemente sostenuto che il papiro costituisse una sorta di *Witzbuch*").

78. See Siegmann 1956; more briefly Andreassi 2004, 23.

79. Aristophanes, *Vesp.* 1427–31.

80. Links with fable: Aristophanes, *Vesp.* 1259. The most recent survey of Sybarite stories is Bowie 2013, 252–55. I am not as confident as Bowie (252) that the genre of these stories must in some form go back to before the destruction of Sybaris (as the place had such proverbial renown), but I am struck that he concludes that the *collection* of these stories only just predated Ovid (255); Aelian, *VH* 14.20 (writing in the late second or early third century CE) implies that he had read a collection. See also, on the tradition of Sybaris, Gorman and Gorman 2007 (usefully showing how much Athenaeus "contributes" to the fragments he cites).

81. The context and characters of the *Deipnosophistae* are well discussed in various essays in Braund and Wilkins 2000, especially Milanezi 2000, on the section on joking, and Braund 2000, on the Roman background (including the identity of Ulpian: see esp. 17).

82. Athenaeus, *Deipnosophistae* 14.614d–e: τοσαύτη δ' αὐτῶν δόξα τῆς ῥαθυμίας ἐγένετο ὡς καὶ Φίλιππον ἀκούσαντα τὸν Μακεδόνα πέμψαι αὐτοῖς τάλαντον, ἵν' ἐκγραφόμενοι τὰ γελοῖα πέμπωσιν αὐτῷ. A similar but shorter version of the story is found at 6.260a–b, citing the second-century CE Hegesander of Delphi as the immediate source.

83. Quotation from Hansen 1998, 273; see also Andreassi 2004, 18–19.

84. As Hansen 1998, 273, carefully concedes.

85. *Deipnosophistae* 14.614c. Athenaeus' gloss: Ἀναξανδρίδης δ' ἐν Γεροντομανίᾳ καὶ εὑρετὰς τῶν γελοίων φησὶ γενέσθαι Ῥαδάμανθυν καὶ Παλαμήδην, λέγων οὕτως; followed by the quotation itself: καίτοι πολλοί γε πονοῦμεν. / τὸ δ' ἀσύμβολον εὗρε γελοῖα λέγειν Ῥαδάμανθυς / καὶ Παλαμήδης.

86. For example, Milanezi 2000, 402, though the chapter is, in general, a useful study of this section of Athenaeus' work. On Palamedes as a mythical inventor and culture hero, see Gera 2003, 122–27; for another appearance of Rhadamanthys, see p. 161; on this pairing, see Ceccarelli 2013, 69 (which is slightly more careful than most on what exactly it attributes to Anaxandrides).

87. Of course, there may have been earlier, now lost, claims about the role of Palamedes and Rhadamanthys as inventors of the joke, but the fact is that this is the only testimony we have—and whatever parallels might once have existed (or not), the slippage in Athenaeus and the effective reinterpretation of Anaxandrides' claim are striking.

AFTERWORD

1. Marzolph 1987 explores the similarities with Arabic traditions. Andreassi 2004, 81–124, collects further parallels in different joking cultures.

2. The work of Barbara Bowen has opened up the world of Renaissance jokebooks. See, for example, Bowen 1984; 1986a; 1986b; 1998. For an earlier period (Cicero's jokes in the culture of the twelfth-century English court), see J. M. Martin 1990.

3. This story goes back to the nineteenth century at least. It makes its point nicely (about both Porson and *Joe Miller*)—though it may not be strictly true; see Baldwin 1983, xii.

4. The joke is less apocryphal than it might seem. It is told in the diary of Powell's fellow politician Woodrow Wyatt (Wyatt 1998, 282–83, entry for 31 January 1987): "There is a very chatty barber in the [House of] Commons who never stops telling MPs whose hair he cuts about politics and what his views are on the world. Enoch Powell went to have his hair cut by him one day, sat down and the barber said 'How would you like your hair cut, sir?' 'In silence,' Enoch replied." Wyatt makes clear that the barber was well known for his chattiness, so Powell would have had ample time to prepare his classical joke. Even better, since first investigating this story, thanks to Gloria Tyler of the House of Commons Library, I have been able to access an interview with the barber himself, Stephen Silverne (British Library, Sound and Moving Image Collection, C1135/14); in this, he gives a very similar account of the story. For another modern version of this gag, see Andreassi 2004, 75–76.

5. Murdoch 1999 [1978], 182; my italics. Her claim that it was Freud's favorite joke is partly intended to resonate with the complex sexual intrigues and anxieties of the novel.

6. Freud 1960 [1905], 107.

References

Alpers, P. 1979. *The Singer of the "Eclogues" A Study in Virgilian Pastoral.* Berkeley and London.

Andersen, Ø., and J. Haarberg. 2001. *Making Sense of Aristotle: Essays in Poetics.* London.

André, J. 1972. *Pline l'Ancien, "Histoire Naturelle," Livre XXIV.* Paris.

Andreassi, M. 2004. *Le facezie del "Philogelos": Barzellette antiche e umorismo moderno.* Lecce.

———. 2006. "Il λιμόξηρος nella Vita Aesopi e nel Philogelos." *ZPE* 158: 95–103.

Arndt, E. 1904. *De ridiculi doctrina rhetorica.* Diss., Kirchain.

Arnott, W. G. 1972. "Targets, Techniques and Tradition in Plautus' *Stichus.*" *BICS* 19: 54–79.

———. 1985. Review of Janko 1984. *CR* 35: 304–6.

Atkinson, R. F. 1993. "Humour in Philosophy." In *Humour and History,* ed. K. Cameron, 10–20. Oxford.

Attardo, S. 1994. *Linguistic Theories of Humor.* Berlin and New York.

Attardo, S., and V. Raskin. 1991. "Script Theory Revis(it)ed: Joke Similarity and Joke Representation Model." *Humor* 4: 293–347.

Bailey, J. F., M. Henneberg, I. B. Colson, A. Ciarallo, R. E. M. Hedges, and B. C. Sykes. 1999. "Monkey Business in Pompeii: Unique Find of a Juvenile Barbary Macaque Skeleton." *Molecular Biology and Evolution* 16: 1410–14.

Bajoni, M. G. 1998. "Lucius Utricida: Per un'interpretazione di Apul. Met. 2,32 pp. 51–52 Helm." *RhM* 141: 197–203.

Bakhtin, M. 1968. *Rabelais and His World.* Trans. H. Iswolsky. Cambridge, MA. Originally published in Russian in 1965.

———. 1981. "Forms of Time and Chronotope in the Novel." In *The Dialogic Imagination,* ed. M. Holquist, trans. C. Emerson and Holquist, 84–259. Austin. Originally published in Russian in 1937–38.

_____. 1986. *Speech Genres and Other Late Essays.* Trans. V. W. McGee. Austin. Originally published in Russian in 1979.

Baldwin, B. 1983. *The Philogelos or Laughter-Lover.* London Studies in Classical Philology 10. Amsterdam.

——. 1986. "John Tzetzes and the *Philogelos.*" *Byzantion* 56: 339–41. Reprinted in *Roman and Byzantine Papers,* 329–31. 1989. Amsterdam.

Ballard, C. 2006. "Strange Alliance: Pygmies in the Colonial Imaginary." *World Archaeology* 38: 133–51.

Barbet, A., and P. Miniero. 1999. *La Villa San Marco a Stabia.* 3 vols. Naples and Rome.

Barchiesi, A. 2005. *Ovidio Metamorfosi.* Vol. 1, bks. 1–2. Milan and Rome.

Barnes, J. 2003. *Porphyry, Introduction.* Oxford.

Barsby, J. 1999. *Terence: Eunuchus.* Cambridge.

——. 2000. "Donatus on Terence: The *Eunuchus* Commentary." In *Dramatische Wäldchen: Festschrift für Eckhard Lefèvre zum 65. Geburtstag,* ed. E. Stärk and G. Vogt-Spira, 491–513. Hildesheim.

——. 2001. *Terence: The Woman of Andros, The Self-Tormentor, The Eunuch.* Cambridge, MA, and London.

Barton, C. A. 1993. *The Sorrows of the Ancient Romans.* Princeton, NJ.

Bataille, G. 1997. "Laughter." In *The Bataille Reader,* ed. F. Botting and S. Wilson, 59–63. Oxford and Malden, MA. Reprint of "Two Fragments on Laughter." 1988. In *Guilty,* trans. B. Boone, 139–43. Venice, CA. Originally published in French in 1944.

Baudelaire, C. 1981. "Of the Essence of Laughter: And Generally of the Comic in the Plastic Arts." In *Baudelaire: Selected Writings on Art and Artists,* trans. P. E. Charvet, 140–61. Cambridge. Originally published in French in 1855.

Beacham, R. C. 1991. *The Roman Theatre and Its Audience.* Cambridge, MA.

Beard, M. 1996. "The Roman and the Foreign: The Cult of the 'Great Mother' in Imperial Rome." In *Shamanism, History and the State,* ed. N. Thomas and C. Humphrey, 164–90. Ann Arbor, MI.

——. 2007. *The Roman Triumph.* Cambridge, MA.

Beard, M., J. North, and S. R. F. Price. 1998. *Religions of Rome.* 2 vols. Cambridge.

Beckett, S. 1963. *Murphy.* London. Originally published in 1938.

Berger, P. L. 1997. *Redeeming Laughter: The Comic Dimension of Human Experience.* Berlin and New York.

Bergmann, B., and C. Kondoleon, eds. 1999. *The Art of Ancient Spectacle.* Studies in the History of Art 56. National Gallery of Art, Washington DC.

Bergson, H. 1911. *Laughter: An Essay on the Meaning of the Comic.* Trans. C. Brereton and F. Rothwell. London. Originally published as three articles in French in 1900.

Bernays, J. 1853. "Ergänzung zu Aristoteles *Poetik.*" *RhM* 8: 561–96.

Bernstein, F. H. 1998. *Ludi Publici: Untersuchungen zur Entstehung und Entwicklung der öffentlichen Spiele im republikanischen Rom.* Stuttgart.

——. 2011. "Complex Rituals: Games and Processions in Republican Rome." In *A Companion to Roman Religion,* ed. J. Rüpke, 222–34. Malden, MA, and Oxford.

Bernstein, M. A. 1992. *Bitter Carnival: Ressentiment and the Abject Hero*. Princeton, NJ.

Bettini, M. 1981. "Introduzione." In *Plauto, Mostellaria, Persa*, 9–31. Milan.

———. 1991. *Verso un'antropologia dell'intreccio e altri studi su Plauto*. Urbino.

———. 2000. "Il Witz di Gelasimus." In *Dramatische Wäldchen: Festschrift für Eckhard Lefèvre zum 65. Geburtstag*, ed. E. Stärk and G. Vogt-Spira, 461–74. Hildesheim.

Bhabha, H. 1994. *The Location of Culture*. London.

Bianco, G. 1971. *La fonte greca delle "Metamorfosi" di Apuleio*. Brescia.

Billig, M. 2005. *Laughter and Ridicule: Towards a Social Critique of Humour*. London.

Bloomer, W. M. 2007. "Roman Declamation: The Elder Seneca and Quintilian." In *A Companion to Roman Rhetoric*, ed. W. Dominik and J. Hall, 297–306. Malden, MA, and Oxford.

Bonaria, M. 1955–56. *Mimorum Romanorum Fragmenta*. Genoa.

Bonner, S. F. 1949. *Roman Declamation in the Late Republic and Early Empire*. Liverpool.

Bowen, B. C. 1984. "Roman Jokes and the Renaissance Prince, 1455–1528." *ICS* 9: 137–48.

———. 1986a. "Renaissance Collections of *facetiae*, 1344–1490: A New Listing." *Renaissance Quarterly* 39: 1–15.

———. 1986b. "Renaissance Collections of *facetiae*, 1499–1528: A New Listing." *Renaissance Quarterly* 39: 263–75.

———. 1998. "Ciceronian Wit and Renaissance Rhetoric." *Rhetorica* 16: 409–29.

Bowersock, G. W. 2006. *Mosaics as History: The Near East from Late Antiquity to Islam*. Cambridge, MA.

Bowie, E. 2013. "Milesian Tales." In *The Romance between Greece and the East*, ed. T. Whitmarsh and S. Thomson, 243–57. Cambridge.

Boyer, P. 1989. "Pourquoi les Pygmées n'ont pas de culture?" *Gradhiva* 7: 3–17.

Branham, R. B., ed. 2002. *Bakhtin and the Classics*. Evanston, IL.

———. 2005. "The Poetics of Genre: Bakhtin, Menippus, Petronius." In *Defining Genre and Gender in Latin Literature: Essays Presented to William S. Anderson on his Seventy-Fifth Birthday*, ed. W. W. Batstone and G. Tissol, 113–38. New York.

Branham, R. B., and D. Kinney. 1996. *Petronius: Satyrica*. London.

Braund, D. 2000. "Learning, Luxury and Empire: Athenaeus' Roman Patron." In *Athenaeus and His World: Reading Greek Culture in the Roman Empire*, ed. Braund and J. Wilkins, 3–22. Exeter.

Braund, D., and J. Wilkins, eds. 2000. *Athenaeus and His World: Reading Greek Culture in the Roman Empire*. Exeter.

Bremmer, J. 1997. "Jokes, Jokers and Jokebooks in Ancient Greek Culture." In *A Cultural History of Humour*, ed. Bremmer and H. Roodenburg, 11–28. Cambridge.

Bremmer, J., and H. Roodenburg, eds. 1997. *A Cultural History of Humour*. Cambridge.

Brendel, O. 1953. "Der Affen-Aeneas." *RM* 60: 153–59.

Briscoe, J. 2008. *A Commentary on Livy, Books 38–40.* Oxford.

Brothers, A. J. 2000. *Terence: The Eunuch.* Warminster.

Brown, P. G. McC. 1992. "Menander, Fragments 745 and 746 K-T, Menander's *Kolax,* and Parasites and Flatterers in Greek Comedy." *ZPE* 92: 91–107.

Brugnola, V. 1896. *Le facezie di Cicerone.* Castello.

Burke, P. 1988. "Bakhtin for Historians." *Social History* 13: 85–90.

Cairns, D., ed. 2005. *Body Language in the Greek and Roman Worlds.* Swansea.

Cameron, A. 2011. *The Last Pagans of Rome.* Oxford.

Cameron, K., ed. 1993. *Humour and History.* Oxford.

Cantarella, R. 1975. "I 'libri' della *Poetica* di Aristotele." *Rendiconti della Classe di scienze morali, storiche e filologiche dell'Accademia dei Lincei* 30: 289–97.

Carey, C. 1981. *A Commentary on Five Odes of Pindar.* New York.

Carey, S. 2003. *Pliny's Catalogue of Culture: Art and Empire in the "Natural History."* Oxford.

Carter, A. 1992. "Alison's Giggle." In *Nothing Sacred: Selected Writings,* 189–204. Rev. ed. London. Originally published in 1983.

Cassin, B., J.-L. Labarrière, and G. R. Dherbey, eds. 1997. *L'animal dans l'antiquité.* Paris.

Cataudella, Q. 1971. *La facezia in Grecia e a Roma.* Florence.

Cèbe, J.-P., 1966. *La caricature et la parodie dans le monde romain antique des origines à Juvénal.* Paris.

Ceccarelli, P. 2013. *Ancient Greek Letter Writing.* Oxford.

Champlin, E. 2003. *Nero.* Cambridge, MA.

Chartier, R. 1987. "Ritual and Print, Discipline and Invention: The *Fête* in France from the Middle Ages to the Revolution." In *The Cultural Uses of Print in Early Modern France,* trans. L. G. Cochrane, 13–31. Princeton, NJ. Originally published in French in 1980.

Chesterfield, Earl of [Philip Dormer Stanhope]. 1774. *Letters Written by the Late Right Honourable Philip Dormer Stanhope, Earl of Chesterfield, to His Son, Philip Stanhope.* 4 vols. London.

———. 1890. *Letters of Philip Dormer, Fourth Earl of Chesterfield, to His Godson and Successor.* Oxford.

Christenson, D. M. 2000. *Plautus: Amphitruo.* Cambridge.

Cioffi, F. 1998. *Wittgenstein on Freud and Frazer.* Cambridge.

Cixous, H. 1976. "The Laugh of the Medusa." Trans. K. Cohen and P. Cohen. *Signs* 1: 875–93. Originally published in French in 1975.

Cixous H., and C. Clément. 1986. *The Newly Born Woman.* Trans. B. Wing. Manchester. Originally published in French in 1975.

Clarke, J. R. 2003. *Art in the Lives of Ordinary Romans: Visual Representation and Non-elite Viewers in Roman Italy, 100 B.C.–A.D. 315.* Berkeley and London.

———. 2007. *Looking at Laughter: Humor, Power, and Transgression in Roman Visual Culture, 100 B.C.–A.D. 250.* Berkeley and London.

Clarke, M. 2005. "On the Semantics of Ancient Greek Smiles." In *Body Language in the Greek and Roman Worlds,* ed. D. Cairns, 37–53. Swansea.

Clausen, W. 1994. *Virgil Eclogues, Edited with an Introduction and Commentary.* Oxford.

Cohen, A. 2008. "Response: Why Is Laughter Almost Non-existent in Ancient Greek Sculpture?" *Cogito* (Athens) 8: 20.

Coleiro, E. 1979. *An Introduction to Vergil's "Bucolics," with a Critical Edition of the Text.* Amsterdam.

Coleman, R. 1977. *Vergil, Eclogues.* Cambridge.

Connolly, J. 2007. *The State of Speech: Rhetoric and Political Thought in Ancient Rome.* Princeton, NJ.

Connors, C. 2004. "Monkey Business: Imitation, Authenticity, and Identity from Pithekoussai to Plautus." *ClAnt* 23: 179–207.

Conte, G.B. 1997. *The Hidden Author: An Interpretation of Petronius's "Satyricon."* Berkeley.

Conybeare, C. 2002. "The Ambiguous Laughter of Saint Laurence." *JECS* 10: 175–202.

———. 2013. *The Laughter of Sarah: Biblical Exegesis, Feminist Theory, and the Concept of Delight.* New York and Basingstoke.

Corbeill, A. 1996. *Controlling Laughter: Political Humor in the Late Roman Republic.* Princeton, NJ.

Corbett, P. 1986. *The Scurra.* Edinburgh.

Cordero, N.-L. 2000. "Démocrite riait-il?" In *Le rire des Grecs: Anthropologie du rire en Grèce ancienne,* ed. M.-L. Desclos, 227–39. Grenoble.

Cristante, L. 1990. "Un verso fantasma di Ovidio." *Prometheus* 16: 181–86.

Critchley, S. 2002. *On Humour.* London and New York.

———. 2005. "Very Funny: An Interview with Simon Critchley," by Brian Dillon. *Cabinet* 17: 78–81.

Crompton, D. 2010. *A Funny Thing Happened on the Way to the Forum.* London.

Crusius, O. 1896. "Excurse zu Virgil." *RhM* 51: 544–59.

Csapo, E. 2002. "Kallipides on the Floor-Sweepings: The Limits of Realism in Classical Acting and Performance Styles." In *Greek and Roman Actors: Aspects of an Ancient Profession,* ed. P. Easterling and E. Hall, 126–47. Cambridge.

Cumont, F. 1897. "Les Actes de S. Dasius." *AB* 16: 5–15.

Cunningham, I.C. 1987. *Herodas, Mimiambi cum appendice fragmentorum mimorum papyraceorum.* Leipzig.

D'Agostino, V. 1969. "Sugli antichi Saturnali." *Rivista di Studi Classici* 17: 180–87.

Damon, C. 1997. *Mask of the Parasite: A Pathology of Roman Patronage.* Ann Arbor, MI.

D'Arms, J.H. 1990. "The Roman *Convivium* and the Ideal of Equality." In *Sympotica: A Symposium on the "Symposion,"* ed. O. Murray, 308–20. Oxford.

Darwin, C. 1872. *The Expression of the Emotions in Man and Animals.* London.

David, E. 1989. "Laughter in Spartan Society." In *Classical Sparta: Techniques behind Her Success,* ed. A. Powell, 1–25. London.

Davila-Ross, M., B. Allcock, C. Thomas, and K. Bard. 2011. "Aping Expressions? Chimpanzees Produce Distinct Laugh Types When Responding to Laughter of Others." *Emotion* 11: 1013–20.

Davis, N. Z. 1975. *Society and Culture in Early Modern France: Eight Essays.* Stanford, CA.

Dawe, R. D., ed. 2000. *Philogelos.* Munich.

Deckers, L. 1993. "On the Validity for a Weight-Judging Paradigm for the Study of Humor." *Humor* 6: 43–56.

Deckers, L., and P. Kizer. 1974. "A Note on Weight Discrepancy and Humor." *Journal of Psychology* 86: 309–12.

———. 1975. "Humor and the Incongruity Hypothesis." *Journal of Psychology* 90: 215–18.

Della Corte, F. 1985. *Le Bucoliche di Virgilio, commentate e tradotte.* Genoa.

Della Corte, M. 1954. *Case ed abitanti di Pompei.* 2nd ed. Rome.

Demont, P. 1997. "Aristophane, le citoyen tranquille et les singeries." In *Aristophane: La langue, la scène, la cité,* ed. P. Thiercy and M. Menu, 457–79. Bari.

Dench, E. 2005. *Romulus' Asylum: Roman Identities from the Age of Alexander to the Age of Hadrian.* Oxford.

Desclos, M.-L., ed. 2000. *Le rire des Grecs: Anthropologie du rire en Grèce ancienne.* Grenoble.

De Waal, F. B. M. 2001. *The Ape and the Sushi Master: Cultural Reflections of a Primatologist.* New York.

Dickie, S. 2011. *Cruelty and Laughter: Forgotten Comic Literature and the Unsentimental Eighteenth Century.* Chicago.

Dolansky, F. 2011. "Celebrating the Saturnalia: Religious Ritual and Roman Domestic Life." In *A Companion to Families in the Greek and Roman Worlds,* ed. B. Rawson, 488–503. Oxford.

Dominik, W., and J. Hall, eds. 2007. *A Companion to Roman Rhetoric.* Malden, MA, and Oxford.

Doody, A. 2010. *Pliny's Encyclopaedia: The Reception of the "Natural History."* Cambridge.

Douglas, M. 1968. "The Social Control of Cognition: Some Factors in Joke Perception." *Man* 3: 361–76. Reprinted in Douglas 1975, 90–114.

———. 1971. "Do Dogs Laugh? A Cross-cultural Approach to Body Symbolism." *Journal of Psychosomatic Research* 15: 387–90. Reprinted in Douglas 1975, 83–89.

———. 1975. *Implicit Meanings: Essays in Anthropology.* London and Boston.

Dugan, J. 2005. *Making a New Man: Ciceronian Self-Fashioning in the Rhetorical Works.* Oxford.

Dunbabin, K. 2008. "*Nec grave nec infacetum:* The Imagery of Convivial Entertainment." In *Das römische Bankett im Spiegel der Altertumswissenschaften,* ed. K. Vössing, 13–26. Stuttgart.

Dunkle, R. 2008. *Gladiators: Violence and Spectacle in Ancient Rome.* Harlow, Essex.

Dupont, F. 1985. *L'Acteur roi: Le théâtre à Rome.* Paris.

———. 2000. *L'orateur sans visage: Essai sur l'acteur romain et son masque.* Paris.

Du Quesnay, I.M.LeM. 1977. "Vergil's Fourth *Eclogue.*" *PLLS* (1976) 1: 25–99.

Dyck, A.R. 2003. *Cicero: De Natura Deorum, Book I.* Cambridge.

Easterling, P., and E. Hall, eds. 2002. *Greek and Roman Actors: Aspects of an Ancient Profession.* Cambridge.

Eco, U. 1983. *The Name of the Rose.* Trans. W. Weaver. London.

Edwards, C. 1993. *The Politics of Immorality in Ancient Rome.* Cambridge.

Ekman, P. 1992. "Facial Expressions of Emotion: New Findings, New Questions." *Psychological Science* 3: 34–38.

———. 1999. "Facial Expressions." In *Handbook of Cognition and Emotion,* ed. T. Dalgleish and M. Power, 301–20. New York.

Elias, N. 1978. *The Civilising Process.* Vol. 1, *The History of Manners.* Oxford. Originally published in German in 1939.

Elsner, J. 1995. *Art and the Roman Viewer: The Transformation of Art from the Pagan World to Christianity.* Cambridge.

Enk, P.J. 1953. *Plauti Truculentus.* 2 vols. Leiden.

Fairer, D.W. 2003. *English Poetry of the Eighteenth Century, 1700–1789.* London.

Fantham, E. 1972. *Comparative Studies in Republican Latin Imagery.* Toronto.

———. 1988. "Mime: The Missing Link in Roman Literary History." *CW* 82: 153–63.

———. 1998. *Ovid: Fasti, Book IV.* Cambridge.

———. 2002. "Orator and/et Actor." In *Greek and Roman Actors: Aspects of an Ancient Profession,* ed. P. Easterling and E. Hall, 362–76. Cambridge.

———. 2004. *The Roman World of Cicero's "De Oratore."* Oxford.

———. 2006. *Julia Augusti: The Emperor's Daughter.* London and New York.

Feeney, D. 1998. *Literature and Religion at Rome: Cultures, Contexts and Beliefs.* Cambridge.

Felice, E.M. 2013. "Putting the ΓΕΛΩΣ Back in *Philogelos* 1." *CPh* 108: 155–58.

Fernández López, J. 2007. "Quintilian as Rhetorician and Teacher." In *A Companion to Roman Rhetoric,* ed. W. Dominik and J. Hall, 307–22. Malden, MA, and Oxford.

Fick-Michel, N. 1991. *Art et Mystique dans les "Métamorphoses" d'Apulée.* Paris.

Fitzgerald, W. 1995. *Catullan Provocations: Lyric Poetry and the Drama of Position.* Berkeley and London.

———. 2000. *Slavery and the Roman Literary Imagination.* Cambridge.

Flohr, M. 2013. *The World of the Fullo: Work, Economy, and Society in Roman Italy.* Oxford.

Flohr, M., and A. Wilson. 2011. "The Economy of Ordure." In *Roman Toilets: Their Archaeology and Cultural History,* ed. G.C.M. Jansen, A.O. Koloski-Ostrow, and E.M. Moormann, 147–56. Leuven.

Floridi, L. 2012. "Greek Skoptic Epigram and 'Popular' Literature: *Anth. Gr.* XI and the *Philogelos.*" *GRBS* 52: 632–60.

Fontaine, M. 2010. *Funny Words in Plautine Comedy.* Oxford.

Fortenbaugh, W. W. 2000. "Une analyse du rire chez Aristote et Théophraste." In *Le rire des Grecs: Anthropologie du rire en Grèce ancienne,* ed. M.-L. Desclos, 333–54. Grenoble.

———. 2002. *Aristotle on Emotion: A Contribution to Philosophical Psychology, Rhetoric, Poetics, Politics, and Ethics.* 2nd ed. London.

Fortenbaugh, W. W., P. M. Huby, R. W. Sharples, and D. Gutas, eds. 1992. *Theophrastus of Eresus: Sources for His Life, Writings, Thought and Influence.* Pt. 1. Leiden.

Fowler, D. 1987. "Brief Reviews: Roman Literature." *G&R* 34: 89–94.

Fox, R. 2001. "Anthropology as It Should Be." *London Review of Books* 23 (9 August): 25–26.

Fraenkel, E. 1922. *Plautinisches im Plautus.* Berlin.

———. 1961. "Two Poems of Catullus." *JRS* 51: 46–53. Partly reprinted in Gaisser 2007, 356–68.

———. 2007. *Plautine Elements in Plautus.* Translation of Fraenkel 1922 by T. Drevikovsky and F. Muecke. Oxford.

Frangoulidis, S. 1994. "The Soldier as a Storyteller in Terence's *Eunuchus.*" *Mnemosyne* 47: 586–95.

Frazer, J. G. 1913. *The Golden Bough: A Study in Magic and Religion.* Pt. 6, *The Scapegoat.* 3rd ed. London and Basingstoke.

Freedberg, D. 2007. "Empathy, Motion and Emotion." In *Wie sich Gefühle Ausdruck verschaffen: Emotionen in Nahsicht,* ed. K. Herding and A. Krause-Wahl, 17–51. Taunusstein.

Freud, S. 1960. *Jokes and Their Relation to the Unconscious.* Trans. J. Strachey. London. Originally published in German in 1905.

Freudenburg, K. 1993. *The Walking Muse: Horace and the Theory of Satire.* Princeton, NJ.

———, ed. 2005. *The Cambridge Companion to Roman Satire.* Cambridge.

Fried, I., C. L. Wilson, K. A. MacDonald, and E. J. Behnke. 1998. "Electric Current Stimulates Laughter." *Nature* 391: 650.

Frischer, B. 1991. *Shifting Paradigms: New Approaches to Horace's "Ars Poetica."* Atlanta.

Gaisser, J. H., ed. 2007. *Catullus.* Oxford Readings in Classical Studies. Oxford.

Garelli, M.-H. 2007. *Danser le mythe: La pantomime et sa réception dans la culture antique.* Leuven.

Garfitt, T., E. McMorran, and J. Taylor, eds. 2005. *The Anatomy of Laughter.* London.

Gatrell, V. 2006. *City of Laughter: Sex and Satire in Eighteenth-Century London.* London.

Geffcken, K. A. 1973. *Comedy in the "Pro Caelio."* Mnemosyne, suppl. 30. Leiden.

Gera, D. L. 2003. *Ancient Greek Ideas on Speech, Language and Civilization.* Oxford.

Gibson, R. 2003. *Ovid: Ars Amatoria 3.* Cambridge.

Gildenhard, I. 2012. *Virgil, Aeneid, 4.1–299: Latin Text, Study Questions, Commentary and Interpretative Essays.* Cambridge.

Giuliani, L. 1986. *Bildnis und Botschaft: Hermeneutische Untersuchungen zur Bildniskunst der römischen Republik.* Frankfurt am Main.

Glinister, F., and C. Woods, eds. 2007. *Verrius, Festus and Paul.* London.

Godwin, J. 1999. *Catullus: The Shorter Poems.* Warminster.

Golahny, A. 2003. *Rembrandt's Reading: The Artist's Bookshelf of Ancient Poetry and History.* Amsterdam.

Goldberg, S. M. 1998. "Plautus on the Palatine." *JRS* 88: 1–20.

———. 2000. "Catullus 42 and the Comic Legacy." In *Dramatische Wäldchen: Festschrift für Eckhard Lefèvre zum 65. Geburtstag,* ed. E. Stärk and G. Vogt-Spira, 475–89. Hildesheim.

———. 2005. *Constructing Literature in the Roman Republic.* Cambridge.

Goldhill, S. 1995. *Foucault's Virginity: Ancient Erotic Fiction and the History of Sexuality.* Cambridge.

———, ed. 2001. *Being Greek under Rome: Cultural Identity, the Second Sophistic and the Development of Empire.* Cambridge.

———. 2006. "The Thrill of Misplaced Laughter." In *Kômôidotragôidia: Intersezioni del tragico e del comico nel teatro del V secolo a.C.,* ed. E. Medda, M. S. Mirto, and M. P. Pattoni, 83–102. Pisa.

———. 2008. "Response: Why Is Laughter Almost Non-existent in Ancient Greek Sculpture?" *Cogito* (Athens) 8: 19.

Gomme, A. W., and F. H. Sandbach. 1973. *Menander: A Commentary.* Oxford.

Gorman, R. J., and V. B. Gorman. 2007. "The Tryphê of the Sybarites: A Historiographical Problem in Athenaeus." *JHS* 127: 38–60.

Gow, A. S. F. 1965. *Machon: The Fragments.* Cambridge.

Gowers, E. 1993. *The Loaded Table: Representations of Food in Roman Literature.* Cambridge.

———. 2005. "The Restless Companion: Horace, *Satires* 1 and 2." In *The Cambridge Companion to Roman Satire,* ed. K. Freudenburg, 48–61. Cambridge.

———. 2012. *Horace: Satires, Book 1.* Cambridge.

Gowing, A. M. 1990. "Dio's Name." *CPh* 85: 49–54.

Graf, F. 1992. "Römische Aitia und ihre Riten: Das Beispiel von Saturnalia und Parilia." *MH* 49: 13–25.

———. 1997. "Cicero, Plautus and Roman Laughter." In *A Cultural History of Humour,* ed. J. Bremmer and H. Roodenburg, 29–39. Cambridge.

———. 2005. "Satire in a Ritual Context." In *The Cambridge Companion to Roman Satire,* ed. K. Freudenburg, 192–206. Cambridge.

Grant, M. A. 1924. *The Ancient Rhetorical Theories of the Laughable: The Greek Rhetoricians and Cicero.* University of Wisconsin Studies in Language and Literature 21. Madison.

Green, P. 2006. *Diodorus Siculus, Books 11–12.37.1.* Austin.

Greenblatt, S. 2007. *Learning to Curse: Essays in Early Modern Culture.* Rev. ed. New York and London.

Grewing, F. 1997. *Martial, Buch VI: Ein Kommentar.* Göttingen.

Griffin, M. T. 1995. "Philosophical Badinage in Cicero's Letters to his Friends." In *Cicero the Philosopher,* ed. J. G. F. Powell, 325–46. Oxford.

Griffith, M. 2006. "Horsepower and Donkeywork: Equids and the Ancient Greek Imagination." *CPh* 101: 185–246, 307–58.

Griffith, R. D. 2008. "Response: Why Is Laughter Almost Non-existent in Ancient Greek Sculpture?" *Cogito* (Athens) 8: 22.

Gruen, E. S. 1990. *Studies in Greek Culture and Roman Policy*. Leiden and New York.

Gruner, C. R. 1978. *Understanding Laughter: The Workings of Wit and Humor*. Chicago.

———. 1997. *The Game of Humor: A Comprehensive Theory of Why We Laugh*. New Brunswick, NJ, and London.

Guérin, C. 2011. *Persona: L'élaboration d'une notion rhétorique au 1er siècle av. J.-C.* Vol. 2. Paris.

Gunderson, E. 2000. *Staging Masculinity: The Rhetoric of Performance in the Roman World*. Ann Arbor, MI.

———. 2003. *Declamation, Paternity and Roman Identity: Authority and the Rhetorical Self*. Cambridge.

Habinek, T. 1990. "Lucius' Rite of Passage." *MD* 25: 49–69.

———. 2005. "Satire as Aristocratic Play." In *The Cambridge Companion to Roman Satire*, ed. K. Freudenburg, 177–91. Cambridge.

Hall, E. 2008. "Introduction: Pantomime, a Lost Chord in Ancient Culture." In *New Directions in Ancient Pantomime*, ed. Hall and R. Wyles, 1–40. Oxford.

Hall, E., and R. Wyles, eds. 2008. *New Directions in Ancient Pantomime*. Oxford.

Hall, N. J. 1983. *The Letters of Anthony Trollope*. 2 vols. Stanford, CA.

Halliwell, S. 1986. *Aristotle's Poetics*. London.

———. 2008. *Greek Laughter: A Study in Cultural Psychology from Homer to Early Christianity*. Cambridge.

———. 2013. "Having a Laugh." *TLS*, 26 April, 23.

Hambartsumian, A. 2001. "The Armenian Parable 'Zoroaster's Laughter' and the Plot of Zoroaster's Birth in the Literary Traditions." *Iran and the Caucasus* 5: 27–36.

Hankinson, R. J. 1997. "Le phénomène et l'obscur: Galien et les animaux." In *L'animal dans l'antiquité*, ed. B. Cassin, J.-L. Labarrière, and G. R. Dherbey, 75–93. Paris.

———. 2000. "La pathologie du rire: Réflexions sur le rôle du rire chez les médecins grecs." In *Le rire des Grecs: Anthropologie du rire en Grèce ancienne*, ed. M.-L. Desclos, 191–200. Grenoble.

Hannerz, U. 1987. "The World in Creolisation." *Africa* 57: 546–59.

Hansen, W., ed. 1998. *Anthology of Ancient Greek Popular Literature*. Bloomington, IL.

Haraway, D. 1989. *Primate Visions: Gender, Race and Nature in the World of Modern Science*. New York and London.

Hardie, P. 2012. "Virgil's Catullan Plots." In *Catullus: Poems, Books, Readers*, ed. I. M. LeM. DuQuesnay and A. J. Woodman, 212–38. Cambridge.

Harris, C. R., and N. Alvarado. 2005. "Facial Expressions, Smile Types, and Self-Report during Humour, Tickle and Pain." *Cognition and Emotion* 19: 655–69.

Harris, C.R., and N. Christenfeld. 1997. "Humour, Tickle and the Darwin-Hecker Hypothesis." *Cognition and Emotion* 11: 103–10.

Harris, W.V. 2009. *Dreams and Experience in Classical Antiquity*. Cambridge, MA.

Harris-McCoy, D.E. 2012. *Artemidorus' "Oneirocritica": Text, Translation, and Commentary*. Oxford.

Harrison, S.J., ed. 1999. *Oxford Readings in the Roman Novel*. Oxford.

Haury, A. 1955. *L'ironie et l'humour chez Cicéron*. Leiden.

Heath, J.R. 1982. "Narration and Nutrition in Apuleius' *Metamorphoses*." *Ramus* 11: 57–77.

Heath, M. 1989. "Aristotelian Comedy." *CQ* 39: 344–54.

Hekster, O. 2002. *Commodus: An Emperor at the Crossroads*. Amsterdam.

Henderson, Jeffrey. 1991. *The Maculate Muse: Obscene Language in Attic Comedy*. Rev. ed. Oxford.

Henderson, John. 1999. *Writing Down Rome: Satire, Comedy, and Other Offences in Latin Poetry*. Oxford.

———. 2001. *Telling Tales on Caesar: Roman Stories from Phaedrus*. Oxford.

Herrenschmidt, C. 2000. "Le rire de Zarathustra, l'Iranien." In *Le rire des Grecs: Anthropologie du rire en Grèce ancienne*, ed. M.-L. Desclos, 497–511. Grenoble.

Hersch, K.K. 2010. *The Roman Wedding: Ritual and Meaning in Antiquity*. Cambridge.

Herzen, A. 2012. "A Letter Criticizing *The Bell*." In *A Herzen Reader*, ed. K. Parthé, 67–69. Evanston, IL. Originally published in Russian in 1858.

Hill, J.D. 2001. "Romanisation, Gender and Class: Recent Approaches to Identity in Britain and Their Possible Consequences." In *Britons and Romans: Advancing an Archaeological Agenda*, CBA Research Report 125, ed. S. James and M. Millett, 12–18. York.

Hirschkop, K., and D. Shepherd, eds. 2001. *Bakhtin and Cultural Theory*. 2nd ed. Manchester.

Hobbes, T. 1969. *The Elements of Law Natural and Politic*. 2nd ed. Ed. F. Tönnies. London. Originally published in 1640.

———. 1996. *Leviathan*. Ed. R. Tuck. Rev. ed. Cambridge. Originally published in 1651.

Hopkins, K. 1983. *Death and Renewal*. Cambridge.

———. 1993. "Novel Evidence for Roman Slavery." *P&P* 138: 3–27.

Hopkins, K., and M. Beard. 2005. *The Colosseum*. Cambridge, MA.

Horsfall, N. 1996. "The Cultural Horizons of the *Plebs Romana*." *MAAR* 41: 101–19.

Hunter, R.L. 1985. *The New Comedy of Greece and Rome*. Cambridge.

———. 2002. "'Acting Down': The Ideology of Hellenistic Performance." In *Greek and Roman Actors: Aspects of an Ancient Profession*, ed. P. Easterling and E. Hall, 189–206. Cambridge.

Huss, B. 1999. *Xenophons Symposion: Ein Kommentar*. Stuttgart.

Hutchinson, G.O. 1998. *Cicero's Correspondence: A Literary Study*. Oxford.

James, P. 1987. *Unity in Diversity: A Study of Apuleius' "Metamorphoses."* Hildesheim.

Janko, R. 1984. *Aristotle on Comedy: Towards a Reconstruction of "Poetics" II*. London.

———. 2001. "Aristotle on Comedy, Aristophanes and Some New Evidence from Herculaneum." In *Making Sense of Aristotle: Essays in Poetics*, ed. Ø. Andersen and J. Haarberg, 51–71. London.

Janson, H. W. 1952. *Apes and Ape Lore in the Middle Ages and Renaissance*. Warburg Institute Studies 20. London.

Janus, A. 2009. "From 'Ha he hi ho hu. Mummum' to 'Haw! Hell! Haw!': Listening to Laughter in Joyce and Beckett." *Journal of Modern Literature* 32: 144–66.

Jennings, V. 2001. Review of *Philogelos*, ed. R. D. Dawe (Munich and Leipzig, 2000). *BMCR* (online publication) 2001.04.05: http://bmcr.brynmawr. edu/2001/2001-04-05.html.

Johnson, S. 1741. "The Pedants, or Jests of Hierocles." *Gentleman's Magazine* 11: 477–79.

Jones, C. P. 1991. "Dinner Theater." In *Dining in a Classical Context*, ed. W. J. Slater, 185–98. Ann Arbor, MI.

Jones, R. E. 1939. "Cicero's Accuracy of Characterization in His Dialogues." *AJPh* 60: 307–25.

Jouanno, C. 2006. *Vie d'Ésope*. Paris.

Joubert, L. 1980. *Treatise on Laughter*. Trans. G. D. de Rocher. Tuscaloosa, AL. Originally published in French in 1579.

Kant, I. 1952. *The Critique of Judgement*. Trans. J. C. Meredith. Oxford. Originally published in German in 1790.

Kassel, R. 1956. "Reste eines hellenistischen Spassmacherbuches auf einem Heidelberger Papyrus." *RhM* 99: 242–45.

———, ed. 1976. *Aristotelis Ars Rhetorica*. Berlin and New York.

Kaster, R. 1980. "Macrobius and Servius: *Verecundia* and the Grammarian's Function." *HSCP* 84: 219–62.

Kawakami, K., K. Takai-Kawakami, M. Tomonaga, J. Suzuki, F. Kusaka, and T. Okai. 2007. "Spontaneous Smile and Spontaneous Laugh: An Intensive Longitudinal Case Study." *Infant Behaviour and Development* 30: 146–52.

Kerman, J. B. 1980. "The Light-Bulb Jokes: Americans Look at Social Action Processes." *Journal of American Folklore* 93: 454–58.

Kidd, S. 2011. "Laughter Interjections in Greek Comedy." *CQ* 61: 445–59.

Kindt, J. 2010. "Parmeniscus' Journey: Tracing Religious Visuality in Word and Wood." *CPh* 105: 252–64.

———. 2012. *Rethinking Greek Religion*. Cambridge.

King, A. 2002. "Mammals: Evidence from Wall Paintings, Sculpture, Mosaics, Faunal Remains, and Ancient Literary Sources." In *The Natural History of Pompeii*, ed. W. F. Jashemski and F. G. Meyer, 401–50. Cambridge.

King, H. 1986. "Agnodike and the Profession of Medicine." *PCPhS* 32: 53–77.

Kipper, S., and D. Todt, 2005. "The Sound of Laughter: Recent Concepts and Findings in Research into Laughter Vocalizations." In *The Anatomy of Laughter*, ed. T. Garfitt, E. McMorran, and J. Taylor, 24–33. London.

Kirichenko, A. 2010. *A Comedy of Storytelling: Theatricality and Narrative in Apuleius' "Golden Ass."* Heidelberg.

Kirkpatrick, J., and F. Dunn. 2002. "Heracles, Cercopes, and Paracomedy." *TAPhA* 132: 29–61.

Klein, L.E. 1994. *Shaftesbury and the Culture of Politeness: Moral Discourse and Cultural Politics in Early Eighteenth-Century England*. Cambridge.

König J. 2012. *Saints and Symposiasts: The Literature of Food and the Symposium in Greco-Roman and Early Christian Culture*. Cambridge.

Konstan, D. 1986. "Venus's Enigmatic Smile." *Vergilius* 32: 18–25.

Konstan, D., and S. Saïd, eds. 2006. *Greeks on Greekness: Viewing the Greek Past under the Roman Empire*. Cambridge Philological Society, supp. vol. 29. Cambridge.

Krabbe, J.K. 1989. *The Metamorphoses of Apuleius*. New York.

Kristeva, J. 1980. *Desire in Language: A Semiotic Approach to Literature and Art*. New York and Oxford. Originally published in French in 1969; reprinted in 1977.

Kroll, W.M. 1913. *M. Tulli Ciceronis Orator*. Berlin.

Krostenko, B.A. 2001. *Cicero, Catullus, and the Language of Social Performance*. Chicago.

Kurke, L. 2002. "Gender, Politics and Subversion in the *Chreiai* of Machon." *PCPhS* 48: 20–65.

——. 2011. *Aesopic Conversations: Popular Tradition, Cultural Dialogue, and the Invention of Greek Prose*. Princeton, NJ.

Labarrière, J.-L. 2000. "Comment et pourquoi la célèbre formule d'Aristote: 'Le rire est le propre de l'homme', se trouve-t-elle dans un traité de physiologie (*Partie des Animaux*, III, 10, 63 a 8)?" In *Le rire des Grecs: Anthropologie du rire en Grèce ancienne*, ed. M.-L. Desclos, 181–89. Grenoble.

La Bua, G. 2013. "Mastering Oratory: The Mock-Trial in Apuleius' *Metamorphoses* 3.3.1–71." *AJPh* 134: 675–701.

Laes, C. 2011. "Silent Witnesses: Deaf-Mutes in Graeco-Roman Antiquity." *CW* 104: 451–73.

Lateiner, D. 1995. *Sardonic Smile: Nonverbal Behaviour in Homeric Epic*. Ann Arbor, MI.

Laurence, R., and J. Paterson. 1999. "Power and Laughter: Imperial *Dicta*." *PBSR* 67: 183–97.

Lautréamont, Comte de. 1965. *Les Chants de Maldoror*. Trans. G. Wernham. New York. Originally published in French in 1869.

Lavin, D., and D.W. Maynard. 2001. "Standardization vs. Rapport: Respondent Laughter and Interviewer Reaction during Telephone Surveys." *American Sociological Review* 66: 453–79.

Lee, G. 1990. *The Poems of Catullus: Edited with Introduction, Translation and Brief Notes*. Oxford.

Leeman, A.D. 1963. *Orationis Ratio: Stylistic Theories and Practice in the Roman Orators, Historians and Philosophers*. Amsterdam.

Leeman, A.D., H. Pinkster, and E. Rabbie. 1981. *M. Tullius Cicero, De Oratore Libri III, 1 Band: Buch I*. Heidelberg.

——. 1989. *M. Tullius Cicero, De Oratore Libri III, 3 Band: Buch II, 99–290*. Heidelberg.

Lefèvre, E. 2003. *Terenz' und Menanders Eunuchus*. Munich.

Le Goff, J. 1989. "Rire au Moyen Age." *Cahiers du Centre de recherches historiques* 3: 1–14.

———. 1992. "Jésus a-t-il ri?" *L'histoire* 158: 72–74.

———. 1993. "Le Roi dans l'Occident medieval." In *Kings and Kingship in Medieval Europe*, King's College London Medieval Studies 10, ed. A.J. Duggan, 1–40. London.

———. 1997. "Laughter in the Middle Ages." In *A Cultural History of Humour*, ed. J. Bremmer and H. Roodenburg, 40–53. Cambridge. Edited version of Le Goff 1989.

Leigh, M. 2004. "The *Pro Caelio* and Comedy." *CPh* 99: 300–335.

Leon, M. 2009. *Molière, the French Revolution, and the Theatrical Afterlife.* Iowa City.

Le Roux, P. 2004. "La Romanisation en question." *Annales, histoire, sciences sociales* 59: 287–311.

Le Roy Ladurie, E. 1979. *Carnival in Romans.* Trans. M. Feeney. New York.

Lessing, D. 1962. *The Golden Notebook.* London.

Levine, D. 1982. "Homeric Laughter and the Unsmiling Suitors." *CJ* 78: 97–104.

———. 1984. "Odysseus' Smiles." *TAPhA* 114: 1–9.

Lévi-Strauss, C. 1997. "The Culinary Triangle." In *Food and Culture: A Reader,* ed. C. Counihan and P. van Esterik, 26–35. New York and London. Originally published in French in 1965.

Lewis, S. 1995. "Barbers' Shops and Perfume Shops: 'Symposia without Wine.'" In *The Greek World,* ed. A.D. Powell, 432–41. London and New York.

Lewis, W., E. Wadsworth, E. Pound, W. Roberts, H. Saunders, L. Atkinson, J. Dismorr, and H. Gaudier-Brzeska. 1914. "Manifesto 1 and 2." *Blast* 1: 11–43.

Lichačëv, D.S., and A.M. Pančenko. 1991. *Die Lachwelt des alten Russland.* Trans. R. Lachmann. Munich. Originally published in Russian in 1976.

Lilja, S. 1980. "The Ape in Ancient Comedy." *Arctos* 14: 31–38.

Ling, R. 2009. "Roman Laughter." Review of J.R. Clarke 2007. *JRA* 22: 508–10.

Lippitt, J. 1994. "Humour and Incongruity." *Cogito* (Athens) 8: 147–53.

———. 1995a. "Humour and Superiority." *Cogito* (Athens) 9: 54–61.

———. 1995b. "Humour and Release." *Cogito* (Athens) 9: 169–76.

Lissarrague, F. 1997. "L'homme, le singe et le satyre." In *L'animal dans l'antiquité,* ed. B. Cassin, J.-L. Labarrière, and G.R. Dherbey, 455–69. Paris.

Long, J. 2000. "Julia-Jokes at Macrobius's *Saturnalia:* Subversive Decorum in Late Antique Reception of Augustan Political Humor." *IJCT* 6: 337–55.

Lonsdale, R. 2009. *Samuel Johnson: The Lives of the Poets, a Selection.* Oxford.

Löwe, G. 1981. *Philogelos oder der Lach-Fan, von Hierokles und Philagrius.* Leipzig.

Lowe, J.C.B. 1989. "Plautus' Parasites and the *Atellana.*" In *Studien zur vorliterarischen Periode im frühen Rom,* ed. G. Vogt-Spira, 161–69. Tübingen.

Lowe, N. 2007. *Comedy: Greece and Rome.* New Surveys in the Classics 37. Cambridge.

Lucaszewicz, A. 1989. "Sarapis and a Free Man." *Eos* 77: 251–55.

Ludovici, A. M. 1932. *The Secret of Laughter*. London.

Malineau, V. 2005. "L'apport de l'*Apologie de mimes* de Chorikios de Gaza à la connaissance du theatre du VIᵉ siècle." In *Gaza dans l'Antiquité Tardive: Archéologie, rhétorique et histoire*, ed. C. Saliou, 149–69. Salerno.

Maltby, R. 1999. "The Language of Plautus' Parasites." http://www2.open. ac.uk/ClassicalStudies/GreekPlays/Conf99/Maltby.htm.

Manuwald, G. 2011. *Roman Republican Theatre*. Cambridge.

Marchesi, I. 2008. *The Art of Pliny's Letters: A Poetics of Allusion in the Private Correspondence*. Cambridge.

Marconi, C. 2007. *Temple Decoration and Cultural Identity in the Archaic Greek World: The Metopes of Selinus*. Cambridge.

Marshall, C. W. 2006. *The Stagecraft and Performance of Roman Comedy*. Cambridge.

Martin, J. M. 1990. "Cicero's Jokes at the Court of Henry II of England." *Modern Language Quarterly* 51: 144–66.

Martin, R. A. 2007. *The Psychology of Humor: An Integrative Approach*. Burlington, MA.

Marzolph, U. 1987. "Philogelos arabikos: Zum Nachleben der antiken Witzesammlung in der mittelalterlichen arabischen Literatur." *Der Islam* 64: 185–230.

Mason, H. J. 1999a. "The *Metamorphoses* of Apuleius and Its Greek Sources." In *Latin Fiction: The Latin Novel in Context*, ed. H. Hoffmann, 103–12. London.

————. 1999b. "*Fabula Graecanica*: Apuleius and His Greek Sources." In *Oxford Readings in the Roman Novel*, ed. S. J. Harrison, 217–36. Oxford.

Mattingly, D. J. 2011. *Imperialism, Power, and Identity: Experiencing the Roman Empire*. Princeton, NJ.

May, J., and J. Wisse. 2001. *Cicero, On the Ideal Orator*. Oxford.

May, R. 1998. "Köche und Parasit: Elemente der Komödie in den *Metamorphosen* des Apuleius." *GCN* 9: 131–55.

————. 2006. *Apuleius and Drama: The Ass on Stage*. Oxford.

McCarthy, K. 2000. *Slaves, Masters, and the Art of Authority in Plautine Comedy*. Princeton, NJ.

McClure, L. 2003. "The Sayings of Courtesans in Book 13 of Athenaeus' *Deipnosophistae*." *AJPh*. 124: 259–94.

McDermott, W. C. 1935. "The Ape in Greek Literature." *TAPhA* 66: 165–76.

————. 1936. "The Ape in Roman Literature." *TAPhA* 67: 148–67.

————. 1938. *The Ape in Antiquity*. Baltimore.

McDonald, M., and J. M. Walton, eds. 2007. *The Cambridge Companion to Greek and Roman Theatre*. Cambridge.

McGettigan, C., E. Walsh, R. Jessop, Z. K. Agnew, D. Sauter, J. E. Warren, and S. K. Scott. 2013. "Individual Differences in Language Perception Reveal Roles for Mentalizing and Sensorimotor Systems in the Evaluation of Emotional Authenticity." *Cerebral Cortex* (online publication): http://cercor. oxfordjournals.org/content/early/2013/08/21/cercor.bht227.full.pdf+html.

McGrath, E. 1997. *Corpus Rubenianum Ludwig Burchard*, pt. 13. 2 vols. London.

McKeown, J.C. 1979. "Augustan Elegy and Mime." *PCPhS* 25: 71–84.

McMahon, A.P. 1917. "On the Second Book of Aristotle's *Poetics* and the Source of Theophrastus' Definition of Tragedy." *HSCP* 28: 1–46.

Ménager, D. 1995. *La Renaissance et le rire*. Paris.

Milanezi, S. 1992. "Outres enflées de rire: A propos de la fête du dieu Risus dans les 'Métamorphoses' d'Apulée." *RHR* 209: 125–47.

———. 2000. "Laughter as Dessert." In *Athenaeus and His World: Reading Greek Culture in the Roman Empire*, ed. D. Braund and J. Wilkins, 400–412. Exeter.

Millar, F.G.B. 1964. *A Study of Cassius Dio*. Oxford.

———. 1977. *The Emperor in the Roman World*. London.

Miller, S.A. 2010. *Medieval Monstrosity and the Female Body*. New York and London.

Millett, M. 1990. *The Romanization of Britain: An Essay in Archaeological Interpretation*. Cambridge.

Minois, G. 2000. *Histoire du rire et de la dérision*. Paris.

Mitchell, T.N. 1991. *Cicero: The Senior Statesman*. New Haven, CT, and London.

Moellendorff, P. von. 1995. *Grundlagen einer Ästhetik der alten Komödie: Untersuchungen zu Aristophanes und Michail Bachtin*. Tübingen.

Monaco, G. 1967. *Quintiliano: Il capitolo de risu ("Inst. Or." VI 3)*. Palermo.

———. 1974. *Cicerone: L'excursus de ridiculis ("De Or." II 216–290)*. 3rd ed. Palermo.

Morales, H. 1996. "The Torturer's Apprentice." In *Art and Text in Roman Culture*, ed. J. Elsner, 182–209. Cambridge.

Morgan, G. 1981. "*Philogelos* 216." *JHS* 101: 141.

Morreall, J. 1983. *Taking Laughter Seriously*. Albany, NY.

Murdoch, I. 1999. *The Sea, the Sea*. London. Originally published in 1978.

Murgia, C. 1991. "Notes on Quintilian." *CQ* 41: 183–212.

Murphy, T. 2004. *Pliny the Elder's "Natural History": The Empire in the Encyclopaedia*. Oxford.

Musurillo, H. 1972. *The Acts of the Christian Martyrs*. Oxford.

Nauta, R.R. 1987. "Seneca's 'Apocolocyntosis' as Saturnalian Literature." *Mnemosyne* 40: 69–96.

———. 2002. *Poetry for Patrons: Literary Communication in the Age of Domitian*. Mnemosyne, suppl. 206. Leiden.

Neil, R.A. 1901. *The "Knights" of Aristophanes*. Cambridge.

Nerhardt, G. 1976. "Incongruity and Funniness: Towards a New Descriptive Model." In *Humor and Laughter: Theory, Research, and Applications*, ed. A.J. Chapman and H.C. Foot, 55–62. London.

Nesselrath, H.-G. 1985. *Lukians Parasitendialog: Untersuchungen und Kommentar*. Berlin and New York.

———. 1990. *Die attische mittlere Komödie: Ihre Stellung in der antiken Literaturkritik und Literaturgeschichte*. Berlin and New York.

Nicholl, A. 1931. *Masks, Mimes and Miracles: Studies in the Popular Theatre*. London.

Nietzsche, F. W. 1986. *Human, All Too Human: A Book for Free Spirits*. Trans. R. J. Hollingdale. Cambridge. Originally published in German in 1878.

———. 1990. *Beyond Good and Evil: Prelude to a Philosophy of the Future*. Trans. R. J. Hollingdale. Harmondsworth. Originally published in German in 1886.

———. 2002. *Beyond Good and Evil: Prelude to a Philosophy of the Future*. Trans. J. Norman. Cambridge. Originally published in German in 1886.

Nimmo Smith, J. 2001. *A Christian's Guide to Greek Culture: The Pseudo-Nonnus Commentaries on Sermons 4, 5, 39 and 43 by Gregory of Nazianzus*. Liverpool.

Nisbet, R. G. M. 1978. "Virgil's Fourth *Eclogue*: Easterners and Westerners." *BICS* 25: 59–78. Reprinted in *Vergil's "Eclogues,"* ed. K. Volk, 155–88. 2007. Oxford.

Nixon, P. 1916–38. *Plautus*. 5 vols. Cambridge, MA.

Norden, E. 1958. *Die Geburt des Kindes: Geschichte einer religiösen Idee*. 2nd ed. Stuttgart.

Nutton, V. 2011. *Galen: On Problematical Movements*. With G. Bos. Cambridge.

Oakley, S. P. 1997. *Commentary on Livy: Books VI–X*. Vol. 2, *Books VII–VIII*. Oxford.

O'Higgins, D. M. 2001. "Women's Cultic Joking and Mockery: Some Perspectives." In *Making Silence Speak: Women's Voices in Greek Literature and Society*, ed. A. Lardinois and L. McClure, 136–60. Princeton, NJ.

Olender, M. 1990. "Aspects of Baubo: Ancient Texts and Contexts." In *Before Sexuality: The Construction of Erotic Experience in the Ancient Greek World*, ed. D. M. Halperin, J. J. Winkler, and F. I. Zeitlin, 83–113. Princeton, NJ. Originally published in French in 1985.

Oliensis, E. 1998. *Horace and the Rhetoric of Authority*. Cambridge.

Pagels, E., and K. King. 2007. *Reading Judas: The Gospel of Judas and the Shaping of Christianity*. New York and London.

Palmer, A.-M. 1989. *Prudentius on the Martyrs*. Oxford.

Panayotakis, C. 1994. "Quartilla's Histrionics in Petronius' 'Satyrica' 16.1–26.6." *Mnemosyne* 47: 319–36.

———. 1995. *Theatrum Arbitri: Theatrical Elements in the Satyrica of Petronius*. Leiden.

———. 2006. "Women in the Greco-Roman Mime of the Roman Republic and the Early Empire." *Ordia Prima* 5: 121–38.

———. 2008. "Virgil on the Popular Stage." In *New Directions in Ancient Pantomime*, ed. E. Hall and R. Wyles, 185–97. Oxford.

———. 2010. *Decimus Laberius: The Fragments*. Cambridge.

Pan'kov, N. 2001. "'Everything Else Depends on How This Business Turns Out . . .': Mikhail Bahktin's Dissertation Defence as Real Event, as High Drama and as Academic Comedy." In *Bakhtin and Cultural Theory*, 2nd ed., ed. K. Hirschkop and D. Shepherd, 26–61. Manchester.

Panksepp, J. 2000. "The Riddle of Laughter: Neural and Psychoevolutionary Underpinnings of Joy." *Current Directions in Psychological Science* 9: 183–86.

Panksepp, J., and J. Burgdorf. 1999. "Laughing Rats? Playful Tickling Arouses High Frequency Ultrasonic Chirping in Young Rodents." In *Toward a Science of Consciousness III: The Third Tucson Discussions and Debates,* ed. S. Hameroff, D. Chalmers, and A. Kaszniak, 231–44. Cambridge, MA.

Parkin, T. 2003. *Old Age in the Roman World: A Cultural and Social History.* Baltimore.

Parvulescu, A. 2010. *Laughter: Notes on a Passion.* Cambridge, MA.

Pelliccia, H. N. 2012. "Where Does His Wit Come From?" *New York Review of Books* 59 (8 November): 36–40.

Pernerstorfer, M. J. 2006. "Zu Menanders *Kolax.*" *WS* 119: 39–61.

———. 2009. *Menanders "Kolax": Ein Beitrag zu Rekonstruktion und Interpretation der Komödie.* Berlin.

Perret, J. 1970. *Virgile, Les Bucoliques: Edition, introduction et commentaire.* Paris.

Perry, B. E. 1943. "On the Manuscripts of the *Philogelos.*" In *Classical Studies in Honor of William Abbott Oldfather,* 157–66. Urbana, IL.

———. 1952. *Aesopica: A Series of Texts Relating to Aesop or Ascribed to Him or Closely Connected to the Literary Tradition That Bears His Name.* Vol. 1. Urbana, IL.

Plaza, M. 2000. *Laughter and Derision in Petronius' "Satyrica": A Literary Study.* Studia Latina Stockholmiensia 46. Stockholm.

Provine, R. R. 2000. *Laughter: A Scientific Investigation.* London.

Purcell, N. 1999. "Does Caesar Mime?" In *The Art of Ancient Spectacle,* Studies in the History of Art 56, ed. B. Bergmann and C. Kondoleon, 181–93. National Gallery of Art, Washington DC.

———. 2005. "The Ancient Mediterranean: The View from the Customs House." In *Rethinking the Mediterranean,* ed. W. V. Harris, 200–232. Oxford.

Putnam, M. C. J. 1970. *Virgil's Pastoral Art.* Princeton, NJ.

Quinn, K. 1970. *Catullus: The Poems.* London and Basingstoke.

Rabbie, E. 2007. "Wit and Humor in Roman Rhetoric." In *A Companion to Roman Rhetoric,* ed. W. Dominik and J. Hall, 207–17. Malden, MA, and Oxford.

Radice, B. 1976. *Terence: The Comedies.* Rev. ed. London.

Ramage, E. S. 1973. *"Urbanitas": Ancient Sophistication and Refinement.* Norman, OK.

Ramsay, W. 1897. *Cities and Bishoprics of Phrygia: Being an Essay of the Local History of Phrygia from the Earliest Times to the Turkish Conquest.* Vol. 1, pt. 2. Oxford.

Ramsey, J. T. 2003. *Cicero, "Philippics" I–II.* Cambridge.

Rapp, A. 1950–51. "A Greek 'Joe Miller.'" *CJ* 46: 236–90, 318.

———. 1951. *The Origins of Wit and Humor.* New York.

Raskin, V. 1985. *Semantic Mechanisms of Humor.* Dordrecht and Boston.

Rawson, E. D. 1975. *Cicero: A Portrait.* London.

Reich, H. 1903. *Der Mimus.* Berlin.

Richlin, A. 1992a. *The Garden of Priapus: Sexuality and Aggression in Roman Humor.* Rev. ed. Oxford.

———. 1992b. "Julia's Jokes, Galla Placidia and the Roman Use of Women as Political Icons." In *Stereotypes of Women in Power: Historical Perspectives and Revisionist Views,* ed. B. Garlick, S. Dixon, and P. Allen, 65–91. New York.

Richter, G. 1913. "Grotesques and the Mime." *AJA* 17: 149–56.

Riggsby, A.M. 1999. *Crime and Community in Ciceronian Rome.* Austin.

Ritschl, F. 1868. *Opuscula Philologica.* Vol. 2. Leipzig.

Robert, L. 1968. "Les épigrammes satiriques de Lucillius sur les athlètes: Parodie et réalités." In *L'épigramme grecque,* Entretiens sur l'Antiquité Classique 14, 181–295. Geneva.

Roberts, D., ed. 1992. *Lord Chesterfield's Letters.* Oxford.

Roberts, M. 1993. *Poetry and the Cult of the Martyrs: The "Liber Peristephanon" of Prudentius.* Ann Arbor, MI.

Robertson, D.S. 1919. "A Greek Carnival." *JHS* 29: 110–15.

Robertson, M. 1975. *A History of Greek Art.* 2 vols. Cambridge.

Rochefort, G. 1950. "Une anthologie grecque du XIe siècle: Le *Parisinus Suppl. Gr. 690.*" *Scriptorium* 4: 3–17.

Roller, M.B. 2001. *Constructing Autocracy: Aristocrats and Emperors in Julio-Claudian Rome.* Princeton, NJ.

———. 2006. *Dining Posture in Ancient Rome.* Princeton, NJ.

Rougé, J. 1987. "Le *Philogélôs* et la navigation." *JS:* 3–12.

Roxan, M.M. 1985. *Roman Military Diplomas, 1978 to 1984.* London.

Ruch, W., and P. Ekman. 2001. "The Expressive Pattern of Laughter." In *Emotions, Qualia, and Consciousness,* ed. A.W. Kaszniak, 426–43. Tokyo.

Rutherford, I. 2000. "Theoria and Darśan: Pilgrimage and Vision in Greece and India." *CQ* 50: 133–46.

Saint-Denis, E. de. 1965. *Essais sur le rire et le sourire des Latins.* Paris.

Sanders, B. 1995. *Sudden Glory: Laughter as Subversive History.* Boston.

Schlam, C.C. 1992. *The Metamorphoses of Apuleius: On Making an Ass of Oneself.* London.

Schlapbach, K. 2010. "The *Logoi* of Philosophers in Lucian of Samosata." *ClAnt* 29: 250–77.

Schlee, F. 1893. *Scholia Terentiana.* Leipzig.

Schmeling, G. 2011. *A Commentary on the "Satyrica" of Petronius.* Oxford.

Schneider, R.M. 2004. "Nachwort." In J. Le Goff, *Das Lachen im Mittelalter,* 79–128. Stuttgart.

Schulten, P. 2002. "Ancient Humour." In *After the Past: Essays in Ancient History in Honour of H.W. Pleket,* ed. W. Jongman and M. Kleijwegt, 209–34. Leiden.

Schulz, F. 1942. "Roman Registers of Births and Birth Certificates." *JRS* 32: 78–91.

———. 1943. "Roman Registers of Births and Birth Certificates, Part II." *JRS* 33: 55–64.

Scott, J.C. 1990. *Domination and the Arts of Resistance: Hidden Transcripts.* New Haven, CT, and London.

Scott, S. 2013. "Laughter—the Ordinary and the Extraordinary." *Psychologist* 26: 264–69.

Screech, M.A. 1997. *Laughter at the Foot of the Cross*. London.

Scruton, R., and P. Jones. 1982. "Laughter." *Proceedings of the Aristotelian Society, Supplementary Volumes* 56: 197–228.

Scullard, H.H. 1981. *Festivals and Ceremonies of the Roman Republic*. London.

Scurr, R. 2003. "The Laughter of Breakdown." *TLS*, 24 October, 23.

Segal, E. 1968. *Roman Laughter: The Comedy of Plautus*. Cambridge, MA.

———. 2001. *The Death of Comedy*. Cambridge, MA.

Selden, D.L. 2007. "*Ceveat lector*: Catullus and the Rhetoric of Performance." In *Catullus*, Oxford Readings in Classical Studies, ed. J.H. Gaisser, 490–559. Oxford. Expanded version of *Innovations of Antiquity*, ed. R. Hexter and D.L. Selden, 461–512. 1992. New York and London.

Self, W. 1997. *Great Apes*. London.

Shackleton Bailey, D.R. 1977. *Cicero: Epistulae ad Familiares*. 2 vols. Cambridge.

———. 1978. "Corrections and Explanations of Martial." *CPh* 73: 273–96.

Sharland, S. 2010. *Horace in Dialogue: Bakhtinian Readings in the Satires*. Oxford.

Sharrock, A. 2009. *Reading Roman Comedy: Poetics and Playfulness in Plautus and Terence*. Cambridge.

———. 2011. Review of Fontaine 2010. *AJPh* 132: 510–13.

Shaw, B.D. 2001. *Spartacus and the Slave Wars: A Brief History with Documents*. Boston and New York.

Sherwin-White, A.N. 1966. *The Letters of Pliny: A Historical and Social Commentary*. Oxford.

Siegmann, E. 1956. *Literarische griechische Texte der Heidelberger Papyrussammlung*. Heidelberg.

Silk, M.S. 2000. *Aristophanes and the Definition of Comedy*. Oxford.

———. 2001. "Aristotle, Rapin, Brecht." In *Making Sense of Aristotle: Essays in Poetics*, ed. Ø. Andersen and J. Haarberg, 173–95. London.

Silk, M.S., I. Gildenhard, and R. Barrow. 2014. *The Classical Tradition: Art, Literature and Thought*. Malden, MA, and Oxford.

Skinner, Q. 2001. "Why Laughing Mattered in the Renaissance." *History of Political Thought* 22: 418–47.

———. 2002. "Hobbes and the Classical Theory of Laughter." In *Hobbes and Civil Science*, vol. 3 of *Visions of Politics*, 142–76. Cambridge.

———. 2004. "Hobbes and the Classical Theory of Laughter." In *Leviathan after 350 Years*, ed. T. Sorell and L. Foisneau, 139–66. Oxford.

———. 2008. "Response: Why Is Laughter Almost Non-existent in Ancient Greek Sculpture?" *Cogito* (Athens) 8: 22.

Smallwood, E.M. 1970. *Philonis Alexandrini Legatio ad Gaium*. 2nd ed. Leiden.

Smith, M. 2008. "Laughter: Nature or Culture?" https://scholarworks.iu.edu/dspace/bitstream/handle/2022/3162/Laughter%20nature%20culture1.pdf?sequence=1.

Smith, W.D. 1990. *Hippocrates: Pseudoepigraphic Writings*. Leiden.

Sommerstein, A. 1981. *Aristophanes: "Knights."* Warminster.

———. 2009. "Talking about Laughter in Aristophanes." In *Talking about Laughter and Other Studies in Greek Comedy*, 104–15. Oxford. Originally published in French in 2000, in *Le rire des Grecs: Anthropologie du rire en Grèce ancienne*, ed. M.-L. Desclos, 65–75. Grenoble.

Sonnabend, H. 2002. *Geschichte der antiken Biographie: Von Isokrates bis zur Historia Augusta*. Stuttgart.

Spawforth, A.J.S. 2012. *Greece and the Augustan Cultural Revolution*. Cambridge.

Spencer, H. 1860. "On the Physiology of Laughter." *Macmillan's Magazine* 1: 395–402. Reprinted in *Essays on Education and Kindred Subjects*, 298–309. 1911. London.

Spengel, L., ed. 1867. *Aristotelis Ars Rhetorica*. Leipzig.

Stackelberg, K.T. von. 2009. *The Roman Garden: Space, Sense, and Society*. London and New York.

Stallybrass, P., and A. White. 1986. *The Politics and Poetics of Transgression*. London.

Stärk, E., and G. Vogt-Spira, eds. 2000. *Dramatische Wäldchen: Festschrift für Eckhard Lefèvre zum 65. Geburtstag*. Hildesheim.

Steel, C. 2005. *Reading Cicero: Genre and Performance in Late Republican Rome*. London.

Stein, E.A. 2006. "Colonial Theatres of Proof: Representations of Laughter in 1930s Rockefeller Foundation Hygiene Cinema in Java." *Health and History* 8: 14–44.

Steiner, G. 1996. "Tragedy, Pure and Simple." In *Tragedy and the Tragic: Greek Theatre and Beyond*, ed. M.S. Silk, 534–46. Oxford.

Stern, H. 1953. *Le calendrier de 354: Etude sur son texte et ses illustrations*. Paris.

Stewart, A. 2008. "Response: Why Is Laughter Almost Non-existent in Ancient Greek Sculpture?" *Cogito* (Athens) 8: 19.

Stylianou, P.J. 1998. *A Historical Commentary on Diodorus Siculus, Book 15*. Oxford.

Sullivan, J.P. 1968. *The Satyricon of Petronius: A Literary Study*. London.

Swain, S. 1996. *Hellenism and Empire: Language, Classicism, and Power in the Greek World, AD 50–250*. Oxford.

Tatum, J. 2006. "Marcus Tullius Cicero, Author of the *Metamorphoses*." In *Lectiones Scrupulosae: Essays on the Text and Interpretation of Apuleius' "Metamorphoses" in Honour of M. Zimmerman*, ed. W.H. Keulen, R.R. Nauta, and S. Panayotakis, 4–14. Groningen.

Taylor, J. 2005. "Introduction." In *The Anatomy of Laughter*, ed. T. Garfitt, E. McMorran, and J. Taylor, 1–10. London.

Taylor, W.S., and J.H. Pringle, eds. 1838–40. *Correspondence of William Pitt, Earl of Chatham*. 4 vols. London.

Thiel, H. van. 1971. *Der Eselroman*. 2 vols. Munich.

———. 1972. "*Philogelos* 237." *Hermes* 100: 509.

Thierfelder, A. 1968. *Philogelos der Lachfreund von Hierocles und Philagrios*. Munich.

Thomas, K. 1977. "The Place of Laughter in Tudor and Stuart England." *TLS*, 21 January, 77–81.

Tilg, S. 2008. "*Eloquentia ludens*—Apuleius' Apology and the Cheerful Side of Standing Trial." In *Paideia at Play: Learning and Wit in Apuleius,* ed. W. Riess, 105–32. Groningen.

Toner, J. P. 2009. *Popular Culture in Ancient Rome.* Cambridge.

Trumble, A. 2004. *A Brief History of the Smile.* Rev. paperback ed. New York.

Turnbull, C. 1961. *The Forest People.* London.

———. 1973. *The Mountain People.* London.

Twain, M. 1889. *A Connecticut Yankee in King Arthur's Court.* New York.

Tylawsky, E. I. 2002. *Saturio's Inheritance: The Greek Ancestry of the Roman Comic Parasite.* New York.

Van der Paardt, R. T. 1971. *L. Apuleius Madaurensis, The Metamorphoses: A Commentary on Book III, with Text and Introduction.* Amsterdam.

Van Dommelen, P. 1997. "Colonial Constructs: Colonialism and Archaeology in the Mediterranean." *World Archaeology* 28: 305–23.

Vasaly, A. 2013. "The Political Impact of Cicero's Speeches." In *The Cambridge Companion to Cicero,* ed. C. Steel, 141–59. Cambridge.

Vasey, G. 1875. *The Philosophy of Laughter and Smiling.* London.

Verberckmoes, J. 1999. *Laughter, Jestbooks and Society in the Spanish Netherlands.* Basingstoke.

Versnel, H. S. 1993. *Inconsistencies in Greek and Roman Religion: Transition and Reversal in Myth and Ritual.* Leiden and New York.

Victor, B. 2013. "History of the Text and Scholia." In *A Companion to Terence,* ed. A. Augoustakis and A. Traill, 343–62. Malden, MA, and Oxford.

Vollgraff, C. G. 1904. "Apuleiana." *Mnemosyne* 32: 252–54.

Vos, M. de. 1991. "La fuga di Enea in pitture del I secolo d.C." *Kölner Jahrbuch* 24: 113–23.

Vout, C. 2007. *Power and Eroticism in Imperial Rome.* Cambridge.

Wallace Collection. 1928. *Pictures and Drawings: Text with Historical Notes and Illustrations.* London.

Wallace-Hadrill, A. 1983. *Suetonius: The Scholar and His Caesars.* London.

———. 1998. "To Be Roman, Go Greek." In *Modus Operandi: Essays in Honour of Geoffrey Rickman, BICS,* suppl. 71, ed. M. Austin, J. Harries, and C. Smith, 79–91. London.

———. 2008. *Rome's Cultural Revolution.* Cambridge.

———. 2011. *Herculaneum, Past and Future.* London.

Wallis, S. T. 1853. *Spain, Her Institutions, Politics and Public Men: A Sketch.* Boston.

Walsh, P. G. 1974. "Bridging the Asses." *CR* 24: 215–18.

———. 1996. *Petronius: The Satyricon, Translated with Introduction and Explanatory Notes.* Oxford.

Walton, J. M. 2007. "Commodity: Asking the Wrong Questions." In *The Cambridge Companion to Greek and Roman Theatre,* ed. M. McDonald and J. M. Walton, 286–302. Cambridge.

Warner, M. 1994. *From the Beast to the Blonde: On Fairy Tales and Their Tellers.* London.

———. 1998. *No Go the Bogeyman: Scaring, Lulling and Making Mock.* London.

Watson, W. 2012. *The Lost Second Book of Aristotle's Poetics.* Chicago.

Webb, R. 2002. "Female Performers in Late Antiquity." In *Greek and Roman Actors: Aspects of an Ancient Profession,* ed. P. Easterling and E. Hall, 282–303. Cambridge.

———. 2008. *Demons and Dancers: Performance in Late Antiquity.* Cambridge, MA.

Webster, J. 2001. "Creolizing the Roman Provinces." *AJA* 105: 209–25.

West, S. 1992. "Not at Home: Nasica's Witticism and Other Stories." *CQ* 42: 287–88.

Whigham, P. 1996. *The Poems of Catullus.* Harmondsworth.

Whitehead, A.N. 1979. *Process and Reality.* Rev. ed. New York. Originally published in 1929.

Whitmarsh, T. 2000. "The Politics and Poetics of Parasitism: Athenaeus on Parasites and Flatterers." In *Athenaeus and His World: Reading Greek Culture in the Roman Empire,* ed. D. Braund and J. Wilkins, 304–15. Exeter.

———. 2001. *Greek Literature and the Roman Empire.* Oxford.

Wilkins, A.S. 1890. *Ciceronis De Oratore, Liber II.* Oxford.

Wilkins, J. 2000. *The Boastful Chef: The Discourse of Food in Ancient Greek Comedy.* Oxford.

Williams, C. 2004. *Martial: Epigrams, Book Two.* Oxford.

Williams, R.D. 1976. "Virgil *Eclogues* 4.60–63." *CPh* 71: 119–21.

Wilson, N.G. 1996. *Scholars of Byzantium.* Rev. ed. London.

Winkler, J.J. 1985. *Auctor & Actor: A Narratological Reading of Apuleius' "The Golden Ass."* Berkeley and Los Angeles.

Winterbottom, M. 1970. *Problems in Quintilian.* BICS, suppl. 25. London.

Wiseman, T.P. 1985. *Catullus and His World: A Reappraisal.* Cambridge.

———. 2008. "'Mime' and 'Pantomime': Some Problematic Texts." In *New Directions in Ancient Pantomime,* ed. E. Hall and R. Wyles, 146–53. Oxford.

Woodford, S. 1992. "Kerkopes." In *LIMC,* vol. 6, pt. 1, 32–35.

Woolf, G. 1994. "Becoming Roman, Staying Greek: Culture, Identity and the Civilizing Process in the Roman East." *PCPhS* 40: 116–43.

———. 1998. *Becoming Roman: The Origins of Provincial Civilization in Gaul.* Cambridge.

Wright, J. 1974. *Dancing in Chains: The Stylistic Unity of the Comoedia Palliata.* Rome.

Wyatt, W. 1998. *The Journals of Woodrow Wyatt,* ed. S. Curtis. Vol. 1. Basingstoke and Oxford.

Yalouris, N. 1986. "Das archaische 'Lächeln' und die Geleontes." *Antike Kunst* 29: 3–5.

Zeitlin, F.I. 1982. "Cultic Models of the Female: Rites of Dionysus and Demeter." *Arethusa* 15: 129–57.

Zimmerman, M. 2000. *Apuleius Madaurensis, Metamorphoses, Book X: Text, Introduction and Commentary.* Groningen Commentaries on Apuleius. Groningen.

Zinn, E. 1960. "Elemente des Humors in augusteischer Dichtung." *Gymnasium* 67: 41–56, 152–55.

Žižek, S. 1989. *The Sublime Object of Ideology.* London.

Zucker, A. 2008. *Va te marrer chez les Grecques (Philogelos): Recueil de blagues grecques anciennes.* Paris.

Illustrations and Credits

Following page 95.

1. Frans Hals, *The Laughing Cavalier,* 1624. Oil on canvas. Wallace Collection, London, P84. Reproduced by kind permission of the Trustees.
2. *Cave Canem* mosaic from the entrance of the House of the Tragic Poet (6.8.5), Pompeii, first century CE. Soprintendenza Archeologica di Pompei. By permission of the *Ministero per i Beni e le Attività Culturali.*
3. Bronze statuette of an actor with an ape's head, Roman date. Private collection.
4. A boy with a performing monkey. Copy of a painting from the House of the Dioscuri (6.9.6/7), Pompeii. Original, first century CE. By permission of the *Ministero per i Beni e le Attività Culturali.*
5. Aeneas as an ape. Copy of a painting from a house (unknown) in Pompeii. Original, Museo Archeologico Nazionale, Naples, inv. 9089.
6. Rembrandt van Rijn, self-portrait as Zeuxis, c. 1668. Oil on canvas. Wallraf Richartz Museum, Cologne, Inv. Nr. WRM 2526.

Index